THE POWER OF
PRAYERFUL LIVING

THE POWER OF
PRAYERFUL
LIVING

HEALING PRAYERS AND SPIRITUAL GUIDANCE
THAT BRING JOY TO EVERY PART OF YOUR LIFE

BY DOUG HILL

REVIEWER: CAROLYN BOHLER, PH.D.

EMMA SANBORN TOUSANT PROFESSOR OF PASTORAL THEOLOGY AND COUNSELING

UNITED THEOLOGICAL SEMINARY, DAYTON, OHIO

RODALE

© 2001 by Rodale Inc.

Photographs © by John Turner/Stone

Printed in the United States of America
Rodale Inc. makes every effort to use acid-free ∞, recycled paper ♻

Interior Designer: Christopher Rhoads
Cover Photographer: John Turner/Stone

Library of Congress Cataloging-in-Publication Data

Hill, Doug.
    The power of prayerful living : healing prayers and spiritual guidance that bring joy to every part of your life / by Doug Hill.
        p.   cm.
    Includes index.
    ISBN 1–57954–200–X   hardcover
    ISBN 1–57954–460–6   paperback
    1. Prayer.   I. Title.
    BL560 .H55   2001
    248.3'2—dc21   00–012329

Distributed to the book trade by St. Martin's Press

2 4 6 8 10 9 7 5 3 1   hardcover
2 4 6 8 10 9 7 5 3 1   paperback

Visit us on the Web at www.rodalebooks.com, or call us toll-free at (800) 848-4735.

WE **INSPIRE** AND **ENABLE** PEOPLE TO IMPROVE
THEIR LIVES AND THE WORLD AROUND THEM

The Power of Prayerful Living Staff

MANAGING EDITOR: Kevin Ireland

LEAD WRITER: Doug Hill

WRITERS: Alisa Bauman, Bridget Doherty, Lois Guarino Hazel, Erik Kolbell, Diane Kozak

ART DIRECTOR: Richard Kershner

COVER DESIGNER: Uttley/DouPonce DesignWorks

INTERIOR DESIGNER: Christopher Rhoads

ASSISTANT RESEARCH MANAGERS: Leah Flickinger, Sandra Salera Lloyd

PRIMARY RESEARCH EDITOR: Anita C. Small

LEAD RESEARCHERS: Lois Guarino Hazel, Janice McLeod

EDITORIAL RESEARCHERS: Molly Donaldson Brown, Jennifer Goldsmith, Jennifer Kushnier, Lucille Uhlman

LAYOUT DESIGNER: Bethany Bodder

MANUFACTURING COORDINATORS: Brenda Miller, Jodi Schaffer, Patrick T. Smith

Rodale Books Group

VICE PRESIDENT AND PUBLISHER: Neil Wertheimer

MARKETING DIRECTOR: Janine Slaughter

PRODUCT MARKETING MANAGER: Sindy Berner

BOOK MANUFACTURING DIRECTOR: Helen Clogston

MANUFACTURING MANAGERS: Eileen Bauder

RESEARCH DIRECTOR: Ann Gossy Yermish

MANAGING EDITOR: Lisa D. Andruscavage

PRODUCTION MANAGER: Robert V. Anderson Jr.

DIGITAL PROCESSING GROUP MANAGERS: Leslie M. Keefe, Thomas P. Aczel

OFFICE MANAGER: Jacqueline Dornblaser

OFFICE STAFF: Susan B. Dorschutz, Julie Kehs Minnix, Catherine E. Strouse

Contents

PART 11
YOUR FAITH LIFE

Foreword

A wise pastoral counselor, Ed Wimberly, relates the story of a man who came to him for counseling to overcome an addiction. Experts suggested that he needed to enter a treatment program for recovery. The man wanted prayer alone to solve his problem.

Wimberly took the man's request for prayer seriously but also prayed with him for guidance as well as healing. After several sessions, the man came to realize that he could not expect prayer alone to change his life in a magical, low-energy manner. He acknowledged that he needed the recovery program, too.

Prayer didn't solve his problem, but it *did* assist his healing. Prayer for guidance helped the man feel secure enough to enter treatment and stay with it. He needed prayer *plus* advice to end his pain.

Within the pages of this book, you will find a similar wedding of prayers and helpful, practical advice. (What a novel and creative idea that is!) There are comforting and inspiring prayers from the Judeo-Christian tradition alongside contemporary psychological advice. Both will help you deal with the issues and crises that occur at every stage of life.

You will also discover wisdom and prayers from other world religions sprinkled throughout to broaden and deepen the ideas expressed here.

Taken as a whole, this mix of new and old, familiar and novel works as a balm to heal your physical, emotional, and spiritual aches and pains. Just as important, the wealth of topic-specific prayers helps you see that you are not alone in your concerns—that throughout the centuries and around the globe, people have struggled and overcome problems like yours by drawing strength from their spiritual lives.

Probably you will dip in and out of the book, locating chapters that are most relevant to your immediate need, eagerly looking for suggestions and prayers that will help you resolve your problems. However, you also can benefit by reading the book cover to cover, meditating upon the myriad life situations in which we all find ourselves.

Browse, enjoy, meditate, reread, ponder, skip sections, consider your own answers. This book is intended to encourage thought, stimulate prayer, and guide action.

Prayer over a lifetime, if it is sincere and searching, reflects the array of emotions and experiences in our lives. Prayer can inspire and comfort, leading us to understanding, wisdom, and change. So too can the words and ideas in *The Power of Prayerful Living.*

This book is a marvelous resource—not just for praying but also for living. It boldly assumes that when we pray, we are fully alive—and open to help and growth. Just as important, it suggests that if we live prayerfully, we will be immersed in life, in touch with our emotions, open to advice from humans as well as wisdom from God—our eyes wide open to the world, even while closed in prayer.

Carolyn Bohler, Ph.D.
Emma Sanborn Tousant Professor of Pastoral Theology and Counseling
United Theological Seminary, Dayton, Ohio

Introduction

Some months ago, when we began work on this book, I visited my mother's study for inspiration. There, she lovingly displays books and Bibles gathered by the several generations of clergy in our family. In the middle of the collection was a small, brown, leather-bound New Testament—my great-grandfather's personal Bible.

The worn pages betrayed his heavy use of this precious book. Penciled in the margins were Great-Grandfather's notes of joy, of praise, of exclamation at the wonder of the words. In the back was a series of dates, each one celebrating another complete Matthew-to-Revelation reading.

Looking through his notes, I was struck by two things: his deep faith and his thorough commitment to a prayerful life. Everything about his comments showed that here was a man zealously pursuing God and a life filled with God's spirit.

We have tried to bring a similar enlightenment to this book, to demonstrate in practical ways how you can apply the philosophy of prayerful living to the many situations you face in life.

Nowadays, many people aren't surrounded and cradled by communities of faith the way Great-Grandfather was. They don't always have convenient places to turn when they need counsel, support, comfort, or guidance. Recognizing that need, we have tried to assemble a community in this book—to provide advice that will help you live a prayerful and satisfying life.

First we carefully chose more than 60 specific concerns of life—from marriage and parenting problems to work and financial concerns, from physical and emotional problems to concerns about faith. Then we consulted leading clergy of many faiths, medical doctors, pastoral counselors, and other recognized experts to get the best advice on how to handle each of those issues prayerfully.

It is our hope that the advice, encouragement, and inspiration they have provided will give you the strength you need to face the challenges of life. We also hope the words of inspiration and the comforting prayers we've included will help you draw closer to God and find Divine guidance for your needs. Finally, we hope you'll draw strength from the "prayer miracle" letters we've included. In these real-life stories, people like you describe in their own words how prayer and prayerful living have helped them solve some of the toughest issues anyone could face.

If you are exhausted by the pressures of life, we believe this book can help. If you're filled with fear over illness, family problems, job problems, and more, again we believe this book will help. Consider it a resource, a road map through your personal prayerful life.

In fact, we hope this book will help you create an entire existence filled with faith and prayer so you can apply the principles of prayerful living to everything you do.

Great-Grandfather spent many hours seeking fulfillment in God's word, especially during the last years of his life, when he dealt with the pain and debility of stomach cancer. For him, prayer and spiritual living were guides along the pathway to peace, to understanding, to an afterlife glorious beyond all comprehension. For him, living prayerfully was a fundamental part of the journey from this life to the next.

May this book help advance your journey on that same sacred path.

Kevin Ireland

Kevin Ireland
Editor

Part 1

THE FUNDAMENTALS OF PRAYER

A Prayerful Life

Leading a spiritual life is more than saying grace at dinner—it is a way of living that puts you in constant and ever-deepening intimacy with God.

One of history's great spiritual masters was a humble, little man known as Brother Lawrence.

Brother Lawrence lived in Paris in the 1600s, where he worked as a footman, as a soldier, and finally as a cook in the kitchen of a monastery. He probably would have been forgotten forever when he died were it not for the fact that several people of considerably higher station urged him to share some of his ideas in letters.

Brother Lawrence lived in a constant state of awareness of the presence of God. In the truest sense, his life was a prayer. "The time of business does not with me differ from the time of prayer," he wrote, "and in the clatter of my kitchen, while several persons are at the same time calling for different things, I possess God in as great tranquillity as if I were upon my knees at the blessed sacrament." He once rejoiced in the fact that pancakes take a minute or so to cook on either side, simply because that afforded him one more uninterrupted minute to give praise to the Lord.

Often, Brother Lawrence was so overjoyed by the intimacy he shared with God that he had to struggle to keep himself from making a scene in front of others. "There is not in the world a kind of life more sweet and delightful than that of a continual conversation with God," he said.

The spiritual focus and holy delight of Brother Lawrence are evidence that living prayerfully is much more than pausing to talk to God for a few minutes on Sunday morning or before falling asleep at night. God is available on an ongoing basis—morning, noon, and night. And you don't have to bow your head or fold your hands to get the conversational ball rolling, nor do you have to close your eyes to notice that God is talking to *you.*

> *I would rather live my life as if there is a God And die to find out there isn't, Than live my life as if there isn't And die to find out there is.*
>
> —*Albert Camus*

Watching for the Presence of God

What does it mean to live a prayerful life?

"It means having a relationship with God, lived out in its fullness, honored and ever-strengthened," says the Reverend Danny E. Morris, a retired Methodist minister who created and for 20 years was executive director of the Academy for Spiritual Formation in Nashville.

You develop the fullest possible relationship with God by consistently thinking about God and being alert for signs of God wherever you go. When you pay prayerful attention throughout the day, you're less likely to rush past the miracles that surround you.

"If we believe that God speaks to us and with us, then we're always on the alert," says the Reverend Walter Wangerin Jr., professor of theology and literature at Valparaiso University in Indiana and author of *Whole Prayer: Speaking and Listening to God.* "We're always watching—in our experiences, in the world around us, in the people who speak to us, in scripture—for that communication from God. That's what it means to live a life of prayer: being in that state of perpetual readiness."

Being in a state of perpetual readiness sounds more difficult than it is. All it really amounts to is focusing on God whenever an opportunity to do so comes along. Brother Lawrence prayed while the pancakes cooked; others living in more modern times pray while waiting in line at the supermarket, for example, or whenever they are stopped at a red light.

A literally endless stream of openings to God present themselves in the course of a given day, says Reverend Morris, and with practice you can make

LORD, TEACH ME TO LISTEN

Blessed Lord! I see why my prayer has not been more believing and prevailing. I was more occupied with my speaking to you than your speaking to me. I did not understand that the secret of faith is this: there can be only so much faith as there is the Living Word dwelling in the soul.

And your Word has taught me so clearly: Let every man be swift to hear, slow to speak; let not your heart be hasty to utter anything before God.

Lord, teach me that it is only through your Word taken up into my life that my words can be taken into your heart; that your work, if it is a living power within me, will be a living power with you; what your mouth has spoken your hand will perform.

—Andrew Murray

the most of them. What takes a conscious effort at first soon turns into a habit that is as natural as breathing.

When you're practicing attentiveness, it helps to remember that a relationship with God, like any other relationship, requires two-way communication. Many of us are better at talking than we are at listening. Taking that attitude to prayer cuts us off from God's response—which is probably why Mother Teresa suggested we keep our prayers short.

True prayer is divided into to four parts, Dr. Wangerin says.

- We speak.
- God listens.
- God speaks.
- We listen.

If you train yourself to listen for God's voice, you will hear it, although God often speaks softly. And since God is infinite, chances are good that when you do listen, you'll learn something.

A Prayerful Attitude

Leading a life of prayer doesn't mean you have to constantly pray with words or even with thoughts. The way you carry yourself throughout the day can also be a form of prayer.

Live as if to die tomorrow.

Learn as if to live forever.

— *Gandhi*

Perhaps no one demonstrated this better than did Jesus Christ, says Dr. Wangerin. People were instinctively drawn to Jesus because he radiated holiness. Jesus inspired trust, love, and reverence because trust, love, and reverence poured out of him. Jesus *embodied* prayer.

Faith radiates from the core of any genuinely faithful person, says the Reverend Thomas E. Clarke, a director of New Bethany Retreat in Highland Mills, New York. For that reason, you can be acting prayerfully even when you aren't consciously at prayer. Prayer bubbles up from your innermost being, reaching out to others around you—and to God. God responds every moment of the day and night—even, some believe, while you sleep!

You can increase the intensity of your inner light by regularly practicing the fundamentals of faith, Dr. Wangerin adds. When you consistently pray, meditate, read scripture, do good works, and share your thoughts and feelings with other believers, it shows.

That is what it means to live a lifetime of prayer. You experience a continual cleansing baptism. The light of the Holy Spirit shines in you and through you. You are blessed, and you are a blessing.

Why Pray?

It's a connection to the Divine—and so much more.

hy pray? For plenty of people you might as well ask, "Why eat?" Prayer, they will tell you, is an essential part of what it means to be human. Why is that? Ask God. God built us that way.

"We pray because it comes naturally," says Larry Dossey, M.D., of Santa Fe, New Mexico, author of *Healing Words*, *Re-inventing Medicine*, and many other books on the healing power of prayer. "There is an emptiness that most people sense in their lives, a space that can only be filled by the Divine. Prayer makes that possible."

You could stop there. Prayer need fulfill no other function than to put us in touch with God. Everything else is secondary.

Having said that, it is also true that you can gather an infinite variety of secondary benefits from prayer, most of them having to do with that fundamental connection to God. Why do we pray? Let us count the ways.

We pray to be healed.

We pray to be comforted.

We pray to be freed from jealousy, from anger, from temptation, from bitterness, from a whole host of human sins.

We pray that others will be healed, comforted, or freed from a host of human sins.

We pray because we're afraid.

We pray because we're lonely.

We pray because we're confused.

We pray because we're filled with despair.

We pray because we're filled with joy.

You get the point. The list of why people pray is endless. Infinite, in fact. Like God.

Prayer is so simple:
It is like quietly opening
a door and slipping into
the very presence of God.
There in the stillness
To listen to His voice,
perhaps to petition or
only to listen.
It matters not,
just to be there,
in His presence . . .
In Prayer

—Unknown

The Practical Power of Prayer

"Thy will be done." For people of faith, no prayer could be more important than wishing that God's will be done, right? Well, yes, but let's be honest: Often we come to God in prayer because *we* want something, because we hope that *our* will might be done.

Does that mean our piety leaves something to be desired? Probably the answer is yes, if we focus on our own desires too much, Dr. Dossey believes. "So often you see prayer portrayed as a way of achieving life's Big Three—health, prosperity, and fulfilling relationships," he says. "In medicine, prayer is often seen as one more tool in the doctor's black bag, something to make illness go away. I think it's very important to emphasize that prayer has nothing to do with getting what we want. It's about making a connection with the Divine."

Having made that point, Dr. Dossey is happy to concede—and to celebrate—an additional truth about prayer: It *works*. You can pray for something and produce a measurable effect in the material world.

This effect has been most thoroughly documented in the area of health. Dozens of research studies have shown that people of faith have lower blood pressure, lower cancer rates, lower rates of addiction to alcohol and drugs, less depression, and higher odds of survival after major surgeries. In fact, people who apply prayer and faith to their lives are less likely than others to die prematurely from any cause.

Does proof exist that prayer can have an impact on the physical world in other ways? Of course it does, if you ask any one of the millions of believers who are fervently and irrevocably convinced that their prayers were miracu-

I'm Too Busy Not to Pray

Too busy to pray, I thought, Lord. I didn't stop to ask you what to do today. I plunged headlong into my own plans. I took too many detours. Slowing me down, frustrating me. How much I need to ask you first to order my day, direct my paths, and help me not to get sidetracked by my "must-get-done" list. I missed our morning talk. Lord, forgive me. In Jesus' name, Amen.

—*Quin Sherrer and Ruthanne Garlock*

lously answered. Finding scientific research documenting that that those Divine intercessions actually occurred, however, is another question.

"The research has been focused on medicine because that's easier to measure," notes Dr. Dossey. "You can come up with numbers and data and figures, and the medical world is oriented toward that sort of thing. But there's every reason to think prayer does have an impact at the social and political levels as well. There's no reason to believe that prayer is ineffective in any area of life."

Be All That You Can Be

You can tell immediately that prayer is effective in your life simply by praying. The benefits occur on many levels. You'll feel better because you've established the link with God that we all need; a sense of reassurance and calm will ensue. You'll feel more connected to the people around you, and often you will gain clarity regarding your problems. Most importantly, you will become more free to be who God wants you to be.

"To grow in prayer is to grow in awareness of what's real," says the Reverend Thomas E. Clarke, a Jesuit priest who has written and lectured about spirituality and prayer for more than 40 years. "We free ourselves from denial, from illusions, from addictions."

Prayer also encourages people to become more fully human, Father Clarke believes. Prayer tends to draw upon your deepest resources, bringing out aspects of you that might otherwise have remained hidden. "The rational mind is only

Prayer Miracles

A Little Child Shall Lead Them

Jonathan, my 5-year-old great-grandson, and I loved traveling on weekends, especially in the fall with the splendor of turning foliage.

One weekend around dusk we were returning from New England. I made a wrong turn on a ramp and we ended up in New York City. I was very concerned about getting lost at night since I had never driven there before. I went around several blocks trying to find the Holland Tunnel and finally I said, "Jonathan, Me-maw is lost; we'll have to find a policeman or taxi driver."

Jonathan looked at me with great faith in his eyes and said, "Me-maw, let's ask Jesus to help us!"

We took hands and told Jesus we were lost and needed his help. It must have been all of three minutes when a taxi pulled up beside us. The driver rolled down his window and asked if we were having trouble. I told him our problem, and he said we were only a few blocks from the Holland Tunnel. He gave me directions and told me he would follow me to make sure I found it.

In amazement I looked at Jonathan and said, "See how Jesus answered our prayers!"

Sylvia Harle
Charleston, South Carolina

part of prayer," he says. "The imagination and the emotions—the heart—have a role to play, too. Prayer helps us make the best possible use of all our human endowments."

The recognition of yourself that you gain in prayer works two ways, Father Clarke adds. On the one hand, you see more clearly your limits as a child of God. This knowledge may be painful, but it is important: Humility helps us all be more accepting of those around us—and of ourselves. Acknowledging your limits also encourages you to pray more: God comes to us in our weakness, Father Clarke believes, and brings comfort and healing there.

In another way, prayer represents an honor that affirms the greatest possible human dignity. "To think that we are worthy of approaching God," marvels Father Clarke, "is amazing!"

A Chance to Grow and Learn

Prayer is an open invitation to God that reads, "Come as you are." And God always does—often taking you by surprise.

You may think you know what you want from God, but God often has other ideas. Prayer can be a learning experience, teaching you to stretch and understand things you would never have contemplated before you bowed your head. And thank God for that, says Guy Finley of Merlin, Oregon, author of *The Lost Secrets of Prayer*.

"We all tend to think that what we need is some new psychological plan that will rescue us," Finley says. "The pitfall in that scenario is the fact that all we can come up with on our own are variations on the old ideas that got us into trouble in the first place. That's why 'Can you help me?' may be the most important prayer we can make. A true call for help doesn't define how help will come. We have to get out of our own way and be open to the answers that come from God."

God can also deliver messages in prayer that you may need but don't necessarily want to hear. As humans, we have a tendency to seek safety and sameness in our lives; we shy away from taking chances. But God doesn't like dull complacency and so likes to issue challenges, says M. Robert Mulholland Jr., vice president and chief academic officer of New Testament at Asbury Theological Seminary in Wilmore, Kentucky.

> *The fruit of silence is prayer, the fruit of prayer is faith, the fruit of faith is love, the fruit of love is service, the fruit of service is peace.*
>
> —*Mother Teresa*

Those challenges can scare you at first, but they can also open doors you've kept closed out of fear or blindness. Dr. Mulholland cites the story of Saul in the New Testament as an example. Saul was happily going about his business dragging Christians off to jail when he was blindsided by the risen Jesus on the road to Damascus.

"Saul, Saul, why do you persecute me?" Jesus asked him.

Saul seems to have been too stunned to answer, but Jesus didn't ask again. Instead, he told Saul to go into the city and await further instructions.

Saul obeyed and went on to embark on a radically different career path—under the name Paul.

This demonstrates the truth of Jesus' promise that if you knock on God's door in prayer, it will be opened.

Only heaven knows what lies on the other side.

What Is Prayer?

A plea for forgiveness, a request for answers. A desire for companionship, comfort, change, reassurance, help, relief. Prayer is all this and so much more.

sk a hundred people to draw a picture of someone at prayer, and chances are you'll get a sketch of a person kneeling piously, hands clasped, eyes shut, and mouth moving.

To most people, this *is* prayer. But in fact prayer is a much richer and more diverse experience. You can pray in a chant; in a quiet, meditative moment behind the wheel of a car; while singing a hymn; or while walking, working, crying, or sleeping.

Each of these acts and many others will open you up to God, help you be received by God, and allow God to enter your life, says the Reverend Fanny Erickson, director of the Ministry of Parish Life at New York City's Riverside Church. That is the essence of prayer. "Prayer is at heart a disposition," says Reverend Erickson. "It may become an activity, but it starts as a mindset, a willingness to be with Christ, or Allah, or Yahweh, or God by any other name."

Put another way, "Prayer entails wanting to commune with God, willing yourself to commune with God, and then—and this is important—finding a comfortable way to make that happen," says the Reverend Alison Boden, dean of Rockefeller Chapel at the University of Chicago. "When you think of it, that leaves the door flung open to almost limitless possibilities."

Prayer in Action

Milewide diversity notwithstanding, we can identify some familiar forms of prayer that most people will recognize.

"There's an old Sunday school saying that's really relevant to most great religions," says Reverend Erickson. "It says the forms of prayer most of us are accustomed to can be found in the anagram 'ACTS'—that is, adoration, confession, thanksgiving, and supplication. One way or another, when we're praying, we're engaging in at least one of these gestures."

Here's a look at each of these four forms of prayer, as well as some advice on how to use them in your communion with God.

God understands our desires not just through the occasional utterances we call "prayers" in the traditional sense, but through every thought we think, every word we speak, and everything we do.

—*Neale Donald Walsch*

1. Prayers of Adoration

When you offer God adoration or praise, you "begin to focus on God as the One who has created both us and all that's around us," says Reverend Boden.

"Think of yourself as a creature of God, connected to everything around you—the Earth, the sky, the stars, the flowers, everything," says Reverend Boden. "The enormity of God is overwhelming, we are reduced to awe, we literally feel an enormous sense of comfort and warmth in our hearts, a sense that we belong to God and to the Earth. This is adoration."

A biblical example of this type of prayer can be found in Ezekiel 6:3, where the prophet, having a vision of God upon a throne as the Lord of the universe, is so moved by God's power and majesty that he prays, "Holy, holy, holy is the Lord of hosts; the whole earth is full of his glory" (RSV).

2. Prayers of Confession

"Think of confession as an admission to God that your relationship is damaged and in need of repair," suggests Reverend Erickson. And, she adds, think of God stepping in and repairing the damage, filling you with forgiveness. "Lord have mercy" may be one of the shortest prayers we can utter, but in these three little words we are acknowledging both our need for mercy and God's ability to grant it.

THE VALUE OF COMMON PRAYER

Although prayers are often spontaneous, those that are travel-tested and well-worn can be immensely useful to us. The Reverend Stephanie Paulsell, Ph.D., director of ministry studies at the University of Chicago Divinity School, tells the story of how a common prayer served both a friend and a complete stranger.

"My colleague was on a train, heading for Chicago, and the train was involved in a terrible crash. There were injuries and fatalities, and as he wandered around the site of the accident, he happened upon one particularly grim scene. Without thinking, he simply dropped to his knees and began reciting the Lord's Prayer. Before he knew it, someone else came over, knelt down beside him, and joined him in the prayer.

"The words to the prayer were the only thing the two of them had in common, but it was enough to form a bond of fellowship in an extremely trying moment."

Prayers of confession and forgiveness have three distinct qualities that you can apply throughout daily life, says Everett Ferguson, Ph.D., professor emeritus of church history at Abilene Christian University in Texas: They call forth sorrow for what you might have done, challenge you to do better, and relieve your conscience of the guilt you may feel for lapses in your life. In this way, as you pray for forgiveness, you can literally feel the weight of sorrow lifted and replaced by the lightness of mercy.

3. Prayers of Thanksgiving

By offering God thanks for some good that has occurred, in a sense you're surrendering to God in worship, writes the Reverend Kenneth Leech, in *True Prayer*. You are showing gratitude for being a loved member of God's creation. And, says Dr. Ferguson, you are giving voice to the knowledge that God is hearing your prayers and acting in your life.

4. Prayers of Supplication

Broadly speaking, supplications can be of two varieties: petitions on your own behalf or intercessions on behalf of others. You can ask for good health for yourself, healing for your neighbor who is sick, strength to face a difficult day at work, or job success for your unemployed friend.

Whatever their focus, prayers of supplication provide the opportunity to ask God for what you want. "Remember," notes Reverend Erickson, "the disciples asked Jesus to teach them to pray, and he taught them the Lord's Prayer, which is a supplication to God for daily bread, forgiveness, guidance, and deliverance."

But what you think you want and what God thinks you need may be two entirely different subjects, so it's wise to include in any prayer of supplication a request for the wisdom to understand God's answer to the prayer, adds Reverend Boden. This affirms faith that God is listening to you and will answer you with your best interests in mind.

Expressing Prayers

Basically, when you pray, you pray with your entire body, says the Reverend Stephanie Paulsell, Ph.D., director of ministry studies at the University

RITUAL AS PRAYER

You needn't voice words to express prayer. "One Sister I know used a ritual as her morning prayer," recalls the Reverend Fanny Erickson, director of the Ministry of Parish Life at New York City's Riverside Church.

She would get up every morning, go into her kitchen, boil water, prepare coffee for herself, pour it, sit with it, let the aroma waft up through her nostrils, and take her first sip. "It gave her comfort and peace," says Reverend Erickson. "It was intensely private. It was done in silence. And in it, she felt God's gentle hand helping her to start her day."

of Chicago Divinity School. But you have many choices about the posture you assume.

"Closing your eyes removes distractions, but opening them, say, in nature, can inspire you," says Dr. Paulsell. "Hands clasped is a way of quieting our bodies, but hands open, with palms upturned, can be experienced as a gesture of openness to God. Kneeling suggests vulnerability, but standing in a group holding hands invites a sense of community. In ancient days, some clergy would lie prostrate on the floor as a symbol of utter surrender."

> *Prayer, to be fruitful, must come from the heart and must be able to touch the heart of God.*
>
> —*Mother Teresa*

How exactly should you express your prayer? Some find that speaking out loud gives their thoughts focus; others find answers by contemplating a problem or meditating on a verse of scripture. Still others draw energy and support from reciting prayers with a group. You may find communion with God through these methods or through any one of your own making.

The avenue you choose really doesn't matter; it's the power in the message. "Regardless of how they travel from our lips to God's ear," says Reverend Boden, "I don't believe God looks dimly upon any prayer if it is heartfelt."

The Unanswered Questions

How can God let bad things happen to good people? If God is all-powerful, why doesn't God answer all prayers? These and other complex faith questions puzzle many who are trying to understand God's presence. Here are some possible answers.

uring an otherwise uneventful day, Joe Grasser's hairdresser got an idea that would change his life forever. "I think you and my neighbor Stephanie Cherrie Crook would make a cute couple," she told him. The next thing Joe knew, he and Stephanie were taking a walk in a local park.

Then they met for ice cream. It didn't take long before the two realized they shared many things in common. They both believed that God played a role in their lives. They had both survived painful relationships. "We enjoyed quiet times, and she really could relate to my two sons, who at that time were 16 and 14," remembers Joe. "We just could share and talk freely about anything."

They married on July 3, 1988, and spent their honeymoon in Ocean City, Maryland.

Then, 4 years later, the unthinkable happened. "We were on vacation in Cancun, Mexico. It was late, about 11:30 P.M. I went to bed and she said she was going to sit on the balcony for a little while. I asked God to watch over her and dozed off.

"When I woke up, she wasn't in bed. The room was still locked from the inside. When I looked over the balcony railing, I saw her, lying on the balcony one floor below. She had suffered an aneurysm and had died almost instantly."

Joe felt bewildered and angry. "I couldn't understand *why* God didn't watch over her. I couldn't understand *why* God did this to me," he says.

Laws of nature do not make exceptions for nice people. A bullet has no conscience; neither does a malignant tumor or an automobile gone out of control. That is why good people get sick and get hurt as much as anyone.

—*Rabbi Harold S. Kushner*

When you hear of random suffering like this, it can fill you with many questions, even if you're a person of real faith. You begin to wonder how God can let bad things happen to good people, why during troubled times there are no signs of God's presence, or why so many other mysteries of faith exist.

Puzzles like these have occupied religious scholars, pastors, and faithful believers for thousands of years. Despite all the study and deep thought, no one in this life may ever know the answers to such questions. Still, pastors and counselors do have some ideas about the "whys" that may guide you as you explore your own faith journey.

Why Do Bad Things Happen to Good People?

The writers of the Old Testament blamed bad things and the suffering they bring on a jealous, wrathful God who punished people for sins. You might suffer because of sins you committed *or* because of the sins of your ancestors. So even if you did absolutely nothing wrong during your lifetime, an angry God might punish you for something a relative did years before.

Others see suffering as a by-product of the evil that has filled the world since the time of Adam and Eve. "God didn't let it loose on purpose. It results from the free will He bestowed upon us," says the Reverend Bruce Miller, pastor of St. Matthews-By-the-Sea in Fenwick Island, Delaware.

GOD, THE SOURCE OF ALL HOPE

Why are you cast down, O my soul,
and why are you disquieted within me?
Hope in God; for I shall again praise him,
my help and my God.

—Psalm 42:11 (NRSV)

There may be another answer, however. Perhaps suffering is a matter of misperception. Perhaps what you see as bad, as pain, is just God's way of opening you up to a deeper relationship with God.

"Humans avoid suffering at all costs, but maybe that's not the way to look at it," suggests Donovan Thesenga, director of Sevenoaks Pathwork Center in Madison, Virginia, and the coauthor of *Fear No Evil*. "Surrender to what God sends you even though you may not understand it." You may find that your suffering will bring you closer to God's master plan for your life, he says.

S. Bryant Kendrick Jr., doctor of ministry, agrees. "Suffering indicates our need for a renewed relationship with God," says Dr. Kendrick, who teaches medical ethics and counseling skills to medical students at Wake Forest University in Winston-Salem, North Carolina. "When we pray to God to end suffering, we may not always get what we ask for. But God does respond. No matter how much pain and suffering we have, nothing can separate us from our love of God, except ourselves."

For Joe Grasser, it took time to accept this truth. "I told God to leave me alone, to get out of my life. I vowed never to go to church or pray again. I just kept asking God 'Why?' and cursing Him for what He had done."

Then 9 months after Stephanie's death, Joe went to a treatment clinic in New Jersey for depression. "During a group session, I met another woman named Sandie, who was also being treated for depression. She also had a failed marriage but, unlike me, still had a deep faith that God would make it all well. After talking with her, I started to see hope that it would be possible for me to love again. Over time, I learned how to resolve my anger at Steph for leaving me and my sadness at not being able to tell her goodbye. Slowly I began to realize that no one could be blamed for Steph's death. She died because she had an

Prayer Miracles

Prayer Helped Me Understand Pain

When I was young my mother began a 3-year ordeal with cancer that slowly turned her into a human skeleton before her death. In time the morphine did not take and her demonstrations of pain were memorable. As I watched the events unfolding around me I spent a great deal of time trying to figure out why those I loved and myself were ever put on this Earth.

A year or so after my mother's death, I was alone in my room one night. I began asking God how He could exist and allow such misery in the world. I asked Him to show me some sign because life to me was totally useless. I was crying and pleading in prayer for understanding.

What I can only describe as a ball of light floated in the room and encompassed me, and I never before or since have felt such love and peace. I heard no words, but I understood that there was a God and that He was love and that everything was going to be all right.

There have been times in my life since then that I have lapsed in faith, but that incident has always been a factor in my return. I have grown to believe that even the most painful experiences in life are only there to assist in the development of our souls.

Richard R. Loucks
Pullman, Washington

aneurysm. She didn't leave me on purpose. God had always been there for her and for me. He had taken her with His love to a better place," he says.

How Do I Know God Is Listening?

You need to open your eyes and your senses to find the answer to this question; God will send you signs that God listens if *you* listen. The signs come in the way God's attitude changes. You may feel despair, and then suddenly with the Lord's presence comes hope. Or you may feel pride, but the Lord brings humility. You may feel sadness, and the Lord brings gratitude.

An even clearer indication that God hears us came during a test that the Reverend Sam Shoemaker conducted when he was rector of the Calvary Episcopal Church in Pittsburgh in the 1950s. Reverend Shoemaker was trying to convince a group of hard-edged businessmen that God listens—and responds, so he challenged them to pray this prayer daily for 30 days: "God, if You are real, reveal Yourself to me."

Reverend Shoemaker instructed the businessmen to pray each morning when they awoke, then whenever they thought of it each day. At the end of the 30 days, the men gathered together in wonder. Every one said God had shown a presence in some way. The men were so moved that they dedicated themselves to God and formed the Pittsburgh Experiment, which is now active in promoting faith around the world.

Of course, you don't need to have proof to believe God listens to your prayers, says Thesenga. If you believe in a loving God then you know you are heard, since listening is a sign of God's love, he explains. And God would no more stop listening than stop loving us. "God is incapable of not listening," says Thesenga. "God is always there."

Why Aren't All Prayers Answered?

"When we ask, 'Why aren't all prayers answered?' we really are asking, 'Why aren't all prayers granted?'" says Reverend Miller. "All prayers are answered, just not as we might wish."

Dr. Kendrick agrees. "God takes all of our requests seriously and responds

FINDING STRENGTH IN GOD

Though the fig tree does not blossom,

and no fruit is on the vines;

though the produce of the olive fails

and the fields yield no food;

though the flock is cut off from the fold

and there is no herd in the stalls,

yet I will rejoice in the Lord;

I will exult in the God of my salvation.

God, the Lord, is my strength;

He makes my feet like the feet of a deer,

and makes me tread upon the heights.

—*Habakkuk 3:17–19 (NRSV)*

by renewing our relationship with Him. We get a deeper relationship with God and a new understanding of ourselves," he says. "We may not always get what we asked for, but we get what we need.

"Maybe we just need to step back from our desire and instead ask, 'What does the Spirit have in store for me?'"

Thesenga takes another tack, saying prayers that are really requests—"please increase my salary," "please make my husband stop cheating"—are just pleas for favors. That, says Thesenga, is an immature way to pray. "To me the more interesting question is not, 'What do I want from God?' but rather, 'What does God want from me?'" he notes.

After all, we don't see the world or our lives the same way that God sees them. By trying to change God's mind through prayer, we may be missing the point. "Our lives are like tapestries that we only view from the backside—seeing the yarn going every which way, great knots of it here and there," says Reverend Miller. "Viewed from the rear, life is a mess. But in heaven we will see the tapestry of our lives from the front—the way God sees it now—and it will make sense."

That's how Joe Grasser sees it today. "Even though you get dealt a bad hand, God sometimes shuffles the cards and makes good come out of bad," says Grasser, who married Sandi three years after Stephanie's death. "God never answered my question of 'why?' But I now realize that He sometimes makes us wait. And His grace and love are forever. I've learned to accept what has happened and move forward," he says.

How Long Should I Persist in Prayer?

Many people worry that they don't pray long enough to get results, but that's not even an issue, says Father Larry Gillick, S.J., director of the Deglman Center for Ignatian Spirituality at Creighton University in Omaha, Nebraska. "God already loves you and will always love you," he says. The amount of time you put into prayer won't affect that, he adds.

Nor will it necessarily improve your chances of getting an answer. Instead of thinking about time, you should look at prayer as a conversation with God: You tell God about your life; God listens.

And if the conversation involves a problem and you aren't led to the answer, just leave your problem with God to deal with. Reverend Miller compares this tactic to a story he once heard about a child who brought a tangled ball of yarn to his mother. "The child went off, supremely confident that she would untangle it. He didn't have to stand around watching her every move. He just knew he could leave it with her and she would work it out," says Reverend Miller.

Why Won't God Give Us a Sign?

Maybe God's tired of signs.

All through the Bible, God gives signs. In Exodus, God performs numerous miracles to convince the Pharaoh to let the Hebrews go. In the Gospels, Jesus performs one miracle after another, including bringing people back from the dead.

Even so, doubters still found a way to explain away the signs. The Egyptians blamed the weather and magic. The doubters of Jesus' time said the people he cured were not really dead, blind, or sick. Even after the resurrection, doubters accused the disciples of hiding the body.

Never are we nearer the Light than when the darkness is deepest.

—*Vivekananda*

Others aren't certain that God has *stopped* giving us signs. Maybe we've simply stopped paying attention. "If you pay more attention to how God is acting in your life, you develop a sense of awe," says Katherine Brown-Saltzman, R.N., a devout Catholic and clinical nurse specialist who uses meditative prayer with her patients at UCLA Medical Center.

"Look for God in all of your experiences," suggests Dr. Kendrick. You might see the sign you are looking for in rainbows, butterflies and sunshine. If you interpret coincidences as God-incidences, you'll suddenly be surrounded by acts of God.

How Do I Know Whether I've Made the Right Decision?

Reverend Miller offers a story from his own life to answer this question. He used to sell insurance, despite the fact that he had a divinity degree.

He did so for many years and used his seminary background to teach adult Sunday school at the church he attended. Then one summer, becoming a full-time pastor suddenly felt right to him. An associate position at another church suddenly opened up. Everything fell into place. Somewhere in his soul, he knew he was ready for full-time ministry.

"For me confirmation that I have chosen rightly has always come in the form of a quiet feeling that affords me peace. There is that proverbial 'peace which passes all understanding' which I attribute to God," says Reverend Miller.

PRAYER FOR
GOD'S WILL

Searching for the True Answer

For centuries, believers wrestling with big decisions, small decisions, and everything in between have prayed to know what God would have them do. And for good reason. When you come down to it, once you know what God's will for you is, not much else really matters.

"I'm never afraid of knowing God's will because I know that God's will is the greatest thing that can happen to me under any circumstance," says the Reverend Danny E. Morris, a retired Methodist minister and the author of *Yearning to Know God's Will.*

Figuring out God's will isn't always so simple, of course. God transmits, but fear, temptation, greed, and a thousand other sources of static create interference on the line. Take heart, though: You can strengthen your receptive skills.

Two qualities are required up front for your prayers in this area to be rewarded, Reverend Morris says. First, you need a sincere desire to know God's will. Second, you must have a genuine commitment to pursue God's will once it's revealed. Asking God to rubber-stamp a decision you've already made won't do—you have to be prepared to go in directions you may not want to go.

To successfully pray for knowledge of God's will, you must first cultivate the habit of listening for God's voice and of feeling the presence of the Holy Spirit in your life, Reverend Morris says. Practicing the fundamentals of prayer and worship will bring you closer to both goals. You'll become accustomed to sensing when God is speaking to you about some issue; you'll feel God nudge you in a certain direction when you're debating what to do.

The actual nudges can come from an infinite variety of sources—perhaps in the words of a friend you're speaking to or from a scripture passage you happen to read or simply from a feeling of certainty that begins to grow in your gut. At some point you realize you can say, "I know what God wants me do." Reverend Morris cites three basic forms of praying for God's will.

- Yes or no prayers: These are prayers for God's guidance on specific, well-defined issues. You probably have an inclination in one direction or another, but you want to run it by God before committing. For example: "Dear Lord, I've been offered this promotion. I think it's the right move for me. Should I take it?"

- Open-ended prayers: These come into play when you know you need to do something but don't have a clue what it is. You need guidance simply to find the right path to walk. The issue at hand can be specific—"Lord, my marriage isn't working, and everything I've tried to mend it has failed. What should I do?"—or it can be more general—"Lord, I don't feel that I'm serving you well in my life. I can't find my calling. Point me in the right direction."

- Spiritual intuition: Many times, God's will becomes apparent without you even asking for it. Let's say you're driving down the street and suddenly you think of an old friend you haven't talked to recently. When you get home, you call her, only to learn she's just been diagnosed with breast cancer.
"How did you know to call?" she asks.
"God willed it," you're thinking, whether you tell her so or not.

"If you live the life of the Spirit, you don't need to sit on a stump and meditate consciously on every decision," Reverend Morris says. "It's as if God has a hand on your shoulder, gently prompting you as you bob and weave through the circumstances of life. You're walking by faith and are open to correction."

If you need to know God's will on a specific issue, make a point of asking for God's guidance in prayer. Be specific and be consistent: Keep praying until an answer comes.

How long should you pray? That depends on how much time you have.

"Sometimes time and circumstances force you to make a move before you're certain," says Reverend Morris. "In those cases, you need to say, 'God, I need to go forward with the light I have on this. Please go with me.' But if time permits, and you still have a chance to tap into the infinite resources of God's wisdom by staying the course in prayer, why not stay the course?"

Part 2

YOUR LOVE LIFE

Dating

Dating can be exciting and wondrous—a time when the seeds of love begin to grow and all of life seems brighter, better, and more meaningful. But finding a partner for the dance that leads to wedlock isn't always easy. Thankfully, prayer, faith, and friends can help you.

Two by two.

It was God's instruction to Noah in the Old Testament, and it's the way of life in relationships as well. You're meant to have a partner to share your life—the adventures, the good times, and the sad times.

Why then do some of us have such a tough time finding a mate? Because of missteps in the dating process itself, say counselors. Some people get caught up in what might be called "serial dating." They date person after person after person with whom they have little in common and never find the meaningful relationship they crave. Others have trouble taking their dating to the next level—making a complete commitment—even when they like the person they're dating.

How do you overcome dating patterns like these? Through three steps, say some counselors.

- First, you need to identify your core values and seek partners with similar beliefs.

- Second, you need to learn to trust and open up to the people you like.
- Third, if you develop a relationship that seems to have promise, you need to affirm you're making the right choice.

"There's a good deal of work that goes into developing a mature relationship and a good deal of guidance to be gleaned from friends, community members, family, and God," says the Reverend H. Scott Matheney, dean of the chapel at Elmhurst College in suburban Chicago.

> *For one human being to love another: that is perhaps the most difficult of all our tasks, the ultimate, the last test and proof, the work, for which all other work is but preparation.*
>
> —*Rainer María Rílke*

Common Values

"A good relationship isn't so much a matter of chemistry, as compatibility," says Herbert Anderson, Ph.D., former professor of pastoral theology at Catholic Theological Union in Chicago.

Yet when many couples start dating they overlook this fundamental truth. They develop a "pseudo-intimacy," remarks Chaplain Matheney. "They feel a strong initial attraction that's a mile high but an inch deep; they mistake scintillation for love and only later discover that this person is not necessarily good for them," he says.

You don't have to share the same set of beliefs or values with a partner to develop a close relationship, but counselors agree that you're in for a rough road if your values don't at least complement the other person's.

"There has to be some similarity in ethics or faith journey, or, more importantly, they should not clash," says Dorothy Becvar, Ph.D., a marriage and family therapist.

So how do you find out if your attraction to someone is more than just a stirring of chemicals? "A relationship is an ongoing process of discernment; we learn as we go," says Dr. Anderson. Here are some of the tools he and the other counselors suggest using along the way.

1. Make a List of Your Values

Take an inventory of what is meaningful to you, maybe even using a scale of one to ten to rate their worth. Ask yourself questions such as: How important is regular worship in my faith life? How much money do I want to earn?

A Prayer for Real Love

Let love be genuine.

Hate that which is evil, hold fast to that which is good.

Love one another with the affection of a sister or a brother.

Outdo one another in showing honor.

Never flag in zeal.

Be aglow with the spirit.

Serve the Lord.

Rejoice in your hope.

Be patient in tribulation.

Be constant in prayer.

Contribute to the needs of the saints.

Practice hospitality . . .

Live in harmony with one another.

—Romans 12:9–13, 16 (RSV)

Do I believe in tithing? Do I want my home to be a place that welcomes strangers? As you meet new people, find out whether they share the things that are important to you. As Jesus said, "For where your treasure is, there will your heart be also" (Matthew 6:21, KJV).

2. Look for Overlaps

If the connections aren't immediately apparent between your core beliefs and those of the person you're dating, look for ways in which they can overlap. Search for at least one activity consistent with both your beliefs that you can share—even if you do the activity for different reasons.

For example, "One of you might believe that politics and faith don't mix and the other might be a strong proponent of faith-based political activism," says Andrew Lester, Ph.D., professor of pastoral theology and pastoral coun-

---

A PRAYER FOR RELATIONSHIPS

Dear God,

We surrender this relationship to You.

May it serve Your purposes and be blessed by You always.

Fill our minds with Your thoughts.

May we always be led to the highest vision of each other.

Remove any obstruction to our highest love.

Thank You very much.

Amen.

—*Marianne Williamson*

---

seling at Brite Divinity School in Fort Worth, Texas. The solution? "Work together for a group like Habitat for Humanity, building homes for the poor," Dr. Lester suggests. "Whether you define it as a social justice issue or an act of religious charity, you both feel the compulsion to do something good and gain the pleasure that comes from doing it together."

Open Your Heart

Dating is a dance in which both partners share the lead. If you want to develop a meaningful connection you have to be willing to reveal what's in your heart. For some people that's a challenge, particularly when it comes to their religious life.

"Spiritual intimacy is a tough thing to develop," says Dr. Lester. "We're afraid that our beliefs will be challenged or even ridiculed by the other person." But if you're trying to create a close relationship with someone you have to open up and trust, says Dr. Lester.

How to do it? When you feel it's appropriate to discuss your spiritual beliefs, Dr. Lester suggests sharing your story, perhaps in the form of a journal. Divide your life chronologically and include both the joyous memories and the rough spots.

If the idea of expressing intimacy in any form is preventing you from opening up, Dr. Becvar has a suggestion: Pray for the ability to follow the commandment spoken by Confucius, Rabbi Hillel, Mohammed, and Jesus—that you love others as you love yourself.

"To me, learning to love someone else starts with self-love," says Dr. Becvar. "I sometimes encourage people literally to look themselves in the mirror and say repeatedly, 'I love you just as you are.' It can be daunting, but only if you have a healthy love of self will you be strong enough to love another person and at the same time remain true to who you are."

Seek Advice in All the Right Places

Once you've found a possible partner, the next step is to decide whether to take the relationship to the next level. This is when you can call in the "angels" for feedback on whether this relationship seems right,

Prayer Miracles

Prayer Brought Me a Wife

Frustrated, I knelt by the couch and poured my heart out to God. "God, I am ready to settle down and get married. Give me a wife. If you don't I will not be responsible for the consequences." It sounds disrespectful now, but this prayer was borne of a real need. I had come to Canada from Holland 3 years earlier and loneliness had settled in.

When I got up from my sincere prayer, the first thought that came to me was "go talk to your Dad." I borrowed money and booked a ticket home for Christmas. Soon I found myself at home. Dad said, "Son, do you have a girlfriend in Canada?" I responded, "No, the way I like them they don't make them anymore."

"Don't be anxious about this," he said. "You will meet the right girl, and when you do all doubt and anxiety will leave, and you will know instantly that she is the one for you."

What a peace filled me. God was at work, and Dad's words turned out to be prophetic. Unknown to me, at about the same time, my buddy Kees's younger sister Truus was praying that she would find a husband.

The very next day, I went off to visit Kees. I talked to his stepmother and learned that he was not there. As I turned to leave I stood face to face with Truus. The peace Dad had talked about came over me like a blanket. I was sure I was face to face with my wife. Truus felt the same way. Truus and I got engaged a month later and married that spring. This year we will celebrate our 40th anniversary.

Ted deCock
Winnipeg, Canada

says Chaplain Matheney. "Although dating is an intensely personal thing, God can speak to us through the people around us who love, know, and care about us," he says.

Counselors identify at least three sources of support.

Q&A: God as Divine Matchmaker?

Q: Can I ask God to find me a good partner?

A: That's probably not realistic, says the Reverend H. Scott Matheney, dean of the chapel at Elmhurst College in suburban Chicago. "But you can ask Him to guide you." Or, as the Reverend Alison Boden, dean of Rockefeller Chapel at the University of Chicago, says, "God can help you ascertain what you need, which is sure to be more useful to you in the long haul than what you think you want."

If you would like to pray for God's help in developing a relationship, pastoral counselors suggest you pray in three ways.

1. Pray for Wisdom
Ask God to help you understand what constitutes a meaningful relationship and what kind of person can create one with you. "God can help us be clear about who this other person is and whether or not we make a good match," says Herbert Anderson, Ph.D., former professor of pastoral theology at Catholic Theological Union in Chicago.

2. Pray for Courage
Ask God for the courage to abide by your sense about what's best for you, even if there is pressure to do otherwise. "People can feel enormous pressure to make an exclusive commitment to their dating partner, become physically involved before they're ready to do so, or perhaps give up time once spent with old friends," says Dr. Anderson, "and because we don't want to drive the other person away, it takes a great deal of courage to assert what we really want."

3. Pray for Guidance
Ask God to direct you and your new partner through your relationship. "God can provide a couple with open hearts and clear minds," says Chaplain Matheney, "so they can better know what kind of relationship they should be creating, at what pace, and whether in fact they should continue to be together."

1. Parents, Friends, and Your Congregation

Ask people who know and care about you if they think your relationship is strong and healthy and if they have any thoughts about how you should begin contemplating whether or not you're ready for marriage.

2. A Pastoral Counselor

Talk to a pastoral counselor about some of the broader issues of a committed relationship. He or she can help you decide where you want to be 5 or 10 years from now, how many (if any) children you want to have, and what religious training you want your children to receive. Also, the pastoral counselor can help you learn how effectively to resolve differences that might arise in your relationship.

3. Couples' Groups

Talk to other couples. Many churches, synagogues, and mosques bring couples together in groups for prayer and conversation about the many aspects of dating. "If nothing else," notes Chaplain Matheney, "when you are with others you begin to realize that you're not such a peculiar couple after all, that others have some of the same questions and anxieties you have."

You . . . alone bear the responsibility for what no one can take from you. . . . But God adds His "Yes" to your "Yes," as He confirms your will with His will, and as He allows you, and approves of, your triumph and rejoicing and pride.

—Dietrich Bonhoeffer

The Loving Marriage

Close, affectionate marriages don't just happen. Nor do they result from blessings bestowed upon a lucky few. Each one takes careful, prayerful work. Here's how to shape your relationship using faith, devotion, and the mysterious languages of love.

opular songs and movies tend to obscure a few nasty secrets about marriage.

Marriage is about more than romance.

Marriage takes work.

Marriage is hard.

For many couples, these facts come as shocks that spark untold disappointment, heartache, and, in many cases, divorce—an option that well over 50 percent of the married people in this country choose.

How can what starts off so tenderly turn so wrong? Part of it is the masking influence of budding love, says Gary Chapman, Ph.D., of Winston-Salem, North Carolina, author of *Toward a Growing Marriage*, *Loving Solutions*, and *The Five Love Languages*.

When people first fall in love, the emotion runs so deep that they close their eyes to the things they may not like about the other person. But "the experience of being 'in love' only lasts, on average, 2 years," says Dr. Chapman. "Once we return to a normal emotional state, all our differences and our conflicts can begin to surface, and we end up fighting the person that a short while before we were in love with."

It doesn't have to be that way. Marriages can be as romantic and fulfilling over the long term as the songwriters and screenwriters say they should be—even more so. There is a depth of satisfaction to a truly loving marriage—the authentic joining into "one flesh," spiritually as well as physically—that the bright burst of first romance can never attain.

> *The best way to know God is to love many things.*
>
> — *Vincent van Gogh*

How can you and your spouse reach this state in your relationship? By paying attention to three key building blocks of lasting love:

- Spiritual intimacy: This is a state of closeness in which you and your spouse transcend your shyness and defensiveness about faith and pray together.
- True communication: More than just talking together, true communication involves listening and empathizing with each other.
- The languages of love: You and your spouse each have an understanding of what love means and how love is communicated. To grow closer to your spouse, you need to figure out each other's "language" and use it regularly.

Pray Together

It would be hard to think of a better way to start building a strong foundation for a marriage than through prayer. One of the deepest forms of intimacy a husband and wife can share is spiritual, and there's no better way to promote this spiritual closeness than to pray together.

"They say three's a crowd, but a threesome can be constructive if the third party is a higher power," says Michael J. McManus, president and founder of Marriage Savers, a consulting group in Bethesda, Maryland, that helps churches establish marriage ministries. "Praying together builds intimacy at a spiritual level that can only help with other forms of intimacy."

Yet many couples find praying together difficult, perhaps for the very reason that it requires spouses to reveal themselves in a kind of nakedness to which they are unaccustomed.

"When you come to God, there's that sense that you want to be completely authentic," says Dr. Chapman. "When you start to be authentic with

God in the presence of your spouse, you're kind of vulnerable, especially if there are some things about yourself you haven't really shared with your spouse."

To get over this initial nervousness, Dr. Chapman recommends starting out by praying silently together, hands clasped and eyes closed. You and your spouse can signal when you're through by saying "Amen." When the two of you become comfortable with that, you can move on to single sentence prayers offered out loud, either alternating prayers or just playing it by ear. One example is this line from Psalm 67: "O God, be gracious and bless us and let your face shed its light upon us" (KJV).

Another option is to offer prayers of praise, which are nonthreatening, Dr. Chapman says. Try thanking God for the specific blessings you've experienced that day, for example, or for the gift of God's presence and guidance in your life. From there you can gradually become more specific and more detailed in your prayers together, as you feel more comfortable.

What if one spouse is uneasy verbalizing prayers? Then be creative in how you express yourself, suggests Carolyn Bohler, Ph.D., professor of pastoral theology and counseling at United Theological Seminary in Dayton, Ohio. Instead of jumping right into prayer, try just spending a minute or two in silence together, taking a quiet walk together, or repeating a simple phrase three times, such as, "We're open to God in our lives."

Whatever direction you decide to take, Dr. Bohler urges that prayer not become a source of discord and division between you and your partner. If one

BRING JOY BACK INTO MARRIAGE

Lord, let the light of your presence bring joy back into our marriage. Burn bright within each of us, to warm us and cheer us so that it breaks down the fog between us.

Dear Lord, shine through me as a person to reach my husband and draw close to him in love and joy, the way you meant us to.

—Marjorie Holmes

THE TIES THAT BIND US

We are the mirror as well as the face in it.
We are tasting the taste this minute
of eternity. We are pain
and what cures pain, both. We are
the sweet cold water and the jar that pours.

—*Rumi, thirteenth-century Sufi poet and mystic*

spouse isn't enthusiastic about the prospect of praying together, she says, don't push it relentlessly.

Another pitfall to avoid is the prayer that's meant more for your spouse's ears than for God's. "I know people who have prayed things like, 'God, please make my partner less angry,'" says Dr. Bohler. "That's not right. If you have something to say to your partner, say it directly. It's not fair to use prayer for that purpose."

Loving Communication 101

Marital counselors will tell you that a husband and wife can't have a fulfilling marriage unless they know how to communicate successfully with one another. This doesn't mean superficial communication—the "you won't believe what so-and-so said at work today" or "I need to get the kids new shorts for soccer" kind of remarks. It means loving, spiritual communication—really listening and identifying with the feelings each of you has.

Unfortunately, there are lots of significant roadblocks to conversational intimacy. Differences in your personal style of communication, misinterpreting what the other partner is saying, and fear of revealing things about yourself are just a few. These and more can block your attempts to really connect.

It is possible to get beyond this and build more spiritual communication in your relationship. Here are some guidelines, compiled by Pastor Steve Carr,

Tools of Faith

The Art of Listening

Learning to listen well is one of the most important skills a loving spouse can acquire. Here are the basic rules, as defined by marital therapists.

1. Maintain eye contact when your spouse is talking.

2. Don't listen to your spouse and do something else at same time.

3. Listen empathically, making an effort to understand the emotions your spouse is feeling. When he or she is finished, confirm your understanding of what's been said by verbally paraphrasing the essence of the message back to your partner. Allow your partner to clarify if necessary.

4. Observe body language. If your mate verbally goes along with something you're proposing but sits staring down at the table, that's a sign that perhaps the agreement isn't as wholehearted as it might be. If you sense the words being spoken don't seem to match the manner of expression, ask for clarification.

5. Don't interrupt. Research has shown that on average people listen for only 17 seconds before interrupting, notes Gary Chapman, Ph.D., a Christian marriage counselor and seminar leader. The point of quality listening is not to interject your own ideas, but to thoroughly and sympathetically hear out your spouse.

founder of Covenant Keepers and author of *Married and How to Stay That Way.*

Be willing. This is where communication—and love—has to begin, Pastor Carr says. With the couples he's counseled, unwillingness to communicate lovingly is more often the cause of marital difficulty than is a lack of ability to communicate. Many husbands, for example, simply don't believe they need to tell their wives how they're really feeling, perhaps because they've been raised to believe that to do so isn't manly. In other marriages the wife is so focused on shuttling the kids from school to soccer practice to ballet lessons to play dates that connecting with her husband assumes a lower priority.

You need to set aside these feelings, turn away from other tasks, and focus on the person you've pledged to love.

Give up your excuses. Pastor Carr has heard them all, from "My parents weren't good role models when it came to talking with each other" to "I had an abusive father, so I don't feel comfortable opening myself up to men." To these he responds with a story from Exodus, in which Moses resisted becoming God's designated spokesman with the excuse that he lacked adequate communication skills.

"O my Lord," he cried, "I have never been eloquent. . . . I am slow of speech and slow of tongue."

To which God answered: "Who gives speech to mortals? Who makes them mute or deaf, seeing or blind? . . . Now go, and I will be with your mouth and teach you what you are to speak" (Exodus 4:11–12, RSV).

The message is clear, Pastor Carr says: Pray to God for help and instruction. Like Moses, you may be surprised at what you can accomplish.

Fess up. Effective communication ends when either partner can't admit weakness. What sorts of weakness? Pastor Carr lists the following examples:

- Stubbornly refusing to acknowledge faults
- Attacking the other person angrily when the two of you disagree
- Exaggerating the facts to make one partner look better

All of these are signs that you're behaving badly. To communicate with love, both spouses need to acknowledge their failures and ask for forgiveness. If you have trouble taking this step, ask God for the ability to do better.

Reduce distractions. Each partner needs attention to feel loved; marriages need it to stay alive. If work or hobbies are taking too much time away from talking to your spouse, pare them down. If your kids keep interrupting, once a week or so leave them with their grandparents or hire a babysitter so you and your spouse can take a break together. Whatever distractions come

LOVE FOR A LIFETIME

I add my breath to your breath

that our days be long on the Earth

that the days of our people may be long,

that we shall be as one person,

that we may finish our road together.

—Pueblo prayer

between you and your spouse, change them. Successful communication has to be an absolute priority.

The Languages of Love

During the "in love" phase of a relationship, it seems as if each partner instantly and intuitively understands the love the other partner feels for him or her. That doesn't last. As the excitement of first love ebbs and each spouse shifts focus to the activities of day-to-day life and work, the sense of love and the little ways you each used to express it can fall by the wayside. Familiarity breeds neglect. Or worse, you and your spouse may just presume that a quick "love ya, honey" is all the other person needs to hear to know your true feelings.

"We all tend to assume that whatever makes 'me' feel loved also makes 'my spouse' feel loved, but that's a false premise," says Dr. Chapman. "We're all different, and we feel love in different ways."

Figuring out what each spouse needs in order to feel truly loved—what love "language" he or she best understands—is a fundamental step toward building a successful, devoted marriage, says Dr. Chapman. He believes that most of us respond primarily to one or two of the following love languages.

What Would **Jesus** Do?

How do partners express love for each other? One way is by performing acts of loving service, says Gary Chapman, Ph.D., author of *Toward a Growing Marriage, Loving Solutions*, and *The Five Love Languages*. The Gospel of John provides a useful model of this "language" of love as Jesus spoke it.

"*Jesus, knowing that the Father had given all things into his hands and that he had come from God and was going to God, got up from the table, took off his outer robe, and tied a towel around himself.* *Then he poured water into a basin and began to wash the disciples' feet and to wipe them with the towel that was tied around him. . . . After he had washed their feet, had put on his robe, and had returned to the table, he said to them, 'Do you know what I have done to you? You call me Teacher and Lord—and you are right, for that is what I am. So if I, your Lord and Teacher, have washed your feet, you also ought to wash one another's feet. For I have set you an example, that you also should do as I have done to you.'*"

(John 13:3–15, NRSV)

1. Words of affirmation: Many people need to be told that they're loved, that they're worthwhile, that their efforts are appreciated. These affirmations are usually verbal, Dr. Chapman says, but written notes count, too. He recommends simple, direct statements. "You look great in that dress," for example, or "I think you're a really good father."

Words of encouragement are another "dialect" in this love language, Dr. Chapman adds. Helping spouses believe in themselves, giving them the courage to overcome their fears or to achieve their dreams, is as powerful a marriage-builder as you can get.

2. Quality time: It's not just the amount of time you and your spouse spend with each other that matters. Time *plus* focus is the formula that produces marital bliss. A husband can spend the day with his wife, sunup to sundown. If he's watching TV the entire time, not much meaningful communication is going on. Dr. Chapman defines quality time as "giving your spouse your undivided attention." You don't have to be sitting across from one another at a table for undivided attention to occur, he points out. Going on a walk together, or on a date, can serve the same purpose.

3. Gift-giving: Studies of cultures around the world reveal that gift-giving is "the universal language of love," says Dr. Chapman. The reason is obvious: When you give a gift you demonstrate that you're thinking of the other person.

Prayer Miracles

Prayer with a Doctor Saved My Husband's Life

On February 2, my husband came home from work, saying he didn't feel well and was going to bed. When I went in 15 minutes later to check on him, I noticed that he looked bad. A short time later he was incoherent. I called 911 and they rushed him to the emergency room where he was diagnosed with bacterial meningitis. The doctor told me and my two daughters to call our son home because my husband would not live through the night. I asked the doctor if he believed in the power of prayer. He said, "I sure do." I then asked if he would pray with me. He said he would be happy to. We prayed, and it was then I felt the Lord's presence. I knew He would save my husband's life. My husband survived, and the doctors called him a walking miracle. I thank the good Lord every day, for every day He gives us all.

Pat Baunsgard
Fullerton, California

Gifts can come in many forms, including companionship. "We can give the gift of self by being present with those we love," reminds Dr. Chapman. If some degree of sacrifice is involved, so much the better. The wife may not particularly enjoy going to football games, for example, but she goes cheerfully because she understands how much her husband enjoys them. The husband may hate antique-hunting, but he patiently accompanies his wife as she scours the shops. The willingness to participate in less-than-desirable activities for the sake of one's spouse is a meaningful gift of loving partnership.

> *Love cannot live without faith; faith cannot live without love.*
>
> —*Unknown*

4. Acts of service: Doing something you know your spouse would like to have done can be another powerful emotional expression of love. Having a meal on the table or keeping the lawn mowed can be just as meaningful as saying "I love you." The Golden Rule says it all: Do unto others as you would have them do unto you. Dr. Chapman adds that in this day and age, we should no longer assume that cooking or mowing, or many other jobs, have to be done by either the man or the woman. Traditional gender roles no longer apply in many cases.

5. Physical touch: This isn't just about sex, although regular intercourse is an important part of a loving marriage. "Meaningful, tender touch"—a stroke of the hair, a squeeze of the hand—speaks volumes, Dr. Chapman says.

To see if you and your partner are meeting each other's needs, try to list, on paper, which of these languages you respond to best and which your spouse responds to. Do this together with your spouse, if possible. You can also watch for clues about your spouse's desires by practicing each language and seeing which one gets the most enthusiastic response. What sorts of things does your spouse most often request from you, for example? What sorts of things seem to bother your spouse most when he or she is neglected or overlooked? Follow those clues to become fluent in your partner's languages of love.

Harmful Arguments

❦

Disagreements are a part of married life. It's how you handle them that determines whether they'll cause your relationship to wither or flourish. The right path lies in learning to fight fairly—and constructively.

T here wasn't anything unusual about the fights Jan and Lee Kremer were having, but that didn't make them any easier to take.

The source of their problem? Money. Lee's daughter from his first marriage would call from college saying that her checking account was overdrawn: Please send money! Lee would agree to send her some, which angered Jan. They would argue, but mostly Jan would withdraw. For a few days not much would be said between them.

Not surprisingly, not much got resolved between them either, until they went to a marriage encounter weekend they'd heard about in church. It was there that the Kremers began to learn how to fight more openly—and more constructively.

"We were told to write down our feelings on paper, and then to talk about them with our spouse," Jan says. "What Lee and I found was that we both had similar feelings. Both of us felt frustrated with the requests and didn't know what to do."

"When I understood how he felt about this money thing, I saw it from a whole different perspective," says Jan.

A whole new perspective that eased tensions significantly.

It may be hard to believe if you're in the middle of a tense argument, but it is possible to find common ground and successfully resolve a conflict if you approach it with a prayerful, loving attitude, say counselors. Three steps can help you begin.

- Learn to pray—together and separately—for understanding, patience, and forgiveness.
- Learn to understand the feelings that underlie your spouse's behavior.
- Learn to argue fairly and constructively.

Turn to God First

The best way to start dealing with marital conflict is to bring God into the picture. "Because God is love, marriages need to have God at the center," says Jan Kremer, who with her husband is now a national team leader for Worldwide Marriage Encounter, an ecumenical organization that is dedicated to strengthening relationships.

> *Be angry but do not sin; do not let the sun go down on your anger, and do not make room for the devil.*
>
> *—Ephesians 4:26–27 (RSV)*

Of course, praying together in the midst of an argument is not always the easiest thing to do. For that reason, Kremer recommends that during calmer times each of you ground yourself spiritually by praying for help in being an understanding and patient listener. These prayers can be written down and shared with your partner, if you like. Such sharing can help establish a loving, prayerful tone for your talks, and it can open an opportunity for praying together for couples who are comfortable with that.

And when an argument starts? It may seem just the opposite of what you want to do, but you should turn to prayer then, too. Pray intensely for your spouse, suggests Everett Worthington Jr., Ph.D., author of *Hope-Focused Marriage Counseling* and numerous other books. "We tend to pray mostly about ourselves," Dr. Worthington says, "but I think the key to getting past conflict is to start focusing on the other person, and you can do that by praying for them. We don't pray for God to show them the error of their ways, but rather for blessing. We pray for the ability to have empathy with our partner."

Prayer can play another important role, says Dr. Worthington. It calls God to actively intervene to help heal the rifts between you and your spouse.

A Prayer for Harmony

United your resolve,
united your hearts,
may your spirits be at one,
that you may long dwell
in unity and concord.

—The Rig-Veda

The Issues behind the Issue

The next step in defusing harmful arguments and resolving conflicts is understanding what's going on below the surface of your marital discord.

All disagreements are not created equal. There are "small ticket" issues—one partner forgetting to put the top on the toothpaste or another leaving the toilet seat up are examples—and "big ticket" issues—such as criticizing a spouse in front of others—says Gary J. Oliver, Ph.D., executive director of The Center for Marriage and Family Studies at John Brown University in Siloam Springs, Arkansas, and coauthor of *How to Bring Out the Best in Your Spouse.* Obviously, the more able you are to shrug off the smaller ticket items, the smoother your relationship will be.

Be aware, however, that small ticket items often become the vehicles through which bigger ticket emotions are expressed. "Toothpaste or toilet seats can become big issues if they become symbols of a power struggle," says Dr. Worthington. "They have a lot of meaning for who is winning the war, who is influencing whom, and who has the say in a given situation."

Failing to appreciate these underlying issues is a major reason why so many married couples can continue to have essentially the same fight, in slightly different guises, for years—even decades.

Many couples also stumble into minefields by failing to appreciate how differently men and women can react to disagreements. Men, for example, are more likely to avoid open conflict by refusing to talk about it, says John Gottman, Ph.D., author of *The Seven Principles for Making Marriage Work.* Women, on the other hand, often prefer to talk through issues.

GOD BLESS THIS RELATIONSHIP

Dear God,

Please make of our relationship a great and holy adventure,

May our joining be a sacred space.

May the two of us find rest here, a haven for our souls.

Remove from us any temptation to judge one another or to direct one another.

We surrender to You our conflicts and our burdens.

We know You are our Answer and our rock.

Help us to not forget.

Bring us together in heart and mind as well as body.

Remove from us the temptation to criticize or be cruel.

May we not be tempted by fantasies and projections.

But guide us in the ways of holiness.

Save us from darkness.

May this relationship be a burst of light.

May it be a fount of love and wisdom for us, for our family, for our community, for our world.

May this bond be a channel for Your love and healing, a vehicle of Your grace and power.

These are not hard-and-fast rules, but it pays to be aware that you may have an entirely different response to an argument than your mate does. The Kremers' problems with his financially strapped daughter are a case in point: When Lee failed to share his own frustration with the requests, Jan assumed he didn't have any discomfort. She was mistaken.

This is exactly why the single most important goal in resolving marital conflicts has to be understanding. Not winning, not comprising, not deciding who is right or wrong, but *understanding*.

"Without being able to understand what is actually going on with your partner, you may never find a solution to whatever it is you're arguing about,

As lessons come and challenges grow, let us not be tempted to forsake each other.

Let us always remember that in each other we have the most beautiful woman, the most beautiful man,

The strongest one,

The sacred one in whose arms we are repaired.

May we remain young in this relationship.

May we grow wise in this relationship.

Bring us what You desire for us,

And show us how You would have us be.

Thank You, dear God.

You who are the cement between us.

Thank You for this love.

Amen.

—*Marianne Williamson*

or you may get a temporary solution that's not going to last," Dr. Oliver says. "When couples really do understand each other, frequently they realize there really isn't a conflict at all."

If you're in the midst of conflict, attempting to understand your partner can soften the hard shell of resistance that makes resolution difficult. "When my wife knows that my heart's desire is to understand, rather than to coerce or convince, that produces freedom and receptivity in her, and vice versa," Dr. Oliver says.

Or, as Dr. Worthington puts it, "Empathy is the key to repairing a relationship. Pray for the ability to get into your partner's frame of mind, and pray that your partner will be blessed with the ability to understand you."

A PRAYER FOR PEACE

O God, through the death of your Son you reconciled us one to another, drawing us together in the bond of peace. In times of trouble and adversity, may your peace sustain us, calming our fretful and anxious hearts, and saving us from all hateful and violent activities.

—Mozarabic Sacramentary

Arguing with LOVE, Step by Step

It's one thing to say you and your partner should strive to understand each other; it's another to know how to achieve that goal. One place to start: regular talks—scheduled, once a week at least—whether or not you're having conflicts at the moment, says Dr. Oliver.

Once you're sitting together, Dr. Worthington recommends four basic principles that can help guide the broad outline of your discussion in fruitful directions. Appropriately enough, the first letters of these four principles spell out the word "LOVE."

L: Listen and Repeat

Arguing couples often stop listening to one another. "When we feel misunderstood, it's usually because we *are* misunderstood," says Dr. Worthington. Being misunderstood creates a vicious cycle. Each partner tunes out when the other is talking, focusing on formulating a response that will finally get his or her point of view across. The other partner senses that lack of focus and becomes equally frustrated and unable to listen.

Using the "Listen and Repeat" method ensures that you are *listening to*, not just hearing, your partner. Here's how it works. After one partner speaks, the other should voice a short summary of what's just been said: "I hear you saying that you feel frustrated when I don't do more to help get the kids off to school," for example.

This technique assures the speaker that he or she has been understood and offers an opportunity for clarification if it's needed. Many couples also find it helpful to pass a physical object back and forth to clarify whose turn it is to talk and whose turn it is to listen. Dr. Worthington suggests a foam ball ("the ball's in your court") or a dollar bill ("the buck stops here").

O: Observe Your Effects

Often there's a difference between what one spouse says and what the other hears. To guard against misunderstandings, Dr. Worthington suggests you each pay attention to the way the other person reacts to your words. If you are explaining that you didn't intentionally insult your brother-in-law at the family picnic but your spouse looks even angrier than before, perhaps you should clarify. Try something along these lines: "I feel like I didn't communicate as clearly as I would like. What I meant to say was . . ."

V: Value Your Partner

In every communication, strive to treat your partner with respect and love, Dr. Worthington says. At all costs, avoid contemptuous expressions, verbal and otherwise—rolling your eyes, criticizing your spouse in front of others, or making ridiculing or disparaging remarks. "Contempt," Dr. Worthington says, "is the poison of family relationships."

E: Evaluate Both Partners' Interests

At all times you should strive to understand what's really going on with your partner, remembering that the surface issue isn't necessarily the "real" issue at hand. Don't get thrown by the positions staked out by you or your partner, Dr. Worthington says. Look instead for the underlying, important goals. For example, a complaint about dirty dishes in the sink may have less to do with the dishes themselves and more to do with one partner's need for a peaceful, orderly home life to balance out the stress of a chaotic job. Always keep your eyes on the primary goal: maintaining a loving, happy marriage.

Q&A: How Can I Avoid Conflicts?

Q: It seems my spouse and I are fighting all the time. How can I avoid future arguments?

A: You shouldn't. What you and most arguing couples don't realize is that conflict can be one of the most constructive tools in a marriage. Why? Because, says Gary J. Oliver, Ph.D., coauthor of *How to Bring Out the Best in Your Spouse*, conflict brings the true issues that threaten your marriage out into the open. Once they're out in the open, you can deal with them. Couples who are willing to deal with their problems come away with stronger, more loving unions.

Stopping the Madness

Disagreements are inevitable. Hand-to-hand combat is not. One way to fight constructively is to keep your disagreements from spiraling into hurtful exchanges of insults and expletives that can permanently damage your marriage.

Before you speak, it is necessary for you to listen, for God speaks in the silence of the heart.

—*Mother Teresa*

Couples who attend the Worldwide Marriage Encounter Weekends run by Jan and Lee Kremer are usually handed a list of guidelines for fighting fairly. (Their definition of the term "fight" never includes violence—physical, verbal, or mental.) If you find yourself in an argument with your spouse, here are nine ways to ensure that your fight produces positive results, rather than more fighting.

1. Avoid name-calling and character assassination.

2. Never fight when one or both of you are under the influence of alcohol or drugs.

3. Don't waste time trying to place blame.

4. Avoid absolute statements ("you never," "every time," "you always"). They are seldom true.

5. Finish the fight. Be sensitive to your spouse's feelings if he or she becomes emotional, but continue the fight *for* your relationship. If emotions are spiraling out of control, take a "time out" until you can resume a constructive discussion. Then schedule a specific time for returning to the issue.

6. Do not bring in third parties. They have no part in your confrontation.

7. Stay physically close to each other. An affectionate touch helps each of you know there is nothing that cannot be worked out in love.

8. Don't let the issue you're discussing become more important than your relationship.

9. Fight for clarification, not to win.

For more information on Worldwide Marriage Encounter Weekends, write to Worldwide Marriage Encounter, 2210 East Highland Avenue, Suite 106, San Bernardino, CA 92404-4666. Another resource for married couples who are struggling is The Coalition for Marriage, Family and Couples Education, 5310 Belt Road, NW, Washington, DC, 20015-1961.

Role Changes

Lost jobs, career shifts, illnesses—changes like these can put strain on you and your spouse and threaten to swamp your marital boat. This is when you need to use faith and teamwork to keep you afloat.

After years as a successful businessman, a husband loses his job— along with his status as the major breadwinner—and has to handle chores around the house while his wife earns the money to pay their bills.

A mother battling breast cancer has to give up the role she loves taking care of her home and her kids.

A wife is elected president of the school board and suddenly becomes more well-known than her husband.

Role changes like these can put a major strain on a marriage. They can threaten each spouse's identity and self-worth and leave both wondering how to restore balance and how to revive the self-respect each one needs. If you reach a crisis like this in your relationship, pastors and counselors recommend three ways to weather the shift gracefully and triumphantly.

- Seek solace and guidance from God and from your spouse.
- Candidly discuss your concerns and look for solutions.
- Look to friends and your faith community for help.

Teamwork First

The first thing to affirm when life throws you a curve is that you are not alone in your crisis.

God is with you. Now more than ever, calling on God in prayer will be reassuring.

Things turn out best for the people who make the best out of the way things turn out.

—Art Linkletter

"God doesn't promise to keep us from going through difficult times, but He does promise to be there with us in the midst of them," says Robert Lauer, Ph.D., an ordained Presbyterian minister and coauthor of *Watersheds: Mastering Life's Unpredictable Crises.* Psalm 23 testifies to that, Dr. Lauer points out: "Yea, though I walk through the valley of the shadow of death, I will fear no evil: for thou art with me."

Your second focus should be on the fact that you and your spouse are a team. Your individual roles on the team may shift, but the joint effort and the stability of the partnership remain.

This may not be as simple to accept as it seems, says Dr. Lauer. You and your spouse have built-in expectations that each of you will fulfill certain roles and perform certain tasks in the marriage. When these roles change, it can create tension between the two of you. For example, if a wife suddenly starts earning more than her husband, the husband can feel threatened emotionally. If he reacts with anger or sullenness, the wife may be upset that her success isn't being appreciated.

If you feel yourself falling into a trap like this, stop. Reaffirm that you love each other and that the two of you are partners. Then resolve to tackle your problem together. "I ask all of my clients who are in this situation to repeat a slogan," Dr. Lauer says. "It isn't 'you have a problem.' It's 'we have a problem.' The key is that couples work these issues out in partnership."

Seek Out Answers

With God and one another, you're well on your way to solving your problems. The next step is to look for explicit answers. Here are four ways you can do that.

God, Show Us the Way

Lord, we beseech thee mercifully to receive the prayers of thy people who call upon thee; and grant that they may both perceive and know what things they ought to do, and also may have grace and power faithfully to fulfill the same; through Jesus Christ our Lord. Amen.

—From the Book of Common Prayer

1. Find the Real Meaning

Many people whose lives are turned upside down question God, wondering why God is punishing them, says Susan Zonnebelt-Smeenge, R.N., Ed.D., a clinical psychologist with the Pine Rest Christian Mental Health Services in Grand Rapids, Michigan, and coauthor of *Getting to the Other Side of Grief.* It's important, she feels, to spend some time on that question. But rather than looking to place blame, look for the deeper message.

God does miraculous work through the crises of life, says Dr. Zonnebelt-Smeenge. As difficult as it may be to accept, when change is forced upon you it can deepen your faith and provide you with a richer understanding of life's deepest meanings.

So use your time now to work through the meaning in your crisis. Explore it in quiet meditation and prayer, in reading, or in conversation with a pastor, priest, or rabbi. Try to envision what new opportunities God might have opened up for you and your spouse.

2. Take Action

Although God is ultimately in control, it is up to you and your spouse to take the steps necessary to get through difficult times, asserts Dr. Zonnebelt-Smeenge. "Our role is not to be passive," she says. "We can trust in God to help, but He also gives us strength so that we can use the abilities He's given us to help ourselves."

How can you help yourself? Start by praying for guidance and the confidence to follow that guidance, Dr. Zonnebelt-Smeenge suggests. An example:

❦

LORD, BRING PEACE TO OUR HEARTS

Lord, lift up the light of your countenance upon us; let your peace rule in our hearts, and may it be our strength and our song in the house of our pilgrimage. We commit ourselves to your care and keeping; let your grace be mighty in us, and sufficient in us, for all the duties of the day. Keep us from sin. Give us the rule over our own spirits, and guard us from speaking unadvisedly with our lips. May we live together in holy love and peace.

—Matthew Henry

"Help me, God, know what I can do." Couples, similarly, can pray together for mutual guidance: "Help us, God, know what *we* can do."

Next, take an inventory of the situation. Sit down with your spouse and assess how the role change is affecting each of you emotionally. Talk about how the crisis will alter your financial situation. Discuss how you'll now handle tasks as simple as who's going to do the laundry and who's going to shovel the snow. Look at every aspect of your lives that may shift. Then, "do some creative planning for the future, too, exploring your options and your resources. Make it a very concrete, deliberate process," suggests Dr. Zonnebelt-Smeenge.

For example, if a husband has lost his job or cannot work for medical reasons, and the wife suddenly becomes the major breadwinner, as a couple they may recognize that the husband needs to feel he's contributing in significant ways to the benefit and maintenance of the household. They can then brainstorm specific ways to work toward reinstating more balance, whether it be looking for a new job, going back to school to prepare to change occupations, or exploring the possibilities of starting his own business. The husband can take similar steps to see that the wife achieves a similar measure of satisfaction with necessary readjustments.

In many instances, there will be no easy or definite answers to these sorts of problems, Dr. Zonnebelt-Smeenge cautions. That's where the crucible of life, and marriage, often lies. A healthy perspective is to do your best, as a team, to creatively make adjustments that work for the well-being of both partners.

3. Take Care of Your Own Needs

A role change crisis can create enormous stress on both of you that can harm your physical and emotional health, warns Dr. Lauer. Thus it's important that you both watch your diet, get enough exercise, and rest when necessary.

Also give yourself ample opportunity to pray and meditate alone, Dr. Zonnebelt-Smeenge suggests, as a means of coming to terms with what's happened. When her husband fell ill with a brain tumor and died at a young age, Dr. Zonnebelt-Smeenge found solace and equilibrium by taking regular walks to a favorite peaceful spot she knew, where she would pray or write in her journal. "Take some time to get away from the busyness, the noise, and the distractions," says Dr. Zonnebelt-Smeenge. "Try to focus on God's continued presence as you work through your pain."

4. Reach Out

When trouble hits, many people tend to withdraw, as if they were ashamed they were struggling. Don't fall into that trap, urges Michele Novotni, Ph.D., a professor of graduate counseling at Eastern College in St. Davids, Pennsylvania. This is a time to draw on your friends and especially your religious community for practical support. Don't try to handle everything on your own.

If one of you is sick and it's hard to get everything done around the house,

HELP US ON THIS JOURNEY

O Lord our God and God of our fathers!
Mercifully direct and guide our steps to our destination
and let us arrive there in health, joy and peace!
Keep us from snares and dangers,
and protect us from any enemies that we might meet along the way.
Bless and protect our journey!
Let us win favor in your eyes and in the sight of those around us.
Blessed are you, O Lord,
who hears and grants our prayers!

—Jewish prayer

ask for help. When you need some help watching the kids because one parent is working and the other parent has a job interview, ask for help. Watching out for each other in times of need is what community is all about.

You also should be prepared to reach out for moral support, Dr. Novotni adds. Working with your spouse as a team doesn't mean that all your emotional and spiritual needs will be taken care of at home. Getting together with close friends or participating in a support group dedicated to people grappling with problems similar to yours can be invaluable. "You may not want to unload some of the things you're feeling on your spouse," Dr. Novotni says. "Having a support group will give you a place where you can share all that stuff so that you can go back home and be supportive again."

> *Each cycle of the tide is valid; each cycle of the wave is valid, each cycle of a relationship is valid.*
>
> —*Anne Morrow Lindbergh*

Check with your religious community for referrals to support groups, or contact the American Self-Help Clearinghouse, St. Clare's Hospital, 25 Pocono Road, Denville, NJ 07834-2995.

Loss of Love

〜⚬〜

Like water poured on a burning flame, the stresses and strains of modern life can douse the love in a marriage. Don't let these things damage yours. Use prayer and persistent attention to keep the fire of love burning bright.

Anybody who thinks the Bible is a boring collection of moral lessons and miracle stories hasn't read the Song of Solomon.

This short book consists of passionate poems exchanged between two lovers, each celebrating the other in the most sensuous terms. Among the most famous images is its description of love as a fire so powerful that all of the trials of life can't put it out.

[F]or love is strong as death,
passion fierce as the grave
Its flashes are flashes of fire,
a raging flame
Many waters cannot quench love,
neither can floods drown it (Song of Solomon 8:6–7, RSV).

All of us probably long for a love like that, and a few of us have been lucky enough to find it. But for far too many couples, passionate love no longer exists—it has been replaced by a coldness that is spiritual as well as physical.

Is it possible to prevent your relationship from cooling, to keep your marital flame burning bright? The answer is most definitely yes, provided that you:

- Avoid the two traits that are most likely to extinguish love.
- Practice the spiritual fundamentals that keep love alive.
- Nourish your friendship with your spouse.
- Keep your sexual love alive.

Two Forces That Kill Love

When love dies it is usually for one of two reasons, says Steve Carr, senior pastor of Calvary Chapel in Arroyo Grande, California, and author of *Married and How to Stay That Way*. The first is inaction. You simply stop feeding the flames.

There is nothing stronger and nobler than when man and wife are of one heart and mind in a house, a grief to their foes, and to their friends great joy, but their own hearts know it best.

—*Homer*

"Anybody who's stood around a fireplace or around a campfire knows that you have to do something to keep the fire going," says Pastor Carr. "You have to keep putting logs on the fire; you have to stir it and you have to stoke it. If you don't, the fire will go out." Love is no different, he notes.

Inaction can take the form of a lack of attention. Never telling your mate "I love you" is one example, as is never noticing when your spouse needs moral support. You can also exhibit inaction by failing to do the things that people who care about each other ought to do, from helping keep the house clean to seeing to it that your mate gets a reasonable degree of satisfaction from your sex life together.

The second force that damages marriages is overtly negative action. Rather than complimenting and supporting one another, each spouse verbally or emotionally knocks the other down. This type of behavior can start so innocuously that you may not even realize it's a problem in the beginning. There may just be sprinkles of negativity in comments and actions, but over the years these grow into a torrent of anger, resentment, selfishness, and judgmental behavior that douse all feelings of love.

In both these cases, the solution is clear: Live your love and express it. How? Read on.

❧

THE PATH BACK TO LOVE

If you have lost heart on the path of love

Flee to Me without delay;

for I am a fortress invincible.

—Rumi, thirteenth-century Sufi poet and mystic

Nurturing Your Love

Much like a fire, deep, affectionate, meaningful love grows from a spark, an essence that you need to nourish at several levels. One key is the spiritual level. If you and your spouse share a faith connection, you open the door for the Holy Spirit, says Pastor Carr. The Spirit penetrates deep within both of you and emerges through you, bringing light to your marriage and all the other relationships of your lives, he says. Pastor Carr recommends these three ways to build your spiritual connection together.

1. Reaffirm Your Faith

Developing a marriage relationship filled with the spirit of God starts with your own spiritual connection, notes Pastor Carr. So practice the fundamentals of a faithful life—pray daily, read scripture daily, worship regularly, and consistently offer service to others.

2. Talk the Talk

As a religious person it's your duty to actively bring the Holy Spirit into the world—particularly into *your* personal world. That means taking "deliberate Godly actions" in your marriage, Pastor Carr says.

For example, Pastor Carr tries to follow Paul's command to the Ephesians to "speak the truth in love." When Pastor Carr goes home each night, he says, "I purposefully walk in that door and deliberately speak the truth in love. That may mean confronting, directly but lovingly, a problem my wife and I are having, or it may just mean telling her that I love her. Anything that God's word

---

❧

A PRAYER OF LOVE

To be said while holding hands:

May the love that is in my heart pass from my hand to yours.

—*From* Grateful Heart

---

commands, I deliberately try to do." He also prays daily for the strength to be able to successfully achieve that goal.

3. Practice Preventive Maintenance

Beyond a spiritual level, it's essential that you and your spouse regularly reaffirm your emotional connection to each other.

For Pastor Carr, that means regularly telling his wife he loves her, for starters, and also regularly investing time in their marriage partnership. "My wife and I go out on a date by ourselves—no children—every single week," he says, "and we have for almost the entire 27 years of our marriage."

The Value of Friendship

After years of scientific research, some of the biggest names in marital therapy today have concluded that happy marriages are based on true friendship. That conclusion is no surprise, says Pastor Carr. "Your friendship with your spouse allows you to steady and encourage one another," he says, "and that's what allows that fire of romance to stay lit always."

The most basic way you and your spouse can have a genuine friendship is to simply resolve to be friends, Pastor Carr says. Practically speaking, that means treating each other with the same respect, courtesy, and concern you would any other friend. The Golden Rule applies here: Treat your spouse as you yourself would like to be treated, and vice versa.

Beyond that, Pastor Carr and his wife take several steps to strengthen the bond of their marital friendship.

Daily Prayer

Friendship flowers when you come before God, individually and together. Pray to God for the strength to be a better friend to each other. Pray together for mutual strength, greater intimacy, and God's guidance.

Daily Talks

Staying in touch with one another by regularly communicating is one of the fundamentals of friendship, reminds Pastor Carr. In the long run, the simple step of having a daily cup of coffee together can save you and your spouse thousands of dollars in counseling or divorce lawyer fees—not to mention two broken hearts, he says.

Absolute Trust

In his role as a marriage counselor, Pastor Carr frequently sees the damage that lack of trust can do. "I have wives come to me who say that their husbands

WALK THIS WAY

You've heard of walking with the Lord? Well, why not try walking with your spouse and the Lord together?

Prayer-walking in tandem is a great way to build communication, love, and faith in a marriage, all at the same time, says Steve Carr, senior pastor of Calvary Chapel in Arroyo Grande, California, and author of *Married and How to Stay That Way*. Plus, you get a little exercise.

Pastor Carr simply prays out loud, spontaneously, as he and his wife stroll along the streets near their home. They keep their eyes open, of course. The topics vary from personal, family, or community needs to world concerns and problems at work. His wife chimes in every so often with words of affirmation; then they trade off and she leads the prayer.

"It builds a tremendous unity between us," Pastor Carr says. "There's something about the freedom of walking together that seems to open naturally the way for prayer."

❦

IMPROVE OUR COMMUNICATION

Lord, you see the weak links in our marriage that need strengthening.

I admit my part in the breakdown of our communication—for my hesitancy to share what's in my heart.

Sometimes he seems deaf and uninterested when I try to talk to him.

Then I give him the silent treatment.

Help me be willing to open up, to be vulnerable, even though I may get hurt.

Lord, it seems when I talk he treats it as idle chitchat.

I yearn to have a strong, happy marriage.

To be able to talk freely to this man I married when he was my best friend.

Give me practical ways to make our marriage better.

To restore the close fellowship we used to enjoy.

Thank you, Lord.

Amen.

—Quin Sherrer and Ruthann Garlock

---

want to know where they are every minute of the day," he says. "That sort of possessiveness—that need for control—is the opposite of love. It destroys love."

Pastor Carr goes out of his way to let his own wife know that he trusts her by telling her so directly. He also prays daily for the strength to be trusting, as well as for the strength to be trustworthy.

Responsiveness

If there is something your spouse needs or desires, you should demonstrate your love and commitment by taking care of it. "Action speaks louder than words," Pastor Carr says. "If my wife tells me she needs something and I don't make an effort to see that she gets it, what I'm really saying is that she's not important enough to me to make the effort."

The Joy of Sex

Speaking of desires, a loving sexual relationship is one of God's great blessings, as well as one of the sweetest gifts a husband and wife can give one another.

Religious traditions consider the enjoyment of sex a legitimate right for wife and husband alike. "The husband should give to his wife her conjugal rights," wrote Paul to the Corinthians, "and likewise the wife to her husband. For the wife does not have authority over her own body, but the husband does; likewise the husband does not have authority over his own body, but the wife does" (1 Corinthians 7:3–4, NRSV).

EQUAL RIGHTS, BY LAW

You wouldn't expect a bunch of male religious scholars in the first century a.d. to be feminists, but in fact some of the oldest teachings in the Jewish rabbinic tradition are decidedly sympathetic to women's sexual rights.

"Rabbinic law states quite clearly that a woman is empowered to demand sexual satisfaction in her marriage," says Rabbi Isaac Jeret of Congregation Beth Ahm in Verona, New Jersey. Why would such a teaching emerge in a time and place where equality between the sexes was, in most respects, unheard of? Because, Rabbi Jeret claims, the rabbis viewed sexuality as a gateway that allowed God's spirit to enter the world.

"Rabbinic tradition understood that a sacred relationship is one in which both parties can enjoy each other equally," he says. "Only then can God's presence be fully manifested within the relationship and in the world at large."

A glance at all the advice books in the "Sexuality" section of most bookstores will tell you, however, that all is not what it could be in too many marital bedrooms. The reasons are numerous, but in most cases, sexual problems begin with a breakdown of marital intimacy and trust.

"Couples have to feel safe enough to abandon themselves to their sexual longings," says Michael Seiler, Ph.D., a marital and sex therapist based in Chicago. "Generally when couples lose their sexual connection, something has happened that has compromised their sense of safety. As a result they have difficulty getting in touch with those very powerful, very primitive sexual longings and sharing them freely with their partner."

Regaining a sense of safety in marriage means addressing many of the issues we've discussed earlier in this chapter and in other chapters in this section. You can't separate sexual intimacy from emotional and spiritual intimacy, claims Dr. Seiler. For just that reason, sex can become one of the tools you and your spouse use to help build and maintain the intimacy between you. Dr. Seiler recommends four key steps.

1. Make Love Prayerfully

Many people are nervous making love with their spouses for the same reason they're nervous praying with their spouses: Both are acts that can be profoundly revealing of their deepest selves. In both cases, however, a couple can reach new depths of emotional and spiritual intimacy if, together, they reveal their deepest feelings and desires to one another.

One way to start to reach this state of intimacy is to pray together before making love, and then carry over that spiritual bond into the act of making love, Dr. Seiler suggests.

The intimacy of making love can also reflect the attitudes and spiritual attention of worship, says Rabbi Isaac Jeret of Congregation Beth Ahm in Verona, New Jersey. "In the Jewish mystical tradition, the Kabbalah, the spirituality of sexual intimacy is about drawing God's energy into the world," he says, "both for the sake of the couple and for the sake of the entire world."

To make love prayerfully, Dr. Seiler recommends that you and your spouse be patient and relaxed and focus on connection and emotion rather than immediate physical gratification. "The point is to get into each other's rhythm," he says. "Open yourself up as much as possible. Let yourself go, and allow yourself to become absorbed in the physical and emotional connection to your spouse. Truly join with the other person. Connect not just with your genitals, but with your soul."

2. Add Spice and Stir

It's been said before, but we'll say it again: Routine sex can easily become boring sex. But it doesn't have to be that way.

"The prevailing view is that monogamy produces monotony," notes Dr. Seiler. "I think that's a myth. If you do the same thing over and over again in the exact same way, you do tend to lose interest, and many couples fall into that trap. But there's a tremendous amount of creativity that can be brought to sex, not just in the positions you use, but in the whole spectrum of sexual activities that you can engage in."

If you and your spouse are nervous with sexual experimentation, Dr. Seiler recommends many books that can help guide the way. Two are *Hot Monogamy* by Patricia Love and Jo Robinson and *For Each Other* by Lonnie Garfield Barbach.

> *The death of illusions is not the death of love. The great advantage of the vow is that it holds people together during this temporary stress and trial, in order to attain a more lasting love.*
>
> —*Bishop Fulton J. Sheen*

3. Work Past the Blocks

Research confirms, Dr. Seiler says, that couples with certain strong religious beliefs often experience conflict over sex because they were raised in religious households where various types of sexual behavior were considered taboo. You and your mate shouldn't let this problem affect your relationship. Frankly but patiently address any concerns you have, suggests Dr. Seiler, and then try to be flexible in the bedroom.

"The person who is uncomfortable with certain sexual behaviors can be invited—in a nondemanding, noncritical way—to examine the source of those beliefs to see if there is some ability for movement," Dr. Seiler says. "Often the religious beliefs we accepted uncritically when we were 5 years old can be reexamined when we're adults and changed without compromising our spirituality."

It also may help if you talk to your pastor about the true tenets of your religious tradition, Rabbi Jeret suggests. You may be surprised to discover that the actual doctrine is more liberal when it comes to sex than the values that have been imposed over time. When he counsels couples, Rabbi Jeret is able to point to 2,000 years worth of rabbinic teachings that unequivocally endorse the mutual enjoyment of sexual pleasure for both the woman and the man in marriage.

4. Try Talk

When there are sexual barriers between couples, the first step in getting over them is dialogue, Dr. Seiler says. "The most critical step is acknowledging the difficulty," he notes. "Whatever the problem is, it needs to be discussed, without blame and without attacks. That's often the most difficult step you have to take in addressing the problem, but unless you take it, nothing's going to happen."

One important note: Avoid talking about your sex problems in the bedroom, Dr. Seiler suggests, and don't talk about them right after you've had some unhappy sexual encounter. Instead, discuss the situation in a safe environment, such as at the kitchen table. It will also help if you talk in positive terms, focusing on the nice places you'd like to go in your mutual sexual journey, he says, rather than on where you haven't been going.

Infidelity

Infidelity doesn't have to be a death blow to your marriage. But to keep your love alive, you and your spouse must uncover what led to the betrayal and then apply prayer, patience, and understanding to heal the wounds.

Ron was a 45-year-old father of three, a devout Christian, and a philanderer. He'd had five affairs during the 23 years of his marriage. After each of them, he had honestly repented and promised his wife he'd do better, only to betray her again.

Why wouldn't Ron remain faithful? He entered therapy to find out. The breakthrough came when his therapist asked him to write an analysis of each of his affairs in hopes that a pattern, and insight, would emerge. They did.

Ron realized that what was driving him to other women was a desperate search for approval. He hadn't found it from his parents when he was younger, and he wasn't finding it now with his wife. Eventually he realized he was struggling with a form of sexual addiction. By combining therapy, prayer, and the steadfast support of his wife, he was able to conquer it.

As Ron and his wife might tell you, an affair is one of the most painful ordeals a married couple can endure—even greater than recovering from a death. "I have counseled a number of people who experienced both the death of a spouse and adultery," says Henry Virkler, Ph.D., the author of *Broken Promises*, "and every one of them has said that losing a spouse to unfaithfulness was worse than losing one to death."

As painful as adultery is, however, it does not have to spell the end of a marriage. Dr. Frank Pittman, a well-known counselor and author of *Private Lives*, found that nearly half of the couples who experienced infidelity stayed together afterward. Dr. Virkler says that in his practice, which involved mostly devout Christians, the number of couples who remained together despite an episode of infidelity was closer to two-thirds. That success rate, he believes, testifies to the fact that prayer and God's grace can help marriages survive.

> *We must make our homes centers of compassion and forgive endlessly.*
>
> —*Mother Teresa*

If you or your partner has had an affair, and together you decide that you want to continue the marriage, you need to address the following fundamental issues.

- Identifying and resolving the reason for the affair
- Reestablishing trust
- Opening a path for forgiveness and reconciliation

Let's look at how you can deal with all three of these.

Why People Cheat

Ron's story demonstrates a fundamental fact about infidelity: Usually, it's about more than just lust. There are many reasons why people become involved in affairs, Dr. Virkler suggests.

Some people are unfaithful because they have deep-seated emotional problems and insecurities from childhood that make them more vulnerable to temptation. Others have midlife crises that include affairs. Some people come into marriage with unrealistic expectations, and when their partner fails to meet those expectations, they look outside the marriage for satisfaction. Other people work in environments where they encounter tempting situations they do not know how to handle. And a small percentage—perhaps 10 percent of people who have affairs—are unfaithful because they have become ensnared in sexual addiction, says Dr. Virkler.

Another cause, he adds, is *realistic* marital expectations that go unfulfilled. For example, individuals may be discouraged when they expect their marriages to provide emotional and sexual intimacy and they do not.

A common thread that is basic to many cases of adultery, Dr. Virkler notes, is a deep and unsatisfied yearning for friendship, connection, and approval.

Q&A: How Can I Confirm There's Been Cheating?

Q: I suspect my spouse is cheating on me. What can I do?

A: If you want to save the marriage, first stop and pray for God's help in calming your emotions, says Henry Virkler, Ph.D., author of *Broken Promises*.

The next step is to confront your spouse with what you know and ask for an explanation. Phrasing the request calmly and politely will encourage a more honest response, Dr. Virkler says. Remember: What looks like sure evidence of infidelity may have an innocent explanation. Dr. Virkler suggests saying something like this: "I've seen x, y, and z and I don't know how to make sense of it. Could you please explain to me what's happening?"

If your spouse claims innocence and you're still suspicious, continue to pray for wisdom, Dr. Virkler recommends, and also pray that God will bring additional information to light that will either confirm that your suspicions are true or prove that they're false. Have confidence that God will reveal the appropriate information.

If you still have suspicions, you can approach your spouse again, saying something like this: "You said this wasn't happening. Here's some more information that confuses me; please tell me what this means."

That's why neither a seemingly happy marriage nor strong religious beliefs are an absolute guarantee against infidelity.

The First Steps to Recovery

The awful secret is out: You or your spouse has had an affair. Despite all the hurt, anger, and mistrust, you want to work to keep the marriage together. What do you do? Dr. Virkler has counseled approximately 100 couples in this situation. He suggests four steps.

1. First, Pray

As always, your first move should be to prayer. Ask God for counsel, healing, and strength.

2. Seek Professional Guidance

Obviously, the affair needs to be ended if the marriage is to survive. Just as obviously, the faithful spouse is going to want it ended immediately.

Surprisingly, Dr. Virkler recommends you take a more moderate approach—if possible. If the affair involves a deep emotional entanglement—as many do—Dr. Virkler says it's best to let the unfaithful spouse end the emotional connection over a short period of time. In the meantime, the faithful member of the marriage should insist that the spouse enter counseling, where he or she can work on understanding how and why the affair developed and begin the process of emotionally leaving the other relationship.

3. Get Counseling

Therapy can help the unfaithful spouse work through any ambivalent feelings about ending the affair. But Dr. Virkler believes it's important that both

A Prayer for Release

Dear God,

I feel such pain, anxiety, and depression.

I know this is not Your will for me, and yet my mind is held in chains by fear and paranoia.

I surrender my life, right now, to You.

Take the entire mess, all of it, now too complicated to explain to anyone but known by You in each detail.

Do what I cannot do.

Lift me up.

Give me a new chance.

Show me a new light.

Make me a new person.

Dear God,

This depression frightens me.

Dear God,

Please bring me peace.

Amen.

—Marianne Williamson

GRANT ME FORGIVENESS

Clean out, O God, the inner stream of my life:
all the duplicity,
all the avarice,
all the falsity.
Search out, O Lord, the hidden motives of my life:
all the conceit,
all the anger,
all the fear.
Root out, divine Master, the destructive actions of my life:
all the manipulation,
all the scheming,
all the guile.
May the operations of faith, hope, and love increase in everything I
am and in everything I do.
Amen.

—*Richard J. Foster*

spouses get individual counseling. This will help each partner resolve the emotional issues surrounding the affair. Also, counseling can give the faithful spouse emotional support during this very stressful time. Without such support, the faithful spouse may act in angry or demanding ways that increase the chance that the unfaithful spouse will be drawn toward the affair partner rather than back to the marriage.

Make sure you find a therapist who believes in the possibility of preserving marriage, Dr. Virkler adds. Some therapists don't, instead allowing the feelings of the moment to be more important than the marriage vows.

After individual therapy, both spouses can come together, preferably with the help of a counselor, and discuss why the affair occurred and what can be done to address the problems that encouraged it. Before embarking on that program, however, you should take another step.

FINDING THE POWER TO FORGIVE

Forgiving is one of the central principles of religious life, and yet few of us have ever been taught how to do it. That's a problem Everett L. Worthington Jr., Ph.D., executive director of the Campaign for Forgiveness Research, is trying to remedy. Dr. Worthington has devised a five-step formula called REACH that can help you learn to forgive. Each letter in the word stands for one of the steps. You can apply this formula to any situation, but it is particularly valuable if your spouse has been unfaithful. Here's how it works.

R: Recall the Hurt

If you've been wounded, it's important to acknowledge and discuss the injury. You should do this in a supportive environment, preferably with a professional counselor.

E: Empathize with the One Who Hurt You

More than anything else, Dr. Worthington says, empathy opens the way for forgiveness. To empathize with your spouse, speculate about what he or she might have been thinking or feeling during the affair.

You might even try writing an imaginary letter from your unfaithful spouse that explains the motives for the affair, suggests Dr. Worthington. This can be very difficult emotionally. For that reason, you might want to do deep-breathing exercises while writing the letter and visualize more pleasant moments in your relationship, he says.

4. Accept Responsibility

Both you and your spouse need to come to terms with your roles in the affair. This is not meant to excuse adultery. Ultimately, we are all responsible for our actions, and therefore the unfaithful spouse cannot blame the other person for what happened. That's fundamental.

Nonetheless, Dr. Virkler says, it's important to underscore that in some cases—not every case, but in some—the faithful partner also bears some responsibility for the conditions that set the stage for infidelity. Obvious examples are the man who strays because his reasonable sexual needs aren't being fulfilled by his wife or the woman who seeks comfort from another man be-

A: Altruistic Gift

Think of your forgiveness as a gift that you unselfishly give to your spouse. It may not be an easy gift to give, but it is what God expects of you, notes Dr. Worthington.

C: Commit to Forgive

It's one thing to forgive someone in your mind; it's another to grant the gift of forgiveness in some tangible way. This is important, Dr. Worthington says, because inevitably the hurt will reoccur in your mind over time, and you'll be tempted to take back your forgiveness unless you've made clear your commitment to forgive.

As a symbol of your commitment, write a "certificate" of forgiveness stating the date you granted it, suggests Dr. Worthington. If you don't feel ready to share your forgiveness with your spouse, you can keep this commitment to yourself at first, or share it just with a trusted counselor.

H: Hold On to Forgiveness

This stage is also aimed at overcoming the powerful tendency to take back forgiveness once it's been granted. Dr. Worthington says we are "hard-wired" biologically to remember hurts—our survival as a species has depended on it. For that reason, painful memories are inevitable. We can work at letting them go, however, by renewing our commitment to forgive each day.

cause her husband isn't fulfilling her emotional needs. Responsibility in marriage is a two-way street, says Dr. Virkler, and if you want to repair the marital rift both of you have to face the truth.

Forgiveness and Reconciliation

If you want your marriage to survive, there's one given: Eventually the betrayed partner has to forgive. That's much easier said than done, of course. Achieving true forgiveness is one of the most difficult spiritual challenges anyone can face.

It may help as you contemplate this challenge to realize that forgiveness is often a process that takes place over time rather than an immediate experience, says Carolyn Bohler, Ph.D., professor of pastoral theology and counseling at United Theological Seminary in Dayton, Ohio. That's an especially important point, she feels, for people of faith. Often, they feel compelled, by scripture or by their religious leaders, to forgive, but they still find themselves struggling. Adding a burden of guilt to the painful burden of being cheated upon is not constructive.

"Forgiveness is not just an act of the will," she says. "You can't just say 'I will forgive' and you do. It's more complicated than that."

One way to approach forgiveness is to simply place the "intention" to forgive in your heart, Dr. Bohler says, trusting that over time the Spirit will gently guide you toward your goal. Day by day, she says, you can endeavor to move your anger and resentment more toward the periphery of your life, so that it occupies less of your center.

If you wish to take a more direct and active approach to forgiving your spouse, there are techniques you can use. For the past decade or so, social scientists and psychologists have begun systematically studying forgiveness and have identified specific ways to address the pain, anger, and other emotions produced by various areas of conflict—from sexual infidelity to international disputes.

One of the leaders in the field is Everett L. Worthington Jr., Ph.D., executive director of the Campaign for Forgiveness Research, in Richmond, Virginia. He and his colleagues have devised a six-stage model that can lead couples through the often long and difficult process of forgiveness and reconciliation. Their approach requires interaction with professional counselors, but you can review the basic elements here to get some idea of the steps you'll need to take.

1. *Decide* you want to reconcile. In the case of infidelity, this is often an open question. Either way, a decision needs to be made.

2. *Talk* about forgiveness. For the philandering spouse this includes admitting committing a wrong, offering a sincere apology, and making a "statement of intention," meaning a promise never to cheat again. Also at this stage the unfaithful spouse should include some explanation of why the wrong occurred—not as an excuse, but as a means of opening the way for greater understanding.

3. *REACH* for forgiveness. REACH stands for the five stages of a process the faithful spouse can use to work toward granting forgiveness. See "Finding the Power to Forgive" on page 74 for the specifics.

RESTORE OUR LOVE

Dear God,

Please bring us big life and big love, deep life and deep love.

We wish to show up now with pure and noble hearts that we might midwife the perfection in each other.

May we see each other's greatness and invoke each other's light.

We surrender all the ways, both those we are aware of and those that remain unconscious, in which we block our love for each other.

We surrender our defenses.

We are ready to bring forth the holiest vibrations of love and healing between us.

Where we are afraid to love, where we have built walls in front of our hearts, may we be healed and set free.

Where we are needy or do not know how to behave or tend to control or to judge or to fix or be dishonest, please, dear God, show us another way.

We surrender ourselves to love.

We surrender our love to You.

May it serve Your purposes.

May it receive Your blessing and carry Your power.

May we never forsake each other.

Thank You very much.

Amen.

—*Marianne Williamson*

4. *Reverse* the negative spiral. Once the faithful spouse has offered forgiveness, the couple can begin to work on the destructive patterns that have infected their relationship, gradually reversing the deterioration that has occurred.

5. *Deal* with small lapses in your spouse's behavior. A spouse who once strayed can't be expected to never again glance at an attractive member of the opposite sex. Nor can you expect perfect behavior in any other way as penance for an earlier untrustworthy act, Dr. Worthington says. The goal is to aim for an "attitude of gratitude"—being grateful for each step forward the unfaithful partner makes—coupled with an "attitude of latitude"—being willing to cut the partner a little slack for occasional mess-ups.

6. *Rebuild* the relationship. In this step you and your spouse should continue to shore up the love and intimacy that are the foundations of a good relationship. Go out on dates, bring each other gifts, make thoughtful compliments—do something every day to build the loving bond between you.

> *No matter what you say or do, I will continue loving you. I may not like what you do, but my love is unconditional and will not be affected—not even if our involvement changes.*
>
> —Ken Keyes Jr.

For more on rebuilding a loving relationship, see the chapters on The Loving Marriage (page 36) and Loss of Love (page 59).

Abusive Relationships

Even marriages with a strong religious foundation can be infected by physical, verbal, or emotional abuse. If you find yourself caught in its grasp, prayer, courage, and counseling can restore your life.

They are a devoutly religious couple who live near Denver. We'll call them Jack and Vickie, although those are not their real names.

Jack believes the Bible gives him the right to be the undisputed head of his family. That means his wife should not question his decisions in any way. If Vickie does question him, Jack sometimes hits her—and he believes he is entitled to do so. "I see it as no different than spanking a rebellious child," he says.

For her part, Vickie vacillates between accepting Jack's abuse and calling the police for help.

Jack has been through a treatment program specifically designed for Christian spouse abusers—twice, says Daryle R. Woodward, Ph.D., owner and clinical director of MOVES, one of Colorado's largest counseling centers for domestic violence. But despite 36 sessions his beliefs haven't changed.

Often abuse victims like Vickie believe there's nothing they can do to alter a harmful relationship. That's not true, say Dr. Woodward and other counselors. With God's help, they—and you, if you're the victim of abuse—can turn things around with the following four steps.

- Learn what drives a spouse to become an abuser.
- Safely demand that the abuse stop.
- Seek help for yourself and for your spouse.
- Build a life for yourself and your family that does not include abuse.

The Roots of Abuse

Physical battering is the most obvious form of abuse, but you also can be abused mentally, verbally, sexually, and spiritually. Belittling or disparaging remarks are abuse, as are threats of physical violence, coercion, and destruction of property. So too is extreme controlling behavior, which can range from refusing to let you participate in family decisions to monitoring your every move.

This above all, I refuse to be a victim. Unless I can do that, I can do nothing.

—Margaret Atwood

All forms of abuse have one thing in common, says Dr. Woodward: "They attack the self-worth of the victim. In a religious context, you might call it dishonoring behavior."

According to statistics, the majority of physical abusers—some 95 percent—are male. Those numbers are assumed to be somewhat biased, however, because husbands are less likely to report they've been abused than wives are.

Why do men abuse? There are many reasons. Research shows a majority of abusers either have witnessed or have been victims of abuse while growing up. Many feel powerless in their lives, particularly in their jobs, and abuse their spouses to feel powerful. Abusers have problems controlling their impulses and resolving conflicts constructively. Alcohol and drug abuse are also often factors.

In some households that claim to be religious, the belief that the wife should submit to the husband may lead to abuse, as it did for Jack and Vickie. Often, the husband will cite certain passages in the Bible to support this view, most notably the passage in Paul's letter to the Ephesians, which states, "Wives, submit yourselves unto your own husbands, as unto the Lord" (5:22, KJV). Biblical scholars, however, vehemently dispute such readings.

"It is mistreatment of scripture to rip passages out of context in that fashion," says Laurence Welborn, Ph.D., associate professor of New Testament at United Theological Seminary in Dayton, Ohio. The Bible says different things in different passages about the proper role of women, Dr. Welborn adds, but the bottom line is that "there is absolutely no sanction for abuse whatsoever in any of those passages."

Another element that's central to abuse but is often overlooked is the relentless intimacy of the marriage relationship, says John Townsend, Ph.D., a clinical psychologist in Newport Beach, California, and coauthor of *Boundaries* and *Safe People*. Because of the closeness of their relationship, a spouse may learn the darkest secrets about her mate, he says, and if those are things the mate is trying to hide, he may consider it a terrible insult when the spouse discovers them. "Sometimes people abuse their spouses because their spouses remind them of who they really are," says Dr. Townsend.

Abuse also follows a clearly defined cyclical pattern. It starts with a tension-building phase in which the ordinary stresses and strains of life and marriage begin to accumulate, says Wilford Wooten, director of the counseling department at Focus on the Family in Colorado Springs, Colorado. This stage can last weeks or months. At some point the tension becomes so great that there's an explosion and an abuse episode occurs.

Q&A: Is It My Fault I've Been Abused?

Q: My husband has been striking me and verbally abusing me. Am I doing something to set him off?

A: "Abuse is *always* the responsibility of the abuser," says John Townsend, Ph.D., a clinical psychologist in Newport Beach, California. "I would never in a million years say that it was a woman's fault that she was abused."

Nonetheless, certain psychological tendencies can increase the chances that a woman will end up with an abusive husband and stay in an abusive marriage, notes Dr. Townsend. You need to recognize these tendencies if you want the abuse to end.

Some abuse victims will take positions of powerlessness in relationships in order to get love. "This is the 'I'll do anything you want, just don't leave me' syndrome," says Dr. Townsend. "Another common characteristic shared by many abuse victims is a sense of feeling guilty about having an opinion, or having difficulty in speaking straightforwardly about what their own opinions are."

If you think you may be prone to these tendencies, you may want to seek counseling to help you deal with them. But regardless of your tendencies, it is important that you learn to ask, forthrightly, to be treated as you expect to be in your relationship, Dr. Townsend says.

A PRAYER FOR COURAGE

Let nothing disturb thee,
Nothing affright thee
All things are passing—
God never changeth.
Patient endurance
Attaineth to all things.
Who God possesseth
In nothing is wanting,
Alone God sufficeth.

—Saint Teresa of Avila

This is followed by what is called the "hearts and flowers" stage: The abuser, plagued with feelings of remorse, promises that the abuse will never be repeated and showers his victim with displays of affection.

This honeymoon phase explains why abused spouses often stay in abusive relationships, Wooten says. They believe that the abuser's promises and affection are sincere. And indeed, they may be sincere. The problem is that abusers typically are as unable to stop the cycle of violence as an alcoholic is to stop drinking. Like the alcoholic, abusers have not learned to control their destructive behavior by themselves. They need help.

Stopping Abuse

Putting a stop to marital abuse is a challenge for anyone, but even more so for those who see themselves as especially religious. Why? Because abuse requires a tough, no-nonsense response that, at least on the surface, doesn't seem to correspond with religious teachings that stress the need for tolerance, acceptance, compassion, and forgiveness.

Make no mistake about it, however; you can love your abuser and still seek safety for yourself. "A spouse demonstrates that she cares when she does something that will bring about change," says Wooten.

You can take the following seven steps to stop the cycle of abuse.

1. Pray for Empowerment

Ask God to help you do what you need to do, says Dr. Townsend. "Most of the time, the abuse victim is in a passive stance where she feels trapped. She needs to pray for empowerment to know what active steps she can take to move from the darkness to the light."

2. Draw the Line

Don't succumb to the temptation to deny that abuse is happening, Wooten says. Call it by its name and declare that you won't tolerate it. "Tell the abuser,

WHERE TO TURN FOR HELP

If you are being threatened or abused and fear for the safety of yourself and/or your children, contact your local police department or a domestic violence shelter in your area. If you or your children have been injured by an abuser, see a medical doctor or go to the hospital emergency room immediately.

Remember, you are not responsible for the abuse committed against you. If your relationship is going to survive, your partner must express true remorse for his behavior, seek your forgiveness, and pursue some type of counseling for his abusive behavior. Then and only then will it be safe to work on restoration of the marriage.

For advice on dealing with abuse, contact the National Coalition Against Domestic Violence, P.O. Box 18749, Denver, Colorado, 80218; phone: 800-799-SAFE (7233). The coalition can put you in touch with the local chapter nearest you. Its Web site (www.ncadv.org) also has information and advice for abused spouses.

Prayer Miracles

Prayer Saved Me from an Abusive Mate

Ten years ago I had no will to live. I was with someone who abused me physically, emotionally, mentally, and spiritually. He took all the good I ever felt about myself and destroyed it with his beating, his lies, his adulterous affairs, and his alcohol and drug abuse. Through this I became a drug addict for 9 years. It was my escape from the pain.

I came to a point where I had no reason to live. I was so lost and alone and there was not a soul around. I told God that I did not want to live anymore. And at that point I found Him. He heard my cry, and He literally saved my life.

He gave me the courage to leave this man, and I never turned back. I am clean from all drugs since the day I found God. I now have life—real life that I never knew existed. I believe in miracles because I am one.

Mary Ellen Vaci
Chicago, Illinois

'You cannot talk to me that way,'" recomends Wooten, "or, 'This is unacceptable behavior. You cannot have a relationship with me if you continue to behave this way. You need to get some help.'"

3. Shine a Light

Abuse thrives in secrecy, Dr. Woodward says. If your spouse refuses to admit he has a problem, bring the issue to the attention of people outside your marriage who can help break down that denial.

You should exercise care, however, in choosing the person or persons in whom to confide. Many people—including some church authorities—don't understand abuse and can make matters worse, says Dr. Woodward. Research has shown, for example, that some church pastors will advise wives to stay with husbands who physically abuse them—advice that can have fatal consequences, according to Dr. Woodward.

Therefore, it's important to seek out the help of individuals or groups who have experience dealing with domestic abuse. Domestic violence shelters, victim services agencies, local police departments, county social service agencies, or the National Coalition Against Domestic Violence can help.

4. Take a Breather

Get away from the abuser, if only for a cooling-off period of a few days, says Wooten. He advises saying something like, "I care about you, I'm committed to you, but I want you to leave for a couple of days and think this over. If you don't leave, then I'm going to."

If you threaten to leave, Wooten adds, it's important to follow through.

❧

SHINE YOUR LIGHT
INTO THE DARK CORNERS

Lord, show me the dark corners of my heart that I need to open up to your light. Give me the courage to allow your grace to heal and restore those areas I've tried to keep hidden. Help me to cooperate with the Holy Spirit; strengthen me to stand against the enemy. I acknowledge that I can't do this by myself. I renounce my pride and ask for your help. Thank you for setting me free. In Jesus' name, Amen.

—*Quin Sherrer and Ruthanne Garlock*

"You've got to be ready to back up your threat with some real action," Wooten says. "If the action doesn't follow, the behavior isn't going to change."

5. Make a Plan

If the abuse continues, you need to move out. But this may require careful planning, especially if you have children or if there is the slightest likelihood your husband will become violent. Abuse counselors suggest you develop a "safety plan" ahead of time, and then implement it quickly when it's clear you'll have to leave. Counselors at domestic violence shelters or hotlines can supply a list of the steps you'll need to take to prepare for an instant departure. Among the things you'll want to do is arrange for safe lodging, make copies of important documents you'll need after you leave (e.g., birth certificates, bank information), keep credit cards, and create emergency reservoirs of cash and clothing. Also, it's often best to leave while your spouse is away from home.

6. Insist on Treatment

You should insist that your spouse undergo treatment in some sort of structured program, notes Dr. Townsend. Treatment takes time—months, sometimes years—to be effective. In the meantime, you should resist the temptation to reconcile. "A lot of abusive husbands say, 'Well, I've stopped the abuse for 6 weeks now, isn't that enough?'" Dr. Townsend says. "The answer is, 'No, it isn't.'"

You and your spouse don't necessarily have to remain separated until the treatment is completed, Dr. Townsend adds, but reconciliation, like treatment, needs to take place in a structured, supervised fashion. Start by getting back together for a trial period of a night or two. The counselors in charge of your spouse's treatment can help you both determine when that's appropriate. Then, if the initial visit works out, increase subsequent stays to a few days together, and then a few weeks.

> *Never grow a wishbone,*
> *daughter, where your*
> *backbone ought to be.*
>
> —*Clementine Paddleford*

7. Come Together in Prayer

When reconciliation starts, you and your spouse may want to pray together for healing. "I don't believe in praying together during conflict," Dr. Townsend says. "She's too frightened, and he's not in the right place for it. But when things are going better the couple can pray together regularly, asking God to help restore their love for one another." This opens the way for repentence, forgiveness, and then genuine healing. (For more on forgiveness, see the chapter on Infidelity on page 69.)

Divorce

A shattered marriage represents one of the greatest tragedies life can offer. If you're in the midst of this painful journey, prayer, faith, and the practical advice offered here can help you emerge whole on the other side.

O ver half of all first marriages in the United States today end in divorce. With momentum like that, you'd think ending a marriage would be simple—the easy way out. Yet talk to anyone who's gone through one and you'll hear a different story: Divorce is almost universally described as one of the most painful experiences in an entire lifetime.

"Divorce is similar to death," says Tom Whiteman, Ph.D., director of Fresh Start divorce recovery seminars in Paoli, Pennsylvania, and coauthor of *The Fresh Start Divorce Recovery Workbook*. "It shocks you, even when you think you're prepared for it. I talk to people all the time who tell me they wouldn't wish the agony of divorce on their worst enemy."

Why, then, do so many people resort to divorce? For some, it may be a case of giving up too soon. For others, however, it may be that a truly bad marriage is simply too painful and too destructive—mentally, emotionally, spiritually—to live with. "Divorce is always a loss, the death of a dream," says Howard Clinebell, Ph.D., professor emeritus of pastoral care and counseling at Claremont School of Theology in California. "But it may also be turning the page to a new chapter, a chapter of real liberation and growth."

Whatever your circumstances, if you're facing the prospect of divorce you're looking out across a fearful expanse of agonizing decisions and frightening change. Rest assured, however, that you can cross it safely, if you seek God's help, pray, and follow these steps.

- Take the time to consider whether divorce is the right decision.
- If it is, learn to accept the divorce, whether it's your choice or your spouse's.
- Learn to forgive your spouse, and start on the road to recovery.

Contemplating Divorce

Given the incredible pressures of family and work and the difficulty of maintaining a loving relationship, perhaps we shouldn't be surprised at how many marriages founder today. Indeed, it's becoming painfully clear that falling out of love is even easier than falling into it.

> *All divorces are the result of sin, but not all divorces are sinful.*
>
> —*Tom Whiteman*

Falling out of love, however, should not automatically be considered grounds for divorce. If you are on the verge of getting a divorce, especially if you and your spouse are separated, there are several steps you should take to make sure the path you choose is the right one.

1. Pray for Solace

If you are undergoing the agony of a broken marriage, your most immediate need is for comfort, says Dr. Whiteman, who has been through a painful divorce himself. "We feel that nobody cares for us, that nobody loves us, that nobody understands us," he says.

God does understand, however, Dr. Whiteman says, and you can pray to God for relief, comfort, and support.

2. Pray for Wisdom

You are making decisions now that will affect you and your family for the rest of your lives, yet emotionally you're a basket case. That's a dangerous combination, Dr. Whiteman points out. Therefore it's important to pray for the wisdom to make the right decisions.

3. Pray for Good Friends

When you're contemplating divorce you can count on receiving lots of well-intentioned advice, some good, some bad. Trusted friends can help you sort it all out and separate the wheat from the chaff, Dr. Whiteman says.

If possible, these friends should be of the same sex as you, he feels. Ideally, they should be able to maintain some objective distance from the conflicts between you and your spouse. They should also be honest enough to tell you things you might not want to hear.

4. Pray Deliberately

Don't make snap judgments. Give yourself time to accurately discern what God's will is for you.

One way to avoid panicky and hasty decisions, suggests Dr. Clinebell, is to practice contemplative or meditative prayer. Such prayer can help you stay in balance or "centered," emotionally and spiritually. "It helps tremendously to realize that God is present in everything, including the messy side of life," he says. "Meditating on that Divine presence can help us avoid being consumed by the huge feelings that are inevitable when we're contemplating a divorce."

5. Visualize Divorce

A constructive way of weighing the implications of a divorce is to use visualization, says Carolyn Bohler, Ph.D., author of *Opening to God: Guided Imagery Meditations on Scripture*.

In this technique, while praying you try to picture in your mind's eye how a divorce would affect each member of your family, including your children, your spouse, and yourself. "We can never be 100 percent sure of God's will at any time," Dr. Bohler says, "but trying to fit all those different perspectives together may be the closest we can come to God's perspective."

What Would **Jesus** Do?

When religious people see their marriages fall apart, often their first reaction is to feel abandoned by God, says Tom Whiteman, Ph.D., director of Fresh Start divorce recovery seminars in Paoli, Pennsylvania. Then that reaction is usually followed quickly by guilt for doubting God's support.

There's no reason for guilt. Even Jesus had doubts when he was on the cross, crying out: "My God, my God, why hast thou forsaken me?"

Jesus' cry demonstrates, Dr. Whiteman feels, that it's okay to cry out to God when we feel abandoned. Acknowledging these feelings, and bringing them to God candidly in prayer, can pave the way for a reconciliation with God and open you once again to the healing power of Divine grace.

Leave the Door Open

Separation for many couples offers a chance to cool off and reconsider their differences, opening the way for eventual reconciliation. Just as easily, however, separation can mean just that—an initial parting of the ways that leads to divorce.

Because the costs of divorce are so steep and the odds of a second mar-

GOD'S BEEN THERE

God hates divorce.

That's what a lot of Bible-believing Christians will tell you, and Tom Whiteman, Ph.D., director of Fresh Start divorce recovery seminars in Paoli, Pennsylvania—a Bible-believing Christian who's been divorced—agrees.

"God hates divorce because He's experienced it himself," Whiteman says.

The story is told in the book of Jeremiah, where God, speaking through the prophet, agonizes over the infidelity of ancient Israel.

"And I saw, when for all the causes whereby backsliding Israel committed adultery I had put her away, and given her a bill of divorce" (Jeremiah 3:8, KJV).

This "divorce" revoked God's grant of the promised land to the Israelites, with the result that Jerusalem fell and the people were exiled to Babylon.

For Dr. Whiteman, learning of this passage was a revelation because it told him that there are times when even God is forced into situations in which divorce, for whatever reason, is the only option. "A lot of people don't know that passage," he laughs, "and they're taken aback when they read it."

riage surviving are even worst than a first, it makes sense for separated couples to leave the door to reconciliation open if they can. Jim A. Talley, Ph.D., a marital and family therapist in Oklahoma City and coauthor of *Reconcilable Differences*, has made a special ministry of reconciliation. He says the seven following "rules of conduct" can help set the stage for healing between estranged couples.

1. Do Kind and Gentle Things for Your Spouse

Make a supportive phone call if you know your spouse is going through a hard time at work, for example. Or offer to fix a leaky kitchen faucet. Offering to help your spouse with no strings attached helps prevent both of you from becoming subsumed in bitterness.

2. Spend as Much Conflict-Free Time with Your Spouse as Possible

If that amounts only to offering a pleasant greeting when you meet in the supermarket, so be it. If it's possible to actually spend some time together and have fun, so much the better.

3. Control Your Expectations

Obviously you have severe differences with your spouse; otherwise you wouldn't have separated. Now is not the time to expect your spouse to completely change ways. Instead, minimize your expectations; this will help minimize your anger.

4. Don't Play Detective

Separated spouses tend to think they have a right to control their mates, Dr. Talley says, and as a result often spy on them or ask questions about their behavior. That's bound to stir up resentment and anger—on both sides.

5. Treat Your Spouse as if He or She Were Already Married to Someone Else

This is another way of overcoming the tendency to assume you have the right to control your spouse.

6. Wear Your Wedding Ring

This is a sign that lets everyone know you're still "committed to your spouse," as Dr. Talley puts it. It announces that you are focusing on reconciliation with your current or former spouse and are not open to advances from other people. And indeed, the sign should mean just what it says.

GIVE ME COURAGE

Lord, I hope in you. I place my trust in you. Give me courage to be strong. I am fully aware that I need courage of heart in order to face the challenges of my life. Through your courage, I will be able to become swifter than an eagle and stronger than a lion. Thank you for this promise, Father.

—*Clift Richards and Lloyd Hildebrand*

7. Make a Commitment

Dr. Talley recommends that you make a written commitment to yourself and to God to remain open and available for reconciliation for 6 months. This means, in addition to following the six rules of conduct just listed, that you make no legal moves toward divorce during that period. Dr. Talley also suggests you seek counseling that will help prepare you for reconciliation.

You can tell your spouse about this commitment if you think it's appropriate and helpful to do so, Dr. Talley says, but he doesn't recommend it. "Chances are they're sick of the talk and they want to see the walk," he says. "Turn it over to God. Let God do the work to bring the other person to it."

At the end of the 6-month period, if your spouse still isn't interested in getting back together, Dr. Talley believes you will still come out the other side a more stable, more clear-headed person than you were going in. If relations seem to be improving between you and your spouse—or at least haven't changed for the worst—there's no reason not to sign yourself up for another 6-month reconciliation contract.

Going Through Divorce

For far too many of us, the dread of divorce eventually turns to the reality of divorce.

If you reach this stage, you'll need all of God's abiding grace and comfort to face it, as well as all the physical and emotional strength you can muster. The following steps can help protect you on your journey through this perilous terrain:

1. Guard Your Health

There is a tendency during times of emotional turmoil to let your health go. Don't, Dr. Bohler says. Make sure you eat properly and exercise regularly. "Not taking care of yourself physically can contribute to a downward emotional spiral," she says.

2. Turn to Your Faith Community

Many people who are going through a divorce shy away from their church because they feel they'll be judged there, says Dr. Bohler. This is a tragedy, she feels, because a faith community can offer just the sort of connection you so desperately need. "Divorce is a time to go *to* church, not away from it," she notes. "If you're feeling judged and unwelcome as a divorcing person in your church," she adds, "perhaps it's time to look around for another church."

3. Don't Turn Away from God

Just as people in the process of divorce often retreat from their church communities, they often retreat from God, either out of guilt or out of anger. For many believers, Dr. Whiteman says, divorce precipitates a huge crisis of faith: "I followed all God's rules," a person may think, "so why didn't God protect me from this calamity?"

This is just the way Dr. Whiteman felt after his divorce. Eventually, he understood, "I needed to reestablish my relationship with God. I had to realize that God never promises that nothing bad will ever happen to me. But He does promise that no matter what happens, He'll be there."

4. Talk to God, Honestly

One thing Dr. Whiteman learned in the process of developing a new view of God was that it is okay to bring his anger to God in prayer. "It's common for people to yell at God," he says, "and that's fine—God is big enough to handle that."

To encourage such honest interaction with the Lord, Dr. Clinebell suggests you try to imagine God sitting in a throne opposite you, listening as you pour out your angriest thoughts and most poisonous emotions.

HELP ME LET GO, GOD

Dear God,

In releasing this man, I surely feel as though my heart is crushed.

I feel as though a limb is gone, a piece of myself now ripped away.

I pray, dear God, for the power to love him so totally that I shall not be in pain.

For my love, I know, shall set me free.

Let me not be tempted to try to constrict him, either in my actions or in my thoughts.

May he fly free.

May I appreciate the rightness of his need to travel.

May I keep my faith in the wisdom of all things.

May I learn to respect his choices to go where he needs to go.

If he finds another love, may that love flourish, for Your sake.

For truly, the arc of love is a blessing on us all.

Wherever he goes, dear Lord, please go with him.

May he be blessed in all his doings.

Please protect him.

Bring him joy.

May he always be happy.

May he always be loved.

May he find his way.

Amen.

—Marianne Williamson

5. Protect the Children

Clearly the biggest tragedy in a divorce is the toll it takes on children.

It is especially destructive, says Dr. Bohler, if you put your children in the middle, between you and your spouse. The counseling term for this is "triangulation." An example is asking your children to pass messages to your spouse. This has the effect of making the children mediators between the parents, and it can be very damaging emotionally, notes Dr. Bohler. Don't let this happen, she says.

Recovery from Divorce

Healing the wounds of divorce seldom happens instantly—nor should we necessarily wish it to. "A lot of people say, 'I gave my pain to God and He healed me instantly,' but that sounds like denial to me," says Dr. Whitehead. "God can do miracles, but if He did that we wouldn't learn anything."

Learning is part of what healing is all about. "Consider what God is asking you to learn from this broken relationship," Dr. Whiteman says. "How are you being called upon to grow?"

Beware, however, of getting stuck in a period of painful development. "There's a difference between staying with the pain and hanging on to it," says Dr. Bohler. "Staying with the feelings will eventually help you come to terms with them and reach closure. On the other hand, you can't go on reliving and obsessing about what's happened to you forever."

How can you discern the line between the two?

1. Listen to Your Heart

There's no substitute for actually sitting down with yourself, and with God, and quietly listening to what's going on in your heart, Dr. Whiteman says. To help get the "conversation" started, he recommends using one of those light devotional books that offer up a line or two of scripture or a meditation topic for each day of the year. Read one topic a day and meditate quietly on it, leaving room for the Spirit to do a healing work in your heart.

2. Don't Rebound

The classic route for circumnavigating the pain of divorce is finding a new romance. Even the "we're just friends" type of relationship can, in truth, be a way to dodge reality, Dr. Whiteman says—and an excellent way to stumble into another marriage mistake. "Research shows that it takes at least two years to grieve the loss of a spouse," he says. "During those two years, you're still not a complete person, and a fraction of a person does not make a whole relationship."

Staying single doesn't mean staying isolated, he adds. "I encourage people to join a singles' ministry or some other form of activity where you do things as a group. Have fun, laugh, and joke—but don't pair off one on one."

3. Work on Forgiveness

You'll know the grieving process is really over, Dr. Whiteman believes, when you can think about your ex-spouse and honestly wish him or her well. That takes time, but you can get there in stages. Try to get the process rolling by forgiving the smaller hurts caused by your divorce, Dr. Whiteman suggests, such as careless remarks made by relatives or insensitive treatment by friends. Work your way up to forgiving the Big One (usually your ex).

> *We do not drown in the tears of healing. We wash away our sorrow.*
>
> —*Unknown*

One step that can help open your heart to forgiveness, Dr. Bohler suggests, is a prayer of "good intention" for your former spouse. "The idea is to hold your spouse in positive regard," she says. "Pray that he or she be guided wisely and that he or she be healed, too."

Remember too that forgiveness is not something you do once and forever. "You make a decision to forgive and then it's a daily practice," Dr. Whiteman says. "Every day you will well up with anger again, and every day you need to confess your anger to God and ask God for help in lifting it from you."

Remarriage

After a divorce, you may wonder whether you'll have to spend the rest of your life alone. Have faith. With patience, a commitment to truth, the support of your friends, and God's help, you can find love again.

Tom Whiteman, Ph.D., director of the Fresh Start divorce recovery seminars in Paoli, Pennsylvania, believed he was happily married—until his wife told him she wanted a divorce. Then he felt as if his life was over. God had other plans.

Now, more than 15 years later, Whiteman says his second wife and their three children have taught him that marriage can be much more satisfying than he ever thought it could be. He also has been able to turn the pain of his divorce into an international ministry that has helped thousands of people recover from their own divorces.

"I wouldn't wish divorce on my worst enemy, but God has been able to take the worst thing in my life and turn it into incredible blessings," says Dr. Whiteman.

Divorce is a tragedy—no doubt about that. But God often works through tragedies. Sometimes the most breathtaking miracles come in the form of healing from the most terrible wounds. Dr. Whiteman experienced such a healing. And so can you, if you prayerfully follow four steps.

- Give yourself time to thoroughly recover from your divorce.
- Take a good look at yourself to find out what went wrong with your first marriage so you can avoid making the same mistakes again.

- Learn how to reach out for new, healthy relationships.
- If you find someone, work together to build a solid foundation for a loving, faithful partnership.

A Healing Season

If you were seriously injured in an automobile accident, you'd expect to recuperate for a period so that your damaged tissue and bones could properly heal. Think of divorce as an emotional head-on collision. Here, also, it will take time, patience, and a positive attitude to recover.

Doctors who specialize in healing emotions recommend you concentrate on healing three major areas of your life.

Nothing in life is to be feared. It is only to be understood.

—Marie Curie

1. Work on Forgiving Yourself

Forgiving your ex is an important step toward recovery from a divorce, Dr. Whiteman says, but so is forgiving yourself. If you don't forgive yourself, shame and low self-esteem can prevent you from moving back into the world of the living—and the loving—which is where God would have you be. "Many people who have been divorced have an overwhelming feeling that they've let everyone down—I know I did," claims Dr. Whiteman. "We have to forgive ourselves for making some mistakes."

Because divorce is seen in some religious communities as a sin, many religious people whose marriages fail feel especially guilty, says Michele Novotni, Ph.D., author of *Making Up with God*. Prayer can help alleviate those feelings, Dr. Novotni says. She suggests meditating on chapter 3, verse 23 of Paul's letter to the Romans: "For all have sinned, and come short of the glory of God" (KJV).

This passage underscores the fact that there are many types of human failure or sin, Dr. Novotni believes. Some people fall short of perfection by lying, some by committing adultery, some by hating their neighbors. Divorce is simply another painful example of human failing. God forgives sins, Dr. Novotni points out. And sinners.

2. Reconnect

Many people come out of the fog of divorce and realize that they've become isolated. They've lost their old social connections, some old friends have faded away, and old associations are just too painful to resume because they are reminders of the former spouse. This isolation is natural, but it's important

SUSTAIN ME, GOD

Steer the ship of my life, good Lord, to your quiet harbour, where I can be safe from the storms of sin and conflict. Show me the course I should take. Renew in me the gift of discernment, so that I can always see the right direction in which I should go. And give me the strength and the courage to choose the right course, even when the sea is rough and the waves are high, knowing that through enduring hardship and danger in your name we shall find comfort and peace.

—Basil of Caesarea

not to let it go on too long, Dr. Novotni says. "Getting together with groups of friends in nonthreatening circumstances is an important step back," she says. "I'm talking about small group activities—not dating. A lot of churches have singles' groups that will go bowling or to the movies. The point is to simply get out of the house and have fun with other people."

Another benefit from this kind of platonic socializing, adds Dr. Whiteman, is that you can expand your capacity for friendship. You'll have a chance to choose friends more carefully, and hopefully more wisely, than you might have when you were younger. You'll also have the chance to learn more about what it means to be a friend yourself. All this is necessary homework for falling in love again. "The ability to find a committed romantic relationship grows from the ability to have committed friendships," Dr. Whiteman says.

3. Take a Look Inside

It may be hard to see any good coming from a divorce, but in reality it can be—and should be—a valuable learning experience. But to benefit from what you've learned—to avoid making the same mistakes again—you need to examine as thoroughly as possible the underlying emotional reasons why your marriage failed.

Concentrate on your role in the collapse, not your ex's—that's what you have control over, says Edward P. Wimberly, Ph.D., author of *Counseling African American Marriages and Families*. Why did you choose the person you did? What did you do—or not do—that might have exacerbated tensions in the

The Cautious Approach

Many churches and synagogues sponsor singles' groups for their members, and by and large they are good places for getting together with like-minded friends of both sexes. That's because church leaders often appreciate that wounded people need, first and foremost, emotional safety. "Finding someone to fall head over heals in love with shouldn't be the goal," says Edward P. Wimberly, Ph.D., professor of pastoral care and counseling at the Interdenominational Theological Center in Atlanta. "You need a safe place to get your act together."

Remember, however, that church groups aren't magically immune from the sorts of predatory behaviors you'll find anywhere men and women get together. "There are barracuda in church, too," says Tom Whiteman, Ph.D., director of the Fresh Start divorce recovery seminars based in Paoli, Pennsylvania.

"In his letter to the Ephesians, Paul talks about walking circumspectly in the world, and that's good advice," says Dr. Whiteman. "There are men who cruise church singles' groups, and you have to watch out for yourself because you won't necessarily be warned. That's why it's a good idea to find people who have a good reputation, who have a history with the group. Even then, it's a good idea to move slowly. You don't have to tell someone everything right off the bat. Share a few things, and then step back and see how the person handles it."

relationship? Perhaps most importantly, what effect did your childhood experiences have on how you behaved?

"Most of the problems that people have in marriage they already had before they got married," Dr. Wimberly says. "Therefore a significant exploration of what therapists call 'family of origin' issues is especially important in order to identify those legacies and patterns."

The best way to explore these issues is with a qualified therapist, Dr. Wimberly says. To find a counselor, Dr. Whiteman recommends that you ask your religious leader, your friends—particularly friends in your religious community—or your family doctor.

Another alternative is to read some of the many self-help books that are available on family and relationship issues. Three recommended by Dr. Novotni are *The 10 Dumbest Mistakes Smart People Make and How to Avoid Them* by Dr. Arthur Freeman and Rose DeWolf, *The Dance of Intimacy* by Harriet G. Lerner, Ph.D., and *Codependent No More* by Melody Beattie.

Go Slowly

Let's say you've found the new love of your life but you're terrified that you might make another mistake. After all, your judgment last time around wasn't the best. What should you do now?

Proceed with caution, says Dr. Whiteman. "There's always chemistry when you see someone who's attractive," he says. "Hormones are screaming in your brain, 'I *need* to be with this person, I *need* to be with this person,' but common sense will tell you that this person isn't the answer to all your problems. When I first met my second wife, we talked once, then we didn't talk for a couple of

GIVE US LOVE AND UNDERSTANDING

Lord, teach me to accept, and in accepting
to see all things as part of your plan
in drawing us closer to you.
When things go wrong between us,
let me see there may be some very good reason for it.
May I see clearly my own mistakes and overcome them.
Teach me to make loving and giving
the center of our every day.

—Rosa George

A PRAYER FOR NEW MARRIAGE

Now we will feel no rain
for each of us will be shelter for the other.
Now we will feel no cold
for each of us will be warmth for the other.
Now there is no more loneliness
for each of us will be companion to the other.
There is only one life before us
and our seasons will be long and good.

—Adapted from an Apache wedding blessing

---

weeks. Even though I was attracted to her immediately, it was several weeks before I asked her out. Then, when we did go out, I asked for a second date in a couple of weeks, rather than the next day. I deliberately slowed down the process."

Some other specific ways you can constructively slow things down are:

1. Make a List and Consult It

As always, when embarking on a scary new path, you should pray to help you stay in touch with God's will and guidance. But there's a tendency, in the heat of the moment, to forget the things you saw clearly in more reflective moments. "We tend to rush into commitments, overlooking what's important to us," Dr. Novotni says. "We need to pay attention to warning signs that maybe this person isn't the right person after all."

Drawing up a relationship "road map" ahead of time can help, Dr. Novotni suggests. Make a list of the qualities you consider to be essential in a prospective mate, from a sense of humor to a loving way with kids. Then, if a serious relationship seems to be developing, pull out your list and see if your new love measures up where it matters most.

Having such a list doesn't mean the new person in your life has to fulfill every item on it, Dr. Novotni adds. You're allowed to compromise—no two people will completely fulfill the needs and desires of one another. But you need to go into a new relationship with your eyes open, since over time the things you're giving up will become very obvious.

2. Seek Mutual Counsel

Ask your new partner to go through joint counseling with you before you make any permanent commitments, Dr. Novotni suggests. A good couples counselor can help you and your prospective partner articulate issues that are important to both of you and test how well—and how honestly—you communicate with one another.

> *I sought the Lord, and he heard me, and delivered me from all my fears.*
>
> —*Psalm 34:4 (KJV)*

3. Pray Together

One way to foster the growth of a healthy new relationship is to read scripture and pray with the new person in your life. For Bible readers, Dr. Wimberly recommends as a good starting place the letters of Paul, especially 1 and 2 Corinthians, Romans, 1 and 2 Thessalonians, and Galatians. There is much about the relationships between husband and wife in these letters—some of it contradictory—that can provide rich fodder for discussion between prospective mates, he says.

An especially fruitful passage to focus on, Dr. Wimberly suggests, is the admonition in Paul's letter to the Ephesians, chapter 5, verse 21: "Be subject to one another." Talking, meditating, and praying together on how each of you can righteously be subject to one another can be an invaluable tool for examining how well suited you might ultimately be as husband and wife, he feels.

PRAYER OF
PETITION

Putting Your Pleas before the Lord

T*he American Heritage Dictionary* defines "petition" as "a solemn supplication or request to a superior authority; an entreaty."

You could quibble with the word "solemn"—there's no reason prayers of petition can't be wailed out or voiced with enthusiasm. But certainly the idea of coming, hat in hand, before a "superior authority"—*the* superior authority, in this case—does capture the mood of what a prayer of petition is all about.

Prayers of petition are prayers that ask for something, for ourselves directly or for somebody else. The request might be for something as all-encompassing as world peace or as specific as the healing of a fracture in your mother's hip. That we would even think to bring such requests to God affirms our dependence on God's power, and so glorifies God, says Romano Guardini, author of *The Art of Praying*. We turn to God, he writes, "as the child in distress turns to his mother or as we turn to a friend when we need comfort or help."

Given how much we humans need help, it's likely that prayers of petition may be the single most used form of prayer there is. The very word "prayer," in fact, comes from the Latin verb *precari*, which means "to entreat or beg." Prayers of petition can be found throughout the Bible. Moses petitioned God for the deliverance of his people, and Jesus prayed to be spared the crucifixion. The psalms are saturated with prayers of petition from beginning to end, while the Lord's Prayer petitions God to "give us this day our daily bread," to "forgive us our debts," to "lead us not into temptation," and "to deliver us from evil."

Some people feel selfish asking God for what they want, but they needn't, says the Reverend Danny E. Morris, a retired Methodist minister who created and for 20 years was the executive director of the Academy of Spiritual Formation in Nashville. God knows what's in our hearts, he says. To pretend that there are areas of our life that are off-limits in prayer is to limit our relationship to the Divine.

Still, there's no harm in petitioning God gracefully, says Carolyn Bohler, Ph.D., professor of pastoral theology and counseling at United Theological Seminary in Dayton, Ohio. Rather than asking for a $70,000 Jaguar, for example, try praying for a safe, reliable form of transportation. Dr. Bohler also suggests praying for *qualities* rather than things: tolerance, for example, or patience, or wisdom.

It's helpful to keep in mind, Dr. Bohler adds, that God cares for the needs and desires of countless people in many communities and nations all over the world. That's why when her son was trying out for a slot on the high school baseball team, she didn't feel she could pray that he win one: There were only 15 slots available, and 45 kids wanted to get on the team just as badly as her son did. Instead she prayed that each boy would be able to do his best and that all would come away from the competition with a positive experience.

Another way to approach prayers of petition, Dr. Bohler suggests, is by offering up a sort of multiple-choice prayer. For example, if your child were going off to war, you might pray for (a) personal safety, (b) a peace treaty, (c) the end of all war, or (d) some solution God can think of but you can't.

Part 3

PARENTS FOR LIFE

Dealing with a Difficult Pregnancy

Pregnancy should be a joyous event, but what if you can't conceive or some serious problems befall your pregnancy? You need to turn to prayer, faith, and some practical advice to see you through.

nder the *best* circumstances pregnancy demands that a couple deal with an inordinate amount of work and worry. When things go wrong—when you and your spouse are dealing with infertility, miscarriage, or a difficult pregnancy—it can amplify your deepest fears and most hardened insecurities.

"Trust does not always come easily to a couple who find themselves in the midst of a problem pregnancy," says Cassandra Cook, Ph.D., clinical psychologist at Columbia University's Parent Infant Program in New York City. "There's often an awful lot of fear attached, not necessarily because the risk of complications is high, but because hope and expectations are high. They want to become parents *so* badly that the thought that something might go wrong can consume them from conception into the first year of the child's life."

But if you and your spouse are having a difficult time conceiving a child or carrying it to term, the experts say there are far more productive things to do than simply succumb to fear. "A couple facing a difficult pregnancy has at least three allies to help them through the hard times," says James Abell, M.D., an obstetrician and gynecologist who works at Prince George Hospital Center near Landover, Maryland. "They have their own strength and common sense, they have the support of their family and friends, and they have their faith in a God who, regardless of what might happen, will see them through it."

See every difficulty as a challenge, a stepping stone, and never be defeated by anything or anyone.

— *Eileen Caddy*

You and your spouse can marshal these appreciable assets in three ways.

- Working through the fear you may be feeling
- Letting go of any sense of guilt you many have
- Turning to family and friends for help

Controlling Fears

From anxiety about conception to worry about having a healthy baby, fear is a large part of pregnancy and parenthood. And that fear is heightened during a risky pregnancy.

"A problem pregnancy can be a real test of faith," says the Reverend Mariah Britton, youth minister at The Riverside Church in New York City. "It forces us to ask ourselves whether we really trust in God to see us through this trying time."

Yet if you open yourself up to God, see your doctor regularly, and take some commonsense steps, you can do much to ease your fears and control your anxieties. The following eight suggestions can help guide you.

1. Take Care of Your Health

With your doctor's guidance, be smart about your diet and get a reasonable amount of exercise. "Eating well may be the simplest thing you can do to help your pregnancy along," says Dr. Abell. "Don't drink alcohol, don't smoke cigarettes, make sure you get plenty of fruits and leafy vegetables. In short, be sensible."

As to exercise, Dr. Abell recommends light activities. "Join an exercise class for pregnant women, get out and walk, perhaps try some yoga," he says.

2. Deal with Your Stress

Each morning, take a moment to write down your fears and concerns for that day, and write, too, your intention to cope with these fears to the best of your ability. By doing this, you are accepting the fact that you will have some stress and fear over your pregnancy, and that it's quite normal.

LORD, GIVE US CHILDREN

Heavenly Father, you see our empty cradle, and you see our great desire to have children. Your Word confirms that you truly are a Father to us, and we know you have a special love for children. Lord, we pray you will answer our hearts' cry for a child, whether by birth or by adoption. But we submit our wills to you and trust your great plan and purpose for our lives. Please, Lord, cause your presence and your peace to sustain us as we wait upon you. In Jesus' name. Amen.

—Quin Sherrer and Ruthanne Garlock

"Women sometimes think they have to let go of all of their fears and be perfectly relaxed about this monumental change, but that's simply not the case," says Dr. Cook. "Instead, they do well to simply define that stress as a normal occurrence. If they want, they can get assurance on this from their doctor or from other mothers. This way they avoid adding to the stress by thinking there's something 'wrong' with them for feeling the way they do."

3. Understand What's Happening to You

If you're experiencing problems in your pregnancy, ask your doctor to explain exactly what is going on. "Having the medical information does two things," says Dr. Cook. "First, it helps you to understand exactly what you're up against and how it can be overcome. It defines the limits of the problem. Second, it prevents you from irrationally blaming yourself for something you had no control over. Just as you don't blame someone who is asthmatic, arthritic, or anemic, there's no need to accept blame when you're having pregnancy complications."

4. Pray for God's Help

God makes no guarantees that your baby is going to be healthy, says Reverend Britton, so you may be frustrated if you pray for something so specific. "Instead, ask God to give you the strength and the gratitude to accept whatever unfolds in your life," she suggests.

❦

FORGIVE ME, GOD

Forgive me my sins, O Lord; forgive me the sins of my youth and the sins of mine age, the sins of my soul and the sins of my body, my secret and whispering sins, my presumptuous and my crying sins, the sins that I have done to please myself and the sins that I have done to please others. . . . [F]orgive them, O Lord, forgive them all of thy great goodness.

—*From* Private Devotions

5. Search the Scriptures

Reading Bible stories that pertain to difficulties in family life can be comforting, says Reverend Britton, "because they reinforce the notion that God is present even in the face of family travail." He suggests the stories of Jacob and Rachel and the struggles they had with one another (Genesis 25) and of Absalom and David and the grave misunderstandings that made parenting so hard for David (2 Samuel 18). Also, says Reverend Britton, to better grasp God's understanding of our plight, read the passages that speak of God as a troubled parent (Ezekiel 20:21, for instance, or Lamentations 1:16).

6. Meditate Every Day

Choose a short Bible passage or prayer and meditate on it daily, either before you get out of bed in the morning or before you go to sleep at night. "A simple passage like 'Thy will be done' or 'Father, into Thy hands I commit my spirit,' recited over and over can strengthen your resolve for the uncertainties that lay ahead," says Reverend Britton.

7. Pray as a Couple

Join with your spouse, hold hands, close your eyes, and pray out loud each evening. "Lifting your concern in this way is extremely unburdening because it reminds each parent that they're not in this alone, that they have each other, and that God is with them," says Dr. Abell.

8. Talk to the Experts

Ask your pastor and/or your obstetrician if they can put you in touch with other couples who have shared the same pregnancy problems you're enduring, says Reverend Britton. "By doing this you can gain strength, understanding, and knowledge from the experience of others," she says.

Dealing with Guilt

When problems develop in a pregnancy, it can be tough for a couple to accept the difficulty simply as the whim of nature or an unfortunate roll of the dice. The temptation instead is to look inward and wonder if they aren't somehow being punished by God for sins or indiscretions of their past.

When you're having trouble getting pregnant or are miscarrying, says the Reverend John Van Regenmorter, director of Stepping Stones, Bethany Christian Services' ministry for infertile couples in Grand Rapids, Michigan, "you look around and feel like the whole world is pregnant. Everyone but you. You look to the heavens and wonder why they're silent, what punishment is being meted out to you and why."

But pastors and counselors point out that we've all sinned—including all of those among us who have borne healthy babies—and that we're all worthy

HELP ME HANDLE THESE TROUBLES

God, help me to remember that life is full of tribulation. And though you do not always deem it right or wise to help me, yet you are helping simply by being there.

My strength comes from you. Thank you.

My courage comes from you. Thank you.

Deep, deep within me, implanted by your very hands, is my determination, my toughness, my will to survive.

—Marjorie Holmes

WHEN YOU HAVE
DIFFICULTIES CONCEIVING

If you and your spouse have difficulty conceiving or have discovered you can't conceive, you may be inundated with feelings beyond the obvious sadness over not having a child of your own.

There might be irrational guilt that you've let your parents down, feelings of being "less of a man" or "less of a woman" for failing to create a child, or perhaps subconscious anger at your mate because of a problem in the other person's biological makeup. But when faced with serious doubt over whether or not you'll be able to conceive a child, the Reverend John Van Regenmorter, director of Stepping Stones, Bethany Christain Services' ministry for infertile couples in Grand Rapids, Michigan, recommends you keep your energies focused in two particular places.

First, don't give up hope. "The Bible is rich with stories of couples who conceived even after they were well past the age of conception," says Reverend Van Regenmorter. "Abraham and Sarah, Zechariah and Elizabeth, Jacob and Rachel all defied the odds. While this doesn't mean God will deliver a child to every childless couple, it does mean miracles are possible."

On the other hand, Reverend Van Regenmorter adds, you also have to be prepared to have your prayers answered in ways other than you want. "God

of God's forgiveness. Instead, separate yourself from guilt using the techniques listed here.

1. Ask Forgiveness

If you think your difficulty in getting pregnant is somehow related to, say, past sexual behavior that you're now ashamed of, pray to God for forgiveness. "There may well be no connection whatsoever between a past misdeed and a present misfortune," says Reverend Britton, "but if problems in a pregnancy call up unresolved issues of guilt, those issues are crying out for forgiveness.

might not grant us a child, or might wait to answer us, or might answer us by saying, 'No, you will not give birth to a child.' When that happens, couples need to be prepared to accept it."

If you need help accepting this situation, seek solace from your pastor, family, or other couples who haven't conceived. You and your spouse should also express your unconditional love for each other and pray as a couple to understand the wisdom of God's ways.

"With an open heart, listen to the pain and sadness you each are feeling and try to understand its depth and texture," suggests Reverend Van Regenmorter.

Infertility reminds all of us that God doesn't always give us what we want, no matter how sincerely we desire it. "I try to encourage people to reach the point of accepting the fact that God really loves them and desires only the best for them," says Julie Parton, manager of Crisis Pregnancy Ministry, Focus on the Family in Colorado Springs, Colorado. "If that best includes being a mother or father, God will somehow, in His own way and time, provide a child."

"But if God's grace for them does not include parenthood, they must accept that as His plan for them, even if that does not line up with their plan for themselves."

"It's time to pray, repent what you've done, ask God's blessing, and know it will be granted. If nothing else, you'll have that burden of guilt lifted from your shoulders," she says.

2. Understand the Biology

As with fear, learning more about what's going on in your body and why can help you overcome guilt, says Dr. Cook. Ask your obstetrician to explain what's causing your problems so you have a scientific understanding. Ask her how many couples go through this sort of thing so you can realize you're not being "singled out" for punishment.

Prayer Miracles

Praying Helped My Unborn Baby Live

Sixteen *weeks into my first pregnancy, I was diagnosed with cancer of the lymphatic system. The doctors recommended four cycles of chemotherapy and then, after the baby was born, six weeks of radiation. I knew I needed to come up with my own plan of attack for my baby and me to get through this successfully.*

I read The Power of Positive Thinking *by Norman Vincent Peale, in which he focused on the power of the mind and prayer to heal. And every day I would lay down and meditate and pray. I would pray and imagine that the powerful drugs that were being given to me were going straight to the tumors, and that the baby was perfectly protected. After one treatment, the tumor shrank from 6 inches in diameter to 1.5 inches. The doctor was shocked and asked me what I was doing. I began to tell him; he said, "Never mind, just keep doing it."*

My son Joey was born perfect and healthy in every way. I continued to pray and meditate through radiation and to this day I still use it to help me in everyday life.

Sue Bauer
Maple Valley, California

3. Accept Whatever Might Happen

Make your prayer for forgiveness an end in itself, not a means to an end. Keep in mind that God's forgiveness doesn't necessarily mean your prayers will be answered in the manner you're hoping. "Our prayers, even ones for a successful pregnancy, are requests, not demands," says Reverend Van Regenmorter. "God will relieve us our guilt and forgive us our sins, but we need to be reconciled to the possibility that we still might not have the child we're hoping for."

4. Give It Time

If you don't feel relieved after asking God's forgiveness, let time help dissipate your guilt. "It's entirely possible to ask God to forgive you and know that He has done so, and still feel the guilt," says Dr. Abell. "That's not necessarily bad. Time is a kind of tincture that slowly heals these sorts of things, and God may decide it will do you well to sit with your unhappiness for a while to make sure the lesson is learned."

5. Practice Forgiveness at Home

Forgive your spouse for past sins and ask him or her to do the same for you. "Even if only one of you feels as though you've committed a sin that is somehow linked to your pregnancy problems, you need to remember that you're in this marriage together," says Reverend Van Regenmorter. "When you pray to God, don't do so as a 'me issue' or a 'you issue,' but as a 'we issue.' There's nothing quite so liberating as knowing your pain is shared with your loved one and not borne alone."

PARENTING IN OTHER WAYS

Couples who can't have children of their own need not despair over never experiencing the joys of helping to share and shape a child's life, says Cassandra Cook, Ph.D., a clinical psychologist at Columbia University's Parent Infant Program in New York City.

"The possibilities are great, even for couples who choose not to adopt a child," says Dr. Cook. "The childless couple can volunteer with their church's youth group or offer to mentor children at their place of work. They can establish special bonds with their nephews and nieces, perhaps more intense and attentive than those with other relatives."

In addition, "They can join up with Big Brothers Big Sisters of America, a program that teams them up with kids who could benefit from a little more guidance and love," says Dr. Cook, "or maybe reach out to a member of their worship congregation, perhaps a single parent who needs help with child care or a father figure for their child."

These may sound like consolation prizes to some who want nothing less than to have children of their own, but what's bad about that?, asks the Reverend John Van Regenmorter, director of Stepping Stones, Bethany Christian Services' ministry for infertile couples in Grand Rapids, Michigan. "There's nothing wrong with consolation. Children console us. We console them. This is the basis of something quite powerful, and quite wonderful."

When Complications Arise

You've managed, with some difficulty, to conceive a child. Your obstetrician is coaxing you along from month to month. You're feeling discomfort and fatigue, but nothing out of the ordinary—or so you assume. Then the doctor gives you the news: There's a serious complication and in order to bring this child to term, you're going to have to spend the rest of your pregnancy—maybe months—in bed. A situation like this can put a strain on many aspects of your life.

Anyone can carry his burden, however hard, until nightfall. Anyone can live sweetly, patiently, lovingly, purely, till the sun goes down. And that is all that life really means.

—Robert Louis Stevenson

"A woman gains a lot when she chooses to get pregnant and does so," says Reverend Britton, "but she can lose a lot, too. She may have a great deal of her personality tied up in who she is professionally, socially, communally, physically. When all of that is suddenly taken away from her, she and her family need to figure out how they're going to cope with it."

1. Expand the Team

When mom or mom-to-be is suddenly taken out of commission, it's time to enlist the assistance of friends and family to pitch in. Ask the members of your church, other family members, friends, prayer groups, and others to help, suggests Dr. Cook. "They can not only lend moral support, but can also prepare meals, clean house, do shopping, even do some laundry," she says.

2. Put Yourself in Charge

If you're physically able, organize the people who are going to help you and the way they will help, says Dr. Cook. For example, "Mom can make plans for how the nursery is going to look, write out grocery lists for the week, etc.," she says. "All of this will help her avoid feelings of powerlessness."

The creation of a child may be the closest we humans ever come to mirroring God's work on earth, and a difficult pregnancy, for all of the heartache and headache, mirrors one part of God's love for all of us. It suggests how God as parent will do everything to nurture even the most fragile among us, with no guarantees that we will emerge and grow as God wishes. Moreover, a difficult pregnancy affirms that the pain of dashed hopes is a risk worth taking if the reward can be something so holy as a newborn child.

Birth of a Child

Life with a first baby is a time of intense and wondrous change for you and your spouse. Thankfully, prayer and spiritual customs can help you celebrate the special moments and cope with the troubling ones.

rom the magic of creating a life to the mystery of changing a first diaper, there is nothing that transforms you as much as the birth of a first child.

It alters your day-to-day life—suddenly your entire focus shifts from your needs and desires to those of someone who needs clothing, feeding, and loving 24 hours a day. But more than that, "having a child changes *you*," says Rabbi Nancy Fuchs-Kreimer, Ph.D., the leader of numerous seminars and workshops on the spiritual challenges of early parenthood. "By creating a new being you become a new being. Childbirth has elements of the profound and the miraculous, and once you cross over that threshold to parenthood, you never cross back."

When an event of this magnitude envelops you and your spouse, you're likely to feel a wide array of emotions—from fear, doubt, frustration, and confusion to wonder, excitement, joy, and delight. From a spiritual perspective, it may lead you to the three following issues.

- How to handle the emotions and pain surrounding birth
- How to bring your faith to bear to celebrate the special first months
- How to prayerfully deal with the feelings and the whirl of events at the

beginning of life—when you're adjusting to the necessity of caring for a helpless newborn and when you and your spouse are adjusting to the changes in your relationship

Each child is an adventure into a better life—an opportunity to change the old pattern and make it new.

—*Hubert Humphrey*

Giving Birth: The Great Unknown

There is perhaps no more profound, emotional experience than that of actually giving birth to a first child. For most couples, the intimate details of the event last a lifetime. But the days and hours before the birth also can be daunting.

"Each woman who goes through the birth experience does it differently," says Pastor Ruth Conard, who has led seminars on Christianity and parenthood. "While we know there is going to be pain, we don't know how much; while we know there will be labor, we don't know how long; and while we know we all have a threshold of endurance, we don't necessarily know when ours will be reached. It's a great mixing of the known and the unknown."

Thankfully, prayer can help you deal with the anxieties and uncertainties that mix produces, says Conard.

Offer God Your Gratitude

As pregnancy winds down and your child's birth date approaches, use prayer to thank God for the opportunity to have served as "co-creator" of this new life. "The creation of life is truly a miraculous partnership," says Conard, and acknowledging God's part in it can ease your fears. It reminds you that "God will be there with you as your child struggles and squirms his way into the world," she says.

Stem the Pain with Prayer

Lessen the pain of childbirth by combining prayer with deep breathing. "Choose a Bible passage and recite it both in anticipation of your child's birth and during labor," suggests Delia Halverson of Ft. Myers, Florida, the author of more than a dozen books on spirituality and family life, including *How Do Our Children Grow.* "This can bring a real sense of calm." Halverson suggests you use short verses that are easy to remember and recite. One

THANKS FOR THIS GIFT OF LIFE

O Creator, who dost all human beings create,
Thou hast a great worth on us conferred
By bringing us this little child!

—Kenyan oral tradition

choice from Ezekiel: "I will make breath enter you, and you will come to life." "Short, succinct verses such as this make wonderful little prayers," says Halverson.

Ask God for Strength

"Birth is separation; it is not only 'giving,' but 'giving up,'" says Conard. "Along with the physical pain and psychological anxiety of birthing a child, there is the emotional trauma of giving up something that has been growing in you for 9 months. Birth is the first in a long line of separations for you and your child, and you need to ask God for the strength to accept this."

Celebrating a New Life

From bar mitzvahs and communions to graduations, weddings, and even retirement parties, we all love to celebrate the milestones in our lives. The first few months of your newborn's life need not be any different.

In addition, because children grow up so quickly, special events and symbols can help you keep fixed in your mind the Divine wonder that is revealed in the early months. Experts recommend several ways you can remember the birth and early life of your child.

Light a Candle

In a prominent place in your home, light a candle each day for a week and make a petition to God to bless your family with health and love. "The candle, and the daily ritual of lighting it, keeps you close to God and reminds you that God is close to you," says Rabbi Fuchs-Kreimer.

THE PERFECT ROLE MODELS

Looking for a role model to inspire you in your position as a parent? Try Mary and Joseph, suggests Ruth Conard, pastor of assimilation at Woodridge Church in Medina, Minnesota.

"If anyone had to weather adversity and come through it with God's grace, it was the two of them," she says. "They had to listen to the direction they received from angels. That requires an awful lot of faith. They had to move the family three times in the earliest stages of the baby's life. That requires an awful lot of cooperation. And they had to endure the gossips and humiliators in the towns they went to. That requires an awful lot of courage.

"I can't believe there has ever been a birth experience that bound a couple more tightly together than that of Jesus of Nazareth, and we all stand to learn from His parents."

Wash Your Baby's Feet

When you first bring your newborn home, wash the child's feet. "When Abraham received three visitors into his home, he washed their feet as a way of welcoming them," says Rabbi Fuchs-Kreimer. Foot-washing is a way of proclaiming to God your joy over this "new visitor" and your pledge to ensure that your newborn will always be welcomed and loved in your home.

Swaddle Your Child

This is a rite sometimes performed in Jewish homes when the parents bring the baby home for the first time, says Rabbi Fuchs-Kreimer. "We strip the child of any garments and then wrap him in a tallith, or prayer shawl," she says. "This symbolizes the fact that we are all exposed to the dangers and uncertainties of the world and yet we are all also enclosed in the love of God."

Remember the First Sabbath

On your child's first Sabbath, ask your pastor to put a rose bud on the altar of your church as a symbol that you offer up your child to God for comfort and protection, suggests Halverson. At the end of the service, take a photograph of the rose, then take the rose home with you, press it, and keep it and the photo with the bulletin from that service as a way of remembering your pledge.

Collect "Icons"

Keep the blanket your child was wrapped in when you came home from the hospital. Save a lock of baby hair from the first month or so. At your first Christmas together, take a photograph of your newborn under the tree—along with all the other presents. "Icons link us with the past, with beginnings, and they remind us that life is truly a joint venture between the human and the Divine," says Halverson.

Adapting to a New Life

While the first few months with your child will be a time of wonder, they can also be a time of trial. You may go weeks without enough sleep. You may have

LORD, PROTECT THIS CHILD

O Lord my God, shed the light of your love on my child. Keep him safe from all illness and all injury. Enter his tiny soul, and comfort him with your peace and joy. He is too young to speak to me, and to my ears his cries and gurgles are meaningless nonsense. But to your ears they are prayers. His cries are cries for your blessing. His gurgles are gurgles of delight at your grace. Let him as a child learn the way of your commandments. As an adult let him live the full span of life, serving your kingdom on earth. And finally in his old age, let him die in the sure and certain knowledge of your salvation. I do not ask that he be wealthy, powerful, or famous. Rather I ask that he be poor in spirit, humble in action, and devout in worship. Dear Lord, smile upon him.

—Johann Starck

GOD, GIVE ME PATIENCE

Dear Lord, sometimes this new baby, this golden light, is just too much for me.

Sometimes when she cries late at night,

and I'm weary from a full day caring for her,

I want to ignore the sound and go back to sleep.

Sometimes when she fusses and fidgets, or spits and wails,

I want to yell at her to stop.

Forgive me.

Bless her.

Help me to remember that loving times are just a moment away.

Help me to understand that with every motion, every cry,

this lovely child is growing, stretching, becoming more the independent person I want her to be.

God, give me the patience, the wisdom, the humor, the strength,

To love her when she is troubling to me.

Just as you love me when I am troubling to you.

to tend to a baby who's unhappy because of illness or a reaction to shots. At the very least, you'll certainly have to adapt your life and daily routine to meet the frequent needs of this helpless new person. As every parent learns, there is nothing as bewitching as a happy baby or as bedeviling as an unhappy one.

"A baby's life is one of permanent change," says Amy Miller, Psy.D., a New York City–based clinical psychologist who works with couples on the verge of parenthood. "This is both a blessing and a curse for the parents. If the baby's going through a tough time, they can rest assured it will pass, but when the child is calm and peaceful, well, that'll change too."

What's important to realize, says Dr. Miller, is your life and your spouse's are in a state of change as well. "When you have a child, you're playing a whole *new* game," says Dr. Miller. "A couple becomes a threesome. And the weakest member of the family is pretty well calling the shots."

So what can couples do to prayerfully deal with the enormous changes brought about by their new baby? Here are some ideas.

Pray Together

Use prayer as a way to solidify the connection between you and your spouse. "In the early going," says Dr. Miller, "couples really need to be reminded that they're in this thing together— that they appreciate the other person's frustrations and fears and that each one of them is valued and celebrated by the other."

A mother spends 9 months holding her child tight and the rest of her life letting go.

Give Yourselves a Break

Allow yourselves time alone as a couple. "Parenthood is wondrous but also relentless, and parents need to take their own little 'retreats' from time to time," says Conard. You may not be immediately able to leave your newborn with, say another family member, says Dr. Miller, "but plan on it, set a date, and go off by yourselves."

Share Your Experience

Join a faith-based support group for new parents (ask your pastor for help finding one). "There's nothing quite as comforting as hearing your own struggles being spoken by another," says Dr. Miller. "We all need to be reminded that we're not alone in this, that we don't have all the answers, and that with God's grace we're going to get through it."

The birth of any child can be taken as a reminder that God is not yet through with us, that we are created in God's image, and that we are alive by virtue of God's grace. In the words of the poet Scriabin, "The universe resounds with the joyful cry I am."

Death of a Child

If your child dies, your world is irrevocably changed by grief and anger. Faith, prayer, and patience can help you find relief—and a path back to the place where God and love still dwell.

t was the middle of the night, and Elsa Riddell had been asleep in her New York City apartment when the call came. The word wasn't good: There'd been a terrible car crash in North Carolina, and Elsa's daughter Anne had been hurt.

How bad was it? No one seemed to know. So Elsa got on the phone and started frantically calling police stations, hospitals, and friends. Finally after 4 hours of calls she reached the doctor who had been in the emergency room when Anne arrived. There was no easy way to put it: Anne was dead, said the doctor, killed instantly when her head had been crushed by the impact of the crash.

"At that moment," says Riddell, "a part of me died too."

There may be no time on earth when God is more needed than when a child has died. It is an event that turns your entire world view upside down, challenging the very basis of your belief in a loving God and inviting you into a level of sadness that can teeter on the brink of outright despair.

When a tragedy like this strikes, you're likely to have three major reactions.

- You may be overwhelmed with emptiness, grief, and possibly even guilt that the death was somehow your fault. This is especially true when death strikes suddenly and there is no time for final goodbyes.
- You may feel anger at God and have doubts about your faith.
- You may wonder how you can ever go on or ever recover from the grief you feel.

Coming to grips with all these feelings will be hard, and the path back will be a difficult one. This is when prayer—and the support of family, friends, and spiritual leaders—can help the most, say counselors.

I lift up my eyes to the hills— where does my help come from? My help comes from the Lord, the Maker of heaven and earth.

—Psalm 121:1, 2 (RSV)

Let the Feelings Flow

Most counselors agree that recovery from the tragedy of a child's death begins inside you, with an honest examination of your feelings and thoughts.

Yes, it will be intensely painful to face your loss and work through the emotions, but you must do it before you can start healing, says the Reverend H. Scott Matheney, who during his nearly 20 years as a university chaplain has counseled numerous parents and young people after the death of a student.

"Let the feelings come," Chaplain Matheney advises. "Let them wash over you, and accept them as a part of the work you must do to be made whole again."

But where do you begin to grieve? With what is in your heart.

Unleash the Tears

If you are filled with sorrow, let it out—just as David did upon learning of the death of his son, Absalom. "My son, my son Absalom!" cried David. "If only I had died instead of you."

Weeping is a healthy way to start to recover, says Chaplain Matheney. "It is a form of cleansing, a kind of prayer of lamentation," he says.

Sometimes, however, you might not feel free to grieve because well-meaning friends get in the way. They may urge you to hold in your feelings because they feel uncomfortable being around when you're tearful. Or they may think the best way to help you recover is to encourage you to move on with your life.

PRAYER FOR THE DEAD

Dear God,

> *Please take the soul and spirit of this dear*
> *departed one into the sweetest corner of*
> *Your mind, the most tender place in Your*
> *heart, that she, and I, might be comforted.*
> *For now she has gone, and I pray, dear God, for*
> *the strength to remember she has not gone far.*
> *For she is with You and shall remain so forever.*
> *She remains within me, for we are all in You together.*
> *The cord that binds us one to the other cannot*
> *be cut, surely not by death.*
> *For You, dear God, have brought us together,*
> *and we remain in eternal connection.*
> *There is no power greater than You.*
> *Death is not Your master, nor mine.*
> *These things I believe and ask my heart to register.*
> *I surrender to You my grief.*
> *I surrender to You my pain.*
> *Please take care of Your servant, my dear one who has passed.*
> *And please, dear Lord, take care of me.*
> *Amen.*

—Marianne Williamson

"When my daughter died," recalls Riddell, "it was as though my friends would allow me a certain period of time to grieve, maybe a few weeks or so, but then they wanted the old me back again. I really wish I could've felt free to express my sadness in their presence because sometimes there was nothing to do but cry." Riddell's solution? She grieved with her family in the privacy of her home.

Celebrate the Life

You can't hope to find a real reason for a child's death, so you shouldn't try to, says Olson Huff, M.D., author of *The Window of Childhood* and a pediatrician who has worked extensively with seriously and terminally ill children and their parents. "Instead we should ask God to help us understand why he or she lived, what great and wondrous purpose this life served in its brevity," Dr. Huff suggests.

Deny the Guilt

Don't hold yourself responsible for something you had no control over, no matter what the circumstances of the death. "Just because we love our children unconditionally doesn't mean we can protect them completely," says Dr. Huff. "Things happen that are simply beyond our power to prevent."

Making Peace with God

When a child dies it not only brings grief but also creates anger and "absolute bewilderment," says Chaplain Matheney. "Children are not supposed to die. We believe it is God's intent that they will one day bury us, not we them," he says. So when our loved one dies, "we look in vain for God's purpose in what has happened."

There's a better course, says Merton Strommen, Ph.D., cofounder of the Youth and Family Institute of Augsburg College in Minneapolis and the father of a child killed by lightning. "I did not believe there was a reason why my son was killed, or that God 'intended' that David die that way," says Dr. Strommen. "But I did believe there were things that we as a family could do that would eventually help us to see that God was still very much at work in our lives." If you're feeling bewildered or angry with God, the four following actions may help you resolve your feelings.

1. Show God Your Anger

Treat anger as a form of prayer. Yell at God if you have to. Pound your fists if you want to. "Feel free to yell your lungs out and direct your fury to the heavens if it will make you feel better," says Dr. Huff. "We need to realize that it's more than okay to be angry at God for seeming to be indifferent to our tragedy."

Prayer Miracles

The Miracle of the Dove

Shortly after the tragic death of my 21-year-old daughter Kristen from asthma, I became very ill. The final diagnosis: I was suffering from extreme anxiety disorder because of my daughter's death.

My husband and I moved to Italy in the midst of my problems because he was stationed with the North Atlantic Treaty Organization. We settled in the small village of Montecchia Di Crosara. Because of the solitude and the serenity of my surroundings, I found it very easy to meditate and pray. During this time, I decided that what I needed was a sign proving that Kristen was being taken care of in the spiritual world. I wanted to see a white dove to know that she was fine and that I could go on with my life.

Days went by and nothing happened. Then one spring evening, my husband and I decided to walk to the little groceria to get bread for dinner. When we returned, suddenly we heard the soft ruffling of feathers and in front of us, gliding through the air and settling peacefully into the trees, were at least 50 white doves. A sign—no, not a sign, an exclamation! It was as if I could hear Kristen shouting joyfully, "Mom, look, I'm fine, I'm more than fine; I am incredible!" From that moment on, my life changed and my body healed.

Six years have gone by since that day. Every now and then I have a "blue" day when I lament over the death of my daughter. All I have to do is look out to my beautiful rose garden where a ceramic dove now sits and once again I am restored in the knowledge that miracles do happen every day.

Janet K. Brennan
Albuquerque, New Mexico

2. Practice Patience

Allow yourself as much time as necessary to get through your feelings. "God's not going anywhere," says Chaplain Matheney. "You don't have to rush the process. Over time, the anger dissipates, and when it does, God will still be there."

3. Build a New Relationship with God

Once you're through your anger, ask God to comfort you, says Chaplain Matheney. Ask God to stand with you and give you the strength and wisdom to heal from your loss.

4. Record Your Prayers

Keep an evening journal, and write down your prayers so you can reflect upon them and chart your journey back from grief.

The Road to Recovery

A child's tragic death is likely to produce an outpouring of support from family, friends, and many others. You should take advantage of it all. Your loved

LOVE LIFE

The thing is
to love life
to love it even when you have no
stomach for it, when everything you've held
dear crumbles like burnt paper in your hands
and your throat is filled with the silt of it.
When grief sits with you so heavily
it's like heat, tropical, moist
thickening the air so it's heavy like water
more fit for gills than lungs.
When grief weights you like your own flesh
only more of it, an obesity of grief.
How long can a body withstand this? you think,
and yet you hold life like a face between your palms,
a plain face, with no charming smile
or twinkle in her eye,
and you say, yes, I will take you
I will love you, again.

—Ellen Bass

ones, along with counselors and support groups, can help you work through your feelings and start on a path to acceptance and closure.

This may be a good time to turn to group prayer with your extended family, suggests Dr. Strommen. "In tragedy, everyone is equal," says Dr. Strommen. His wife, Irene, recalls one moment in their grief that brought home this point. "Mert was leading our family through prayer when he couldn't finish. He was too broken up," she says. "So without explanation he simply stopped, and when he did, our little granddaughter stepped in and finished his prayer for him."

Three other ways to work toward recovery are recommended.

1. Express Your Love

One of your loved ones may be gone, but many more remain. Remind all family members how important they are to you. "We've always been a close family," says Dr. Strommen, "but since David's death we always hug each other when we greet and when we say goodbye, and we always end conversations by telling one another that we love them."

2. Seek Help from a Group

Keep company with others who have been through what you've been through. Riddell joined a group called The Compassionate Friends, which is comprised solely of families that have suffered the death of a child. There, you can be candid about your grief and receive unconditional love. "People can pray if they want to, listen to one another's anger or sadness if need be, hold each other, and support one another in ways that no one else can. It truly is a healing ministry," she says. The Compassionate Friends has chapters nationwide. Call your local church, synagogue, or funeral home for help locating one near you.

3. Seek Counsel

The enormous confusion that attends the death of a child can be particularly overwhelming. If you feel lost in anguish and confusion, talk to a pastoral counselor.

Keeping the Spirit Alive

Beyond the death itself, there are many other regrets that may come when a child dies. You may grieve personally for the grandchildren you'll never enjoy. Or you may mourn in a broader sense because the world has lost the talent, the caring touch, whatever the special spark your child brought to this life. Yes, there has been a great loss, but death doesn't have to be the end of all the goodness your child represented.

Mert and Irene Strommen understood this. After their son's death, they decided that they "could never make his death worthwhile, but we could make it worth something, and we knew God would lead us to what that would be," says Dr. Strommen. The result? The Strommens established an endowment fund in their son's name to support a youth and family ministries center at Augsburg College in Minneapolis, his hometown. In this way they are sustaining their son's work as a minister to young people.

Helping Others Deal with a Child's Death

Sometimes it's not our child but the child of a friend, neighbor, or coworker who has died. When this happens you want to help, to do God's will in a time of great pain, but you may be at a loss as to what to do. Here are some suggestions.

Help Them Grieve

Let the grieving person know that it's okay to weep when you're there, to rage, to talk through the sorrow, whatever helps relieve the feelings. Your willingness to be a witness to the griever's pain can provide incredible comfort.

Don't Try to Explain the Death

Remember how Job reacted when his friends came to comfort him after the death of his children? He welcomed their visit when they sat with him in silence. But when they began to tell him why he was in the predicament he was in, they drove him crazy! Your words may have the same effect if you try to explain why the grieving person's child died. Keep your opinions to yourself.

Feed Them

"A good pot roast is always better than a bad theology when ministering to someone who has suffered such an incalculable loss as this," says the Reverend H. Scott Matheney, chaplain and dean of the chapel at Elmhurst College in suburban Chicago, who during his nearly 20 years as a university chaplain has counseled numerous parents and young people after the death of a student.

Let Your Children Take Part

If the child who has died is a friend of your children, let them attend the funeral to say goodbye. Encourage your children to talk about the friend. Remind them that you always do everything in your power to protect and watch out for them.

You can remember your child in many ways. Use the suggestions that follow as a starting point.

I know that when my son died, as the waves closed over the sinking car, God's heart was the first of all our hearts to break.

—*Reverend William Sloane Coffin Jr.*

Create a Living Memory

Follow the Strommens' example and create something enduring that will remind people of your child. It could be a tree planted in your child's memory to fill some barren place with life, a scholarship program that will help other children fulfill their dreams, or anything else that fits with what was important to your child in life. Irene Strommen calls the program she and her husband established "a kind of 'bricks-and-mortar' expression of our love for our son and our faith in the enduring power of God's love here on earth."

Do Good Works

Use your own experience to help others. You might join a cause, such as Mothers Against Drunk Driving, that helps keep other children alive. Or you might offer emotional support to other grieving families. If you're unsure how to contact other families, Chaplain Matheney suggests visiting your clergy or local funeral directors to make them aware of their willingness to help.

For related material see the chapter on dealing with the Death of a Loved One, on page 226.

The Trials
of Toddlerhood

*A time of curiosity and tantrums, insecurity and independence,
toddlerhood is when your child needs your loving presence
most. Faith, ritual, and prayer can help you both ride out the
rough spots.*

W hen you've spent your entire life believing you're the center of
the universe, it comes as a bit of a shock to discover otherwise,
even if you've only been living that life for 9 months. But this is
what children begin to come to terms with when they reach toddlerhood—
some time late in their first year. And your ability to help manage this transition will impact both your child's psychological development and spiritual
growth.

During this time, you'll face three major challenges.

- Reassuring your toddler as she begins to understand the world is a big,
  potentially scary place
- Helping your child develop an understanding of God, faith, and prayer
- Working through your frustrations—and hers—as your toddler begins to
  assert her independence

The Age of Uncertainty

To put it kindly, newborns tend to have a provincial view of the world. To them, it is a place designed solely to meet their needs and wants. Whether it's a clean diaper, a full belly, or a comfortable crib, whatever they desire is provided by a magical team of people whose role in life—as far as they can tell—is to love them and keep them happy.

Train up a child in the way he should go: and when he is old, he will not depart from it.

—*Proverbs 22:6 (KJV)*

Then toddlerhood hits. The protected life gives way to what Olson Huff, M.D., pediatric medical director of The Ruth and Billy Graham Children's Health Center in Asheville, North Carolina, calls "the discovery of separation." This, he says, is the realization that their needs are not always immediately met.

"This is a profound time in the child's life," says Dr. Huff. "She discovers that the world is not really under her control—that for the first time she must learn to trust, to have faith that people will care for her, will protect her."

This is when your child needs comfort and reassurance most. One of the best ways to provide them is in a spiritual context.

1. Use "Quiet Prayer" to Soothe

As bedtime approaches each night, offer your child a kind of quiet prayer she can understand: Hold her in your arms, rock her gently, and speak softly. "Because children are so much more aware of the world than they once were, they need a transition from the alertness of the day to the tranquility of the night," says Dr. Huff, "and when we hold them quietly we are praying with them insofar as we are transmitting comfort, reassurance, and calm."

2. Do as God Would Do

This may seem like a tall order, but remember that many of the qualities we look for in God are those that our children look for in us. "Just as we ask it of God, we need to prayerfully assure our children that we will always be there for them, that we will love them unconditionally, and that they can always turn to us for guidance and direction," says the Reverend Chris Erdman, senior pastor at University Presbyterian Church in Fresno, California. "If your 3-year-old is caught in a crying fit because it's the end of the day and he's just too tired to think straight," says Pastor Erdman, "just by picking him up, stroking the back of his head, telling him everything is okay, and rocking him in your arms, he'll begin to feel safe, protected, and calm."

THE VALUE OF QUESTIONS

Children always surprise us with the thoughtfulness of their questions, and here is one example from the Reverend Chris Erdman, senior pastor at University Presbyterian Church in Fresno, California:

"My young son once asked me—totally out of the blue—why God makes bugs," recalls Pastor Erdman. "I suppose I could've gone on at great length about life cycles and food chains and such, but instead I asked him what he thought, to which he answered, 'I think He makes them to punish mean people.'"

What ensued from this little nugget of wisdom was a rich conversation between father and son about how God works in their lives, why there are "mean" people, and what God wants us to do when we encounter them.

"It's important to nurture your toddler's questioning mind," says Pastor Erdman. Rather than trying to answer every question your child raises, meet her questions with questions. "The opportunity is not one of providing data," says Pastor Erdman, "but of encouraging your child's eagerness to explore the great questions of life."

3. Introduce Comforting Rituals

Punctuate each day with important rituals, such as grace before dinner or Bible stories before bed. "In ritual we open ourselves to God, and by incorporating this into the child's daily life she becomes increasingly secure in the knowledge that God is a benevolent presence in her family's life," says Dr. Huff.

The Age of Curiosity

Toddlerhood is also a time of great exploration. As your child starts to understand there's a world beyond her own, she also begins to realize this big place is just begging to be discovered. Now is a good time to help your child begin to explore her relationship with God.

"Because a young child's mind is so open to discovery, toddlerhood provides an excellent opportunity for parents to present to their children some fundamental ideas about God's love and purpose in the world," says Andrew Lester, Ph.D., professor of pastoral theology and pastoral counseling at Brite Divinity School in Fort Worth, Texas.

The key, says Dr. Lester, is to meet the child on her terms. "Kids are naturally curious; they see a lot of things going on around them, and they can't always articulate how they think or feel about those things," says Dr. Lester. "What we need to do is encourage their curiosity by engaging them in activities and conversations that allow them to express those feelings and thoughts." Experts advise that you do this in three ways.

1. Explore God through Play

Draw pictures that show how you feel about one another and how God feels about the two of you. Use puppets to act out Bible stories. Steps like these help you relate to your child in terms she understands. "Play is the work of the child," says Dr. Lester. "It is where she can be both expressive of her thoughts and feelings and receptive to yours."

2. Set Aside Time for Reflection

Give your toddler quiet time each day in her room, with no television, radio, or electronic games to grab her attention. "Prayer entails learning how to reflect on our world," says Ruth Conard, master of divinity, pastor of assimilation at Woodridge Church in Medina, Minnesota, who has led seminars on parenting. "We all need reflective time, but children won't necessarily seek it out

LORD, HELP US TRAIN THIS CHILD

Almighty God and heavenly Father,

we thank you for the children which you have given us:

give us also grace to train them in your faith, fear and love;

that as they advance in years they may grow in grace,

and may hereafter be found in the number of your elect children.

—*John Cosin, seventeenth-century bishop*

A Mother's Prayer

Dear Lord, It's such a hectic day,

With little time to stop and pray,

For Life's been anything but calm,

Since you called me to be a Mom,

Running errands, matching socks,

Building dreams with matching blocks,

Cooking, cleaning, finding shoes,

And other stuff that children lose,

Fitting lids on bottled bugs,

Wiping tears and giving hugs,

A stack of last week's mail to read,

So where's the quiet time I need?

Yet, when I steal a moment, Lord,

Just at the sink or ironing board,

To ask the blessings of Your grace,

I see them, in my small one's face,

That you have blessed me all the while,

And I stoop to kiss that precious smile.

for themselves. If you begin a daily regimen when they're young—with just 10 minutes a day—they learn to use that time to think about themselves, their family, and the world they inhabit. It is a discipline that they'll be able to carry throughout life."

3. Teach by Example

Let your children see you in daily prayer. "By seeing you regularly praying, a time will come when your child will ask you what you are doing and why," says Pastor Erdman. "It's then that you can explain how and why prayer is an integral part of our lives.

The Age of Irrationality

With all of the changes a child experiences when toddlerhood hits, it's no surprise that the experience can change her attitude from sweet to ill-tempered.

In automobile terms, the child supplies the power but the parents have to do the steering.

—Dr. Benjamin Spock

This puts a strain on the child and on you. But it is possible to get through the really difficult parts of toddlerhood with your sanity intact and your faith in command. The key, says Cassandra Cook, Ph.D., a clinical psychologist at Columbia University's Parent Infant Program in New York City, is recognizing that a child's temper is often an expression of her feeling of helplessness in the big world. Your goal, says Dr. Cook, is to "keep your own cool and at the same time help them learn how to whittle away at that helplessness." To do this, she recommends the following:

1. Ride Out the Storm with Your Child

When your child loses her temper or composure, stay with her. "It seems like a simple matter," says Dr. Cook, "but the child is afraid of being abandoned, which is one of the reasons for the loss of control. A parent's quiet presence is calming and reassuring."

2. Manage Your Feelings

Remain calm when your child starts a fit. Pray quietly to yourself if you have to, and ask God to help you both deal with the problem. "Anger met with more anger, louder voices, or sharper tongues only escalates," says Dr. Cook. "If your child is kicking you in the legs because he's angry that you didn't take him to the playground, you do a world of good if you can look at him sternly but calmly and tell him it's okay to be angry but not okay to hit and that he needs to get control of himself."

3. Take a Break

If you have been enduring the brunt of the work, ask your spouse or a friend to take over for a while. "Sometimes we need to take little 'mini-retreats,'" says Dr. Cook, "even if for only an hour or so. It allows us to gather ourselves, recharge our batteries, and get our strength back."

All in all, whether you are teaching your child how to tie a shoe, say her prayers, or survive the tempest of her own feelings, you are equipping your toddler with the tools she will need to meet her own needs," says Dr. Huff, "be they of the body, the mind, or the soul."

The Rebellious Years

Even good teenagers have their bad moments. Here's how to prayerfully guide your kids through the rocky shoals of adolescence.

There may be no greater exercise in humility than being the parent of a teenager.

Go ahead and discard whatever wisdom you think you've accumulated in your life: it's now worthless. What you wear, what you read, what you listen to, whom you admire—it's all absurd. Ditto your most cherished beliefs. And don't even think about uttering those corny jokes your teen used to love, or in any other way acting like yourself around the house. In fact, it's best to just keep a low profile at home. To the teenager who lives there, you've become a complete embarrassment.

It's not pretty, but it is survivable. In fact, as brutal as teenage rebellion sometimes seems, experts will tell you not only that it is a normal stage of human development, but also that it's a healthy one. (Within limits, of course: We're not talking here about teen pregnancy, drug abuse, criminal behavior, and other types of serious trouble.)

There is much that prayerful parents can do to help their children—and themselves—navigate the adolescent rites of passage safely and sanely. The path lies, the experts say, in the following basic rules:

- Pray to God for the ability to stay connected to your teen and the wisdom to handle your own emotions as well as theirs.

- Be ready to guide your teens around the most dangerous pitfalls of adolescent experimentation.

Stay Cool

The tortured teenager is a familiar stereotype, immortalized forever by James Dean's performance in the 1950s movie classic, *Rebel without a Cause.* Since that film was made, however, social scientists have come to realize that the sort of extreme teenage rebellion it portrays is not nearly as inevitable as many believe.

It's a little like wrestling a gorilla. You don't quit when you're tired. You quit when the gorilla is tired.

—*Robert Strauss*

Virtually all teens do go through a process of trying to sort out who they are and how their individual identity is distinct from their parents' identity, says Patricia H. Davis, Ph.D., associate professor of pastoral care at Southern Methodist University in Dallas. There are also physical changes underway—in addition to sexual maturity, there are vast changes in the brain—that contribute to the mood swings, sleep disruptions, and physical awkwardness often associated with adolescence.

It's almost inevitable that these changes will produce some attitudes and actions that make you, the parent, squirm. Don't panic! In the vast majority of cases this behavior won't add up to the sort of full-scale teen rebellion every parent fears.

"We now know that teenagers definitely want to remain in connection with the adults in their lives," Dr. Davis says. "They want to figure out who they are on their own, as newly formed individuals, but they don't want to disconnect totally."

Most often, teens express their rebellious impulses through relatively superficial tastes and fashions, adds Kathleen J. King, Ph.D., a psychologist in Kansas City, Missouri, who has specialized in teen issues. For bigger life decisions, Dr. King says, most adolescents still look to their parents for guidance.

Experts recommend the following to help you minimize the surface turmoil while keeping that deeper connection firmly in place.

1. Pray for Guidance

It goes without saying that you should ask God to protect and keep your children, but don't forget to pray for yourself as well, says Dr. Davis. Ask God

FOR A CHILD WHO HAS STRAYED

Lord God . . . You have a Father's heart and know the anguish we feel over the straying of our child.

Lord, he/she whom You love is sick in his soul. Recall him/her from him/her straying, and restore him/her once more to the joys of fellowship with You and to the security which comes to those who rest securely in Your fold.

Where we have sinned, forgive us, Lord. If we have been neglectful, unkind, thoughtless, cold, or unreasonable, pardon us and help us to make amends. Preserve us from an unforgiving spirit and a haughty heart in our relationship with our child. Comfort us by Your Spirit, and teach us to rely on You.

Be gracious to us, good Lord, and reunite us before Your throne of mercy, for Jesus' sake. Amen.

—*From* My Prayer Book

to give you an open spirit so that you can listen carefully to what your teenager is saying. "Teens are not the best at communication," she says. "Sometimes they come at things in a sideways fashion."

Perhaps most of all, pray for the wisdom and the patience you'll need to handle the difficult situations that may arise.

2. Pray for Insight

Adolescents are very good at pushing their parents' buttons. Rather than simply reacting when they do, try to see what these upsets can tell you about your own character and about your relationship with your child, says Stephen P. Greggo, Psy.D., chairman of the department of pastoral counseling and psychology at Trinity Evangelical Divinity School in Deerfield, Illinois.

A mother who goes nuts when her daughter dyes her hair green, for example, may be too focused on what other people think. It's also possible that

GUIDE THESE CHILDREN IN YOUR WAY

Father, may my children fulfill your plan and purpose for their lives. May the spirit of the Lord be upon them . . ." the Spirit of wisdom and of understanding, the Spirit of counsel and of power, the Spirit of knowledge and of the fear of the lord . . ." (Isaiah 11:2). Lord I release my children into your hands. Thank you that you love them more than I do, that your plans for them are plans for welfare and peace, not for evil, and that will you give them a future of hope (Jeremiah 29:11). Amen.

—*Quin Sherrer and Ruthanne Garlock*

a daughter who dyes her hair green may be trying to get a reaction from parents who she feels haven't been paying enough attention to her.

Pray for insights into these sorts of connections, Dr. Greggo suggests. Remember, too, that your child is not doing whatever he or she is doing only to make you mad. "A lot of parents have a tendency to think, 'he's doing this *to me,*'" says Dr. King. "In truth, he's not doing it to you, he's doing it because he's 15 years old or because his friends are doing it—for a whole host of reasons that may have nothing to do with you. Try not to take it personally."

3. Be Unconditional

Most parents love their children unconditionally, but sometimes they fail to let their kids know that, says Dr. King. There's a tendency to get too hung up on grades, sports performance, or a thousand other forms of personal achievement. Don't forget to let your kids know that you love them regardless of their achievements—the same way, Dr. King points out, that God loves you.

4. Get Support

As the parent of a teenager, you need help. One way to get it is by finding a support group of other parents with whom you can share your woes as well as your joys, your successes, your failures, your techniques, and your lessons learned. Many churches offer support groups where parents regularly meet to share and commiserate, says Dr. Greggo. If your church doesn't have one, find one at another church or set one up yourself.

Look for Balance

Being the parent of a teenager is a lot like being an ambassador to the United Nations. Your skills at diplomacy will be in constant demand, and the last thing you should do is assume that the person you're dealing with sees a given issue the same way you do.

Take heart: Virtually everyone is as unprepared going into this as you are, and you'll definitely learn as you go. These suggestions can help you handle the negotiations.

1. Back Off

One knee-jerk reaction to guard against with your teens is the impulse to say "no." Resist that temptation.

HELP THEM CHOOSE THE RIGHT PATH, LORD

Great God, with heart and tongue, to thee aloud we pray,

That all our children, while they're young, may walk in wisdom's way.

Now in their early days, teach them thy will to know,

O God, thy sanctifying grace on every heart bestow.

Make their defenceless youth the object of thy care;

Cause them to choose the way of truth, and flee from every snare.

Their hearts to folly prone, renew by power divine;

Unite them to thyself alone, and make them wholly thine.

—Anonymous

STAKING A CLAIM

If you've got a rebellious teenager on your hands, chances are good that one thing he or she is rebelling against is God—or, more accurately, your God.

For a devout parent, the prospect of having a child stray from the righteous path can be distressing indeed. But psychologists who study teen development say that teens who question can be something to celebrate rather than mourn.

"Adolescence is a special time in a child's spiritual life," says Patricia H. Davis, Ph.D., associate professor of pastoral care at Southern Methodist University in Dallas. "Religions recognize this with various ceremonies—confirmations, bar mitzvahs, and the like. Hopefully, when a child asks questions, that indicates that a process of 'claiming' the religion is underway."

Teens often feel they can't adopt their parents' religious beliefs for themselves without first subjecting those beliefs to a rigorous cross-examination, Dr. Davis

---

This is not to say that there aren't times when a clear and definite "no" isn't appropriate: Parents must set boundaries and enforce them. The point is not to fall into the habit of fearfully restricting your children's every move. Teenagers want to try new things, which goes against the parent's instinct to stay with the tried and true. Scary as it may be, the most effective way for them to learn is to make a mistake.

"Let your kids go about two steps beyond where you feel comfortable," says Dr. Davis. "That's not to say you should let your kids do something dangerous, but to allow your kids to grow, you need to push yourself past your own comfort zone. Pray for the courage you'll need to give your child that space."

2. Set Clear Boundaries

If your teens are going to follow your rules, they need to know what those rules are. Sit down with your children and clearly discuss not only what rules you insist on, Dr. King says, but also what the consequences will be if they're broken.

says. They're asking themselves what makes sense and what sounds false; they're on the lookout for hypocrisies and contradictions. Kids these days are exposed to so many different religious opinions that it takes a while to sort that out.

"The comfortable homogeneity of religious experience is disrupted for them," Dr. Davis says, "and that causes them to call into question the very basis of their faith."

Some teens decide the struggle isn't worth the effort. Either they just go through the motions of worship or they withdraw from it altogether. For that reason, Dr. Davis believes that the teens who are seriously wrestling with religious questions may be best off in the long run because those are the ones for whom questions about God truly matter.

Don't discourage or ignore those questions, Dr. Davis recommends. Honor them and discuss them.

Hard as this may be to believe, teens actually *like* to know what the boundaries are, says Dr. Davis. But be careful you don't make the limits too numerous; a long list that tries to cover every possible contingency only creates confusion and resentment. Dr. King used three rules to raise her teenage son: Let me know where you are, be home by the agreed-upon time, and don't watch TV until your homework's done.

Similarly, don't make punishments too onerous. Kids who are grounded for 6 months tend to give up in despair: Why change if you won't get the reward for changing? Punishments need to be specific, related to the offense, and brief, Dr. King believes.

3. Be Forgiving

Giving your kids the freedom to learn from their mistakes means forgiving them when they make the mistakes. "Tell them, 'We're going to get through this and we're going to start over,'" says Dr. King.

4. Be Flexible

Rigid enforcement of rules also sets the wrong tone, Dr. King believes. If you have a curfew of 11:00 P.M., and your child comes in at 11:10, don't fly off the handle. Again, allowing the child some room to grow and experiment, within limits, is important to growth and to self-esteem. Be willing to talk over rules with your teen, and be willing to bend on occasion.

If, in instructing a child, you are vexed with it for want of adroitness, try, if you have never tried before, to write with your left hand, and then remember that a child is all left hand.

—J. F. Boyse

4. Pay Attention

Part of setting effective boundaries is keeping an eye on what your teen is up to, Dr. King says. That means listening to the music they're bringing home and watching the movies they rent. It also means getting to know their friends. This needs to be handled gracefully—kids will react badly if they feel they're being given the third degree. If you have problems with what you learn, that's the time to sit down and directly discuss your concerns with your teen.

You can also help steer your child—literally—toward fruitful activities and friendships. Dr. Greggo always makes himself available to drive his teenage daughter to social activities he approves of. He also lets her know that he will be happy to come pick her up immediately if something is going on that she feels uncomfortable with. All she has to do is call.

5. Take the Pressure Off

The stresses of modern life affect teenagers just as they do adults. Academic pressures, competition to succeed in sports and other activities, working to earn the money to pay for fancy clothes and other luxuries—all take a tremendous toll. Lots of kids are burning out—or breaking down. Just as your teens need to be reminded that your love for them isn't contingent on grades or sports performance, they also need help in not becoming overwhelmed with the competitive demands of school and social activities.

"I love it when my daughter gets an A," Dr. Greggo says, "but sometimes she studies harder than I think she should. At that point I have to say to her, 'Hey, I realize I've probably been responsible for putting some of the pressure you feel to do well in school, but I think you've done enough studying for this exam. Why don't you goof off tonight?'"

Serious Problems

Every parent fears the forces that might draw a child into deep trouble. But with prayer, faith, and a balanced response, you can keep your children on the right path—and deal with the consequences if they stray.

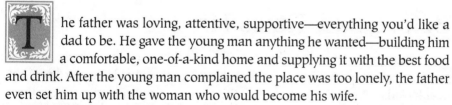

The father was loving, attentive, supportive—everything you'd like a dad to be. He gave the young man anything he wanted—building him a comfortable, one-of-a-kind home and supplying it with the best food and drink. After the young man complained the place was too lonely, the father even set him up with the woman who would become his wife.

Yet none of it was enough.

Eventually, the young man got involved with an unsavory character and stumbled into a problem with the law. When his father found out, the young man tried to cover up and lied about what he'd done. In the end, all the father could do was watch as the young man was punished—for life.

Yes, it sounds like a scenario that's all too familiar these days—a doting parent and a troubled child. But this one was played out between God and Adam. As the story proves, children have been getting into serious trouble—and anguished parents have been dealing with it—since the beginning of time.

These days, kids find trouble (and vice versa) for any number of reasons. It might be contact with the wrong friends, broken homes, negligent parents, or psychological frailties. Or, as the Reverend Colleen Holby, chaplain to Children's Village shelter in Dobbs Ferry, New York, points out, it might just be the mix of a whole slew of little problems that in and of themselves don't amount to much, but when taken together result in good kids getting involved in bad stuff.

How do you keep your children from taking a fatal step into an unwanted pregnancy, gang membership, drug addiction, criminal activity, or some other serious problem? And what do you do if your children do get into serious trouble? Counselors and pastors suggest the following:

> *When a child is in serious trouble, his parents should walk through the fire with him. Not for him, but with him.*
>
> —*Reverend Jeremy Montgomery*

- Build a family life filled with prayer, faith, love, and trust to head off trouble before it hits.
- Watch for signs your children are moving in a bad direction and react quickly when something seems wrong.
- If your children get involved in serious trouble, pray, listen, and never stop loving.

Before Bad Times Hit

A good gardener knows that growing a healthy crop starts early on, with careful preparation of the soil and the plants. The same holds true for "growing" healthy kids—you have to start when they're young and carefully nurture them so they can fend off the bugs and blights of life.

What's the best way to nurture? "Build a relationship with them, be active in their lives, show an interest in what they do, let them know they're precious in your sight," says the Reverend Jeremy Montgomery, youth coordinator of the Ten Point Coalition, a Boston group organized to prevent youth violence.

Active parenting, experts say, also includes the way you love your kids and the way you discipline them, often two sides of the same coin. Starting when your children are young, you need to apply consistent discipline when they do something wrong, but it should be discipline mixed with love, says Brother Larry Backus, C.S.C., director of jail ministries for the Diocese of Albany, New York.

"Children have to know that when they've done something wrong you're angry at what they've *done*, but you still love *them*," says Brother Backus. "A

WHAT YE SOW . . .

"Our kids are less likely to be enticed by the bad stuff if they're enjoying the good," says Father Placid Stroik, director of pastoral ministry for the international youth haven Covenant House in New York City. "A gang isn't going to seem like an attractive 'family' if her own family gives her the attention she needs. Drugs aren't going to have appeal if he discovers the rewards of a healthy body out on a playing field. A child won't be prone to depression or despair if she's learned early in life that she can take her problems to her parents and her God and work them out there.

"We plant these seeds early, we sow them when they're young, and they'll reap them when they're older."

---

child who feels the security of that unconditional love will be free to turn to his parents when he's made a mistake or gotten himself into a jam."

Here are some other prayerful ways you can parent children to minimize their susceptibility to serious trouble.

1. Give Them Your Time

Spend time alone with your children—schedule it if you have to. "For all the gifts you can bestow on your children, nothing is as sacred as your time," says Alan Ross, executive director of Samaritans, a New York City–based suicide prevention organization. "Nothing shows the child that you care quite like giving hours in your day, whether it's to talk, have a meal, go for a walk, go to worship, throw a ball around, or play with dolls."

2. Be Consistent

Establish fair rules and apply them consistently. "We are a spiritual people in part because we appreciate the security that comes from knowing that God will look out for us and deal justly with us," says Reverend Montgomery, "and our kids want the same things from us." Reverend Montgomery

GOD, HELP THE YOUNG

Lord, the world needs

this marvelous wealth which is youth.

Help young people!

They hold the inexhaustible wealth of the future. . . .

Do not allow an easy life to corrupt them

Nor obstacles to crush their spirit.

Free them from the worst danger of all—

That is getting used to being

Old within themselves

And only young on the outside.

—*Dom Helder Camara*

---

recommends that families have set rules—written if necessary—that the rules be honored, and that the child understand the consequences if they're not.

3. Admit Your Mistakes

When you make a mistake, acknowledge it. "Children who see their parents making mistakes and taking responsibility for them will be freer to do the same," says Ross. Confession and forgiveness, adds Brother Backus, are useless on Sunday if they're not practiced the rest of the week.

4. Fix the Problem, Not the Blame

"Rather than establishing blame for the things your kids do wrong, simply hold them responsible for fixing them," says Father Placid Stroik, director of pastoral ministry for the international youth haven Covenant House in New York City. Say, for instance, your child breaks a window in his bedroom. Instead of scolding or punishing him for being careless, simply point out that the problem isn't him, it's the broken window, and the way for the problem to be solved is for him to repair it with his time and his money.

When Danger Is on the Horizon

Wouldn't it be nice if you had a high-tech wireless alarm that would ring the instant your kids were about to get into serious problems? Truth is, however, it's not always easy to see when trouble is on the horizon.

"I've known kids who look like the toughest dudes on the block but who would never so much as smoke a cigarette," says the Reverend Daniel Hahn, doctor of ministry, pastor to students and families at Mission Hills Church in Los Angeles, "and I've known ones who look squeaky clean from head to toe and then wind up getting busted or arrested. You simply can't always tell."

But even as an inexact science, experts say there are still ways to identify danger signs in the children you love. If you see the signs early enough there are ways to respond with swiftness, thoroughness, and confidence—before your children get in too deep.

1. Look for Difficult Behavior

"If a child starts rejecting the authority of parents, teachers, clergy, and the like, there's a good chance that child is angry and might not even know why," says Reverend Montgomery. Adds Amy Miller, Psy.D., a New York City–based psychologist, "When indiscriminate anger and rejection appear seemingly out of nowhere, you owe it to your child to be suspicious. Look around their room, their personal effects, and see if there is evidence to justify your suspicion. Then, if there is, be ready for a gentle but firm conversation with your child about seeking help."

2. Look for Denial

Watch for signs that your children are blaming others for any and all of their own perceived shortcomings, says Reverend Holby. "This is a child in denial, and it means she's losing touch with herself. For whatever reason, she's afraid to face her problems and you need to help her do so.

"Say for instance your son is arrested for shoplifting and he immediately starts blaming his friends for setting him up," says Dr. Miller. "You sit him down, and you begin by saying 'Well, then clearly one of your problems is the friends you have, so how do you want to go about losing the ones you have and making new ones?' While you're giving the child some input, you're also making it clear that you insist on the need for change to be made in his life."

3. Look for Help

When your children seem to be troubled, look for an authority figure they respect and become allies with that person. It could be a coach, a teacher, a

Deliver My Child from Addiction

Lord, I praise you for being the Great Deliverer. I ask you to move mightily on behalf of our child, _____. Deliver him/her from evil. Show him/her a way of escape. Convict him/her of this destructive sin that prevents him/her from receiving your love.

Father, thank you for the promise in your Word that "the seed of the righteous shall be delivered" (Proverbs 11:21). I am righteous because of the blood of Jesus, and _____ is my seed. So, Lord, I'm trusting you to deliver him/her from this trap and establish his/her life in your perfect plan.

Amen.

—Quin Sherrer and Ruthanne Garlock

mentor, or a youth worker. "Pray with them, ask God to work through them, and ask them to sit and visit with you and your child so that your child knows you all hold his interest in your hearts," says Brother Backus. Also, adds Dr. Miller, "tell them your kid really enjoys the time you spend together, and ask that they continue to show interest."

4. Encourage Other Interests

If you fear your children are engaged in friendships with the wrong people or are taking part in dangerous activities, spend time with them and help them find alternatives. "Our children rely on us more than we imagine, " says Dr. Hahn. "They're hungry for us to look out for them, and that includes giving direction to their free time."

5. Punish Proportionately

If your children do start to stray, make the punishment fit the "crime." "Punishment should be instructive and loving," says Father Stroik. "If a child is caught shoplifting at a local grocery store, ask the manager if he can spend a week carrying groceries for the elderly. This is how you redeem bad behavior."

6. Tackle Problems One by One

Each morning help your children make a list of troubling behaviors that they can work on that day. Perhaps the list will include things like "control my temper," "do my homework," or "be kind to my sister." Then, at day's end, go over your children's list, encourage what they've done well, and discuss what will be on tomorrow's list. "The child needs to see what he has control over and what he thinks is out of his control," says Reverend Holby.

When Trouble Strikes

For all of your efforts, your children may reach the point where they are in serious trouble—when hope seems so far away that it's not even a glimmer. Of course at a time like this your first act should be to turn to God, says Dr. Hahn. "Acknowledge just how faint hope seems, and ask God daily to restore your faith that you can work things out," Dr. Hahn suggests.

But beyond this, what actions can you take to build a hopeful future for your children—and the rest of the world? Pastors and counselors offer six suggestions.

1. Acknowledge Your Grief

Talk to God and to your close friends and family about the heartache and grief you feel over your child. "Pretending you're not wounded is exhausting and ultimately futile," says Brother Backus. "You need to acknowledge before God and friends the severity of the situation and its effect on you."

2. Listen to Your Children

Without making judgments or suggestions, hear what your children have to say. Let them begin by unburdening themselves of their thoughts and feelings. "A sign that says 'Shut up and Listen' hangs over my office door," says Ross. Why? To remind him that too many of us forget that at first blush a kid in trouble doesn't necessarily want to be 'fixed'; he wants to be listened to. "You might not agree with what they have to say, and that's fine, because they're not expecting to be agreed with, they're simply expecting to be heard," Ross says.

3. Let Your Children Pay the Debt

If your son or daughter has done something illegal, such as vandalize a home or steal a car, don't try to buy their way out of the trouble. Let the child deal with the consequences of the act. "The only way we learn how to live in society is the way the prodigal son learned," says Reverend Montgomery. "He had to endure the sufferings he brought upon himself, and only then was he able to return home."

Reverend Montgomery believes this lesson even extends to possible jail time. "As caregivers and parents, our instinct is to rescue our youth and children from the natural consequences of their negative choices," he said. "But if we allow them to reap the consequences of a vandalistic act by sitting in a jail cell for a while, then the message will be clear to them that vandalism is not a positive choice."

> *O God, give us serenity to accept what cannot be changed, the courage to change what can be changed, and wisdom to know the difference.*
>
> —*Reinhold Niebuhr*

4. Don't Abandon Your Children

Tell them, repeatedly, that you still love them and will always leave the door open to them. "One of the reasons the prodigal was able to come home in all his humiliation," says Reverend Montgomery, "is that his dad never lost faith and waited for him. It's a story worth telling a troubled kid."

5. Ask Your Loved Ones to Pray

Your children need to be in everyone's prayers during times of trouble. Ask all of your relatives to pray for your family. Ask them to do it in private and anonymously during worship services.

6. Don't Ignore the Rest of the Family

It's easy to neglect other family members when a child is in desperate trouble. That can hurt the other family members. Pray regularly as a family, follow it with time when each member can talk about the pain and struggles you're engaged in, and ask each other how you can be of help to one another.

"Children wander, but they're never fully lost unless we turn our backs," says Father Stroik. "This is not what God intends of us, nor, do I think, is it what we expect of ourselves."

Older Children

Your children are grown and ready to go out on their own. How can you help them become loving, successful adults? Through prayer, support, and thoughtful advice.

Y ou bring them into this world. You care for them through scrapes, illnesses, first dates, and disappointments. You help them learn to drive and prepare for college. Then one day your children are ready to go out on their own.

After you've spent years attending to your children's needs, it can be difficult to give up that role. But you must if you want them to become successful, independent adults. Parenthood, after all, is a wondrous—but temporary—vocation, says the Reverend Lex Baer, doctor of ministry, a counselor at the Professional Pastoral-Counseling Institute in Cincinnati.

"We can only do parenthood well enough to get fired," says Dr. Baer.

Pastors and counselors agree that you must do three things to make this passage easier for you and your children.

- Prepare the family for the children's departure.
- Develop a new relationship with adult children.
- Fill the void after your children leave.

On the Path to Separation

Although most parents of older children can pinpoint the exact day their kids moved out and set up life on their own, the departure in many ways is—or should be—a gradual process. "You should slowly loosen the reins until their actual leaving is momentous but also something you're both well prepared for," says Robert F. Stahmann, Ph.D., professor of marriage and family therapy at Brigham Young University in Provo, Utah.

My role is to release my children full force on the world, loving themselves, loving what's different about themselves, embracing what's different about other people, and up for some kind of adventure.

—Susan Sarandon

Here's how you can reach that stage.

1. Covenant with Your Child

Just as God did with Abraham, make a covenant of expectation and promise with your children. "You once provided everything for them," says Dr. Stahmann, "but now the lines of responsibility are blurred. If, say, your child is going off to school, be clear about what part of his education you will pay for, whether he needs to maintain a certain grade point average in order continue to receive financial support, what will happen if he wants to take a year off, and so forth. If he's going out to seek a job, be clear about whether he's welcome to live with you if things don't work out."

You should enter into this covenant prayerfully, writing it down if necessary, and both you and your children should agree to it. And if for some reason your children balk at the terms, says Dr. Stahmann, they need to be reminded that these are the only terms under which they can rely on your continued support.

2. Share Your Wisdom

Offer advice, but don't legalize or moralize. "You are still the 'matriarch or patriarch,' who your children will want to turn to for direction," says the Reverend H. Scott Matheney, chaplain and dean of the chapel at Elmhurst College in suburban Chicago. However, you are no longer in a position to dictate how your children must behave. "If, for instance, your child announces she'll be giving up her new job to go off and explore the South Sea Islands for an indefinite period of time, you can no longer say to her, 'Here is what you must do,'" says Dr. Baer. But you can say, "I want you to know where I stand on this."

Then you can offer impartial feedback that puts your child's dream in per-

Help Us Let Go

Father, we commit to your care our child who is leaving home. We thank you for the years of happiness and shared experience, for the laughter, tears, and talking together. We thank you for every sign of your grace in his life. We commit to you the failures and disappointments too.

Now give us the humility to stand aside from his life and choices. Give us wisdom, tact, and love that we may support without being intrusive and be at hand without getting in the way.

Take him into your strong keeping for your love is greater than ours.

—*From* The Doubleday Prayer Collection

---

spective. So, following up on the South Seas example, you might tell your child, "From where I stand, this is what your decision looks like: The South Seas are beautiful and romantic, but on the other hand they're expensive, you won't know anybody, and there's little chance of your making a living there. Also, keep in mind that you won't have a job to come back to, so you'll need to have some savings to live off when you return. Maybe what we want to think about is how long you can afford to take a trip like this, what you want to do with it, and what you'll do when you when you return." In other words, says Dr. Baer, your job is just to lend your experience to tighten the threads of a loosely fitting dream.

3. Help Them Design Their Exit

What if the opposite is true and your children reach adulthood and still are reluctant to leave home or go to work or school? Then you need to push them out of the nest compassionately. "Very often all a parent needs to say is something along the lines of, 'You're an adult now; it's time you went off on your own, either to school or to work. But I know this can be an enormous challenge, so we all need to talk as a family about how we can work with you to make this happen,'" says Chaplain Matheney. "By saying this you're nudging them out of the nest without abandoning them."

COMING OF AGE

O you four Powers of the universe, you wingeds of the air, and all the peoples who move in the universe—you have all been placed in the pipe. Help this young man with the knowledge which has been given to all of you by Wakan-Tanka. Be merciful to him!

O Wakan-Tanka, grant that this young man may have relatives; that he may be one with the four winds, the four Powers of the world, and with the light of the dawn. May he understand his relationship with all the winged peoples of the air. He will place his feet upon the sacred earth of a mountaintop; may he receive understanding there; may his generations to come be holy!

All things give thanks to You, O Wakan-Tanka, who are merciful and who help us all. We ask all this of You because we know that You are the only One and that You have the power over all things!

—Sioux rite of initiation

4. Pray for Strength

Whatever course your children take, pray with them for God to support all of you in the uncertain days that lie ahead. "We all move into new circumstances with a certain amount of dread," says Chaplain Matheney. "When children are leaving home, the one thing they share in common with their parents is a fear of the unknown. But fear and the faith to overcome it can be a powerful family bond at a time like that."

Building a New Relationship

When your children first go out on their own, your relationship with them develops a new rhythm. You still think of them late at night, still pray for their safety and well-being, but they're no longer under your roof where you can see daily how they're getting on in life.

This is a critical time in a parent-child relationship, says the Reverend Peter Bridge, doctor of ministry, clinical director at The Samaritan Counseling Center in Philadelphia, because you and your children may be tempted to lapse into familiar parent-child roles that can harm their development.

You need to encourage them to be independent—to be your peers in some ways. Here's how experts suggest you make that happen.

1. Seek Their Counsel

Ask your children for their advice in matters they have some knowledge of. It might be choosing a car or buying a stock. The goal is to start to show your children you view them as equals and you value their ideas. By doing this, "you pass the mantle to the next generation of sage, just as Elijah did with Elisha in the first chapter of Kings," says Chaplain Matheney. "It's a way of affirming adulthood."

2. Reverse Roles

Let your children take over control for some aspect of the family. For example, "when college students tell me they want their parents to acknowledge that they're no longer little kids," says Chaplain Matheney, "I sometimes en-

MY NEST IS EMPTY, LORD

How I miss my children since they've all left the nest, Lord. It seems their years at home just evaporated. Now they're off to college or to distant jobs, and the house is strangely quiet. I find myself imagining what one of them may be doing at any given moment. When the phone rings, I hope it might be one of them calling home.

Thank you, Lord, that your eye is upon each of my children and that your protection continues to cover them. Prepare them for the future. Help them resist evil and be examples of godliness wherever they go. You know all about their mistakes, Lord. But how grateful I am that you can redeem the mistakes all of us have made! Help me fulfill your purpose for my life now that the nest is empty. In Jesus' name, Amen.

—Quin Sherrer and Ruthanne Garlock

courage them to demonstrate it by taking their parents out to dinner. It may not seem like much, but when they explain to their parents that it is both a meal of appreciation for all the parents provided and a statement of independence, it becomes a rather poignant rite of passage."

Don't try to force anything.

Let life be a deep let-go.

See God opening millions of flowers every day without forcing the buds.

—*Bhagwan Shree Rajneesh*

3. Create New Traditions

Establish new ways of celebrating birthdays, anniversaries, summer vacations, and holidays. "Parents and children should look at the times of year that are sacred to them as a family and decide how to celebrate them now that the children have their own lives," says Dr. Stahmann. "This keeps the 'sacred moment' alive but accommodates new realities as well: Christmas or Thanksgiving at home might have to alternate between homes, but as old traditions are laid to rest new ones take their places."

Filling Your Empty Nest

A house long filled with the sound of children is peculiarly quiet when they grow up and leave. At times like these, "children aren't the only ones to experience transition," says Dr. Bridge. You are just as likely to feel a loss—both of companionship and of identity. After all, you're no longer the caretaker, the provider, and the decision maker your children call upon.

Here's how experts suggest you handle the loss.

1. Spend Time with Others

Seek the company of other friends whose children are grown and gone. Draw from their experiences, ask them to pray for you, and, as Chaplain Matheney suggests, "in your own prayers, ask that God grant you the *imagination* necessary to create your new life."

2. Volunteer

Identify charitable groups—perhaps a children's organization or your church's Sunday school—to which you and your spouse would both enjoy donating your time. "Part of the richness of parenting is that it entails working toward a common aim," says Dr. Bridge. "Giving your time likewise to your faith community, or even to total strangers, can be similarly enriching."

The Returning Child

When a grown child decides to move back home it can create disruptions and tension—if you let it. Here's how you can use prayer and compassion to work through the potential problems.

In their mid-fifties and with all their children grown and out of the home, Chuck and Nancy Norton were beginning to enjoy their life together as a mature couple. Then Chuck's 30-year-old son, Ken, called.

Ken said his divorce and financial difficulties had left him in a bad way. After some prayerful thought, Chuck and Nancy offered to let him move back with them—if Ken would abide some basic rules. The key ones: Ken would not be allowed to host parties in their home, and he had to participate in weekly financial planning meetings with Chuck and Nancy to help him work out of his debts. "We wanted him to be responsible, a good citizen," says Chuck.

Ken agreed, and after 9 months of nesting he felt he was ready to fly solo again—and Chuck and Nancy were relieved. Things were stressful at times, but Chuck and Nancy know that letting Ken move in helped him.

Three out of every 10 adult children will move back home at some point in their lives, and in many cases, the return of a "boomerang" child creates stress and unhappiness for everyone. It doesn't have to be that way. If you handle the situation with prayer, faith, and planning, you can develop a deeper, more fulfilling relationship with your grown child while helping ease the child out of the nest and into a productive and independent life. The key, say pastors and counselors, is concentrating on three steps.

- Explore what's triggering your child's desire to return.
- Create rules you all can live with.
- Help your child return to independence.

Examining the "Why"

Before you fling wide the doors in welcome, you first need to find out what's brought your child back to your doorstep. If you let the child return for the wrong reasons, you're not doing either of you any favors, says the Reverend Peter Bridge, doctor of ministry, clinical director at The Samaritan Counseling Center in Philadelphia.

You may give them your love but not your thoughts, for they have their own thoughts. You may house their bodies but not their souls, for their souls dwell in the house of tomorrow, which you cannot visit, not even in your dreams.

—*Kahlíl Gibran*

Usually, a child's request is prompted by either a developmental issue or a responsibility issue, suggests Dr. Bridge. If fears, difficulties, or just plain immaturity have left your child with a temporary confidence crisis, it's developmental. Example: Maybe college overwhelmed Junior and he needs time to regroup in familiar surroundings. In cases like this, it's appropriate to show compassion and welcome your child home, says Dr. Bridge.

But if you're hearing that your daughter wants to return because her "stupid boss" cost her her third job in 2 months, she might be shirking adult responsibilities and wanting to nest simply because it's a nice place to hang out, says Dr. Bridge. In that case, your child *can* make it on her own—she's just backtracking, suggests Dr. Bridge. You still may choose to let your child move back, "but you jolly well better set some terms."

For example, you might limit how long she can stay and require that she pay rent. Barter household chores or errands until she's able to contribute cash. The goal is help her gradually earn her way back to independence

When the Answer Is No

There also may be times when it's not appropriate to let your child move back, suggests Art Sprunger, Ph.D., director of New Hope & Freedom Counseling Center in Geigertown, Pennsylvania. If the child has drug or alcohol

FOR THOSE WE ARE TRYING TO HELP

Oh, God, I sometimes get so discouraged trying to pray character into other people.

Over and over I ask: Give them honor. Give them self-discipline. Give them determination, give them courage. And when they falter my disappointment is overpowering. I am bewildered. I am stung.

Why don't you hear me? I wonder. Why don't you stir the fires within them? Why don't you rouse them to a sense of their own values? Why don't you take them in hand and make them the strong fine people they were meant to be?

Then I realize—you can't do it for them. I can't do it for them. They've got to do it for themselves.

And how can I help to give them strength if I weaken? How can I be a channel of courage if I become afraid?

—*Marjorie Holmes*

problems, for example, his homecoming could disrupt or destroy family life—especially if there are younger kids still in the house.

A better choice in a case like this would be to ask if any extended family member could help. Or offer to pay for your child's stay at a halfway house. Then gradually withdraw your financial support as the child overcomes the addiction and becomes self-sufficient.

Mother May I?

Remember that childhood game? The association may be painful if you're trying to determine appropriate boundaries for an adult child. While you don't want your child to feel like he has to ask permission for everything he wants to do, you do want him to realize there are limits in your house.

"There should be a prayerful awareness by both child and parents that everything is a privilege rather than a right," says Dr. Sprunger. But how do you establish rules, then live under them without creating any unnecessary tension?

1. Speak Frankly

If you have concerns about language, hours, friends, money, whatever, discuss these "hot buttons" and let your child know what's unacceptable, suggests Robert Brantley, managing director of The Brantley Group, a Christian counseling center in Baltimore.

2. Be Flexible

Yes, you may be setting limits, but that doesn't mean you can't be open to change if your child suggests an alternative.

"Parents who do best with boomerang kids are those who have a real sense of openness about their own growth," says Dr. Bridge. If your child wants to investigate other faiths, for example, be open to learning about his choices—while expressing your concerns, if appropriate.

Saying something like, "This scares me, but tell me more," helps to keep the lines of communication open. And if you overreact to some situation, don't be afraid to tell your child, "I blew it," says Dr. Bridge.

A PARENT'S PRAYER

Dear Father in heaven, I thank You for having made me a parent. I pray You, help me fully to realize my parental responsibility and the privilege of rearing children for You.

Give me a calm and even temperament, and help me to lead my children patiently and surely toward physical and emotional maturity. Make them useful and helpful in all things.

Amen.

—From My Prayer Book

3. Focus on the Issues, Not Each Other

If a problem arises over the rules you've set, don't let feelings from the past creep into your statements. You'll only create a crisis if you start screaming about the fact that Junior has been a slob all is life when the current problem is only that he's left his dirty socks on the side of the tub. Remember, you're living in an adult-to-adult relationship now, says Dr. Sprunger.

The Road to Self-Reliance

When a grown child returns to what feels like dependency, it almost always steals something from his identity, Dr. Sprunger says. That's not healthy for either of you.

There are two lasting bequests we can hope to give our children. One of these is roots; the other wings.

—*Hodding Carter*

Instead, the goal should be "interdependence and a mutuality of respect," suggests says Dr. Sprunger. "You're reattached, but not reabsorbed."

Here are a few suggestions on peacefully coexisting.

1. Visualize Independence

While helping your child, your aim should be to make the time back in the nest as short-lived as possible, advises Dr. Sprunger. Establish a clear time line for departure.

2. Live Your Own Lives

Parents often foster a returning child's dependence by trying to fix everything for the child—from the emotional damage of a painful divorce to the erratically stacked CDs in the reclaimed bedroom. While it may be easy to slip into this comfortable role, you don't do you or your child any good by fixing problems.

3. Don't Expect Obedience

The Bible may admonish that a child should "obey" the parents, but when the child is over 20, the goal changes to "respect and honor," says Dr. Sprunger.

4. Remember Who They Are

Chuck and Nancy Norton pray for their kids daily. No matter what happens, "they're always family," says Chuck. Hold that thought and it won't matter if the nest is empty or filled to capacity. You'll have your priorities straight.

DAILY PRAYER

Staying in Tune with God

Gracefully incorporating prayer into your daily life is not a matter of the more prayer the better, says Elizabeth J. Canham, doctor of ministry, an Episcopal priest who directs the Stillpoint Ministries in Black Mountain, North Carolina. Think in terms of quality, not quantity. Also think in terms of rhythm and tone.

Dr. Canham sets a prayerful tone for her day by spending about an hour in prayer each morning. (If you're unused to prayer, she recommends you start with a much shorter period of time and build up gradually.) She has a sacred space in her house set aside for prayer, and she usually begins by lighting an oil lamp and doing some stretching and deep-breathing exercises. She also sips a cup of coffee. "It took me a while to realize that there's nothing unspiritual about praying with a good cup of high-test coffee," she says.

A typical morning's prayer session for Dr. Canham includes some time spent in silent prayer, some time meditating on scripture, and some time journaling. She recommends that you use one of the many available books of daily scripture readings or daily meditations rather than choosing passages at random. As an Episcopalian, Dr. Canham follows the daily rites suggested in the Book of Common Prayer. Often her journal-writing expands on thoughts she has while meditating on scripture.

Morning prayer establishes a sort of spiritual set-point for the day, says Dr. Canham. Her goal then is to apprehend as much as possible the presence of God in all things. To aid in this, she often tries to find a line or two of scripture to think about as she goes about her daily business. Once, for example, she had a line in her head from the psalms about God giving strength to those who follow him. That thought gave her comfort as she ruminated during her morning walk about some anxieties she was experiencing in her work.

Dr. Canham also has identified events that routinely crop up during her day—"triggers," she calls them—which signal her to repeat specific prayers. Whenever she comes to a red light, for example, she silently repeats to herself the opening words of Psalm 63 (as translated in the Book of Common Prayer): "For God alone my soul in silence waits." These help her appreciate what Jean-Pierre de Caussade, an eighteenth-century Jesuit priest, called "the sacrament of the present moment."

The second major prayer session in Dr. Canham's daily regimen comes at night. In her book *Heart Whispers: Benedictine Wisdom for Today*, she outlines the five-step exercise with which she routinely ends her day.

1. Give Thanks

Reflect back on the day, looking for all the gifts God has given you, and also for the moments in which your needs might have been revealed. Express your gratitude to God for gifts received and allow that gratitude to sink into your heart.

2. Ask for Insights

Pray that the Holy Spirit will reveal to you insights about the day's events that you might not have seen by yourself.

3. Look for God

Go over the day's events again, this time focusing on the various moods and emotions you experienced. What might those emotions have been telling you about the will of God? Was God pulling you in a particular direction? Were you especially aware of God's presence in another person during the day? How did you respond to these experiences or situations?

4. Express Repentance and Gratitude

Ask God to forgive you for those moments when you were unresponsive to the Divine presence, and pray that you receive the willingness to be more responsive in the future. Give God thanks and praise for those moments when you were responsive to the Divine will.

5. Receive Help and Guidance for Tomorrow

Ask God to give you whatever you will need to move faithfully through tomorrow. Pray specifically for the strength to deal with your spiritual struggles, such as fighting anger or finding the ability to forgive.

Part 4

Preparing
for Retirement

*Life after work can be a time of leisure and inactivity—or a
time of spiritual, emotional, and mental growth. The key lies in
how you approach these precious years.*

uring his career, Chandra had been a pillar of the community.
He was dedicated to his work as a merchant and used his earnings to help sustain a large household—including his wife, their two
sons and daughters-in-law, and a number of servants. Then after living a
rich, full life—his moral duties to society fulfilled—it was time for Chandra
to retire.

But retirement didn't mean a life of leisure. According to the *Laws of Manu*,
the ancient Hindu text he followed, Chandra renounced his home, family, and
career and retired to a forest dwelling. There, he lived austerely while pursuing
life's truest goal: achieving union with God.

Few of us would be willing to spend retirement foraging in the woods like
Chandra, who lived out his life some 1,700 years ago in India. But we can learn
from his example, says Drew Leder, M.D., Ph.D., author of *Spiritual Passages:
Embracing Life's Sacred Journey*. The crucial point: Life after work isn't the beginning of the end. It is a time of promise and growth

"We tend to view aging as painful. We try to deny it as long as possible, defeat it by compulsive productivity, or be distracted from it with activities and games," explains Dr. Leder. "The Hindu model suggests a different approach: Rather than mourn all that is slipping away, we can turn toward a realization of the Divine. Retirement opens up time and space for an inner contemplative life."

Hold fast to dreams
For if dreams die
Life is a broken-
winged bird
That cannot fly.

—Langston Hughes

If, like Chandra, you want to make retirement a time of renewed possibilities and spiritual growth, you need to take three steps.

- Prepare your mind and spirit for retirement.
- Cope with your grief over the career you're leaving.
- Embrace retirement as a new beginning.

Beyond Dollars and Cents

Financial advisers will tell you that it's never *too* early to begin preparing for retirement. But they're talking about money only. You also need to plan for your emotional and spiritual needs. That should start about 10 years prior to the time you expect to leave work, says pre-retirement planning expert Dorothy Madway Sampson, coauthor of *The Healing Journey through Retirement*.

Five actions can help you prepare for life after you end your career.

1. Face Your Feelings

Retiring can conjure up a whole range of emotions—from exultation to bitterness. It's important that you let those feelings out, particularly the negative ones, says Sampson. Otherwise, they may trigger inappropriate behavior like misplaced anger, overeating, or even alcohol abuse.

If you're unsure what exactly is bothering you, make a list of the emotions you're feeling. The list might include words like *angry, afraid, happy, bitter, dejected, disappointed, free, overwhelmed, at peace,* or *sad.* Next, focus on *each* word. Try to understand what's causing that feeling; then plan how you can overcome it. For example, if driving by your old office building makes you feel sad or depressed, take a different route.

Also, keep in mind that "experiencing a range of feelings during times of big change is normal," says Sampson. "Try not to fret too much about your

---

HELP ME USE MY MANY GIFTS

You have blessed me with many gifts, God, but I know it is my task to realize them. May I never underestimate my potential, may I never lose hope. May I find the strength to strive for better, the courage to be different, the energy to give all that I have to offer.

—*Rabbi Naomi Levy*

---

state of mind today, or this afternoon. Effective planning for retirement requires a long-term focus."

2. Take Inventory

Imagine yourself, like Chandra, going off to the forest to pursue enlightenment, suggests Dr. Leder. What in your life would you leave behind? "Think of particular chores, distractions, and habits that you'd like to be free of—paying bills, always feeling rushed, dealing with car problems," says Dr. Leder. Make a list, and then symbolically renounce your burdens by drawing a line through them.

Next make a second (and hopefully smaller) list of the things that you would bring with you on your forest retreat. Your list might include the Bible, a particular person to serve as a friend or guide, or special objects from art or nature that help raise your awareness.

Then start setting aside time to escape the things that trouble you and work with the spiritual tools you've chosen. You may, for instance, want to establish a daily quiet hour devoted exclusively to prayer and meditation.

3. Get More Involved in Church

It's natural to feel drawn to God as you approach the end of your career. This is a good time to strengthen that connection because the spiritual and social support network your church can provide will help you navigate the transition to retirement, says Sampson. How do you get more involved now? Scan the weekly church bulletin for news of upcoming activities. Sign up to teach

---

PREPARE ME FOR WHAT WILL COME, LORD

Gracious God, heavenly Father, I must confess that I am sometimes upset by the many changes that come in life. I find it difficult to make the necessary adjustments. I do not ask to understand, but help me, I pray You, always to realize that no matter what happens to me, and what changes must be made, You still love me and will make every experience work together for my good.

Give me the faith to trust Your promise, "My grace is sufficient for you." In mercy forgive all grumbling and complaining of which I have been guilty in the past. Teach me to follow the example of Jesus, my Savior and Lord, who in trial and tribulation said, "Not My will, but Thine, be done." In that spirit I shall be able to meet whatever life has in store for me. For Jesus' sake. Amen.

—*From* My Prayer Book

Sunday school, join the choir, become a church lector, or simply volunteer to help wash dishes at the next church supper.

4. Become an Elder, Not Just Older

Thanks to scientific advances, we're leading longer, healthier lives today than past generations did. "But what's the point of this elongated lifespan if we don't put it to some positive use?" questions Dr. Leder. Aging brings precious lessons and a wealth of wisdom you can share as an "elder-sage," he says. And passing on your knowledge will bring you fulfillment, too.

Unsure how to share? Contact an organization like Big Brothers Big Sisters of America. Volunteer as a foster grandparent. Give time as a literary volunteer at a local school. The opportunities are endless.

5. Try Out New Hobbies Now

Many people who planned to fill their days with new activities discover when they retire that they don't enjoy woodworking, golf, puttering around in the garden, or whatever they'd planned to do. To avoid this trap, "try out hobbies that you think you might want to invest a lot of your time in before you build your life around them," says Sampson.

Grieving a Work Life That's Ending

No matter how well you prepare for the end of your work career you will still experience a sense of grief and loss when it actually comes time to retire. Leaving a career represents a loss of identity, power, structure in your life, relationships, and possibly income.

To get through this phase, you must "acknowledge the loss and give yourself time to grieve," says the Reverend Marilyle Sweet Page, doctor of ministry, a pastoral counselor in Rochester, New York. Here are some suggestions for working through the process.

1. Ritualize the Event

In our culture we tend to have rituals early in life—for instance, baptism, marriage, and graduation. "But we don't have many to sanctify later life transitions," says Dr. Leder. But these later rituals are important because they allow you to pause for a moment to mourn, grieve, and celebrate life's passages, he says.

The solution? Construct your own ritual. It could be a formal event like a special retirement service at church that includes family and friends, or something more private, such as writing a list of gifts that God has given you in your work life and then offering a prayer of thanks.

2. Resist the Temptation to Stay Busy

Many people are so afraid that retiring will leave a void in their lives that they try to fill every waking moment of their time off with busyness. This circumvents the grieving process. Instead, "honor the opening that has come into your life," suggests Dr. Leder. "You can use this time to deepen your spiritual and emotional life. Pray, write, listen to music, take walks in nature—do anything that helps you get in touch with your soul."

3. Pray for Acceptance

Perhaps you're struggling with feelings of anger after being forced into an early retirement. You can find comfort and direction, says Sampson, in the words of what has become known as the serenity prayer: "God, grant me the serenity to accept the things I cannot change, courage to change the things I can, and wisdom to know the difference."

A Prayer of Surrender

Oh my father, I surrender my whole self to you.

Do with me as you please! Whatever you do, I will thank you for it.

I am ready for anything, ready to accept whatever comes. As long as your will is accomplished in me and within all creation, I ask for nothing else.

Into your hands I hand over my life. To you I give it, my God, with all my heart's love.

I love you, and so I feel compelled to do as lovers do—to give myself, to put myself entirely in your hands, with infinite trust, for I know you are my Father!

Amen.

—*Charles de Foucald (translated from French by Charles Cummings)*

"Recognizing the difference between the things you can and cannot change is an important ingredient in acceptance and personal growth," she affirms.

To help with the process, get a piece of paper and write down four things that are difficult to accept during this time in your life. For example, "fear of getting older" might be on your list. Evaluate whether each issue is something you can change. If not, ask yourself if there is another way to look at it. For instance, you can't change how old you are, but you can change how you view age. Think of it not as a time of decline, but as a time of renewed possibilities.

4. Defeat Stereotypes

Having a healthy, happy retirement means conquering some of the conventional views in our culture about what it means to age, says Sampson. "Although some progress is being made, the older person is still often portrayed as either a creaky, white-haired, hearing impaired, semi-invalid eating a bowl of fiber-packed cereal or the recipient of frequent chin tucks, face lifts, and any number of procedures to keep looking young at all costs," she says.

You can do a lot to make the most of your later years without buying into either image. Take care of yourself physically with a healthy diet and regular exercise. As far as attitude goes, learn to accept wrinkles, baldness, and graying hair as merit badges in living, rather than as stigmas, says Sampson.

Harvesting a New Life

Through the story of Abraham and Sarah we know that in life's second half we can start anew. When Abraham was 99 years old, God appeared to him and said that his wife, Sarah, would give birth to a son. "Abraham fell face down; he laughed and said to himself, 'Will a son be born to a man a hundred years old? Will Sarah bear a child at the age of ninety?' " But it happened. Sarah became pregnant and bore a son they named Isaac. Sarah said, "God has brought me laughter, and everyone who hears about this will laugh with me" (Genesis 17:17; 21:2, 6, NIV).

The name Isaac is derived from the Hebrew word *yitzchak*, meaning "he will laugh," explains Dr. Leder. "He's the symbol of the laughter, joy, and generativity possible in later life," he says. "We can give birth, if not to a baby, then to a renewed self."

It may be difficult to envision a renewed self if you increasingly confront the physical limits that may come in the second half of life. Here again, Sarah's story can give you inspiration. She joyfully exceeded her limits, not by her own power, but by the power of God.

Here are some suggestions to help you discover inspiration and guidance.

1. Be a Beginner Again

To realize the spiritual and emotional rewards of retirement, you have to be willing to start over again—to try things that may seem unfamiliar. The first step in doing this is to look deep within your own head and heart, says Sampson. Think back. When you were a child, what did you want to be when you grew up? Many people retiring now are products of the Depression. The aspirations they held as young people were buried by circumstance, she says.

Her uncle is one example. As a young man he dreamed of becoming a doctor. During World War II he was drafted, and his dream was cast aside—but not entirely forgotten. Fifty years later, he began volunteering in a hospital emergency room. "No, he's not a doctor. But he's found a great deal of satisfaction in working with doctors to help people," she says.

2. Take a Retreat

Devote a week or even just a few days exclusively to prayer and meditation, suggests Dr. Leder. Ask yourself, "What is my new direction? What is my heart calling me to do?" During periods of quiet contemplation, it is easier to listen for God's guidance. Listen for what makes you most enthusiastic. Pay attention to outward signs—perhaps a series of conversations or coincidences that seem to point in a new direction, says Dr. Leder.

> *I think the purpose of life is . . . after all, to matter: to count, to stand for something, to have made some difference that you lived at all.*
>
> —*Leo C. Rosten*

3. Write Your Memoirs

Join an autobiography-writing group at a retirement center, church or synagogue, or local college campus. Thousands have popped up across the country. More than reminiscence, gerontologists call recording your experiences *life review*, *guided autobiography*, and *spiritual autobiography*. It's a way to search for meaning in your life, to find your voice, to leave a record. It's also a way to pay attention to yourself.

"We're living in a world where people say, 'Oh get over it. Don't think about the past. Just move on.' What life review is saying is, 'No, think about the past. Work it through," says Harry R. Moody, Ph.D., author of *The Five Stages of the Soul*.

By examining the past, you can make the most of the years to come.

4. Redefine Your Relationships

Most marriages don't simply change after retirement—they enter a whole new era. Suddenly it's total togetherness 24 hours a day. Even the strongest marriage is bound to experience some stresses. Start early to minimize conflict, says Sampson. Think about the strains on your relationship that retirement will bring. For example, a seemingly simple issue such as what time to prepare lunch can affect the texture and quality of everyday life. Learn to negotiate—not nag—to resolve large and small issues.

Being a Good Grandparent

Beyond the love and affection you can offer, grandchildren need
you to be a friend, supporter, and spiritual guide. Here's how
to prayerfully live up to that responsibility.

In Native American cultures, grandparents hold positions of exceptional esteem. Native Americans refer to the planet as Grandmother or Grandfather earth. They expect the grandparents, rather than the parents, to provide the wisdom, patience, understanding, spiritual guidance, and unconditional love that children crave.

These roles as teacher and nurturer are ones for which all grandparents are well suited, says Arthur Kornhaber, M.D., founder and president of the Foundation for Grandparenting in Ojai, California. Often removed from the daily pressures of raising young children, and also more secure both emotionally and financially, grandparents have the time, energy, and ability to give children the extra attention and affection they want, he says. Plus, some would say, grandparents and grandchildren have an intuitive spiritual connection with each other.

"Grandparents offer spirituality with the unconditional love they give. There's no purer form of love," says Dr. Kornhaber.

Perhaps you already may have a wonderful relationship with your grandchildren. Or perhaps you're not as close as you'd like to be. Either way, there are steps you can take to strengthen the relationship and help them develop into the moral, spiritual young adults you pray they'll become.

- Strengthen your ties to their parents, if necessary.
- Form a direct bond with your grandchildren.
- Set a religious and spiritual example for them.

Building Ties of Love

In any relationship between you and your grandchildren, their parents are the "linchpin," says Dr. Kornhaber. Without a good relationship with your child and son- or daughter-in-law, it will be difficult to have a healthy, spiritual relationship with your grandchildren. For many families this is not an issue, but if you have a less-than-perfect relationship because of difficulties with your children, here's how you can use prayer and understanding to improve it.

Children require guidance and sympathy far more than instruction.

—*Anne Sullivan*

1. Learn to Listen

With all your parental experience, you may want to offer suggestions and tell the children how to raise your grandchildren. But more than anything, parents need someone to listen—without offering opinions. "You should be a kind, compassionate, nonjudgmental support system for the parents," Dr. Kornhaber says. To truly help, be a sounding board when your son or daughter calls to complain that Junior is acting up at school or the youngest one refuses to be potty trained. You can offer advice, *if asked*, but otherwise just listen. For ideas on how to be a great and supportive listener, turn to the chapter on Helping Friends in Need, page 281.

2. Fight the Urge to Disagree

There could come a time when you don't agree with how your grandchildren are being raised. It might involve the parents' disciplinary style or religious preferences—or lack thereof. While it may be difficult, try not to criticize. In many cases, it will only drive a wedge between you.

"Grandparents need to respect their place in the life of the grandchildren, even if they disagree with the parents. No one knows the perfect way to raise a child," says Robert S. Henderson, doctor of ministry, director of the Pastoral Counseling Center in Glastonbury, Connecticut.

Help Me Fill This Role, God

Lord, teach me to love my grandchildren as a grandmother should:

not interfering, only understanding;

not pushing myself, just being there when wanted.

Teach me to be the sort of grandmother

my children and my children's children

would want me to be.

—Rosa George

How do you know whether you should voice a concern? "The proof is in the pudding. If the child is fine and happy, then it's not your place to butt in," Dr. Kornhaber says.

3. Share the Power of Prayer

When her daughter became a new mom, LaVerne K. Jordan, Ph.D., a professor of psychology at Olivet Nazarene University in Bourbonnais, Illinois, happily prayed for her, asking God to help her daughter make the right decisions. But she made it clear to her daughter that a grandmother's prayers were not enough. "You need to pray for God's direction in this situation," she told her daughter. "God will talk directly to you. You don't have to wait for God to talk to me about this."

Develop an Unconditional Bond

Like any good relationship, the grandparent-child bond does need a little attention to thrive. The best ways: Spend time with your grandchildren and show interest in their lives.

1. Play One-on-One

It may seem obvious, but it bears repeating: If you spend time alone with your grandchildren—just you and them, not other family members—they'll take

---

❧

A Prayer for the Parents

Heavenly Father, from whom all fatherhood in heaven and earth is named, bless, we beg you, all children, and give to their parents and to all in whose charge they may be, your Spirit of wisdom and love; so that the home in which they grow up may be to them an image of your kingdom, and the care of their parents a likeness of your love; through Jesus Christ our Lord.

—Leslie Hunter

---

you into their hearts and souls. "The connection between you and your grandchild grows when the child has your undivided attention," Dr. Kornhaber says. How to do it? "Go to their school. Go to their doctor. Become computer literate. Attend their recitals and baseball games. Get involved in their world," he suggests.

2. Overcome the Miles between You

In today's world, where families may be spread across the entire country, it not always easy to find time together. If you're caught in a situation like this, there are several ways you can develop a closer relationship.

Schedule a special visit. Use your vacation time to visit your grandchildren or have them come out to see you. During these visits, get as much one-on-one time as possible, suggests Dr. Kornhaber. His foundation sponsors "grandparent-grandchild summer camps" for those who live far away from each other. "The people who attend have a wonderful time," he says.

Contact them daily. Stay in touch by phone, letters, faxes, videotapes, or e-mail.

Surprise them with random gifts. Send something as simple as a card that says, "I love you," or an inexpensive little toy will make your grandchildren squeal with delight. Don't wait for a birthday or holiday to send a treat.

Set a Prayerful Example

Because of the bond between grandparent and grandchild, some children learn more of their spiritual and moral perspective from their grandparents than from any other role models. In fact, this is a role many grandparents are eager to play. In an American Association of Retired Persons poll of over 800 people, grandparents listed passing on morals and religion to their grandchildren as among their top priorities.

"Grandparents teach more by experience than by preaching. With this nonpressure, unconditional love example the grandchildren absorb it better," Dr. Kornhaber says. Here's how you can pass on your spiritual treasures to your grandchildren.

There is no exercise better for the heart than reaching down and lifting people up.

—*John Andrew Holmes*

1. Let Them Watch You

When your grandchildren spend time with you, be open about how you include God in your life. "We hold up God as the guidance in our own daily lives so they see God through us," says Charles A. Turnbo, president of Positive Solutions in Evergreen, Colorado. Just by the way you live your life, you give them a moral and spiritual compass to live by. As the Bible says, "Set the believers an example in speech and conduct, in love, in faith, in purity" (1 Timothy 4:12, RSV).

2. Read to Them

Whether it be the Bible or religious bedtime stories, the Turnbos read and discuss spirituality with their grandchildren. "We read daily devotions every day, and if they are around we include them in that. They see us read the Bible and talk about the important issues. They've gotten into it even though they are only little tykes," Turnbo says. And if you live far away? You can call to read or pray with them, suggests Turnbo.

Caring
for an Aging Parent

Helping your parents as they grow older and frail can be incredibly stressful. But if you approach the task with a prayerful, loving attitude, it also can be incredibly rewarding.

One day a patient at a medical clinic paid a visit to the pastoral counselor on staff. She wasn't there because of her own medical problems, she said. She had another concern, that, while straightforward, was not exactly simple:

"I want to know what it means," she told him, "to honor my father and my mother."

Honoring your mother and father as they grow older may be one of the greatest challenges you'll ever face. You may be called upon to help make decisions for them when they can no longer keep up their own home, shop for themselves, or drive. You may have to take over their care if they develop a degenerative condition such as Alzheimer's disease. You may have to do all this from a very long distance, without the help of brothers and sisters.

Prayer can help you sort through difficult questions, especially, experts say, if you lay a firm foundation of faith by following two general goals.

- Understand and respect your parents' emotional needs.
- Prayerfully handle the challenges that arise with flexibility, teamwork, humor, and grace.

Walk Hand in Hand

Not everything that is faced can be changed. But nothing can be changed until it is faced.

—James Baldwin

One of the most powerful stories in the New Testament tells of the night Jesus was arrested in the Garden of Gethsemane. Before the soldiers came, Jesus asked three of his disciples—three times—to "stay awake" with him. They couldn't do it.

It's tempting to dismiss the disciples as hopeless reprobates, but in fact this story demonstrates a painful truth about human nature, says Drew Leder, M.D., Ph.D., author of *Spiritual Passages: Embracing Life's Sacred Journey*. It can be tremendously hard to "stay awake" with your loved ones as they suffer. You constantly have to fight shutting down emotionally and mentally because the psychological cost of staying involved is so high, especially when there's nothing you can do to "fix" their problems.

America's obsession with youth represents another form of abandonment of the elderly, says David Maitland, Ph.D., chaplain emeritus at Carleton College in Northfield, Minnesota. It's not an accident that with rare exceptions you see only the young and beautiful on television, in movies, and in advertising. Sometimes it seems as a society we do everything we can to pretend that old folks don't exist.

Staying awake and aware are the first challenges in honoring your father and mother as they age. The following seven steps can help:

1. Seek God's Help

For most of your life, your parents took care of you. Now it's necessary for you to start taking care of them. That's a huge psychological and spiritual shift that needs to be shared with God, says Dr. Maitland.

Spend some time praying and meditating on who your parents are today, Dr. Maitland suggests, and on who they no longer are. For example, your parents may not have the energy to counsel you through every crisis the way they once did. Nor will they necessarily remember all the children's birthdays the way they used to. Appreciating clearly your parents' physical, emotional, and

---

❧

A Prayer for Our Parents

Father, hear our prayer for our parents and elderly relatives. You have promised to care for your children till the time that their hair is gray. Look down with love and pity on these members of our family and care for them in their frailty and need.

Give us the wisdom to know how to do what is best for them. Guide our decision making. Give us patience and understanding, especially with those who are difficult or obstinate. Supply us with the strength to follow out the course we feel we should follow and give us your love for them.

—Anonymous

---

mental capabilities *today* will help you address the changes in your relationship without being immersed in a fog of denial and false assumptions.

2. Help Open Doors

We tend to see aging as a gradual closing down of the opportunities and experiences a person can have, but in reality the opposite may be true, says Dr. Leder. Many people feel emotionally liberated by old age, even as their physical strengths diminish. That's because they're no longer so worried about what other people think, no longer weighed down with obligations and ambitions.

As a result, old age can be a joyful time of self-discovery and personal growth. If you're aware of that potential you can help your parents celebrate their new freedom, encourage it, learn from it, share it, and be inspired by it.

3. Record Their Story

"Aging is at least as much biographical as it is biological," says Dr. Maitland. By that he means that our lives form a narrative, and many people seem to have a strong natural instinct as the end of life nears to make sense of the journey they've taken.

Writing a journal or autobiography can help that process, Dr. Maitland believes. If your parents haven't thought of this themselves, suggest it, and ask to read anything they produce. Also tell them that you would like to have a record of their lives to pass on to your own children.

4. Recognize the Seasons

Our obsession with youth denies that aging is a natural part of life, Dr. Maitland says. Such an obsession also denies that aging is a natural part of God's plan. For that reason, accepting and embracing the natural beauty of aging can be a deeply spiritual exercise.

The four seasons offer a perfect model for reflecting on life's natural cycles, Dr. Maitland suggests. Take walks in the park with your parents, and ponder the leaves in fall as well as the buds in the spring. As you stroll, talk to one another about the order of life, death, and rebirth that God has given.

5. Back Off

It's easy to think that your parents want nothing more than to be with their loving children at every possible moment. You may also assume that they want to be regularly involved with their peers in various social activities, whether they be dances at the nursing home or bridge games at the club.

Maintaining community and family ties is vitally important, Dr. Leder agrees, and you should do whatever you can to help your parents keep such ties intact. At the same time, he adds, you should be aware that many aging people feel a longing for solitude.

"In Hinduism, there is a recognition that at certain stages of life, it is appropriate for people to take a kind of extended retreat," he says. "The idea is to disconnect to some degree from their community, from their responsibilities, and from their social identity. They embark on an inward journey of prayer and meditation—to seek to realize God within."

Because such a retreat is not taken for granted in American culture, it may not be as easy for your parents to articulate their need for solitude. In fact, if they withdraw, your parents' caregivers may easily mistake the move for depression. If testing shows that your parents aren't depressed, your job is to be aware of their needs and support them, whether they feel either a need to be connected to a community or a call to solitude. "Both of these desires should be honored and supported," Dr. Leder says.

6. Be Thankful

There's a tendency to dread the responsibility of taking care of your parents—understandably so, given the challenges such a responsibility often entails. But those challenges can also be seen as one of life's most fulfilling tasks—a gift to be grateful for, rather than a burden.

❧

MAY I SEE YOU TODAY

Dear Lord, may I see you today and every day in the person of your sick and, while nursing them, minister unto you. Though you hide yourself behind the unattractive disguise of the irritable, the exacting, the unreasonable, may I still recognize you and say: "Jesus, my patient, how sweet it is to serve you."

—*Mother Teresa*

"Because our culture emphasizes autonomy and individualism, we tend to feel ashamed when we need help," says Dr. Leder. "Often as not, though, when one member of the family is in physical or financial need, it brings out the best in people, which in turn brings families closer together. Just as parents enjoy taking care of their children when they're young, many children see taking care of their parents as an opportunity to express their love."

If you consider caring for your parents an opportunity rather than a burden, then by all means make a point of letting your parents know that, Dr. Leder says. Such reassurances will go a long way toward alleviating any embarrassment they feel for being less independent than they used to be.

7. Learn the Lessons

Some things don't change as your parents age. Since childhood, your parents have been your role models, for better or for worse, demonstrating what living is all about. The same is true now, Dr. Leder says. Your parents are traveling a road you'll be on yourself some day, and you may never have a better opportunity to observe what you're in for than by watching them.

It will pay to pay attention.

Working Together

Week in and week out, the old man had always been in church, a part of a small congregation in the small town of Riverside, Iowa. Then, suddenly one

Sunday, he wasn't there, and word spread that his children had flown in from some city on one of the coasts and put him in a nursing home.

The old man's friends in church were outraged, says William Clements, Ph.D., professor of pastoral care and counseling at the Claremont School of Theology in California. Dr. Clements was one of those friends. How could the old man be so abruptly locked away from everything he'd known and loved? Then the man showed up the following Sunday, smiling and looking better than ever—pleased with his new life of assisted care.

"Let me tell you what I don't have to worry about anymore," he said. "I don't have to worry about grocery shopping. I don't have to worry about washing my clothes. I don't have to worry about slipping on the ice when I get the newspaper in the morning."

The list went on like that for some time, and his church friends were stunned as they listened. No one had ever realized how hard it had been for the old man to appear in church each Sunday, or how his life outside of church had grown more and more restricted by his growing frailty. In fact, coming to church was about the only time he still managed to get out at all.

The tendency to put up a good front is another reflection of how much we Americans worship independence and self-reliance. God help us if we ever have to ask anyone for help—even our children. "A lot of parents express the sentiment that they don't want to become a burden on their children," says Dr. Leder. "They would rather die before they become incapacitated."

Other parents, of course, aren't embarrassed in the least to demand help from their children—constantly! In either case, if you intend to keep watch with your mother and father in their old age, it's important to get a clear vision of what exactly their needs are.

How can you do this? The following five steps can help you assume your caregiving responsibilities gracefully as well as effectively.

1. Ask

The simplest way to avoid making wrong assumptions about what your parents need and don't need is to ask, says Dr. Leder. "How can I help?" is a direct question that goes to the heart of the issue, he says, and opens the way for effective action, including prayer.

Taking a direct approach can also be constructive when it comes to dealing with things both you and they may be afraid of, including the physical decline of old age and the prospect that for your parents death may be near. "The best you can offer is your truth," Dr. Leder says. "Often in these situations, a conspiracy of silence takes over, which makes everybody feel that much more distant from one another. You can penetrate that by speaking the unspeakable.

LET US REMEMBER

As we make our way through our busy and often lonely days, may our thoughts lead us back to time of smiles and laughter. May our tears and pain be eased by the comfort of our memory. And may God offer us strength and comfort now and always.

Amen.

—*Rabbi Naomi Levy*

Ask, 'What are you going through?' or say, 'Yes, I'm afraid, too.' Nothing will get worked out unless people are willing to share what's really happening."

2. Pray Together for Guidance

As people age, they dearly want to hold on to their independence, and their children are often urged not to violate that wish by imposing decisions on them. This is fine, up to a point, says Dr. Leder, but it also overlooks the fact that families sometimes need to make decisions collectively. Should Mom move in with you and your family? Should Dad be playing the stock market when he can no longer balance his checkbook?

"The children will be affected by these choices, too," Dr. Leder points out. The question to ask, therefore, is "What can *we* do to solve this problem?" Emphasize that you are a family working together.

Prayer can be the perfect medium for collectively weighing important decisions, Dr. Leder believes. He suggests that everyone gather in one place, perhaps the living room, to pray and meditate on the issue at hand. "Invite the Holy Spirit into the discussion," he says.

3. Lighten Up

Face it: Getting old involves certain indignities. Memory problems. Moving problems. Bladder problems. Bowel problems. Sometimes it's not pretty.

One way to make these indignities easier to handle is to laugh at them. Humor can inject the light of the Spirit into the darkest situations, Dr. Leder says, and in that sense can be considered a form of prayer.

One man Dr. Leder knew had a debilitating neurological disease that caused him to constantly lose his balance and fall. He decided to turn falling into an art form, striving to lose his balance as stylishly as possible. He also usually wore a T-shirt that read, "It's better to be over the hill than under it."

In this way, the man was able to turn the indignities of his condition on their head. Bringing humor to situations in which your parents are struggling can give them the same power.

4. Be Respectful

You won't always be able to laugh at the indignities of old age, of course. At some point your parents may lose their ability to act and think on their own, and you'll have to make decisions for them. These can be some of life's most stressful moments, and for that reason it's easy as they unfold to slip into authoritarianism and anger, Dr. Maitland says.

Dreams are renewable. No matter what our age or condition, there are still untapped possibilities within us and new beauty waiting to be born.

—*Dr. Dale Turner*

Try to circumvent that pitfall by praying for calm and patience, keeping God's love for creation uppermost in your mind. "Nobody learns anything by being shouted at or coerced," he says. "The respect for this person has to be there."

5. Share the Load

Too often when a parent needs care, one of the children ends up taking on all the responsibility, Dr. Clements points out. That can be unfair—not only to the sibling who's doing the work but also to other siblings who may want to participate but aren't given a chance to.

Here again, collective prayer can help. Getting everybody together in one place—even if that place is a telephone conference call—to pray for God's guidance can defuse potential conflict with the light of the Holy Spirit.

Dealing
with Chronic Illness

*Upbeat and happy one moment, downcast and sad the next.
Life with a chronic illness can spin you physically and emotionally—if you let it. Here's how you tap into your faith to feel
better.*

hen Steven M. Tovian, Ph.D., assistant professor of psychiatry and behavioral sciences, wants to stump the medical students at Northwestern University in Chicago he asks them to name an illness that doesn't have psychological consequences. They throw out possible answers:

"The common cold."

Nope. People get frustrated with their lack of energy.

"A broken arm."

No again. Broken bones can leave people feeling frazzled, lost, and fearful they'll get hurt again.

It goes on. And each time Dr. Tovian comes up with psychological ramifications.

Given the problems that can arise even with small, short-term conditions like these, it's no wonder that when you have a chronic illness it takes such an emotional and spiritual toll.

Unlike a cold or a broken bone, a chronic illness never goes away. Whether it takes the form of a heart condition, recurrent back pain, asthma, arthritis, or a dozen other long-term maladies, a chronic illness can send you on an emotional roller coaster. One day you're positive and upbeat, convinced that you're cured or soon will be. The next you're angry at doctors and treatments that don't work and depressed with thoughts that nothing ever will, says S. Bryant Kendrick Jr., doctor of ministry, associate professor of medicine at Wake Forest University in Winston-Salem, North Carolina.

When dealing with a chronic illness you are likely to confront a number of emotional obstacles.

- You may feel vulnerable, fearful, guilty, or angry about your illness.
- The treatment you receive—possibly including invasive hospital procedures and experimental medications—can be confusing and overwhelming.
- As your illness continues you may even question the very meaning of your life.

How can you overcome these hurdles? With a combination of faith, prayer, and practical advice.

"What did I do to deserve this?" is an understandable outcry from a sick and suffering person, but it is really the wrong question. . . . The better question is "what do I do now, and who is there to help me do it?"

—*Rabbi Harold S. Kushner*

Putting Emotions in Their Place

In her book, *On Death and Dying*, author Elisabeth Kubler-Ross defines five stages that people go through as they come to grip with death: denial and isolation, anger, bargaining, depression, and, finally, acceptance. A chronic illness can raise some of the same emotions, says Debra S. Borys, Ph.D., a psychologist and assistant clinical professor of psychology at UCLA.

You're likely to feel mad that you're the one saddled with a sickness that won't go away. You may wonder if God is punishing you for something you've done. You may even grieve for the more active life you've lost.

These are natural reactions. But they're not healthy ones over the long haul. If you want to find peace and satisfaction in your life, it's important to prayerfully work through these and your other feelings.

I Am Healed!

God, it is Your spirit of life within me that heals me. I am refreshed by an energy that surges throughout my body in a healing flow of Divine life and love. I am alive with Divine life that awakens me to both the wholeness of my physical body and the holiness of my spiritual identity. I feel Your joy and peace filling me with strength as I gratefully affirm, "I am healed!"

—from Daily Word for Healing

1. Face Your Anger

In the midst of unrelenting pain you may feel like angrily complaining to God or anyone else who's around you for letting you suffer. Don't feel ashamed if you do. Instead, let out the anger.

- Pray without words. Many people dealing with the emotions of chronic illness are able to find peace by practicing "contemplative prayer," says the Reverend Clayton L. Thomason, J.D., assistant professor of spirituality and ethics at Michigan State University in East Lansing. Choose a symbolic word like "Jesus," "Father," "Peace," "Creator," "Mother God," "Wisdom," or "Calm." Close your eyes and meditate on that word silently. When you become aware of thoughts intruding on your prayer, just reintroduce the word to yourself. Try to breathe deeply as you contemplate your word. You'll find that your angry thoughts may drift away, and they may even be replaced by new insights.
- Talk with someone you trust. A spiritual counselor, a close friend, a psychologist, or even members of a support group can all lend a caring ear and help you sort through your feelings.
- Start a journal. Write how you feel. Make up poems or short stories or simply write whatever comes out. There are no rules to journal writing. Do what best helps unburden you.
- Draw a picture. Many people find release and eventually understanding

by drawing, doing watercolors, even sketching cartoons. Often you'll pick up on subtle imagery that can offer a clue to your inner world. One woman Dr. Borys counseled had done abstract paintings before her illness. After her illness she switched to cartoon drawings where she could more easily vent her anger.

2. Probe Your Guilt

Chronic sickness also can leave you questioning whether your illness is a punishment from God for something you've done, says Dr. Borys. After all, you may think, bad things shouldn't happen to good people.

Feeling that you are being punished is not a healthy response, nor is it an

---

BLESSINGS FROM GOD

Bless the Lord, O my soul: and all that is within me, bless his holy name.

Bless the Lord, O my soul, and forget not all his benefits:

Who forgivith all thine iniquities; who healeth all thy diseases;

Who redeemeth thy life from destruction; who crowneth thee with lovingkindness and tender mercies;

Who satisfieth thy mouth with good things; so that thy youth is renewed like the eagle's. . . .

Bless the Lord, ye his angels, that excel in strength, that do his commandments, harkening unto the voice of his word.

Bless ye the Lord, all ye his hosts; ye ministers of his, that do his pleasure.

Bless the Lord, all his works in all places of his dominion: bless the Lord, O my soul.

—Psalm 103:1–5, 20–22 (KJV)

Prayer Miracles

Hands-On Prayer
Cured My Arthritis

In 1975, I was diagnosed with pre-rheuma-toid arthritis. For a year I suffered greatly with swollen joints. My fingers were so bad that the only way I could lift a plate was to slide my hands under it. I began attending a women's prayer group and asked for prayer. They had me sit in a chair, gathered around me, put their hands gently on my back and arms, and began to pray according to Mark 11:24: "[W]hat things soever ye desire, when ye pray, believe that ye receive them and ye shall have them." They also prayed 1 Peter 2:24: "[B]y whose stripes ye were healed." They then asked Jesus to set me free from this infirmity. I felt such peace and joy and went home to tell my husband that Jesus had healed me of my arthritis. Every day, I thanked and praised God for healing me. Although I still had pain, in my heart I felt it was done.

Six weeks later I had a blood test and X rays taken. The doctor told me he could find no trace of arthritis. I have been totally free of any prob-lems since that time. I do take good care of my body—eating well, exercising, walking, and praying. But all of this came after my heal-ing that was caused by prayer and the power of God.

Jo Sweatt
DeSoto, Kansas

accurate one. However, it could be a sign that you are repressing guilt for some-thing else in your life. If you feel guilt, try to pin-point what's creating it. Do you feel you should have done a better job raising your children? Do you feel that you were less than kind to a friend? Do you need to forgive anyone? Do you need anyone to forgive you?

Work out the answers on your own or with the help of a trusted friend or counselor. The important thing is to find the source of your guilt and then make amends, suggests Reverend Thomason. Ask for forgive-ness if you need to. Then move on.

3. Express Your Grief

It's okay to grieve for your lost health, says Rev-erend Thomason. It's fine to mourn the damage your illness has caused. Eventu-ally you want to come to an emotional and spiritual place where you can focus on all of the things you still can do. But right now, you may not be ready to do so, and that's perfectly normal. For now, meditate on one of Mother Teresa's say-ings: "Yesterday is gone. Tomorrow has not yet come. We have only today. Let us begin."

Coping with Medical Treatment

When Reverend Thomason used to make rounds as a hospital chaplain, he made sure to tell the patients he visited: "I'm the one person you can tell to go away if you want."

The phrase usually made the patients laugh. But Reverend Thomason was serious. If your illness takes you to the hospital, you'll experience an incredible invasion of privacy. Doctors, nurses, friends, and family all may drop by unannounced. Suddenly, you no longer control your social calendar. And few people ever think to ask whether you'd like to have company—or not.

This is just one aspect of medical care that takes getting used to. You also may face scary medical tests, abrasive staff member, and invasive procedures.

The following tips can help you cope.

1. Identify Your Fear

If you are feeling nervous about an upcoming test or medical procedure, probe that fear, says Reverend Thomason. Are you scared of the actual procedure or of the results it will uncover? If you're afraid of the results, sit down with your nurse, physician, or hospital chaplain and talk about your emotions.

If you're afraid of the procedure, talk with the technician or surgeon who will do it and find out the answers to your questions. Make sure to ask:

- Will it hurt?
- What are the risks?
- Why do I have to have this done to me?
- What exactly does this test/procedure entail?

MAKE US WHOLE

O God, who gives the day for work and the night for sleep, refresh our bodies and our minds through the quiet hours of night, and let our inward eyes be directed towards you, dreaming of your eternal glory.

—The Leonine Sacramentary

Aren't sure whom to speak to? Start by asking a nurse to recommend someone who can help you find information about your case, suggests Dr. Kendrick.

2. Surf the Net

If you find the medical staff unhelpful—or if you are too shy to ask the questions you need answered—go to the library or the Internet (many libraries now have access) and research everything you can about your illness, medications, and medical procedures.

One woman Dr. Borys counseled did so much research that she was able to diagnose her own ailment. Her doctor—who had been baffled by the illness—agreed with her finding.

An important caution: Make sure to talk with your physician about what you discover. Some Web sites offer information that may not be credible.

3. Coach Yourself

If you get sick of people who come into your hospital room to poke and prod your body, mentally remind yourself: "These people are here to help me." And remember, says Dr. Borys, it is okay to tell someone to go away if you don't feel you can deal with them at that moment.

What Would Jesus Do?

Do you fear that you'll never be able to move beyond your illness? While Jesus was never ill (or at least the Bible never mentions that he was), he suffered plenty, especially on his last day of human life. With nails through his feet and palms, Jesus hung dying on a cross sandwiched between two thieves. Jesus endured onlookers who cast bets on who could take his clothes after he died. Some heckled him.

"Then said Jesus, 'Father forgive them for they know not what they do.' And one of the malefactors which were hanged railed on him saying, 'If thou be Christ, save thyself and us.'

"But the other answering rebuked him, saying 'Dost not thou fear God, seeing thou art in the same condemnation?

"'And we indeed justly; for we received the due reward of our deeds: but this man hath done nothing amiss.'

"And he said unto Jesus, 'Lord, remember me when thou comest into thy kingdom.'

"And Jesus said unto him, 'Verily I say unto thee, Today shalt thou be with me in paradise.' "

(Luke 23:39–43, KJV).

A Prayer for a Loved One Who Is Ill

Bless thy servant (insert name) with health of body and of spirit. Let the hand of thy blessing be upon his head, night and day, and support him in all necessities, strengthen him in all temptations, comfort him in all his sorrows, and let him be thy servant in all changes; and make us both to dwell with thee for ever in thy favour, in the light of thy countenance, and in thy glory.

—*From the* HarperCollins Book of Prayers

Find Meaning in Your Illness

We all should be focusing on the meaning in our lives long before illness strikes, but few of us ever do. When everything is well, we go about our jobs, family life, spare time, and church life without a care. Rarely do we stop to wonder whether all the things that keep our days full really keep our souls fulfilled.

That is, until something forces us to reflect. It's not uncommon for people who develop chronic illnesses to do an about-face on their career tracks, to abruptly change their hobbies, and to decide to nurture some friendships while letting others languish.

Far from a negative, this time of change can be a rich opportunity for you to set new goals that give your life more meaning.

1. Make a Value List

Write up a list of the things that are important to you—the things that give your life purpose, suggests Reverend Thomason. If you have a hard time coming up with ideas, imagine you're at the end of your life. What do you want people to say about you when you are gone? Whom do you want to remember you? What do you want those people to remember?

2. Ask Questions

Once you've developed a list of goals, ask yourself: How does this illness interfere with those goals? Is there any way to modify your goals so you can still accomplish them with the illness? For instance, if one of your goals is to help others, and you can no longer accomplish that goal by building homes as part of Habitat for Humanity because of persistent back pain, consider a new approach. How about reading to children at the local library?

God is the very life that animates me, filling every cell of my body with the energy and ability to function. God is the master creator of life, and it is God who makes me whole and well.

—*Richard N. Bolles*

3. Learn from Your Illness

You can choose to see your illness as an adversary or as a teacher. If you make it an adversary, you'll be fighting it all the time. If you choose to see it as a teacher, then you can explore how your illness might enhance your understanding of what it means to be human, suggests Dr. Kendrick. Maybe it can help you empathize with others or become more accepting of people's differences. Figure out how this illness helps you become a better person.

Getting On with Your Life

A chronic illness may force you to make some changes in your lifestyle, but it doesn't mean you have to give up life altogether. In fact, staying active and involved with others actually can improve the way you feel.

Some people who are chronically ill find relief by taking part in charities that raise money for their illness and by lobbying for research dollars and legislation, says Dr. Borys. Such activities can help take the focus off your own pain and suffering and give you a sense of purpose in helping others.

Another option for improving the way you feel is to focus on the small things you still can do rather than on the things your illness prevents you from doing. One woman who was bed-bound became the communication link in her faith community, says Dr. Kendrick. She called congregational members to congratulate them on marriages and babies. She called others to soothe them during times of grief. Another woman confined to a wheelchair ran errands at her local hospital, getting things for patients who couldn't get around. "There's always a place of service where you can be needed," says Dr. Kendrick.

Physical Restrictions

You may feel discouraged or spiritually abandoned if pain and physical problems begin to limit your life. But there is much you can learn from your situation if you approach it prayerfully as the next step in your relationship with God.

fter the Last Supper, Jesus went with his disciples to a place called Gethsemane. Deeply troubled, he asked Peter and the two sons of Zebedee to stay awake with him, and then went off and prayed, "My Father, if it is possible, may this cup be taken from me. Yet not as I will, but you will."

With that simple prayer, Jesus showed the way. Returning, he found the three disciples asleep and said to Peter, "What, could none of you stay awake with me one hour? Stay awake and pray that you may be spared the test. The spirit is willing, but the flesh is weak."

Later Jesus suffered at the hands of Pilate's soldiers, who placed a crown of thorns on his head, spat on him and beat him before leading him away to be crucified (Matthew 26, 27, NIV).

Just as Jesus faced extraordinary trials in his final days, so may you, if you experience a crippling physical problem as you grow older. And your reaction may be similar, suggests Drew Leder, M.D., Ph.D., a professor of philosophy at Loyola College in Baltimore and author of *Spiritual Passages: Embracing Life's Sacred Journey.*

You may pray for relief that may not be granted. You may feel the pain of anticipated losses, such as the loss of your health, your independence, and even life itself. Like Jesus you may wonder why the spirit is still willing yet the flesh so weak.

I'm tired, Lord, but I'll lift one foot if you'll lift the other for me.

—*Saidie Patterson*

Yes, this time can be trying, but it also can be a gift that helps you know yourself better and grow spiritually. To make profitable use of your experience, you need to take three steps.

- Accept the physical limitations that you cannot control.
- Have the courage to face and change what you can.
- Draw spiritual wisdom from your journey.

Accept Your Aging Body

The first line of the well-known serenity prayer reads, "God, grant me the peace to accept the things I cannot change." That is the best attitude to take toward physical infirmities, although admittedly it may be a hard philosophy to adopt.

Faced with the physical limitations that come with aging, you're likely to feel frustrated, sad, and angry. "There is an old self that has died off—that person who could move around with ease," says Dr. Leder. Yet beyond there waits a new person you can become. By accepting the condition of your body, you can discover that, yes, life may be different, but it can also be just as delightful.

As you pray for peace and serenity, remember the comforting words of Jesus: "Peace I leave with you; my peace I give you. Do not let your hearts be troubled and do not be afraid" (John 14:27, NIV).

1. Stay Awake

To come to grips with the pain of your restrictions, you must first allow yourself to experience it, spiritually and emotionally—just as Jesus did. "In Gethsemane, though others around him were sleeping, Jesus stayed awake and faced his suffering," explains Dr. Leder. "He went through it all—anxiety, sadness, and the grief of loss."

To "stay awake" with your pain, start by acknowledging your feelings about loss, illness, and aging. Often people escape or "sleep" through what hurts by practicing denial. "Everything's fine," they may say. "I've never felt better."

STAY HERE WITH ME, LORD

God, I need to know that You are with me; that You hear my cry. I long to feel Your presence not just this day but every day. When I am weak and in pain, I need to know You are beside me. That in itself is often comfort enough. . . . The lot you have bestowed upon me is a heavy one. I am angry. . . . There are times when I want to have nothing to do with You. When to think of You brings nothing but confusion and ambivalence. And there are times, like this time, when I seek to return to You, when I feel the emptiness that comes when I am far from You. . . . Help me to appreciate all that I have, and to realize all that I have to offer. Help me to find my way back to you, so that I may never be alone. Amen.

—*Rabbi Naomi Levy*

While there certainly isn't anything wrong with a positive attitude, you shouldn't mask your fears with it.

"There is often a fantasy that facing unpleasant feelings will overwhelm us if we let them come to the surface. We might drown in fear, sadness, or anger. The truth is more the opposite: By allowing ourselves to feel, we begin to heal," says Dr. Leder.

2. Explore the Reason for Your Pain

Why some should suffer while others don't is a question as old as faith itself, says Kent Richmond, doctor of sacred theology, chaplain at the Lutheran General Hospital in Park Ridge, Illinois. "A lot of people feel that their faith should have protected them from a disabling condition—should have made them special, if you will. The discovery that that doesn't happen is often difficult."

Consciously and unconsciously you may find reasons to blame yourself for your situation. But the reality is that bad things happen. Instead of asking, "Why me?" the question should be, "Why not me?" says the Reverend Marilyle Sweet Page, doctor of ministry, a pastoral counselor and Episcopal priest in Rochester, New York. "Suffering isn't something that God visits upon us. When I have been in the most pain, whether it's emotional, physical, or interpersonal, my prayer life has been strengthened and has grown more intense and meaningful than when I've been on Easy Street."

So, don't fall into a lament. Instead, pray to God to help you discover some of the spiritual lessons in suffering—compassion, humility, and dependence on God.

3. Learn to Be a Receiver

Physical restrictions may force you to become more dependent on others, a thought that may make you shudder. Here, the story of Jesus' last days also offers some help in learning to be better receivers of God's love for us.

At the Last Supper, Jesus washes his disciples' feet. Peter, one of those who fell asleep in Gethsemane, is shown as reluctant to receive. "You shall never wash my feet," he says. But Jesus is adamant. "Unless I wash you, you have no part with me" (John 13:8–9, NIV). Peter gives in to the call.

"This passage is often interpreted as a lesson in giving, but we also see here a profound lesson in receiving," says Dr. Leder. "Receiving, no less than giving, is an act of love that brings you closer to God."

Every Minute

Through every minute of this day, be with me Lord!

Through every day of all this week, be with me Lord!

Through every week of all this year, be with me, Lord!

Through all the years of all this life, be with me, Lord!!

So shall the days and weeks and years be threaded on a golden cord.

And all draw on with sweet accord unto thy fullness, Lord, that so, when time is past,

by grace I may, at last,

Be with thee, Lord.

—*John Oxenham*

Change What You Can

The serenity prayer is equally the courage prayer, says Dr. Leder. As you accept and realize that changes in your body may be inescapable, you also need to take steps to reduce those aspects of your suffering that you are able to—from pain to immobility to discomfort. Here are three suggestions to reach this goal.

1. Make the Most of Medication

Medication offers a window of opportunity—periods during the day when you may feel better. Be aware and take advantage of these times to stay as active as possible, suggests Douglas Rosenau, Ed.D., a Christian psychologist in Atlanta. For example, if your arthritic joints seem to feel their best at midday, plan to go grocery shopping then or do some activity you enjoy rather than scheduling things for times when you body isn't working as well.

Also, if you aren't getting the relief you need from your medication, share your concerns with your doctor, suggests Dr. Rosenau. Ask whether changes in medication or diet might help improve your sense of well-being.

2. Exercise If You Are Able

Studies show that much of the physical frailty attributed to aging is actually the result of inactivity. The good news is many long-term problems, such as back pain, adult-onset diabetes, hypertension, osteoporosis, and arthritis, can improve if you increase your physical activity, says Dr. Leder.

Physical exercise also releases endorphins, hormones that act like natural opiates in the body. Endorphins are also thought to directly improve your tolerance for pain. By promoting a sense of calm and well-being, endorphins may enhance the body's self-healing process, says James G. Garrick, M.D., director of the Center for Sports Medicine at Saint Francis Memorial Hospital in San Francisco.

Talk to your doctor about the health benefits of adopting an exercise plan that will improve your strength, flexibility, and endurance.

3. Change Your Surroundings

You can alleviate some of the suffering and discomfort caused by physical restrictions by making changes to your home, says Dr. Leder. Don't be afraid to rebuild a section of your house to make it more accessible. Even small changes can make like easier and more pleasant. For example, if adding larger knobs to your kitchen cabinets would make it easier to prepare meals, throw away the old ones and head to the hardware store.

A PRAYER FOR RELIEF

Send down your angel who in his mercy gives comfort and relief to those who suffer. Let the sick and infirm be healed. Lighten and relieve their pain. Let them have respite from suffering that they may see your light. Let healing come swiftly with the dawn.

Blessed are you, O Lord, who uphold the sick on their bed of sorrow! May their days once more be good and their years happy!

Blessed are you, who uphold, save, and restore the sick.

—*From* Praying in the Jewish Tradition

Transform Your Faith

The apostle Paul, who also endured a chronic physical problem, made it clear that his suffering helped transform his faith. "I will not boast about myself except about my weaknesses. To keep me from becoming conceited because of these surpassingly great revelations, there was given to me a thorn in my flesh, a messenger of Satan, to torment me. Three times I pleaded with the Lord to take it away from me. But he said to me, 'My Grace is sufficient for you, for my power is made perfect in weakness.' That is why I delight in weakness. For when I am weak, then I am strong" (2 Corinthians 12:5–10, NIV).

Paul doesn't tell us what his thorn is, but some suggest that it was malaria, epilepsy, or a disease of the eyes. It reminded him of his need for constant contact with God.

Like Paul, you will be changed by your "thorn." Your prayer life will determine whether you become hard-hearted and bitter or softened and humbled by the experience.

1. Cope with One Day at a Time

Just as physical restrictions often test your faith, the day-to-day task of coping with limitations tests your strength—not just physical strength, but also emotional and spiritual strength. Invite courage, hope, and strength into your life each morning with this prayer suggested by Dr. Page from the Book of Common Prayer: "This is another day, O Lord. I know not what it will bring forth, but make me ready, Lord, for whatever it may be. If I am to stand up, help me to stand bravely. If I am to sit still, help me to sit quietly. If I am to lie low, help me to do it patiently. And if I am to do nothing, let me do it gallantly. Make these words more than words, and give me the Spirit of Jesus. Amen."

2. Realize That Suffering Is Universal

When you are suffering, it is helpful to remember that you are not alone, says Dr. Leder. "Understanding that everybody faces aging, sickness, and limitations helps you to bear it with grace and dignity," he says. Sharing your pain with someone else can help lighten the load. You may even want to join a support group.

But what if you have no one with whom you can share your burden?

Turn to God, who also suffers with you. Far from being aloof and unmoved, God actively participates in our pain. "Your suffering can be a source of growing recognition of your dependence on God," says Dr. Page.

> *Old age is like climbing a mountain. You climb from ledge to ledge. The higher you get, the more tired and breathless you become, but your views become more extensive.*
>
> —Ingmar Bergman

3. Think about Others

Dr. Leder recalls the time a chaplain friend was visiting a nursing home to comfort an ill-tempered woman with cancer. She was bitter and downright nasty about her situation. The staff was at a loss about how to handle her. Then the chaplain had an idea. Another couple down the hall was also dealing with serious physical problems: the wife from multiple sclerosis and the husband from Hodgkin's disease. He suggested to the woman, "Why don't you offer up your suffering to take away some of their pain?"

When the chaplain checked back at the end of the day he was surprised to find that the woman had cheered up quite a bit and needed less medication. She was curious to know if her prayer had helped the other couple. By praying for the other couple, she had diminished her pain.

"Instead of isolating us in pain, suddenly that suffering can begin to make us seem more connected to others when we offer it up as a gift," says Dr. Leder. As you pray, first ask that it be used to somehow relieve the pain of others. You may even imagine yourself holding a symbol of the pain in your hands, like a broken heart, and offering it up in prayer.

Terminal Illness

If you learn you're terminally ill, you're likely to feel fear and regret for yourself and deep concern for loved ones you'll leave behind. Prayer, faith, and the practical advice offered here can help you cope with these reactions and bring you peace.

L et's begin with this idea: Everyone knows they're going to die, but nobody believes it.

So begins the central chapter in *Tuesdays with Morrie*, the bestselling true story about a terminally ill college professor who teaches a final "course" on the lessons that can be learned from dying. Lesson number one: No one is immune.

But it's one thing to realize in the back of your mind that one day you will die; it's quite another to be told that your time is at hand. A diagnosis of terminal illness strips away the armor of denial with which we all protect ourselves. Suddenly you shift from thinking about the daily details of a seemingly infinite life to worrying about the particulars of inevitable death.

At times like this, say doctors and pastoral counselors, you're likely to feel four emotions.

- You may fear the suffering that may come in the weeks or months ahead.
- You may be terrified about losing control over even the most basic aspects of your life.

- You may have sadness and regrets that your life is ending so soon.
- You may be anxious for the loved ones you'll leave behind.

These concerns are natural and are part of the dying process. But you don't have to let them overwhelm you. You *can* handle these issues and prepare yourself spiritually and physically for a peaceful passage.

Before All Else Be Hopeful

> *Do not seek death. Death will find you. But seek the road which makes death a fulfillment.*
>
> —*Dag Hammarskjöld*

When you first learn you're ill, your spirits are likely to flag. After all, everything about your life is turning upside down. But once you're beyond that initial reaction your goal should be to look for hope—real, profound hope—for it can be one of your staunchest allies at a time when seemingly everything is working against you.

How can hope help? First, if you hope and pray for a miraculous cure, you may get it, says Dale Matthews, M.D., of Washington, D.C., coauthor of *The Faith Factor: Proof of the Healing Power of Prayer*. The Bible is filled with stories of miraculous healing, Dr. Matthews points out, from Jesus curing the blind man in the Gospel of John (9:1–7) to Peter raising a woman from the dead in Acts (9:36–41). Nor is the miracle of healing confined to Biblical times: Thousands of people are alive today who, according to their doctors, should have passed away long ago. So by all means, if you feel called to pray for healing, do so. "All things are possible for the Lord," Dr. Matthews affirms.

Also, hope itself may nourish you. The University of Michigan, Louisiana State University, and Duke University Medical Center conducted a joint study that investigated the emotions of 147 women suffering from various stages of gynecologic cancer and benign gynecologic disease. Researchers found that those women who retained the mind and heart of a "fighter" and who had strong faith maintained a level of hope that was life-sustaining.

Finally, hope can put you at ease, says James E. Miller, doctor of ministry, author of *When You Know You're Dying*. If you can keep optimism alive, you'll be less likely to feel sorry for yourself or fixate on the disabling elements of your illness. So dare to hope; hold on to it for all it's worth.

A PRAYER FOR HEALING

Dear Lord, our loved one is ill. Touch him, I beseech Thee, with the healing grace of Jesus Christ and make him well.

You gave our loved one life and You have the power to renew his life. We put him in Your kindly and loving hands, knowing that no harm can come to him while in Your care, whether on earth or in heaven.

I believe in Thy power to heal the sick. Through faith the tremendous healing force of God the Creator re-creates. I hold our loved one up to Thee and humbly ask that You will lay Your hands upon him and restore him, even as You did to those about whom we read in the Bible.

Jesus Christ is the same yesterday, today, and forever and You, Dear Lord, can give new health and strength to our dear one. This we humbly and earnestly request in Thy holy name. Amen.

—Norman Vincent Peale

Calming the Fears

Once they learn they have a terminal illness, most people enter a period of fear that can last as short as moments or as long as days or months. You'd hardly be human if you didn't share this feeling. But rest assured that you can overcome your fears and die peacefully, counselors say, in part because the realities of death are often not as frightening as most people imagine.

Most of us fear dying in pain, for example, but today, nearly all pain can be controlled. "We have pain relief agents now that can pretty much keep you out of pain 99.9 percent of the time," says David Kessler, R.N., the author of *The Rights of the Dying*, who has worked with dying patients for nearly 20 years.

Sometimes getting relief means you'll need to be forceful and make it clear to your nurse or doctor that you want medication. "Do not take no for an answer," Kessler says. "Pain may, at times, be unavoidable, but suffering—consistent, ongoing pain—*is* avoidable."

The attitude you adopt toward death can also reduce your fears, says Patricia Weenolsen, Ph.D., author of *The Art of Dying*. She suggests you help put yourself at ease by visualizing death as a doorway to a peaceful, loving place where you will be reunited with loved ones who have passed away before you.

One woman Dr. Weenolsen treated imagined that when she died she would be returning to a favorite beach where she and her late husband had spent many happy hours. They had vowed to one another before he died to meet there when both of their lives were over.

Besides adjusting your attitude there are other ways you can overcome your fears. Counselors suggest the following:

1. Talk to God

It's hard to imagine a more appropriate time to pray than when you're facing death. If you take God your fears, your sorrow—and yes, even your anger—over your illness, He will help you bear them. "I can do all things through him who strengthens me," said Paul in his letter to the Philippians (4:13, NRSV).

What Would Jesus Do?

You are not alone if you have prayed to have the threat of death lifted from your shoulders. The night Jesus was arrested, He prayed desperately in the Garden of Gethsemane for a reprieve from the trial and crucifixion He was about to endure. It is one of Christ's most human moments, and it shows that He truly understands the suffering we are going through. Just as importantly, it sets an example for us, since in the end Jesus was willing to accept God's desire, whatever it was.

"Then Jesus went with them to a place called Gethsemane; and he said to his disciples, 'Sit here while I go over there and pray.' He took with him Peter and the two sons of Zebedee, and began to be grieved and agitated. Then he said to them, 'I am deeply grieved, even to death; remain here, and stay awake with me.' And going a little farther, he threw himself on the ground and prayed, 'My Father, if it is possible, let this cup pass from me; yet not what I want but what you want.' "

(Matthew 26:36–39, NRSV)

2. Talk to Someone You Trust

"Often people in crisis anticipate that nobody else can help them or understand, but almost always there is tremendous benefit in confiding in another human being," says the Reverend Mel Lawrenz, Ph.D., director of the Elmbrook Christian Studies Center in Brookfield, Wisconsin, and coauthor of numerous books, including *Life After Grief.*

This isn't always easy, admits the Reverend Jennie Malewski, staff chaplain at The University of Kansas Medical Center in Kansas City, especially if you've made a habit during your life of keeping your troubles to yourself. Remember, however, that people genuinely *want* to help you, and they will usually feel honored that you've chosen them to confide in.

In addition to speaking to family, friends, and pastors, you can connect

THE ROAD AHEAD

My Lord God, I have no idea where I am going.

I do not see the road ahead of me.

I cannot know for certain where it will end.

Nor do I really know myself, and the fact that I think I am following your will does not mean that I am actually doing so.

But I believe that the desire to please you does in fact please you.

And I hope I have that desire in all that I am doing.

I hope that I will never do anything apart from that desire.

And I know that if I do this you will lead me by the right road, though I may know nothing about it.

Therefore I will trust you always though I may seem to be lost and in the shadow of death. I will not fear, for you are ever with me, and you will never leave me to face my perils alone.

—Thomas Merton

with other people who will listen sympathetically and prayerfully. Most hospitals have social workers or chaplains who have extensive experience and training in counseling people who are terminally ill, says the Reverend Richard B. Gilbert, a chaplain and Anglican priest who directs the World Pastoral Care Center in Valparaiso, Indiana. In addition, there are dozens of support groups dedicated to helping people who have specific diseases.

3. Talk to Members of Your Church

You also may find it helpful to seek the support and prayers of your broader faith community. Many churches set aside time in their regular services to pray for members who are ill, says Reverend Malewski. Others have prayer chains that will pray for you throughout the week. To connect with these services, simply call the pastor or church office and ask for help, she suggests. You can make your requests for prayers as general or as specific as you like, she adds. Some people ask for healing prayers, others for prayers of strength for them and their families.

4. Talk to Yourself

As helpful as being around others will be during this time of trial, it can also be extremely calming to take some time for yourself. Take walks in nature: to a favorite hill, perhaps, to the beach, or to a favorite park, suggests Peg Elliott Mayo, a psychotherapist in Blodgett, Oregon, and coauthor of *Rituals for Living and Dying*. The main point is to quiet the turmoil that is raging within.

Being surrounded by creation reminds you of your place in it, she says, which can help you come to terms with the fact that death is a natural part of life. If your illness makes walking difficult, Mayo adds, you can put a potted plant on the windowsill to create a connection to the natural world.

Maintaining Control

We're taught at a young age to be as independent as possible. After a lifetime of acting that way, there are few things as troubling as the thought of losing control at the end of your life. You imagine that as your illness progresses others will begin making decisions about your meals, your treatment, your medication, even about what you wear. And you worry how you'll feel if you lose control of your body and bodily functions.

Some of this may come to pass, but you can still exercise control over your life by taking these steps.

Tools of Faith

Friendly Surroundings

Taking control over your physical environment can have a major impact on how you feel when you're seriously ill. This is the message of the hospice movement, which stresses that dying at home is more satisfying than being surrounded by the cold impersonality of a hospital.

How can you build a comforting environment?

• Photographs: Pictures of family and friends can create a cocoon of emotional warmth around you.

• Spiritual objects: Crosses, rosaries, Bibles, St. Christopher medals—spiritually meaningful objects can be very helpful to hold on to, especially if we become too weak or ill to read, pray, or participate in other spiritual activities.

• Keepsakes: A shell from a favorite beach, perhaps, a cherished childhood toy, a piece of pottery, a lock of your spouse's hair—all can provide comfort and prompt warm memories.

• Aromatherapy: Smells, whether from the essential oils used in aromatherapy or scented candles, can provoke soothing emotions. Be forewarned, however, that some smells can provoke nausea when you're ill. Your best bet, says Peg Elliott Mayo, a clinical social worker and psychotherapist in Blodgett, Oregon, and coauthor of Rituals for Living and Dying, *are scents that have a clean, refreshing smell, such as lemon, lavender, or mint.*

• Music: Listening to music—classical or new Age music in particular—can be a vital source of comfort, especially when other activities become difficult physically.

1. Write an Advance Directive

If you're concerned about the treatment you'll receive at the very end, talk to your family and your physician now and let them know how far you want to go to prolong your life. Create an advance directive or Do Not Resuscitate order spelling out your decisions and the point at which you want treatment to end. Chaplains, social workers, and hospice counselors can help guide you in developing one.

2. Close Out Personal Affairs

Another way to exercise control involves wrapping up your personal affairs. This includes practical matters, such as making a last will. But there is also more sentimental business to consider, such as giving away belongings that will have special meaning to special people in your life. Any personal object—from a favorite piece of jewelry to a shaving kit—can help your loved ones feel connected to you after you're gone. Also at this time you may want to make plans for your own funeral.

A NATIVE AMERICAN PRAYER

Oh Great Spirit,

Whose voice I hear in the wind,

Whose breath gives life to the world,

Hear me!

I come to you as one of your many children.

I am small and weak.

I need your strength and wisdom.

May I walk in beauty.

Make my eyes behold the red and purple sunset.

Make my hands respect the things that you have made,

And my ears sharp to hear your voice.

Make me wise so that I may know the things

That you have taught your children—

The lessons that you have hidden in every leaf and rock.

Make me strong, not to be superior to my brothers, but to be

able to fight my greatest enemy: myself.

Make me ever ready to come to you with straight eyes, so that

When life fades as the faded sunset

My spirit will come to you without shame.

—John Yellow Lark

Far from being morbid, many dying patients turn these types of house-keeping chores into celebrations of their lives and of the people they love, says Reverend Malewski. She recalls one young woman dying of cancer who chose a series of scripture readings, reminiscences, poems, and songs that captured, joyfully, some of the experiences that had been especially meaningful to her in her life.

3. Put Things in Perspective

Yes, you'll probably reach a point where others need to make decisions for you, but that is nothing about which you should be ashamed. Remember, says Dr. Weenolsen, the problem is not that you have somehow lost control of yourself—the problem is that a disease is taking control from you. This is not a personal failing on your part; it's simply part of a disease process.

4. Accept What You Can't Control

You'll have no choice if your body becomes so weak you can no longer care for yourself, but you do have options about how you view it.

Morrie Schwartz, the college professor whose graceful dying is documented in *Tuesdays with Morrie*, dreaded what he called "the ultimate sign of dependency"—needing help "wiping his bottom." Despite that dread, he learned to adjust by simply allowing himself to enjoy being taken care of. "After all," he laughed, "I get to be a baby one more time."

It may also help to be reminded again that your loved ones are often happy to have something that they can do for you in your time of need. "Taking care of those we love is one of the joys of life," says Bernie S. Siegel, M.D., founder of Exceptional Cancer Patients, an organization for people with serious illnesses, and author of *Love, Medicine and Miracles*.

Managing Regrets

For you it might be the life story you never wrote, the mountain you never climbed, the grandchild you'll never see, or the angry words you said to an old friend many years ago. Whatever the issue, you're bound to have regrets when you realize your life is nearing the end.

How can you come to resolve these feelings?

1. Take Stock of Your Life

You may never achieve all you'd hoped to; that doesn't make your life a failure. Indeed, it's likely you've already had a profound impact on

THE PEACE IN DEATH

Oh, God, death is so still, so utterly still.

Death is more still than the quietest meadow on a summer day. Stiller than the whitest snows of a winter hillside. More deeply still than the deepest stillness of a starry night.

There is such peace in death, for the spirit is lost in the bliss of some absolute dream.

Death is perfect acceptance, perfect understanding.

Death is the perfect knowing.

"Be still and know that I am God," you said. The living can never attain that absolute perfection of stillness and knowing. Only the dead.

But so profound is their stillness this we do know: In you they live.

—*Marjorie Holmes*

the people around you. Now is the time to acknowledge that by performing what counselors call a *life review*. Remember your experiences, achievements, and regrets; sum up the good and the bad. Yes, you may recall major disappointments, but recognize that despite them you have come a long way and achieved a lot, says Kessler. There is much you can celebrate.

Besides showing you how far you've come, your review can serve as a witness of your existence that will live on after you've gone. Keep a journal or dictate your thoughts into a tape recorder, advises Joyce Rupp, author of *Praying Our Goodbyes* and coauthor of *May I Walk You Home? Courage and Comfort for Caregivers of the Very Ill*. Or record your comments on a videotape.

Q&A: How Can I Put Friends at Ease?

Q: It's clear my family and friends are having trouble dealing with my illness; what can I do to make it easier for them?

A: The best way to help is to be frank and truthful, say counselors. "Tell people that you feel uncomfortable when they tiptoe around the subject of dying," says David Feinstein, Ph.D., a psychologist based in Ashland, Oregon, and coauthor of *Rituals for Living and Dying.* "It will usually be a relief for everyone."

Grief counselors recommend being frank with young children as well. "Keep it simple, but tell the truth," says the Reverend Jennie Malewski, staff chaplain at The University of Kansas Medical Center in Kansas City. "Use the word 'dying.' A lot of people will use euphemisms like 'going to sleep,' or 'passing on,' but that just confuses children and sometimes frightens them. If the person is dying, say so. Use the 'D' word."

Reverend Maleswski advises that you tell a child something along the lines of, "Grandma is dying, dear, so she will be leaving this life and going to heaven soon."

2. Set Short-Term Goals

You can help keep your spirits high by identifying some goal that you'd like to accomplish before the end arrives, says Dr. Weenolsen. She calls this having "active" rather than "passive" hope—it's active because you're *doing* something. The challenge you set for yourself may be as complicated as finishing that novel you've always dreamed of writing or as simple as taking a pottery course. In either case, Dr. Weenolsen recommends you try to focus on the pleasure of the process—the feeling of being engaged with something you care about—rather than on the results.

3. Say "Thank You"

It's easy to let a lifetime go by without telling those you love how much they've meant to you. You still have time to correct that oversight. Whether in person, by letter, on the telephone, or in prayer, you can speak to family and friends as part of your final farewells. This can pay debts that need to be paid and at the same time provide some genuinely sacred moments.

4. Say You're Sorry

If you're like most of us, you can compile an entire list of people you've slighted or angered in some way. Now is the time to apologize. "Freely saying you're sorry will help free you," says Dr. Siegel. "Tell your children, your spouse, whoever, 'I'm sorry if I hurt you. I wasn't smart enough, I'm still learning, and I want you to know I love you and I'm sorry.' Let that healing begin."

5. Forgive the People Who Have Hurt You

Grudges are tethers that bind people to this world, Dr. Siegel says. Forgiving those who have wronged you during your life dissolves those bonds of bitterness.

Let's be honest: Some wrongs simply can't be forgiven. But the more you can forgive, the greater the relief you are likely to feel.

6. Tell Your Secrets

Often people who are dying feel the need to unburden themselves of some secret in their past. In their book, *May I Walk You Home? Courage and Comfort for Caregivers of the Very Ill*, Joyce Hutchison Carpenter and Joyce Rupp tell of one woman who desperately wanted to make a confession. Dying of breast cancer, she couldn't let go of life until she'd told her nurse about the baby she'd had as an unmarried teenager. The baby had died at birth, and the memory had always haunted her mother. Making the confession was such a relief that she was able to accept her approaching death.

Fears for the Family

If you've always been the strong one—the breadwinner or the one who made most of the major decisions for your family—you are likely to be worried about how they'll get along after your death. In truth, your illness itself may help prepare them, say counselors, since you'll be turning more and more decision making over to them as time passes.

Beyond this, you may worry about the emotional gap your death will leave in their lives. Counselors recommend the following steps to reduce that void.

1. Tell Them How Much You Love Them

Let your family and friends know you appreciate who they are, all they've accomplished, and how much they've meant to you, especially during your illness. By doing this, you will protect your loved ones from the feelings of guilt that plague many survivors who fear that they didn't do enough for their loved ones when they were alive, Dr. Weenolsen says.

How to Help a Loved One Who Is Dying

Helping loved ones who are dying can be one of the most difficult—and most rewarding—responsibilities you'll ever have. Here is some advice to guide you, from Joyce Hutchison Carpenter, R.N., director at Mercy Hospice–Johnston in Iowa and coauthor of *May I Walk You Home? Courage and Comfort for Caregivers of the Very Ill.*

• Be honest but sensitive. Giving false promises—"You'll be fine," for example—only makes your loved ones distrust you. At the same time, you need to avoid brutally offering information they may not be ready to handle. This sometimes requires walking a fine line. Try to follow their lead. If they say, "Do you think I'm going to die?" you can answer, "I don't know, what do you think?" If they answer, "Yes, I feel weaker, I think maybe I'm dying," then it's okay to say, "Yes, I sense that you're losing ground, too."

• Listen. Dying people can be vulnerable and may have trouble expressing themselves. Resist the temptation to put words in your loved ones' mouths.

• Offer prayers when appropriate. Here, too, some sensitivity is in order. Many people will be grateful to receive prayers, but others may not. When in doubt, you might say, "I have a sense that you might enjoy it if I said a prayer for you. Am I right about that?" If the answer is yes, you can

2. Share Memories

Gather your family around and share memories of all your joyful times together. This can be one of the happiest and most moving moments in your shared lives. Dr. Siegel says that when he's on his deathbed, he plans to watch his family's entire collection of home movies. His goal is to die laughing, and he figures that's one sure way of getting there.

also ask if they prefer a spontaneous, conversational prayer, or something more structured, like the Lord's Prayer.

• Touch. Back rubs, foot rubs, and holding hands can be very important to people who are dying. In part that's because touching signals that you truly are committed to their care: It's a way of saying that you are with your loved ones on the journey. Keep in mind, though, that some people are less comfortable being touched than others.

• Look for joy. Death is not always sad. A sense of humor is allowed. Nor does the environment have to be sterile or somber. Let your loved ones set the tone: If telling a few jokes or singing funny songs is something they've always enjoyed, chances are they still will. Keep in mind that kids can instantly bring happiness into a room.

• Give them permission to die. Don't hold on to your loved ones when they are ready to go. If you sense they are struggling to hang on for your sake, say something like, "I know you've been really sick for a long time, and it's been a hard struggle for you. If you don't want to struggle any more and you want to let go, you have my permission to do that. I'll be okay without you. I will miss you, but I'll be okay."

3. Talk about Their Futures

You may not be around when a grandchild gets married or a son earns a coveted degree, but you can live such experiences now by discussing them with your loved ones. Imagine with them what the event will be like and offer advice if it's appropriate. For a spouse, you might discuss the relief and rest they'll get when your battle is finally over, suggests Dr. Weenolsen. That can comfort them and relieve any guilt they're feeling about not being able to help you more.

4. Hear Them Out

Your illness and coming death are painful for your loved ones too. And they may have issues they want to discuss with you before you die. Encourage them to speak their minds, Dr. Weenolsen says. You may want to do so gently and indirectly, she adds—some-times simply hinting that you're open to listening can be better than confronting a subject head-on.

5. Let Them Know You'll Always Be There

Assure your loved ones that, if you can, you'll visit them after you're gone and lend them strength.

When It's Time to Let Go

In a way, a life of faith is directed toward death—we all know that time on earth is temporary, says the Reverend Norman J. Muckerman, editor of *Preparation for Death: Prayers and Consolations for the Final Journey*. Then why the reluctance to leave? Perhaps because this is "home," and what's ahead is uncertain.

> *Death—the last sleep?*
> *No, the final awakening.*
>
> —*Sir Walter Scott*

Yet you can take comfort in knowing that your faith serves you best in the final days and hours of your life. Some final steps can help you let go more gracefully.

Grant Yourself Permission to Die

When death nears, you may feel ready to let go of your life before your loved ones are ready to let you go. This is a common experience, Reverend Malewski says, and it can create a sense of conflict that causes many dying people to hang on, even when it is agony for them to do so. This is probably why many people die in the middle of the night, Dr. Siegel believes, when no one is around, or when their loved ones leave their bedside for a moment.

It's important to grant yourself permission to die when you are ready. "Don't keep fighting for someone else and put yourself through hell," says Dr. Siegel. "It's all right to say, 'I'm tired. I'd like to leave my body.'"

Look Forward

For the faithful, dying is as much a beginning as an end; it is nothing less, in fact, than the gateway to paradise. "God is waiting to welcome us," says Father Muckerman. "He made us to bring to Himself."

Pastoral counselors often compare dying to childbirth. Both are filled with fear and uncertainty, both take work, and both are natural processes over which, ultimately, we have little control. One other thing they have in common: Both produce a miracle. "I'm sure as a baby in our mother's womb, we were afraid to come into the world, and it's just like that going out of the world," says Reverend Malewski. "It's an unknown, but God wants what is good for us, and we can trust him."

Death of a Loved One

The death of someone close can leave you feeling lost, confused, and overwhelmed with grief. This is when you need your faith, friends, and family most, for they more than anything else can help you realize there's hope beyond the pain.

D eath is the one thing in life of which you're certain, yet it never fails to shock when it decides to pay a visit.

As a child you may first confront it in a fallen bird you find in the backyard or the old family dog that your parents "put to sleep." With age comes more familiarity—as death claims grandparents, great-grandparents, or perhaps the kindly old woman who lived by herself in your neighborhood. And later still, it becomes a closer companion, as you say goodbye to your own parents, to friends, perhaps even to your spouse.

Yet despite the frequency with which death strikes, despite the scriptures' assurance that life on this world is only a beginning, the fact is that death hurts, and it hurts deeply. When someone close to you dies, you are left with a dull ache that can take years to heal. And even the smallest thing—a song you and your loved one shared, a chance comment from someone at church—can revive the pain.

Thankfully, your faith, friends, and memories can do much to soothe your suffering and restore your life after the death of a loved one. Specifically, pastors and counselors suggest three ways they can help.

- Friends, family, clergy, and church members can offer emotional support and advice.
- Symbols of your loved one can keep alive the memories of your happy times together.
- Prayer and faith can help you handle the hard work of "starting over."

Look To the Living

When you're deep in grief there's no greater comfort than talking about it with people who understand what you're going through. They can soften the loneliness you're sure to be feeling, remind you that others share your suffering, and voice emotions you may not be able to verbalize yourself.

We do best homage to our dead when we live our lives most fully, even in the shadow of our loss.

—*Jewish prayer for the High Holy Days*

Just as importantly, other people can serve as the listening board you need, letting you release your pain, relate your fears, or voice your anger and possible doubts you may have about God's love, says David Carroll of Tappan, New York, who has led seminars and workshops on grieving.

It's important, however, to choose carefully whom you talk to. You want comfort and support, not advice from people who want to jolt you out of your grief. "You don't want to be 'edited' in your grief,'" says Carroll. "You don't want to be told, 'Stop feeling that way, cheer up, don't dwell on the past.' What you want is to be heard."

So where, exactly, should you turn?

1. Turn to Caring Friends and Family

People who know you and knew your loved one well can relate best to the pain you're suffering. And they'll be less likely to sermonize or try to short-circuit the mourning you need to do before you become whole again.

2. Seek Out Other Grievers

Ask your pastor for the name of a grief support group in your community, and attend at least one meeting. "In grief groups, people remind you that whatever you're feeling is quite legitimate, and that mistakenly setting two places at the dinner table instead of one or waking up feeling lousy but going to bed feeling okay is perfectly all right," says Carroll. "In grief groups

---

❧

IF DEATH MY FRIEND
AND ME DIVIDE

If Death my friend and me divide,

thou dost not, Lord, my sorrow chide,

or frown my tears to see;

restrained from passionate excess,

thou bidst me mourn in calm distress

for them that rest in thee.

I feel a strong immortal hope,

which bears my mournful spirit up

beneath its mountain load;

redeemed from death, and grief, and pain,

I soon shall find my friend again

within the arms of God.

Pass a few fleeting moments more

and death the blessing shall restore

which death has snatched away;

for me thou wilt the summons send,

and give me back my parted friend

in that eternal day.

—*Charles Wesley*

---

you get the collective wisdom of experience and the compassion that comes with it."

3. Speak to God

Bring your grief to God in private prayer. "Even if you're angry at God, tell Him so," says the Reverend John Davies, chaplain of Hospice Care in Westchester and Putnam counties in New York State. "If you feel He's far, far away, tell Him that, too. Or if you simply need the strength to face the day, tell Him that. God has promised to provide for us, and you do well to take Him at His word."

4. Consult Your Pastor

Here's your opportunity to work through whatever "unfinished business" might have existed between you and your loved one. "Often times there are things that weren't said, apologies that weren't offered, amends that weren't made," says Reverend Davies, "and talking them out with a clergy member who you have faith in can help you reconcile yourself to the fact that death often doesn't wait for loose ends to be tied up."

5. Recall Memories with Your Family

Gather children, parents, and other relatives together and let each person discuss one event in your loved one's life from their perspective. By doing this "you gain an appreciation for the richness of the person; how many things he or she was to how many people, and how you each experienced your loved one in your own way. It's like taking something plain—a story—and making it something sacred—a 'gospel,'" says the Reverend Thomas Brown, doctor of theology, dean at the Interdenominational Theological Seminary in Atlanta.

Keeping a Memory Alive

One of the reasons you take photographs of special events is because you want to remember them and having a tangible object you can look at, feel, and run your fingers through, helps transport you back to the event itself. In the same way, symbols keep memories of your loved one alive.

"You need benchmarks, anchors, real things with weight and form and texture that will recall a memory you don't want to lose," says Carroll. "They're like the communion wafer; they don't fully satisfy the hunger but they provide you with proof that the memories are real."

What might you use as anchors?

1. Create a Marker

Mark your loved one's grave with a stone, or, if their body has been cremated, erect a memorial marker. "The gravestone or marker provides a place to commune with the memory of the loved one," says Reverend Davies. "It is often segregated from the common paths of your daily life, so visiting it can be like a retreat for you, a place to get away, clear your head, and think only about the person."

FINDING STRENGTH IN GOD

You, Lord God, are my strength. By your Spirit I shall prevail. Your "weakness" is stronger than men, and your strength is made perfect in man's weakness. Because this is true, I know that when I am weak I shall be strong because you are with me, and I will be strong in you, Lord, and in the power of your might.

—*Clift Richards and Lloyd Hildebrand*

2. Choose a Special Place

Pick some place that was of special significance to your loved one, and visit it when you want to recall the person's memory. "I remember performing a service for a woman who had died of cancer," recalls Reverend Davies. "We spread some of her ashes near a favorite grove of hers in a botanical garden. Now, family and friends can return there and recall with great joy the hours of pleasure she used to derive from that grove."

3. Write a Eulogy

Even if you have no intention of delivering it publicly, write a remembrance of your loved one. "It feels good to gather your thoughts, articulate them, write them down, and go back and revisit them from time to time," says Dr. Brown. "It can serve you the same way a beautiful poem serves you even after you've read it several times. It stirs wonderful, grateful remembrances."

4. Keep a Memento

Keep a small item that belonged to your loved one and simply hold it from time to time. "Little things—maybe a rock or a seashell they picked up on a walk with you, maybe a favorite hat, or an old war medal—provide you with something tactile that you can hold in your hands and that recalls some facet of the person's life," says Reverend Davies.

5. Keep Only What Matters Most

It's not uncommon for a husband or wife to keep all of a spouse's possessions because it's too painful to relinquish them, says Reverend Davies. But this makes it difficult to accept the finality of the death and get on with life. Reverend Davies offers a better suggestion: "If, for instance, a wife has left her husband's dresser just the way it was when he died 7 or 8 years ago, I would encourage her to pick one item from it—perhaps a hair brush or a tie tack—and put it on her dresser," he says. "Having held on to something of his

BRING PEACE TO THIS TROUBLED SOUL

O Lord, our heavenly Father, almighty and most merciful God, in whose hands are life and death, who givest and takest away, castest down and raisest up, look with mercy on the affliction of thy unworthy servant, turn away thine anger from me, and speak peace to my troubled soul.

Grant me the assistance and comfort of thy Holy Spirit, that I may remember with thankfulness the blessings so long enjoyed by me in the society of my departed wife.

Make me so to think on her precepts and example, that I may imitate whatever was in her life acceptable in thy sight, and avoid all by which she offended thee.

Forgive me, O merciful Lord, all my sins, and enable me to begin and perfect that reformation which I promised her, and to persevere in that resolution, which she implored thee to continue.

And now, O Lord, release me from my sorrow, fill me with just hopes, true faith, and holy consolations, and enable me to do my duty in that state of life to which thou hast been pleased to call me, without disturbance from fruitless grief, or tumultuous imaginations; that in all my thoughts, words, and actions, I may glorify thy Holy Name.

—Samuel Johnson

memory, she would then be free to dispose of the rest of his personal effects and by doing so signify the need to move on with her own life."

Starting Life Again

You may feel it would be insulting to the memory of your loved one to get on with your life, laugh again, enjoy a good meal, or be entertained by a favorite piece of music or old movie.

But experts maintain that while grief and mourning can take a long, long time, one crucial part of the recovery process is moving yourself back into life again.

"It's not easy to mourn," says Carroll, "but it can be even tougher to start pushing yourself beyond it. Still, it's what your loved one would want for you and what you would want for anyone who mourns your passing."

Help yourself begin healing in the following ways.

1. Start Slowly

Fully recovering from the loss of a loved one is a long process. Some experts suggest it may take 3 or 4 years. During this period, it's important you not rush the process—either out of your own impatience or that of your friends and family. "Many people around you will be wanting you to get 'back on your feet' more quickly than you can," says Reverend Davies. "You need to have patience, and you need to tell them not to abandon you while you're weathering your storm." Adds Carroll, "you need to let nature run its course. You can't make grass grow by pulling at it."

2. Accept the Void inside You

Draw a picture of a heart; inside of the heart list everyone who is important in your life, but leave a blank space for your loved one. By doing this you acknowledge that this was a special person whom no one can replace, but you also acknowledge that your heart is filled with people who care about you. "The emptiness signifies the sacred bond you had with this person," says Reverend Davies, "but it also reminds you that the Holy Spirit will use the people still around you to help you rebuild your life."

3. Be Prepared for Ups and Downs

Mourning is a very uneven process, says Dr. Brown. "You think you're out of the woods or having a good day, and then, 'wham!' you get hit with it again," he says. You can help yourself get through the down periods by writing a short prayer you can recite to yourself when you're feeling particularly sad. "It helps if you have a few words, maybe nothing more than, 'Thy will be done,' to keep yourself conscious of God's presence with you," says Dr. Brown.

4. Revisit Old Sites

A year or so after your loved one's death, go back to some of the places the two of you frequented. "When you first go back to the restaurant or park, it can be awfully difficult," says Carroll. "But it will gradually get easier, and it's a way of affirming your need to keep living. It's the beginning, if you will, of a new history."

5. Rearrange Family Rituals

If certain activities have been altered by the death of your loved one, consciously restructure them. For example, "if mom and dad always hosted Thanksgiving but mom has since died, gather together as a family and discuss how and where you want to celebrate the holiday hereafter," suggests Reverend Davies. "This is a way of affirming the life that God has given us by creating new rituals."

> *I have lost my seven best friends, which is to say God has had mercy on me seven times. He lent a friendship, took it from me, sent me another.*
>
> —*Jean Cocteau*

In the book of Genesis, when Jacob wrestled with the angel it was because he was about to become a new being. His old identity was dying and a new one was emerging in him. He struggled with the adversary all night, until, badly bruised in the joint of his hip, he finally prevailed. The story closes with Jacob, now renamed Israel (meaning "to have struggled with God"), limping, forever wounded, but walking nonetheless, to the dawn of a new day.

And so it is when you wrestle with life and death, that through your faith and prayers and those who love you, you limp along until you reach the new day.

For more advice on coping with death, see the chapter dealing with the Death of a Child, page 126.

PRAYER OF
RELEASE

Unlock the Chains of Resentment

Bitterness is a prison.

It chains you to the wounds you've suffered, whether they occurred in childhood or last week. It chains you as well to the people who inflicted those hurts, whether they're still in your life or not.

Yet forgiveness, as anyone who's tried it knows, is not an easy task, which is why you need God's help to pull it off. Prayer is the answer.

"The most loving thing you can do for your enemies—for anyone, really—is pray for them," says the Reverend Siang-Yang Tan, Ph.D., professor of psychology at Fuller Theological Seminary in Pasadena, California, and senior pastor of the First Evangelical Church in Glendale, California.

Praying for someone who's slighted you in some minor way is a fairly straightforward matter. If the hurt is a serious one, however, Dr. Tan recommends a two-step prayer prescription. First, he says, you need to pray for the Holy Spirit to heal the hurt that's in your own heart. Only then are you ready to take the second step: praying for the strength to forgive the person who's hurt you. Your prayers of forgiveness are not likely to succeed, Dr. Tan believes, until some "inner healing" has been accomplished.

1. Begin with a prayer for God's guidance and protection. For example, "Dear Lord, please come and bless me and protect me from evil."

2. Spend a minute or two relaxing. Take several slow, deep breaths and allow the tension to drain out of your body as much as possible. Talk soothingly to yourself: "Just relax. Take it easy. Be at peace." Visualize pleasant, peaceful scenes in your mind's eye: a favorite beach, perhaps, or a favorite meadow.

3. When you feel relaxed, close your eyes and picture in your mind's eye the painful event that occurred. Relive it in your imagination. Don't hurry past this, Dr. Tan says. Wait for the memory to be clear. Pay attention to how you feel as you relive it; let your emotions emerge.

4. Once you have the image of the wounding incident clearly in mind, pray aloud, asking God to heal the hurt. For example, says Dr. Tan: "Spirit of God, I pray in the name of Jesus that you will come and minister to me right now. Let me experience your healing grace."

5. Having prayed, wait. Think about what you're feeling right now. Be patient; give God's grace time to work. Often, helpful feelings, thoughts, or visions will come, Dr. Tan says, but they may not. You don't always feel the Spirit working right away. Give this step as much time as it requires or as much time as you can.

6. Close with a brief prayer, thanking God for what has occurred.

7. Later, perhaps that evening or the next morning, "debrief" yourself, Dr. Tan suggests, either by discussing what has happened with a trusted advisor or by writing down what you've experienced in a journal.

Having completed this preparatory prayer of inner healing, you are now ready to pray for the release of the person who inflicted the wound. "The prayer of inner healing must always have as its final goal forgiveness of the other party," Dr. Tan says. "The point is not to make yourself feel good and go on holding a grudge against someone. Christ commanded us to forgive." This step is simpler, but every bit as vital.

"In the name of Jesus, I forgive John for hurting me so badly. I release my anger, my resentment, my bitterness, and my hatred. I pray, Lord, that You will take it all away from me. Show me and sustain me with Your grace and Your Holy Spirit's presence. I truly let go of this resentment against John, and I ask You to bless him."

It is important to remember, Dr. Tan says, that forgiving someone for a wrong he or she has committed is not the same as excusing it or forgetting it. The memory of the hurt you've suffered is likely to remain with you, and you may feel the need to repeat these steps many times.

The hope is that by doing so you will be able to gradually reverse resentment's momentum: Instead of sinking ever deeper into your soul, its grip will gradually be loosened. Eventually, with God's grace, you will be freed.

Part 5

YOUR FAMILY LIFE

Family Conflicts

The people you love the most sometimes can be the ones who cause you the most sorrow. If you're stuck in a damaged relationship, here's how you can get past the hard feelings and mend them through prayer.

hey were what a lot of us might call a "model family": a husband and wife whose love spanned nearly 30 years and two happy, successful children—all living in a comfortable home in an affluent suburb of New York City.

Then the daughter chose to marry a man their parents didn't approve of, and "the wheels started falling off," recalls the Reverend Gregory Sutterlin, a minister at Ascension Lutheran Church and a psychotherapist in Franklin Square, New York.

"Her parents fiercely opposed the wedding, her brother fiercely encouraged it, even the grandparents were split, right down the middle," says Reverend Sutterlin. "The whole thing created deep and lasting divides throughout three generations of what by every indication was an otherwise solid, committed, and close knit family."

Although most families will never see strife this extreme, conflict is an inevitable part of every family's life. We may argue over the way one family member dresses, another member's political views, still another's way with money—all sorts of things. And there is nothing wrong with that, say counselors and pastors. The secret to having a happy family life doesn't lie in avoiding conflict but in working through it.

"It can in fact be useful," says Robert Stahmann, Ph.D., professor of marriage and family therapy at Brigham Young University in Provo, Utah, "because it challenges us to be selfless, forces us to think of someone other than ourselves when we're deciding what we want to do and how we want to do it."

If we really want to love we must learn how to forgive.

—Mother Teresa

If you're having a difficult relationship in your family—perhaps with a grown child, a parent, a grown brother or sister, or another close family member—you can take three steps to resolve it, say experts.

- Create an atmosphere that encourages everyone to speak their mind.
- Establish rules for fighting fairly.
- Look for creative ways to solve your problems.

Conflict—It Does a Body Good

Often, people feel guilty about admitting there's ever been a conflict between themselves and another member of the family. The reason: They've been conditioned to believe that if they have serious conflicts and get angry with someone, it means their relationship lacks love, says the Reverend William Hiebert, executive director of Marriage and Family Counseling Services in Rock Island, Illinois. So rather than address their problems, they hide them behind a curtain of apparent harmony.

"But that unrest is like steam in a radiator," says Reverend Hiebert. "It's only going to build until either it's ventilated, aired out, or it blows things sky high." The truth is that you can only manage family conflict when you acknowledge that it's okay to get angry and encourage people to speak their minds. Here are three ways to do this.

1. Examine Your Beliefs

With other family members, compile a list of your attitudes and beliefs about conflict and anger, says Reverend Hiebert. Do you regard conflict as a "bad" thing? Do you think a spiritual person shouldn't express anger? When someone you love expresses anger toward you, do you think they no longer care about you? Are you afraid of anger? If your responses show that you ap-

HELP US THROUGH THESE TOUGH TIMES

How comforting to know you hear us when we cry out to you, Lord.
Thank you for your promise to be with our family in our heart-
breaking situation. We are trusting you to show yourself strong as
our Deliverer and to extend your mercy to all of us. Thank you for
your grace that has brought us this far and for the love that binds
our family together. We offer you the sacrifice of praise in the midst
of our tough times, knowing you will receive all glory in the end.

Amen.

—*Quin Sherrer and Ruthanne Garlock*

proach conflict and anger with great discomfort, you can set some rules for expressing your anger.

2. Say It Constructively

When you feel yourself getting angry, don't yell. Instead, stop and think about what's really causing your feelings. Try to break down your emotions into three components: behavior, feeling, and feared consequences, says Dr. Stahmann. "If, for instance, you feel particularly uncomfortable when you and your brother argue, respond to him by saying, 'When you do X (behavior), I feel Y (feeling), and I fear that Z will happen (feared consequences),'" he says.

So, you might say to him: "When you yell at me I feel sad because I fear you don't love me anymore." Once he hears your side, he can reassure you that his anger is momentary but his feelings for you are enduring. "By doing this over and over you begin to lose the fears you have about the consequences of expressing anger and experiencing conflict," says Dr. Stahmann.

3. Let It Out—Within the Family

Agree to express anger openly—within the safe confines of the family. "The family is a protective body," says Reverend Hiebert, "and it can withstand the winds of rage that need to blow through from time to time. Sometimes anger needs to be let out before a family can get down to the hard issues of negotiating their way through whatever conflict has given it birth."

What if you're so wound up you're afraid your fury will hurt the other person? Then vent first at something that won't care. "It's sometimes helpful to yell at an empty chair, or even take a tennis racket and light into an old pillow," says Reverend Sutterlin. "Then, when you're ready, you and the other family member will be able to focus on the essence of the conflict itself."

The Rules of Engagement

So now you know that it's okay to let your anger surface. The next step in handling conflicts is to learn to resolve them without damaging your relationship. That means making compromises, says Dr. Stahmann. "An essential element in any life of faith is your willingness to sacrifice, to engage in the kind of give and take that makes a family both loving and alive," he says. "Remember, even the disciples had their share of disagreements, but they still managed to found a community of faith that's lasted 2,000 years."

It's one thing to acknowledge the need for give and take, however, and quite another to actually make it happen in the midst of conflict. "When we're arguing with a loved one," says Reverend Sutterlin, "give and take usually means you give and I'll take." But that attitude doesn't square with the advice of Jesus and other great religious leaders. They suggest you be patient and calm in the face of strife, turn the other cheek, bless the meek, and even love your

THE VALUE OF CONVERSATION

"Communication among family members is like water running through pipes," says the Reverend William Hiebert, executive director of Marriage and Family Counseling Services in Rock Island, Illinois. "When the water doesn't run, the pipes corrode, wear out, and die. If your family is to stay alive and vital, you have to keep the water running, even if you sometimes don't like the way that water tastes."

enemy, says Reverend Sutterlin. Or, put simply, fight fairly. How do you fight fairly? By establishing some ground rules ahead of time.

1. Decide What You Want to Accomplish

Agree on the purpose for your argument. For example, a family might have a mother who insists her new daughter-in-law promise that she and her husband will come over for Sunday supper at least once a month and a daughter-in-law who finds this too much to ask. The two of them could engage in a tug-of-war over whether the daughter-in-law will capitulate to the mother's demand. Or they could look at the bigger picture—decide what the common goal is and work to reach that.

In this case, the goal might be establish how much time they all wish to spend together. Once they've established a common goal, they can work together to determine how that time is arranged. "You can accomplish one of three things in an argument with a loved one," says Reverend Hiebert. "You can prevail over them, hurt them, or find a

Prayer Miracles

A Miracle Reunited Me with My Sisters

During my father's last months fighting lung cancer and Alzheimer's disease, the old tensions between me and my three sisters resurfaced, causing much divisiveness. My sister Anne and I were on one side, my other two sisters were on the other side. We made no bones about telling each other how much we hated each other.

My father was filled with a great sadness at all this. He and I would sit together for hours with Father Joe from the hospice, and pray for peace. As my father's condition deteriorated, we four sisters divided visits to him into shifts to avoid being with each other. Then one Monday morning I suddenly had a mental picture of my father and the word Go. I turned to Anne and said, "I'm going to visit Dad now." She reminded me that our sisters would be there, but I said I didn't care.

When we got to my father's room, I knew I was there to say goodbye. I took his hand, stroked his hair and told him to feel the love in the room. Anne whispered her last words to him, then my other sisters took their turn. My oldest sister then opened my father's Bible and read aloud Psalm 23. Halfway through the psalm, he opened his eyes, looked at us, and then left us.

And I knew we had witnessed a miracle. For that moment we sisters were united in our purpose and our love. It was the culmination of my father's endeavors to bring his four daughters together. And it was the joyful culmination of all our prayers for his inner peace.

Karla Murphy
Winthrop, Massachusetts

solution you can both live with. The first is bullying and the second abusive, but the third holds the seeds for a strong and healthy relationship."

2. Agree on the Tactics You'll Use

For example, you and the other family members might promise to make a genuine attempt to understand each others' feelings about the issue in conflict. Or you might agree to hear each other out without interrupting to defend your own views. Or you might promise to listen, then feed back exactly what the other person is saying so you are sure you understand the other person's point of view.

If need be, write down the rules to help you stick to them. The important thing is to create some parameters that will ensure that everything that needs saying will be said—without things getting out of hand. "If you really trust the other person, and if you trust that God will guide you through rough times, then you can dare to work out your conflicts without aggression or recrimination," says Reverend Sutterlin.

3. Take "Time Outs"

If you feel you and another family member just aren't getting anywhere, or if you fear you're on the verge of saying something you might regret, take a time out. Go for a walk, cool off, pray or read scriptures, and agree to come together in an hour or so for another crack at it.

Taking the Creative Approach

Sometimes you can get stuck in a conflict because you treat it like a high school algebra problem and think there's only one right answer.

But one of the keys to solving problems is to think more broadly. "Conflicts might have any number of solutions," says Reverend Sutterlin, "each one as valid as the next. What families need to do is open themselves to the possibility that any number of roads may take them to their desired destination."

1. Brainstorm Solutions

Get together with the rest of the family and write down every possible solution you can think of to deal with the issue—no matter how crazy it may initially sound. Then, go through your list and see which ones all of you might agree on. This exercise may provide the foundation for some kind of solution, says Reverend Sutterlin.

SISTER ETERNAL

I loved you when, as cherubs
We played in heavenly spheres.
And then as children, growing,
Sighing, singing through the years.
I love you now, as women,
We share our hopes and fears,
Our laughter and our dreaming,
Our memories, prayers and tears.
But I'll love you even deeper
When our life on earth is done
And its sorrow and its heartaches
Are the wars that we have won.
Then when we are Guardian Angels,
Reassuring those still here,
I will love you even sweeter,
Oh my gentle sister, Dear.

—Sharon Lawlor

2. Use "Outsiders"

If brainstorming still leaves you stuck, ask a skilled but disinterested third party—perhaps a pastor—to come in and mediate the dispute. "Sometimes we're 'too close' to a problem to see the solutions," says Reverend Sutterlin. "At those times, a mediator might be useful in making suggestions or offering new perspectives that open up doors of possibility you didn't know were there."

3. Love, Honor, Cherish, and Tolerate

If despite your best efforts you can't solve your problem, or if the same problem keeps coming back and the stakes aren't very high, maybe it's time for one of you to shrug it off and let it go. "Living with one another can be a fairly

❧

A Prayer for Inward Peace

O Lord Jesus Christ, who didst say that in thee we may have peace, and hast bidden us to be of good cheer, since thou hast overcome the world: give us ears to hear and faith to receive thy word; that in all the tensions and confusion of this present time, with mind serene and steadfast purpose, we may continue to abide in thee.

—*Frederick MacNutt*

messy affair," says Dr. Stahmann. "The pieces don't always fit." Just as the Hebrews had their squabbles on the way to Canaan and the King didn't always agree with Jeremiah on issues of governance, "sometimes one of us simply has to give up the fight."

Healing Old Wounds

Sometimes disputes get so out of hand that family members stop speaking to one another. Sometimes communication is cut off for years. It can be difficult for a family to get back together after an impasse like this—old slights die hard. But it's not impossible to renew the relationship. Here are some suggestions to get your family back on the right track.

1. Approach the Family Member Gently

Open up a dialogue with a brief note, a postcard, or a holiday card with a note attached, and simply say something like, "I was thinking of you and hoping you're well." "When years of bad blood have accumulated, a bold overture might be met with suspicion or fear," says Dr. Stahmann. "It's best to move cautiously."

2. Let Things Proceed at Their Own Pace

Ask God for the strength to endure what will be a very long process of discovery and healing, says the Reverend Peter Bridge, doctor of ministry, a marriage and family therapist, pastoral counselor, and clinical director at The Samaritan Counseling Center in Philadelphia. When you're trying to tear down barriers built in anger you need to work one brick at a time. Trust takes a long time to construct and requires immense amounts of prayer, patience, and faith that God will steer this relationship to a healthier place.

3. Find a Safe Way to Communicate

If you send a note and the other family member responds, write another one, and ask if the two of you can talk on the phone some time. If the phone call goes well, perhaps you can agree to meet for coffee and a longer conversation. Or, if the issues between you are too volatile to discuss alone, perhaps you can both agree to sit with a pastor or pastoral counselor and air your pain and anger in a safe setting.

> *Make sure you never, never argue at night. You just lose a good night's sleep, and you can't settle anything until morning anyway.*
>
> —*Rose Kennedy*

4. Put the Past in the Past

When you do meet, tell the family member you don't want to relive the past. "In the case of two brothers, for instance," says Dr. Stahmann, "one might want to say to the other, 'You know, when we were younger it seems as though the script for our relationship was for you to bully me around and for me to make a pest of myself with your friends. But you know, now I'd like to write a new script for us.' By doing this you identify the reality of the problem, cast it in the past, and invite the other person to move on to a new relationship."

5. Affirm Each Other's Goodness

When you speak, tell the other family member you care about them and hope this can work out. Then once or twice a week, reflect on the other person's goodness. "In a deeply entrenched crisis you can lose sight of the fact that you still care deeply for this person who you wounded or who wounded you," says Dr. Bridge. Thinking about the other person in a positive light can restore the good feelings, he says.

Overbearing Relatives

The mother-in-law who's forever criticizing your cooking, the uncle who outstays his welcome—these and other difficult relations can try the most patient souls. Here's how to deal with them prayerfully.

or years, Mary Dyer Hubbard, a pastoral counselor with The Samaritan Counseling Center in Ambler, Pennsylvania, suffered with a father-in-law who basically defined the word "overbearing."

He showed her little respect—"women didn't matter much in his scheme of things," says Hubbard. And he continually ordered around her and others, even going so far as to tell relatives what to eat at a family picnic. His actions created such a wall between them that even during the last month of his life as he lay dying of a brain tumor she found it difficult to be by his side, let alone show her familial foe compassion.

So she decided to pray to God to help her see another side of this controlling man. "I really prayed to help me see him as a son of God," says Hubbard. "By doing that, I was able to stroke his hair and hold his hand as he lay dying in a hospice. It felt like it was God's grace, not mine. I couldn't do that with sheer willpower."

Like Hubbard, you may have problems with a relative who drives you to the brink of insanity. The constant nagging, criticizing, and controlling ways may make you wonder what on earth anyone sees in the person, let alone God.

Relationships like this can become poisonous to you and to your entire family. But if you approach them with a prayerful attitude and take some practical steps, you may find you can live in peace with a difficult relative. Even if that's not possible, you can learn to reach a place of peace within yourself that will make it easier to deal with the person. How?

- Use prayer and understanding to see the person in a different light.
- Resolve your conflict in a peaceful and spiritual way.
- Set boundaries to protect yourself.

> *Behind every adversity lies a hidden possibility. . . .*
>
> —*Sufi saying*

Look with Different Eyes

After years of dealing with a domineering and oppressive relative, it may be hard to view the person as anything but a painful family appendage. That's unfortunate, for while you're focusing on your relative's exhausting manner or pushy delivery, you may be missing valid points the person has to make and other good things. The key to overcoming your feelings? Just as the blind man asked Jesus to help him see, ask God to open your eyes to your relative's perspective.

1. Honor the Divinity Within

In the Hindu religion, people greet each other by saying "Namasté," meaning, "The Divine within me honors the Divine within you." Using this principle as your guide, try to view your overbearing relative as someone who by virtue of simply being alive carries God's spirit within. "No matter what the person does, they have a Divine Entity that can be honored," says the Reverend Siegfried F. Haug, master of divinity, a psychotherapist and director of the Farmington Valley Counseling Service in Simsbury, Connecticut.

Not only will this make the relative easier to tolerate, but it may also improve your relationship. "To bring that kind of respect to a relationship often changes how they react back to you," Reverend Haug says.

2. Search for the Source

As a child of the 1960s, LaVerne K. Jordan, Ph.D., a professor of psychology at Olivet Nazarene University in Bourbonnais, Illinois, can't stand it when her mother tells her what to do and how to feel. Yet instead of losing her temper, Dr. Jordan tries to picture what's motivating her mom. "I know it is a

❦

LOVE ONE ANOTHER

Almighty God and most merciful Father, who has given us a new commandment that we should love one another, give us also grace that we may fulfill it. Make us gentle, courteous, and forbearing. Direct our lives so that we may look to the good of the other in word and deed. And hallow all our friendships by the blessing of your Spirit, for his sake who loves us and gave himself for us, Jesus Christ our Lord.

—*Brooke Foss Westcott*

deep sense of protectiveness, a deep sense of not wanting to see me get hurt," she says. Realizing that makes it easier to accept her mother's intrusions.

Also keep in mind that a relative's verbal slings and arrows may have little to do with you. In truth, your relative may be reacting because the situation strikes a chord within her. "If we are able to grasp where they are coming from, we might be able to notice a hurt in their past," Hubbard says.

Before reacting to your relative's assault, dwell on why the person feels the need to treat you badly. Prayer is a great way to see past your feelings and into the other person's heart, Dr. Jordan says. First, ask God for the ability to see the situation from your relative's perspective. Then ask for the ability to see it through God's eyes.

3. Pray for Your Relative

When Hubbard comes across someone she doesn't necessarily like, she prays for the person. She doesn't tell God what she thinks the person should do or how God should handle the person. She just leaves that up to God. "I pray that God gives them what they need," she says.

If you intentionally pray for your relative every day, you may find it easier to see the person in a different light. Hubbard used this technique with an overbearing colleague, and through daily prayer she learned to tolerate and then form a half-decent relationship with the person. "Within a month and a half I started to observe positive things about her. Praying for her enabled me to see her as a whole person instead of focusing on the faults that really bugged me," she says.

Try to Make Peace

When family members lock horns, a small squabble can quickly escalate into combat. "Any time you end up in a war situation everyone loses," Reverend Haug says. A better choice? "Use spirituality to align yourself with something above and beyond the conflict." Here's how.

1. Turn the Other Cheek

As it says in Proverbs 19:11, "A man's wisdom gives him patience; it is to his glory to overlook an offense" (NIV). Not every verbal jab or underhanded attempt at control deserves a response. Sometimes the best course of action is

GIVE ME STRENGTH

O Lord,

keep my lips from speaking evil, untruth, and deceit.

Give me the strength not to react against anyone who insults me.

Let it be my delight to keep your commandments

and help me to a full understanding of your laws.

Let me not be proud.

May the wicked plans of those who seek to harm me be brought to nothing.

Grant me wisdom, patience and understanding, mercy and compassion,

and give to me the means to live.

O God, who established the harmony of creation,

give peace to mankind and to Israel.

—Closing meditation of the Amidah

to do nothing, especially if it's a minor infraction that's not worth getting all upset about, suggests Charles A. Turnbo, president of Positive Solutions in Evergreen, Colorado. Just let it roll off your back. If that seems like a hard cross to bear, murmur a quick prayer to God asking for the strength to do so, suggests Turnbo.

2. Open Your Ears

If a nagging relative won't let up, your best defense might be to listen. Take a second to say: "You obviously feel the need to get this across. Why do you feel this way? I want to understand your point of view," Reverend Haug suggests. By simply showing some interest, your relative may give you some space, feeling that you've finally heard. When you show interest in the other person's perspective, it can lead to an "opening up of the heart," he says.

3. Explain How You Feel

When Dr. Jordan's husband says something that upsets her, she doesn't shoot back with angry rebuttals. Instead, she tells him how she interpreted his comments and why they bothered her.

His usual response: "I didn't mean it that way."

This same technique may get your overbearing relative's attention. Look at the alternative. "Leaving the room and getting angry doesn't let them know what they have done. They don't know how they are being perceived," Dr. Jordan says. Knowing that they come across as controlling or rude may make them back down, or at least express themselves in a less abusive manner.

Taking Care of Yourself

While you want to protect the feelings of even the most trying of loved ones, there comes a time when you must put that aside and protect yourself. After all, even the Bible says you can confront a relative if you feel the person has hurt you. "If your brother sins against you, go and show him his fault, just between the two of you" (Matthew 18:15, NIV). Here's how to state your case and stand your ground.

1. Pray for the Strength to Stand Up for Yourself

For many people, confronting a tyrannical person paralyzes them with fear. They'd rather tolerate the insults and injustices for the sake of family harmony. If this is the case for you, ask God for the ability to speak your mind in a loving and positive way. "Pray that you may have the courage to speak," Hubbard says. "Also pray to find out what prevents you from setting clear boundaries to protect yourself."

2. Set Some Limits

Your pushy daughter-in-law drops her two kids off unannounced—again—saying that she's got to meet some friends for lunch. But this time you look her in the eye and say: "I have no problem watching the children as long as you give me a few days notice. You are no longer to drop them off without calling ahead and getting my approval."

When nobody around you seems to measure up, it's time to check your yardstick.

—*Bill Lemley*

There's nothing wrong with laying down the law, says Hubbard. You're not being unreasonable by setting your own rules. You're not saying you'll never do it, just that from now on it's got to be on your terms.

3. Make the Consequences Clear

Hubbard's father-in-law often ruined the annual family picnic with his obnoxious ways. One year, she told him point blank that she would not tolerate it. "If you are going to be agitating and it is going to end up in conflict, I won't come," she told him. He backed down and she had a peaceful time.

If you don't declare what will happen if your relative continues to berate you, the person will often keep right at it, Hubbard says. But if you set forth the ramifications, your relative just might comprehend how important this is to you—or at least fear the consequences. "You need to make it clear: This is what I want, this is what I don't want. If you are not able to do this, this is what will happen," Hubbard says. "It is not an ultimatum. But you need to protect your own interests."

Shocking Family Revelations

When skeletons jump out of the closest, it can disrupt your life and bring you shame, doubt, and more. Here's how to use prayer and your faith to keep an event like this from ripping you and your family apart.

o many Bob seemed like the ultimate upright citizen: Wonderful husband with two lovely children, a former Eagle Scout and a scout leader, and vice president at a major banking corporation. His family and friends knew if there was one person you could always count on, it was Bob.

Until one day when Bob didn't come home for dinner. The next time his family saw him, it was on the evening news. He was being taken away in handcuffs for stealing almost $1 million from his bank and fleeing the country—with his mistress. For Bob's wife and family, it was as if their entire reality were a lie. The rock on which they based their lives crumbled right before them.

Whether it involves theft and bigamy, shameful secrets, or another traumatic situation, a shocking family revelation like Bob's has the impact of several deaths at once: It represents the death of your reality, the figurative "death" of someone you thought you had known well, the death of your way of life, and even the death of the trust you had in other people.

Clearly, while a secret itself is damaging, what it can do to you and your family after it's revealed can be just as destructive. For all these reasons, you must learn how to handle this skeleton in the closet in a prayerful and constructive way. Here's how.

- Be open with your emotions.
- Try to understand the why's of the situation.
- Release yourself and the problem to God.

Dealing with Your Emotions

Let us not look back in anger, nor forward in fear, but around us in awareness.

—*James Thurber*

Family secrets can be so overwhelming that people fall into a state of shock when they come into the open. In that state of shock, they don't truly deal with their feelings. "People often react with emotions when they find something out, but they never actually analyze what this means to them," says LaVerne K. Jordan, Ph.D., professor of psychology at Olivet Nazarene University in Bourbonnais, Illinois. To help yourself heal, you have to come to terms with these raw emotions.

1. Confront Your Anger

Once the initial amazement wears off, you're often left with one overpowering emotion: anger. You're furious with the person who did this terrible thing, angry with yourself, enraged at other family members who may have harbored this secret, and often angry with God. Instead of hiding or denying this fury and letting it eat you up inside, be open with it by taking it to God in prayer.

"Our relationships with other people are based on our relationship with God. If we can be honest with God we can be honest with the people around us," says Jerry F. Mock, Ph.D., a pastoral counselor in Carlisle, Pennsylvania.

So rage at God if you need to, admit how much you've been hurt. Then pass the anger to God, and "Let go, Let God."

2. Let Yourself Grieve

Before you make judgments about the person who has hurt you, before you take actions against him or her, mourn what you have lost. "When a family secret comes out, people need to go through a grieving process," says Sister Maureen Harrison, director of the Foundation for Religion and Mental Health of Wyoming Valley in West Pittston, Pennsylvania. Cry if you feel the need.

FOR A PERSON IN TROUBLE

O merciful Father, who hast taught us in thy holy Word that thou dost not willingly afflict or grieve the children of men: Look with pity upon the sorrows of thy servant for whom our prayers are offered. Remember him, O Lord, in mercy, nourish his soul with patience, comfort him with a sense of thy goodness, lift up thy countenance upon him, and give him peace; through Jesus Christ our Lord. Amen.

—*From the Book of Common Prayer*

Mourn the loss that this shocking event signals. Through prayer and meditation, ask for God's help to get through this grieving period.

3. Write It All Down

With all the confusion swirling around you, it may be hard for you to clearly get a grip on the emotional damage it has caused. To clear your mind, put pen to paper. Keep a journal or write a letter to someone—perhaps the person who betrayed you, or maybe even to God, Dr. Mock says. Write how this act made you feel, or write out just how this has affected you and your family. Even if you never send it, it often lets you straighten out your thoughts.

Walking in the Other Person's Shoes

Some shocking family revelations are so horrible that they require no processing to understand that they are wrong: Uncle Charlie is a bigamist, cousin Fred deals drugs to minors. But there are cases where condemnation is not so simple. Not everything people do in life is perfectly black or white. If you learn your father is not your biological father or that an aunt's "stay" at a hospital was really a commitment to a mental institution, you initially may be angry at being kept in the dark. But seemingly unthinkable acts like these may be what people thought best under the circumstances. So in some instances you may want to try to understand what prompted the family member to act. How can you gain this understanding?

1. Seek Another Perspective

Long after her mother died, Mary learned that she was not an only child. Her mother had another baby girl years before she was married and had given up the infant for adoption. Her mother never said a word to anyone. Mary only found out when the adopted woman approached her while looking for her birth mother.

Of course, Mary felt angry and betrayed, but it was important that Mary not stop at that point, says Dr. Jordan. She needed to look past her pain and think about the situation in which her mother made her decision. "Think about the times her mother was in. A single woman in the early 1940s with a baby didn't have many choices," Dr. Jordan says. Also, the stigma attached to her secret may have made her fearful of revealing it to anyone even as she grew older.

Looking at the situation through the other person's eyes can help you better understand why they did what they did, even if you don't approve of it, Dr. Jordan says.

HELP THESE TROUBLED LOVED ONES

Lord, I come to you on behalf of my loved ones who are going through a stormy situation right now. I hang my hope, faith, and trust on your strong right arm reaching out to save. Use me as an instrument of peace and reconciliation in my family. I stand as an intercessor for them, asking you to continue to give me a prayer strategy until they come through this crisis. Just as you quieted the storm for your disciples who were so afraid, I pray you will quiet the storm in the lives of _____. In Jesus' precious name I pray, Amen.

—Quin Sherrer and Ruthanne Garlock

2. Pray for God's Perspective

Perhaps you need the input of a third party to help you come to grips with the objectionable behavior. If so, turn to God, suggests Dr. Jordan. Ask God for the ability to see the situation as objectively as possible. Your prayers may help you understand—or at least come to terms with—what the person did.

3. Focus on the Whole Person

Each person's life is a tapestry of actions and events. To follow just one thread doesn't give you a complete picture of the entire work, Dr. Jordan says. That's not fair to the person you know has good qualities.

To put things in perspective, make a list of the good things about the person who betrayed you: Was he kind to you? What good has she done for others? Were there happy times? By looking at the good with the bad, you may be able to accept the person, if not the action. In some cases, one mistake should not tarnish a lifetime of goodness.

Learn to Let Go

No matter how traumatic a revelation may be, one fact is clear: There is probably not much you can do about it. That's not to say you must just forgive and forget. But you must not let something over which you have no control de-

REVIVE MY TRUST

It is hard to trust when we have been hurt. It is hard to hope again when we have known tragedy. It is hard to stop flinching, to stop responding to past pains. It is hard to face the present with an open heart. Help me, God. Restore me. Revive in me all the optimism that I once had. Remind me of the person I used to be. Help me to return to life, to openness, and to You, my God.

Amen.

—Rabbi Naomi Levy

stroy your own life. After grieving and coming to terms with the revelation, you must move on by using steps like these.

1. Create a "Letting Go" Ritual

To get past a serious problem, many people find it helps to perform an act to represent letting go. "Rituals enable you to visually and emotionally release yourself from a situation," Dr. Mock says. If you're caught in an emotional web, plan a private prayer service where you'll release your anger and frustration to God. If the family secret involves someone who has passed away, you might perform a ritual at his grave. Whatever you decide, make it personal, Dr. Mock says.

We have been created to love and to be loved. As the Father has loved me, we will love one another.

—Mother Teresa

2. Surrender It to God

If you have trouble accepting your inability to fix or undo a shocking revelation, pray for the power to accept this truth and move on. "If we think that we are in control of everything, that's when we go crazy," Dr. Mock says. "You must say to yourself and God: I can only do what I can do, then I need to let go. Surrender it to the power that is outside of us."

3. Ask God for the Ability to Trust Again

When the people you trust the most do something outrageous, it's hard to have faith in anyone else. While it may be difficult, keep in mind that the actions of one person do not reflect everyone. Also, pray to God and ask God to restore your trust in those who earn and deserve it.

CENTERING PRAYER

Opening Yourself Up to God

Noise. Our lives are filled with it. The noise of commitments, of distractions, of stress. We're too busy being busy to be with God.

Centering prayer is an antidote to that, a way of saying: Stop the world, I want to get off. Centering prayer quiets you down and lets you listen to the whisper of the Spirit, leading you beside still waters, calling you home.

The practice of centering prayer is ancient, going back at least to the "desert fathers" of the second century A.D. These Christian hermits lived in the deserts of the Middle East, praying constantly. For centuries the centering prayer tradition was kept alive mainly in Catholic monasteries, but that changed in the 1970s. The growing popularity of Eastern meditation techniques caused two Cistercian monks, Father Thomas Keating and Father M. Basil Pennington, to begin teaching centering prayer to outsiders. A contemporary movement was born that has now been widely adopted by various Protestant groups.

There are two things you need to practice centering prayer: 20 minutes of quiet time and a prayer word. The prayer word will become your signal, to yourself and to God, that you are ready and willing to recognize the presence of God within you and around you. It is the prayer equivalent of saying, "I do." "Abba," "Mother," "Father," "Jesus," "Mary," "Love," "Yes," and "Shalom" have all been used as prayer words. Choose one of these or another word that feels right for you and begin.

Sit comfortably with your eyes closed. Settle briefly, then silently begin saying your prayer word to yourself. When you become aware of thoughts, sensations, feelings—any perception whatsoever—return your attention gently to the sacred word. Do this for 20 minutes or so. At the end of that time, remain in silence with your eyes closed for a couple of minutes. Take a deep breath and open your eyes. You're done.

The power of centering prayer derives in large part from its elegant simplicity, says the Reverend Carl Arico, a priest in the archdiocese of Newark, New Jersey, who has studied and practiced centering prayer for more than 25 years. You present yourself to God, you listen for God, you rest in God. Nothing more, nothing less. For Father Arico, the word "consent" captures the essence of what centering prayer is all about. "You consent to the presence and action of God," he says.

Centering prayer bears some similarities to Zen meditation, but there are important differences. The point of centering prayer is not to empty the mind of thoughts, but simply to allow thoughts to gently come and go. The mind is cleared of distractions not so much to transcend the self, but to experience the presence of God.

Nor is the sacred word a "mantra" on which you focus your attention, as in Hindu and Buddhist meditation. Rather, it is a reminder. By restating it, you remind yourself that you are in God's presence and that all you want to do is to remain attentive to that Divine presence. Father Arico compares it to being in a sailboat on open water: You put your sail up and trust that the wind will carry you forward. "God takes care of the rest," he says.

Father Arico recommends practicing two 20-minute sessions of centering prayer a day, one in the morning, one at night. The peacefulness of that time will begin to spill over into everything you do, so that more and more you will be conscious of walking with the Lord on a continuous basis.

Part 6

FRIENDSHIPS FOR LIFE

Finding True Friends

Friends can be among the most important blessings in your life.
If you're struggling to find some, here's advice on where to look,
how to nourish your relationships, and how to show your
friends you cherish their company.

riendship is in danger of becoming a lost art.

Through much of history, friends were placed on a par with marriage and family in the well-bred person's constellation of meaningful relationships. Now, all too often they've become an afterthought. "Whatever happened to friendship?" asked a headline in the *Wall Street Journal*, adding, "In this overstressed, hyperlinked age, some people seem wired to everything but each other."

What we forget as we rush from here to there is that friendship can fulfill needs in us that work and family don't. That becomes painfully clear when a breakdown occurs on either of those two fronts. Getting fired or divorced makes us appreciate—too late, in many cases—how isolated we've become.

We also tend to forget that friendship is a holy thing. God uses our friends as channels of the Holy Spirit: We are nourished and healed by the love they give us and guided by the wisdom they convey. "Friendship is one of the most overlooked means of grace in our lives and one of the most overlooked sources of support for spiritual growth," says Timothy Jones, from Nolensville, Tennessee, author of *Finding a Spiritual Friend*.

If you'd like to rediscover the blessings friendship can bestow, Jones and others who have studied the spiritual dynamics of friendship say the path lies in following three basic steps.

There is nothing on this earth more to be prized than true friendship.

—*Saint Thomas Aquinas*

- Open your eyes wide and look for true friends where true friends can be found.
- Learn how to build meaningful friendships that stand up to the tests of time and temperament.
- Take the risks necessary to turn good friends into spiritual friends.

Looking in All the Right Places

It can be one of life's sadder realizations: You wake up one day and realize you don't really have any true friends.

What happened? Any number of things. You may have gotten divorced or moved to a new city, or maybe you simply weren't paying attention. It happens. The question now is, what are you going to do about it?

A lot of people say they have trouble finding real friends, but good friends *are* out there. You just need to know where and how to look.

1. Pray for Friends

If it's true that God speaks to us through our friends, then it stands to reason that God also will put those friends in our path. Therefore prayer is "the first and perhaps the most important step" in seeking true friendship, says Jones.

How should you pray? In his book on friendship, Jones quotes a close friend of his who asked for God's help using this simple prayer: "Lord, bring along the kind of person I need."

2. Plug In Where You Fit

If you want to meet people who might turn into friends, the obvious places to look are those where people with similar values and interests congregate: church, the PTA, another friend's dinner party. But don't stop there. Try volunteering. Working alongside people on a project for Habitat for Humanity or the Sierra Club can make getting to know them easy and fun.

Another smart move is to tell your pastor that you're lonely and need his advice on finding friends. Church leaders are often connected to vast social networks and can help tie you in.

Bring Us Together

Oh, God, we go through life so lonely, needing what other people can give us, yet ashamed to show that need.

And other people go though life so lonely, hungering for what it would be such a joy for us to give.

Dear God, please bring us together, the people who need each other, who can help each other, and would so enjoy each other.

—*Marjorie Holmes*

3. Keep Your Eyes Open

You've heard about missing the forest for the trees? The same thing applies to finding a friend, Jones suggests. Your new friend may be sitting next to you on the bus, standing in line behind you at the supermarket, or working out on the next treadmill at the health club. Keeping yourself open to chance encounters will prevent you from walking past the friends God would have you meet.

The Art of Being a Friend

When it comes to defining the rules for successful friendship, The Beatles probably said it best: "The love you take is equal to the love you make." To have a friend, it's important that you know how to *be* a friend.

Here are some basic rules of thumb that will help you reach that goal.

1. Pay Attention

Perhaps the most fundamental obligation you owe a friend is presence, says Robert M. Hamma, coauthor of *A Circle of Friends: Encountering the Caring Voices in Your Life*. Presence means that you make yourself available to your friends, that you're *there* for them, consistently.

Sometimes being there entails giving advice, sometimes helpful criticism, but most of all it means offering encouragement, support, and an attentive, sym-

HELP ME VALUE FRIENDSHIP, GOD

*When I am feeling self-pity, God, help me to see beyond myself.
When I am feeling despair, restore me to hope. When I shut people
out, help me to believe in the healing power of companionship. Remind me that I am not alone, that I am needed, that I am heard,
and that You are with me, now and always.*

Amen.

—Rabbi Naomi Levy

pathetic ear. Whether you're talking over a morning snack or over the Internet,
whether you're sending a card on your friend's birthday or making a point to call
when she's down, loving presence is the essence of what friendship is all about.

2. Keep Your Commitments

If friendships are vehicles of grace, then time spent with a friend is "sacred
time," says Mary E. Hunt, Ph.D., cofounder and codirector of the Women's Alliance for Theology, Ethics and Ritual (WATER) in Silver Spring, Maryland, and
author of *Fierce Tenderness: A Feminist Theology of Friendship*. This is true even
if you just intend to meet for coffee. "Once that date is in your appointment
book, it's as important as going to synagogue or church," she says.

3. Practice Patience

Friendships inevitably evolve and change. Roles shift, needs fluctuate. One
month you're the one who's in a crisis; the next month the role may be reversed
and it's your turn to listen. Maybe you and your friend have attended the same
church forever, but now the pastor is leaving to start a new parish across town.
You're going to change churches with the pastor but your friend wants to stay
put. Or maybe a couple you love gets divorced and suddenly your friend starts
dating someone you don't really like.

Can friendships survive these sorts of fluctuations? Only with patience,
Hamma believes. "Patience is the willingness to stay with the relationship as
both friends evolve, sometimes in different ways," he says. "Patience is also re-

alizing that 'I will be there to meet my friend's needs, as much as he'll be there to meet mine.'"

4. Persevere

A friendship can resemble a marriage. Its very intimacy makes both partners vulnerable to disagreements, misunderstandings, and hurt feelings. Friendships that last are those in which the partners stick with it.

In ancient times, monks entering monasteries took a "vow of stability," Jones says. "This vow signified that the monk intended to stay with the community, even though he realized there'd be times he wouldn't be able to stand the people he was living with."

As friends we need to take similar vows, even if we do so only silently. "In any friendship, there's going to be ups and downs," Hamma says. "During the bad times, we need to remember the good times we had in the past, and also hope for where we might go in the future."

5. Tell the Truth

While it's true that your main job in a friendship is to offer encouragement and support, Hamma says, at times it may be necessary to tell a friend something he or she may not want to hear.

MAKE ME A GOOD FRIEND

Lord, where would we be without our friends?
They give us of themselves unselfishly,
they stand by us in trouble,
in happiness they share our laughter,
they make life more colorful.
Make me a good friend,
ready to help but not to interfere,
loyal but not uncritical,
open rather than exclusive,
dependable at all times.

—From More Everyday Prayers

If your friend is about to take a new job you feel certain she'll hate, at some point you probably owe it to her to tell her your opinion. If another friend is infatuated with some sweet young thing and is about to divorce his loving wife, you need to warn him before he plunges off the cliff.

Sometimes the warning you're sounding won't be welcomed, Hamma acknowledges, but that's a risk a true friend will be willing to take.

Many Christian evangelicals take on this practice by hooking up with "accountability" partners. Such friends get together and call one another on a regular basis to discuss problem areas in their lives. Say one person is prone to fits of anger that are often directed at his wife and children. The person would let his accountability partner know that this was an issue he's struggling with, and the friend would make a point of checking in with him regularly to see how he's doing in his battle with that particular sin.

The point is not to become a scold or a moralizer, says Jones, but to help one another remember what may have been forgotten. "A friend can remind us what we know deep down," he says, "but may have forgotten in the press of the moment."

Taking It Deeper

All friendships are not created equal.

Some friends are great to talk to about kids, others share your love of music, others are there for you when you're angry at your spouse. And then there are the friends with whom you can talk about God.

"Spiritual friendships," Jones calls them, and if you have one, you know they can be the most fulfilling friendships of all.

"A lot of times I'll hear people say that they want to be more attentive to either their friendships or their prayer lives, or both," Jones says. "What we often fail to recognize is that those two can go hand in hand."

Make no mistake about it: Every friendship is in some ways a spiritual friendship, and all friendships can be honored as vessels of the Holy Spirit. The difference with spiritual friendships is that the movement of the Spirit is discussed and explored, openly and actively.

Sometimes spiritual friendships come about effortlessly. If you meet someone in a Bible study class, religion will find its way into the conversation without too much effort. Other times you may need to take more concerted action to turn a "normal" friendship into something deeper. "Would you mind if we prayed about this together?" is one way to begin that process. Or simply begin, naturally and gently, to talk about whatever spiritual issue is on your mind that day.

However the door is opened, spiritual friendships, like any friendship, can be nurtured and cultivated.

1. Pray Together

Perhaps the essence of a spiritual friendship is that you pray together. Many people fall into this comfortably and easily; others do not. For the latter, there are alternatives to the more traditional forms of prayer, says the Reverend Carter Heyward, Ph.D., a professor at the Episcopal Divinity School in Cambridge, Massachusetts and author of *Saving Jesus from Those Who Are Right*.

> *Friendship is like a step to raise us to the love and knowledge of God.*
>
> —*Aelred of Rievaulx*

For example, Dr. Heyward has a Buddhist friend with whom she regularly meets for lunch. Afterward, they often make a point of simply sitting together in silence for 15 minutes or so. Both are keenly aware of the deep connection between them during this time.

Another possibility is to simply take a quiet walk together. Participating in some form of social action or ministry together also can be a particularly powerful form of mutual prayer with spiritual friends, Dr. Heyward adds.

2. Acknowledge What You Have

Friendships, like romantic relationships, have their own rhythm, and you probably won't feel it's appropriate to declare your spiritual friendship to someone you've only had coffee with once or twice. But when the time is right, confirming the specialness of a spiritual friendship explicitly can cement the bond between you in a meaningful way. "Naming something is a powerful statement," says Hamma.

You don't have to be gushy about it, he adds. Saying something along the lines of, "I'm really grateful for being able to talk about these kinds of things with you" will get the point across nicely.

3. Keep the Balance

Spiritual seekers throughout history have often associated themselves with mentors or teachers who lead them on the path to enlightenment—Jesus and the twelve disciples are one familiar example.

Ideally, in spiritual friendships, you and your friends will shift back and forth between the roles of mentor and student, says Hamma. Sometimes you'll offer the spiritual guidance; other times you'll receive it.

A spiritual friendship is more balanced in that way than a master-student relationship is, Hamma says, and is also more intimate.

Saving a Friendship

❦

Harsh words. A broken promise. Misunderstandings. Simple mistakes. These types of things can harm or destroy even the closest of friendships. Thankfully, with prayer, God's help, and some commonsense steps you can reverse the damage.

Phil is a photographer in Montclair, New Jersey, who is mourning a lost friendship.

He'd known Russell, another photographer, for about 10 years. They used to see each other regularly and confide in one another when either was having any sort of problem. Phil believed the bond between them was solid.

But eventually Phil began to feel that Russell was neglecting their friendship. Phone calls went unanswered, favors unacknowledged. Hurt and angry, Phil finally called Russell to ask him what was going on.

"I was kind of leading up to the subject," Phil recalls, "but then he actually broached it. He said he wasn't getting enough out of the friendship."

Phil was stunned and told Russell he'd like to hear more, but Russell said he was rushing out to a movie. That was the last time they talked.

"It totally mystified me," Phil says. "I don't know why it fell apart. It made me sad when I was making up the guest list for my 50th birthday party that I didn't feel I could invite him."

Friendships can be fragile things. An unreturned phone call, a misinterpreted remark, not to mention some overt betrayal of trust, and the fabric that ties two people together can be rent forever.

If you have all the friends you want, read no further, but if there's a torn relationship in your life that you'd like to heal, you can. People who have studied the art of friendship recommend you follow two basic steps.

> *Good friendships are fragile things and require as much care as any other fragile and precious thing.*
>
> —*Randolph Bourne*

- Heal the breach with insight, forgiveness, and grace.
- For more serious injuries, follow the Twelve Step approach to make your friendship new again.

First Aid for Friendships

We've all heard it said that "you only hurt the one you love," and perhaps that's because the people you love trust you *not* to hurt them. Trust makes us vulnerable, which is why so many friendships—like Phil's with Russell—get thrown off track so easily.

Many times, minor damage to a friendship can be repaired fairly quickly, if you take steps promptly to address the problem. Phil and Russell might still be buddies today, for example, if Russell had simply told Phil that he wanted their friendship to go deeper.

If you have a friendship that's struggling, use this five-step first aid program to restore its vitality.

1. Pray for Insight and Healing

It's often said that if we were able to understand what motivates people's behavior as God does, we'd have no trouble loving them as God loves them. That's one reason why prayer should be our first step in tending a wounded friendship, says Robert M. Hamma, coauthor of *A Circle of Friends: Encountering the Caring Voices in Your Life*.

If your friend does something that baffles and hurts you, ask God for insight into what might underlie her actions. Pray, too, for insights into any behavior of yours that might have caused or contributed to the tensions between you.

2. Pray for Forgiveness

If you can forgive your enemies, as Jesus urged, then forgiving friends ought to be a piece of cake. Right?

❧

BROKEN FRIENDSHIPS

*Dear God, lover of us all, do not let us go down into the grave with
old broken friendships unresolved. Give to us, and to all with whom
we have shared our lives and deepest selves along the way, the
courage not only to express anger when we feel let down, but your
more generous love which always seeks to reconcile and so to build a
more enduring love between those we have held dear as friends.*

—Kathy Keay

Maybe, maybe not. The fact is that forgiveness can be tough in any situation, says the Reverend Carter Heyward, Ph.D., professor at the Episcopal Divinity School in Cambridge, Massachusetts. So what should you do if you're finding it tough to forgive a friend? Turn to prayer, she suggests.

It may help to think of forgiveness as an act of generosity, a gift you can offer your friend out of love. So says one of the world's leading experts on forgiveness, Everett L. Worthington Jr., Ph.D., executive director of the Campaign for Forgiveness Research and author of *Dimensions of Forgiveness: Psychological Research & Theological Perspectives*. To grant forgiveness, Dr. Worthington recommends that you first state your commitment clearly and firmly to yourself. You may also at some point wish to express your forgiveness to your friend.

Having given that gift of forgiveness, Dr. Worthington adds, don't think that's the end of it. Resentments and hurt don't automatically go away forever just because you've said you forgive the person who harmed you. It's likely you'll need to renew your commitment to forgive—in your own heart, if not out loud—as long as the hurt keeps returning. (For a description of Dr. Worthington's five-step program for achieving forgiveness, see page 74.)

3. Acknowledge the Problem

Wounds tend to fester in the dark, but healing can begin when they're exposed to the light. That's why openly acknowledging that a problem exists between you—putting the issue on the table—is a key step in mending a broken friendship, says Dr. Heyward.

TWELVE STEPS TO FRIENDSHIP

The Twelve Steps of Alcoholics Anonymous (A.A.) have been adapted here to apply specifically to saving a troubled friendship. (To see a copy of the steps as originally written for A.A., see page 424.)

1. I admitted that I was powerless over the problems in my friendship and that they had become unmanageable.

2. I came to believe that a Power greater than myself could restore my friendship to sanity.

3. Made a decision to turn my will and my friendship over to the care of God, as I understand God.

4. Made a searching and fearless inventory of my side of my relationship with my friend.

5. Admitted to God, to myself, and to another human being the exact nature of the wrongs I've been responsible for in this friendship.

6. Were entirely ready to have God remove the defects of character which have contributed to the problems in my friendship.

7. Humbly asked God to remove those shortcomings.

8. Became willing to make amends to my friend.

9. Made direct amends wherever possible, except when to do so would injure my friend or others.

10. Continued to take personal inventory and when I was wrong promptly admitted it.

11. Sought through prayer and meditation to improve my conscious contact with God, as I understand God, praying only for knowledge of God's will for my friendship and the power to carry that out.

12. Having had a spiritual awakening as a result of these steps, I will try to carry this message to my friends and to practice these principles in all my affairs.

Tell your friend in plain but gentle English when you have a problem that's bothering you. Make clear as you do so that you're raising the issue because you value your friendship and don't want to see anything damage it.

Sometimes tensions, once brought to the surface, will simply melt away in the warmth of the mutual affection you feel for one another. If remedial action is necessary, Dr. Heyward says, a frank discussion of the problem is the best starting point. Talking things through can also help keep you from stumbling over the same issue again later.

4. Go Back to the Basics

When a surface chill has fallen over your friendship, Hamma says, you may be able to warm things up by going back to the interests that attracted you to one another in the first place. Let's say you first met at a book club: You could suggest reading a new novel together. If baseball is a mutual passion, tell your friend you have two tickets right behind home plate, and ask him to join you.

"Go back to your foundations," Hamma says. "Let something that you share in common that's not threatening be a way for you to reconnect."

5. Bring In a Third Party

If tensions are creating a distance between friends, sometimes a third party can help, suggests Dr. Heyward. Look for a mutual friend who can play the role of mediator and work with you and your friend to reduce tension. Mediation, Dr. Heyward points out, is a tool that is increasingly used in all sorts of negotiations, from arbitration of labor disputes to divorces—and it echoes the role Jesus often played in the Bible.

Work the Program

If you're looking for somebody who's had a lot of experience ruining friendships, ask an alcoholic.

No one knew this better than Bill Wilson, cofounder of Alcoholics Anonymous (A.A.). "The primary fact that we fail to recognize is our total inability to form a true partnership with another human being," Wilson wrote to his fellow alcoholics in the book *Twelve Steps and Twelve Traditions.*

For just this reason, restoring shattered friendships is one of the things Wilson and the other founding members of A.A. paid close attention to as they constructed the Twelve Step program. Although the steps are intended to be a model for reforming all aspects of the alcoholic's life, they also can be applied

RESTORE THIS FRIENDSHIP, GOD

My God, I must admit I'm not handling something well right now. What I mean is there's conflict in me. Some things just don't match, add up, allow for inner peace. At best, today the usual joy seems remote.

I confess that I'm angry, hurt, resentful, sad. So sad, my God. So sad.

What doesn't match is that for (fill in name) I feel deep compassion, tenderness, an ache so cavernous that only you can fill it.

She's yours and I love her perhaps not as much as I must right now. But you ask no more of me in this moment. I thank you: That I don't have to hide behind artificial feelings. That I can come to you just as I am, just as I feel. That you can restore all things that are damaged, broken.

Restore me.

Restore us.

—Reverend Virginia Hall Wilcox

to many specific problems, including damaged friendships, says Bill Lagerstrom, founder and director of Lazarus Ministries, a lay ministry program, based in New York City, focusing on the spiritual development of people in recovery from addictions.

Below is an overview of how A.A.'s program can help restore a friendship gone awry. (See page 424 for a list of the original 12 steps.) Some of its principles are similar to those just outlined, but they are applied in a more thorough and systematic way. As you work through the program, it will be helpful to keep a notebook in which you can write your thoughts on each step.

Be forewarned that the Twelve Step approach focuses on "cleaning up your own side of the street," as A.A. members put it, which means that it asks you to focus on your issues, not your friend's. This doesn't mean you need to accept responsibility for your friend's faults, Lagerstrom stresses. To the contrary, you may come to the conclusion when you've worked through the steps that you need to let a particular relationship go because your friend isn't willing to take responsibility for his or her part in the tensions between you.

For that reason, Lagerstrom recommends that before working each step, you repeat to yourself the serenity prayer:

> *God, grant me the serenity to accept the things I cannot change,*
> *the courage to change the things I can,*
> *And the wisdom to know the difference.*

1. Turn It Over

The first three steps ask that you recognize clearly that there are problems that are damaging your friendship, that you don't have the ability to control these problems, and that God can help mend them.

Note that step three specifically asks you to let God take over. "The implication is that there is something wrong with my approach, something that probably has to do with self-will," Lagerstrom says. "I need to turn my will over to God because at this point I don't know how to change that."

This is a clear invitation to pray. The book *Alcoholics Anonymous* (known in A.A. circles as "The Big Book") suggests this prayer for the third step:

"God, I offer myself to Thee—to build with me and to do with me as Thou wilt. Relieve me of the bondage of self, that I may better do Thy will. Take away my difficulties, that victory over them may bear witness to those I would help of Thy Power, Thy Love, and Thy Way of life. May I do Thy will always!"

2. Take an Inventory

Once you've acknowledged that there is trouble, the next step is to thoroughly examine the problem—take a fearless and thorough "inventory," as A.A. puts it.

Pay special attention as you complete your inventory to the role resentment may play in your troubles. "Resentment is the 'number one' offender," says *Alcoholics Anonymous*. "From it stem all forms of spiritual disease." Your focus, A.A. insists, needs to remain on your *reactions* to harms that were done, rather than on the harms themselves.

"We realized that the people who wronged us were perhaps spiritually sick," The Big Book says. "We asked God to help us show them the same tolerance, pity, and patience that we would cheerfully grant a sick friend."

After you complete the inventory, discuss what you've discovered with God and with a third party (another friend, a spiritual advisor, a therapist). Now you've completed steps four and five.

3. Pray for Release

In steps six and seven, you again ask God's help in healing the faults in you that have contributed to the problems in the friendship.

For this process to succeed, you must be, as the sixth step says, "entirely ready" to change. Many of us find it difficult to let go of certain troublesome characteristics that can stand in the way of healing our friendships. For example, perhaps your friend has withdrawn from your relationship in part because she feels you're too quick to tell her how she ought to run her life. You may tell yourself that you'll refrain from handing out advice, but if you still secretly believe you know better than she does what she should do, that attitude is likely to come across. And it will continue to damage your friendship.

4. Make Amends

The word "amend" means more than simply apologizing, says Lagerstrom: It means to "make as new." And that is what you will do by following steps eight and nine in the A.A. program.

State directly to your friend that there has been an issue between you and that you are willing to accept responsibility for your part in it. Also, express your willingness to make up for whatever harm you might have caused.

RELEASE THIS RESENTMENT

Soften my hardened heart, God. In my suffering I have grown callous and unforgiving. Secretly I've been wishing for my friends to fall. Teach me, God, to cherish all that I am, all that I have, all that I have yet to offer. Help me to rejoice in the joy of others even when I am in pain; to take pleasure in their pleasure; to wish them nothing but blessings and peace.

Amen.

—Rabbi Naomi Levy

Besides being willing to change your own behavior, repairing the relationship may include forgiving your friend his faults. "This is where wisdom and generosity come in," Lagerstrom says. "You put aside your own resentments to help the other person if he was at fault."

> *There is a magnet in your heart that will attract true friends. That magnet is unselfishness, thinking of others first. . . . [W]hen you learn to live for others, they will live for you.*
>
> —*Paramahansa Yogananda*

5. Practice Ongoing Vigilance

Once your friendship is back on track, you need to exercise vigilance to keep it there. Steps ten, eleven, and twelve, which A.A. members often call the "maintenance steps," are designed for just that purpose. "We save our friendships every day," says Lagerstrom. "This is ongoing work."

The tenth step specifies that we continue to look for emotional land mines—resentments, emotional baggage from the past, personal weaknesses—that can go off, damaging the friendship once more. If you discuss these issues honestly with your friends, the relationships will continue to grow deeper, more honest, and closer over time.

The eleventh step encourages you to keep bringing God into your friendship, Lagerstrom says. Ask yourself, "What does God want from this friendship?" and "What is God telling me through this friendship?"

The twelfth step wraps it up. By working through the twelve steps, you prepare yourself to move forward with your friendship on a much sounder basis than before, practicing the principles of the program on a daily basis. Having had a spiritual awakening, you now can appreciate what friendship is worth and what you need to do to ensure that your friendships stay healthy.

Helping Friends in Need

When misfortune strikes a true friend, surely you'll want to open your heart and help. But being effective requires more than good intentions, say counselors. You need to set aside your opinions and desires and prayerfully help your friend work through the problem on her own.

I f ever there was someone in need of a friend, it was Job.

To prove Job's faith was steadfast, God let the devil inflict him with all sorts of woe. Job's 10 children, most of his servants, and all of his livestock were killed on the same day. Job himself broke out in painful, ugly boils. People even began to talk about him behind his back, questioning whether he'd committed some horrible sin that incurred such wrath from God.

How did his true friends react? They went to his house to comfort him and sat with him for seven days and nights, never uttering a word.

This may seem an odd way for friends to respond, but religious counselors say listening quietly is actually one of the four best prescriptions for helping a friend in need. The other three:

- Probing thoughtfully
- Showing you care
- Maintaining your own energy so you can provide the support your friend needs

Let's take a look at each of these solutions.

Loving Acts of Silence

One of the best things you can offer a friend in need—whether your friend has an emotional dilemma or a life threatening illness—is a quiet ear. Sounds simple enough. But few people can master the art of quiet listening, says the Reverend Clayton L. Thomason, J.D., assistant professor of spirituality and ethics at Michigan State University in East Lansing.

To console does not mean to take away the pain but rather to be there and say, "You are not alone, I am with you. Together we can carry the burden."

—Henri J. M. Nouwen

He speaks from experience. During the workshops he runs for medical school students, Reverend Thomason divides participants into groups of three. One person in the group unloads a problem, another person guides the conversation, and a third simply listens. No uh huhs. No interrupting. Just listening. "It's very hard for people. When you look at them 10 minutes into the exercise you would think they were having their teeth pulled without anesthetic," says Reverend Thomason. "Then, a little longer and they are liberated. They're one with simply being present."

While difficult, quiet listening is important, say counselors. Your friend needs to talk and needs someone to hear her concerns. Your role isn't to solve your friend's problem or make things better. Rather, by listening quietly, you are offering the best type of comfort a friend can offer—your time. By listening, you are saying "I love you."

You can lend quiet support in five ways.

1. Make Sure You're Welcome

Some people need space when struggling with a problem. So always ask, "Is this a good time?" or "Would you like to talk about it?" Sometimes the an-

GIVE US PEACE

O God, give us peace, give us contentment, give us good fortune.

Let no one curse us. Let no one have evil thoughts about us. Let all think well of us.

Give us rain when we sow our crops. Give us sunshine when we harvest our crops.

Let those who are sick be healed. Let those who are ready to die go in peace.

—Prayer of the Wapokomo tribe

swer will be yes, sometimes no. Be prepared for either. If your friend doesn't want to talk, ask, "Is it comforting for you to have me here?" If the answer is yes, just sit quietly, says Reverend Thomason.

2. Put Your Ears to Work

Focus on listening, really *hearing* what your friend is saying. Resist the urge to interrupt or to relate the words you hear to your own life. If you're unsure you can curb the impulse to speak, practice your quiet listening skills in a regular conversation first.

3. Don't Project

Even if you think your friend must feel a certain way about some problem, don't assume you're right. Ask, says Reverend Thomason. You could be completely misreading your friend's feelings.

4. Don't Play Judge

If your friend is in an emotional or physical crisis—such as suddenly being laid off from a job or finding out her spouse has been cheating—she may not be thinking as clearly as you are. For instance, your friend may say things you know aren't true, such as, "That company was run by a bunch of

PRAYER FOR A FRIEND

O God, You care for Your creation with tenderness. In the midst of greatest pain, You offer hope. We are praying for our loved one, (insert name), whose spirit is lost, whose soul is in despair. She curses the day she came into life and longs for oblivion.

Let her feel Your pure love. Let her believe in the miracle of rebirth so that she can experience now a foretaste of the joy she will know in eternity. Amen.

—*Dimma, seventh-century Irish Christian monk*

---

evil sadists anyway," or "He'll come crawling back to me any day now." Comments such as these are okay at this stage. Don't shoulder the responsibility for setting your friend straight. Be there as a witness to what your friend has to say, not to what you have to say. And don't offer your opinion unless your friend asks for it.

5. Don't Play God

Realize that you're not expected to provide all the answers. "Once you recognize that the most valuable gift you have to offer is the gift of your presence, you'll feel liberated," says Reverend Thomason.

Exploring the Wound

When someone you know is struggling with one of life's biggest issues—a serious health problem, the death of a loved one, the loss of a job—you may feel uncomfortable being there. After all, your friend may be angry, depressed, or both. And sickness and grief are hard to deal with for most of us because they tend to make us think about our own mortality, says Reverend Thomason.

You may feel even more uneasy if your friend asks you one of those unanswerable questions, such as, "Why is this happening to me?" Yes, times like these are difficult, but there are thoughtful, spiritual ways to respond to your friend's needs. If she asks you a question or indicates a desire for verbal consoling, it's perfectly appropriate to break your silence and try to comfort in one of the following ways.

1. Share Your Feelings

Say your friend asks your opinion about her problem. Feel free to say, "This stinks," "I wish this wasn't happening to you," or "I wish I could do or say something that would make you feel better." While none of those statements will make the hurt go away, they help make your friend feel more comfortable talking to you about her problem, says the Reverend J. William Lentz, senior pastor at Wesley United Methodist Church in Bethlehem, Pennsylvania.

2. Be a Faithful Guide

If your friend asks you for guidance and you feel at a loss to provide an answer, you can:

- Ask questions that open a dialogue and help your friend find a solution. Possible questions: "Why do *you* think this has happened?" "What do

WHAT NOT TO SAY

Many times when comforting a sick or grieving friend, we unconsciously say things that make the hurt even worse, says the Reverend W. Sanford Ostman, associate pastor at Wesley United Methodist Church in Bethlehem, Pennsylvania. Avoid the following phrases:

- It was the will of God.

- Adversity builds character.

- No pain, no gain.

- There's nothing to be afraid of.

- You think you have it bad . . .

Q&A: How Can I Help Someone Who's Dangerously Troubled?

Q: I fear my friend may harm herself or someone else. What can I do?

A: Intervene, says the Reverend J. William Lentz, senior pastor at Wesley United Methodist Church in Bethlehem, Pennsylvania. When life is at stake, you need to move beyond your friend's feelings and focus instead on your friend's best interests, even if your friend personally wouldn't agree with you.

Reverend Lentz dealt with a situation like this while working as a peer counselor at Albright College in Reading, Pennsylvania. One day a student came to talk. She said she was doing poorly in her classes, that her parents had high expectations of her, and that she could not bear to let them down. She was contemplating suicide.

After talking with her and explaining that he didn't feel suicide was the right option, Reverend Lentz then told the university chaplain, who immediately visited with the female student. "She never talked to me again," says Reverend Lentz. "But I felt that her life was much more valuable than her never talking to me again."

you think is the meaning of (fill in the blank) in your life?" "Where is God in this experience?"

- Say, "I don't know." For instance, if someone asks: "Why has my husband left me?" respond: "I'm sorry there's no easy explanation for what happened. I don't have the answers but I'm here if you want to talk."
- Join your friend in prayer. When a bad thing happens, people often wonder how a God who cares for them could let it take place. Don't try to solve that mystery. Turn it over to God, suggests Reverend Thomason. Hold your friend's hand and pray out loud, "God, why is this happening?" Most people really aren't interested in your theology; they are looking for your approval and comfort, Reverend Thomason says.

3. Concentrate on Things Your Friend *Can* Change

If your friend is angry or depressed, help her focus on the present. For example, if your friend has a terminal illness you can help by asking: "How are you going to get your personal affairs in order?" or "Is there anyone you need to thank, forgive, or remind of your love?"

4. Share a Personal Narrative

If your friend feels hopeless and no amount of quiet listening or thoughtful questioning seems to help, feel free to share a story from your personal experience. How have you coped in your life with pain and suffering? What got you through it?

The Comfort of Small Acts

When a dear friend is hurting, you'd like to make everything better. You'd like to wipe away the pain, restore happiness, and set everything right in the world so your friend doesn't have to suffer, says Reverend Lentz.

MAKE ME A GOOD FRIEND

Help me, O God, to be a good and a true friend;

to be always loyal and never to let my friends down:

Never to talk about them behind their backs in a way which I would not do before their faces;

never to betray a confidence or talk about the things about which I ought to be silent;

always to be ready to share everything I have;

to be as true to my friends as I would wish them to be to me.

This I ask for the sake of him who is the greatest and truest of all friends, for Jesus' sake.

—William Barclay

THE VALUE OF FAMILIAR PRAYERS

One of the best ways to prayerfully comfort a friend is with familiar prayers, say counselors. These prayers can soothe because they bring back memories of when you learned them—when times were better.

Good examples include:

The Lord's Prayer

Psalm 23

The Apostles' Creed

The Rosary

That's just not realistic. And it's not a role you should try to play. Still, you can offer your friend comfort by thinking on a smaller level.

Kathleen Norris tells a story in her book *Dakota: A Spiritual Geography* about how her grandfather comforted a neighbor simply by doing the laundry. The neighbor's wife had died and left him with several small children. The neighbor began drinking heavily. But one day Norris' grandfather walked into the house, did the family's laundry and left, without chastising the man for drinking. The neighbor eventually pulled himself together and never forgot his friend's small gift.

As Sir H. Davy once said, "Life is made up, not of great sacrifices or duties, but of little things, in which smiles, and kindnesses, and small obligations, given habitually, are what win and preserve the heart and secure comfort."

Here are some suggestions of ways you can do such "little things" for your friend.

1. Fill Your Friend's Physical Needs

During times of sickness or crisis one of the best ways you can support a friend is by helping meet her everyday needs. That gives your friend the time she needs to work through her emotional or spiritual concerns, says Reverend Thomason. So, when you visit, consider offering comfort in one of the following ways.

- Bring a meal along or simply drop one off.
- Bring along some groceries.
- Offer to take care of various tasks like watering the plants, cutting the grass, or cleaning the house.
- If your friend is sick, offer to mop his or her brow or cover his or her feet with a blanket, or get your friend something to drink.

2. Offer Your Touch

Holding your friend's hand, hugging, and even rubbing your friend's back, shoulders, or feet will make her feel loved, says Reverend Lentz.

3. Say You Care in Little Ways

Send a sympathy card. Send inspiring quotes or stories by e-mail. Call and simply say, "I was thinking

Prayer Miracles

The Christmas Prayer

When I was newly married and had a child, we moved to Otis Orchards, Washington. Our nearest neighbor was acres away from us and I knew no one but an old lady by the name of Bea Culbert, who introduced me to the Lord.

Come wintertime, it was very, very cold and we ran out of propane to heat our little mobile home. I had to do what I could to keep the house warm for the baby and me. As I burned my books I cried. Then I broke apart the bookshelves to burn as well. By Christmas, there was no food, no propane, and no presents to offer my one-year-old, who had been born December 26.

I quietly knelt down and prayed, "Help me Lord not to feel so sad and selfish when so many in the world out there don't even have a roof over their heads. Please help me to be grateful for what I do have." I wiped my face and was preparing to boil the last potato when we heard a car approaching.

It was my neighbors from a couple orchards away. They said they remembered my son and me taking walks during the nice weather. They just wanted to stop by and drop off some things for the holiday. Following this neighbor came another, then another until a dozen cars had come and gone—each leaving a box containing gifts for our son, small amounts of cash or gift certificates, some propane or food, and so very much more.

When they left, my husband said, "I was never raised knowing this God you pray to but I now know He is real and that He hears you."

Franny Alvidrez
Rio Rancho, New Mexico

about you." Send flowers. All are small, nonencroaching ways to show you're concerned, says the Reverend W. Sanford Ostman, associate pastor at Wesley United Methodist Church in Bethlehem, Pennsylvania.

Nurture Your Soul

As chaplain for the LaGrange, Kentucky, police department, the Reverend Don Wright, assistant pastor at Covenant United Methodist Church in LaGrange, faces some challenging situations. One in particular left him feeling drained. A local teen had committed suicide. It was Wright's job to inform and comfort the teen's parents, who happened to also be close friends of his.

Too often we underestimate the power of a touch, a smile, a kind word, a listening ear, an honest compliment, or the smallest act of caring, all of which have the potential to turn a life around.

—Leo Buscaglia

After telling them what had happened, hugging, comforting, and listening, Reverend Wright was drained. He knew he would not be able to help much more unless he replenished his reserves. So he went for a run. Even though he felt dead-legged and sluggish, Wright knew the time spent alone in the outdoors would help. And it did.

Helping others is physically and emotionally draining, especially if you're helping someone you care about deeply. If you don't take time to nourish your own soul, as Reverend Wright did, you won't be able to really help. Here are some ways to replenish.

1. Educate Yourself

While distancing yourself may help in the short term, it doesn't do much for your friendship. So move out of that stage by researching what your friend is going through. Look up articles on the Internet or in the library that deal with your friend's problem. Talk to others.

2. Set Boundaries

People who are hurting or ill often take out their anger and frustration on the people who love them most, explains Debra S. Borys, Ph.D., a psychologist and assistant clinical professor of psychology at UCLA. If this happens in your relationship, remind your friend that you are only trying to help. If your friend still snaps at you, express what you are willing to do and what you are not willing to do. If you have to, leave and give your friend time to cool off, says Dr. Borys.

3. Replenish Yourself

Do whatever helps you release stress and rejuvenate your mind. For instance, when Pastor Lentz needs to replenish his soul after helping others all day long, he turns to friends to comfort him. He talks about what's on *his* mind. Other people get a massage. Others turn to prayer. Still others to nature or exercise. All are ways to give yourself space.

"Helping others can drain you. Allow yourself to walk away when you must," says Pastor Lentz.

PRAYING WITH
OTHERS

Gathering in the Presence of the Lord

When you say the word "prayer," the image that probably comes to mind is of an individual speaking to God alone. After all, that's how Jesus said we should pray in the Sermon on the Mount. But Jesus also said that wherever two or three are gathered in his name, he would be present among them.

Which way is right? Both, of course. In the first instance, Jesus was warning against making a show of praying in public to prove how pious and righteous you are. In the second instance he was discussing the way in which communities of believers can be confident and strong in the presence of God.

There is nothing quite like the sense of unity and community that group prayer can engender, whether the group consists of 3 believers, 30, or 30,000. Indeed, group prayer in a very real sense *creates* communities, says the Reverend Charles M. Olsen, a Presbyterian minister who directs the Worshipful-Work Center for Transforming Religious Leadership, based in Kansas City, Missouri.

"Group prayer turns 'I' prayers into 'we' prayers," he says. A transformation takes place: Separate individuals become members of a unified group. This group shares what Reverend Olsen calls a single "story," a collective history—a "family" history, as it were—that represents their journey of faith with God.

There are an infinite number of ways to pray with others, from prayers by the congregation on Sunday morning to a weeknight e-mail exchange between two or three believers sitting at their computers. Many Christian leaders consider the small prayer group movement, in which a handful of believers gather on a regular basis to discuss their spiritual lives and pray together, to be the single most powerful force in religion today.

Be creative in coming up with your own ideas for group prayer, Reverend Olsen suggests. Here are three unusual approaches he has found particularly powerful. All apply to groups of any size.

- Silent prayer: This is "the growing edge" of group prayer, Reverend Olsen says. A group of people simply sits, stands, or kneels in silence, focusing its attention on the presence of God. Make a point of allocating enough time here for the Spirit to begin moving within the group; five minutes would probably be a minimum.

  Silent prayer in groups takes some getting used to for those who haven't practiced it before—"people tend to get antsy and uncomfortable," Reverend Olsen says—but the results are worth the effort.

- "Popcorn prayer": This is a spontaneous form of group prayer in which the people gathered voice short prayerful thoughts. It helps to set a theme for the session—thanksgiving, for example, or confession, or requests for Divine intercession. The key is that the prayers be brief, popping out as the Spirit moves people. In a session, someone might offer thanks "for new life today," the next "for the grace of our children," a third "for the beauty of spring."

  "The beauty of popcorn prayer is that people don't have to frame their prayers in 'official' language," says Reverend Olsen.

- Singing prayer: This is a form of invocation-and-response prayer using as its recurring theme a line from a hymn. Individual members of the group offer up brief, one-sentence prayers, as the Spirit moves them. The group as a whole then follows by singing the chosen line.

  For example, Reverend Olsen has used this line from Charles Wesley's hymn, *Come Thou Long Expected Jesus*: "From our fears and sins release us/let us find our rest in thee." Each member would voice some sin or fear of the church or of his own. "Our fear of reaching out to the poor," for example. Or "Our sins against one another in gossip." After each confession, the group sings: "From our fears and sins release us/let us find our rest in thee."

  The repetition and rhythm of this approach cause the impact of the hymn's words to sink deeper and deeper into the hearts of the worshipers, Reverend Olsen says, with powerful results.

Part 7

YOUR WORKING LIFE

Difficult Boss
or Coworkers

What do you do if your time at work is more hell than heaven? Draw on your faith and prayer. They can help you build the courage to face your problems and the peace of mind to get beyond them.

A wake, awake, to love and work . . ."
At least that's what the old hymn encourages us to do. But what happens when work is not so much a labor of love as it is a test of faith?

If you work in a world where demanding bosses, unpleasant coworkers, and unyielding pressure are the norm, you may find that they challenge your religious strength every day. Yet your faith also can serve you best in an environment like this, say pastors and counselors.

Faith, along with prayer and some practical responses, can help you handle many of the conflicts and problems that arise. If the challenges get too great, your faith can help you develop the courage to walk away.

Pastors and counselors say you are likely to face three major threats at work.

- Coworkers who are deceitful, complaining, or threatening
- Bosses who are abusive or overly demanding

- Moral dilemmas involving the business your company is in or the people with whom you work

Here's how you can handle each one prayerfully.

Problem Coworkers

> *I will not permit any man to narrow and degrade my soul by making me hate him.*
>
> —*Booker T. Washington*

If you're surrounded by coworkers who are constantly hurtful, opportunistic, or deceitful, it not only makes your workday unpleasant but can also threaten your emotional and physical health. You have one goal in a situation like this—to keep *their* afflictions from infecting *your* life.

"The last thing you want is to let the circumstances of the workplace take you over," says Kirk Farnsworth, Ph.D., psychologist and author of *Wounded Workers: Recovering from Heartache in the Workplace and the Church*. "Even when you can't change everything that's wrong in your work environment, you can protect yourself from its poisons."

Specifically, here are five suggestions.

1. Pray before Work

While you're on your way to your job, ask God to give you the strength to cope with the coming day, suggests Michael Santorsa, a retired human resources consultant from Pocasset, Massachusetts, and former Passionist priest. "Ask God to be with you when things get rough. Ask that your heart be focused on good things. Ask that your actions embody good. And ask that your mind be open so you'll be aware if you stray from the right path," he says.

2. Avoid Trouble—When Possible

Stay away from the gossips, the saboteurs, the backbiters, and the chronic malcontents. "When you give credence to the inveterate troublemakers, you lower yourself as a human being," says Dale Klamfoth, a human resources consultant and area director of Drake Beam Morin in New York City. "And this is not what God asks of you." As it says in Proverbs 10:20, "The tongue of the righteous is choice silver; but the mind of the wicked is of little worth" (RSV).

3. Don't Play the Game

Let's say someone you work with is making unflattering and untrue remarks about you. They're not career-threatening—just hurtful. How should you react?

A Prayer for Serenity

Before me, may it be delightful.

Behind me, may it be delightful.

Around me, may it be delightful.

Below me, may it be delightful.

Above me, may it be delightful.

All, may it be delightful.

—*Navajo prayer*

Reject the remarks firmly—without emotion, without discussion—then, get on with your life, says Father William J. Byron, S.J., pastor of Holy Trinity Parish in Washington, D.C., and author of *Answers from Within: Spiritual Guidelines for Managing Setbacks in Work and Life.* "If someone rolls a ball in your direction, you don't have a game of catch unless you pick it up," says Father Byron.

4. Be Candid and Firm

What if a coworker is doing something that could damage your career? Then you should confront the person face to face. "Be calm, but direct," says Klamfoth. "Meet with the person in private. Say something like, 'Here's what I've noticed, and it needs to stop.'" This, says Klamfoth, sends the message that you're on to the coworker, that you're treating the problem seriously, and that you won't let it pass you by.

5. Appeal to a Higher Authority

If direct confrontation doesn't work, take your case to your boss, your foreman, or your human resources director.

Coping with a Difficult Boss

Bosses can be kind, wise, generous, and reasoned. They also can be vindictive, petty, stingy, irrational, and abusive. How do you keep your composure when the person you work for falls into the latter category? Start with prayer, say pastors and counselors.

What Would Jesus Do?

A coworker—perhaps someone you've trusted—has betrayed you by spreading malicious rumors or sabotaging your work. How should you react? Your first thought might be for revenge, but a better course is to follow Jesus' lead.

When Judas, one of His most trusted companions, agreed to hand over Jesus to the crowd in exchange for 30 pieces of silver, Jesus didn't react with rage. As Judas approached, Matthew relates that He greeted him as "friend" and bid him "do what you came here to do."

"There is sadness and resignation in that line, but no hint of anger or revenge," says Father William J. Byron, S.J., pastor of Holy Trinity Parish in Washington, D.C., and the author of *Answers from Within: Spiritual Guidelines for Managing Setbacks in Work and Life*. "A managed sadness, far stronger than anger, is the appropriate response to betrayal."

In fact, Jesus asked His companions to put away their swords when they moved forward to defend Him, saying in Matthew that "all who take the sword will perish by the sword." "This message is worth considering," says Father Byron. "If you try to live by the sword of retaliation in the workplace, you will surely die a workplace death by someone else's sword." A much better course is to greet betrayal with peace, patience, faithfulness, gentleness, and self-control, says Father Byron. "These values are your arms and armor."

First, pray for the power to stand up to what your boss may throw your way—this is your shield against all that may come. Then, pray for your boss. "No one can know what secret pain or fear or sadness might dwell deep inside your boss to make him act the way he does," says Klamfoth. "But what you can't get at, God can." As Jesus said in the Book of Matthew, "Love your enemies, and pray for those who persecute you" (Matthew 5:44, RSV).

2. Don't Flinch

Many bosses use rage to intimidate their staff. The quickest way to defeat this treatment is to greet it with calm and confidence. So if your boss blows her stack, be cool, meet her gaze, and recite to yourself: "Those who are hot-tempered stir up strife, but those who are slow to anger calm contention" (Proverbs 15:18, NRS). You may not change your boss's ways immediately, says Klamfoth, but if, over time, she learns that anger won't frighten you she'll have no choice but to respect you.

3. Carry an Icon with You

If you feel frightened by your boss's conduct, keep a favorite religious symbol—a cross, a star of David, a replica of a saint—in your pocket. When you're in a tense situation with the boss, slip your hand into the pocket and feel it; let it comfort you and remind you that you're not alone. "I wear a ring with the inscription 'Love one another as I have loved you,'" says Santorsa, "and it always gives me comfort in the midst of a stressful situation."

4. Meet the Issue Head-On

If your boss openly torments or abuses you, speak up. "In a calm manner, say to your boss something like, 'I think it would be helpful for you to know I'm uncomfortable with the way you're treating me,'" suggests Klamfoth. "Then tell him of your difficulties."

It's particularly important to address the issue head-on if the problem involves sexual harassment, says Father Byron. Immediately tell your boss that the attention is unwanted and unacceptable. You may even want to hold out your hand in a "stop" gesture and say "stop!"

5. Go over Your Boss's Head

As with a difficult coworker, your boss has people she answers to, and you can appeal to them to monitor the situation. Consult your employee manual or your human resources director to learn how to do this, and let your boss know that you have no other option but to bring someone else in on the problem.

When Morals Clash

Your boss has asked you to submit her dinner bill to the office comptroller as a business expense, even though you know she was entertaining friends.

LEAD US, LORD

In You we live and move and have our being;
We humbly pray that You will guide us
so that in all the cares and occupations of our life
we may not forget You.

—From the "Prayer for Guidance"

Your company's just been bought out by a firm that manufactures a product you find objectionable.

You find evidence that the shop foreman is covering up shoddy workmanship.

Issues like these can lead to a quick collision between your personal ethical code and your job. What do you do?

"It's desirable, of course, to be morally pure," says Dr. Farnsworth, "but it's complicated too; you have mixed allegiances and you need to sort them out very carefully."

There's no cut-and-dried formula for how to handle morally ambiguous work situations, the experts do offer some helpful guidelines.

1. Analyze the Situation

Be sure that there is a concrete moral breach. "If you think someone is passing off substandard work, or padding their expense account, or engaging in some other kind of immoral behavior, you have to be as certain as possible that it's not just speculation," says Santorsa. To make sure, you might talk to a trusted coworker and ask that person if she sees things the same way you do.

2. Meet with Your Pastor

Discuss the problem with your pastor so you can better discern God's will and guidance, says Klamfoth. You want to understand the consequences of any action you decide to take and allow God to direct your thinking.

3. Meet with the Offender

If you're certain something immoral is being done, confront the person you hold responsible and let him know your moral concerns, particularly if you are being asked to have a hand in what's being done. "If, for instance, your boss is asking you to submit falsified reports, you can tell him you don't feel comfortable with doing so because the report doesn't add up," says Santorsa. "Then ask him to handle it himself."

4. Report the Problem

If all else fails and you decide that morally you must act, report the situation to a higher-up, says Klamfoth. "See if your company has a code of conduct or a code of ethics and if the offending behavior violates that code," suggests Klamfoth. "Then, take the situation to your company's human resources director and ask, in confidence, what the company's procedure is for handling such concerns."

When Leaving Is the Best Answer

You may reach a point where the situation at work is so intolerable you feel you have to leave. Obviously, that will cause you some concern. "We all feel a tremendous amount of anxiety at the prospect of leaving jobs," says Dr. Farnsworth, "because they represent our livelihood, our income, and *us*. A large part of our identity, of *who we are*, we define ourselves by *what we do*."

If you find your anxiety rising, says Dr. Farnsworth, keep two things in mind: "First, you are who you are by God's grace, not by virtue of what you do to provide for yourself and your family. And second, God emboldens you to do what you have to do, because He stands by you, and in prayer and faith you know that you will not be abandoned." Then, with the right attitude in place, use your faith and the following steps to locate your next job.

> *When I'm in a well-paying job that supports my family but makes me miserable, I need to remember that my family may be getting the benefits of my work, but they're also getting my negative emotional baggage.*
>
> —*Kirk Farnsworth*

1. Pray with Your Spouse

With your spouse's help, ask God for the wisdom to know what to do and the courage to do it. By doing this, you define your decision as a family matter rather than one you are facing alone.

2. View Your Problem as an Opportunity

Don't just search the want ads for a similar job. Look at your problem as a wake-up call to pursue a new career. "God does speak to us in mysterious ways," says Klamfoth, "sometimes with the subtlety of a hint. When you feel stuck in a miserable job situation, you need to pray for discernment, to understand if it's God's will that you look at other ways to earn your living. After all, the apostles were all second career men!"

3. Create a Cushion

As a practical matter, if you think you may have to leave your job without having an immediate replacement, start saving. If possible, accumulate between 6 months' and 1 year's salary in the bank to carry you through your job search, says Klamfoth. "With all the pressure you can feel looking for another job, the one thing you don't want is a financial pinch that'll force you to take another job that's no better than the one you lost."

Job Pressures

❧

The strain and demands of work can overwhelm you if you let them. Instead, use these sensible tips and a spiritual attitude to shut them down.

P ermanent white water."

That's the term psychologists use to describe today's workplace. And it's appropriate. We live in an era where corporate mergers and downsizing are par, where long hours at a frenzied pace are the norm, and where the stress of coping with new technology is a given. It's no wonder many people feel overwhelmed by the pressures of their jobs.

But it's at times like these when your faith can be most valuable, says Krista Kurth, Ph.D., codirector of Renewal Resources, a management consulting firm in Potomac, Maryland, that helps people implement spiritual principles in the workplace.

When things are turbulent all the time, says Dr. Kurth, "the only way to navigate it is through spiritual renewal. To deal with job pressure, we have to come back to ourselves."

How do you do that?

- Bring your stress level under control.
- Integrate prayer into your work life.
- Cultivate job satisfaction.

Turning Down the Current

Job stress is something like overloading the electric current in your house, says Greg Schweitzer, a stress management counselor and owner of Stress Reduction Resources in Sinking Spring, Pennsylvania. Your lightbulbs work fine as long as they're running on 110 volts of electricity. But if you turn up the juice to 220 volts, you'll sizzle the filaments and end up sitting in the dark.

They who have steeped their soul in prayer can every anguish calmly bear.

—*Richard M. Milnes*

On the job, you're that lightbulb. And when you're overwhelmed by your work, maybe doing the work of three people, you simply burn out.

In a study on work trends, 88 percent of people said stress is a factor in their jobs, according to the National Institute of Business Management. So the chances are slim you can escape stress. But you can learn how to minimize it. Here's how:

1. Start with the Basics

Eat lots of fruits, vegetables, and whole grains. Get enough sleep, and exercise at least 30 minutes a day three times a week. A healthy regimen helps fortify body and soul against stress, says Diana Dale, doctor of ministry, executive director of the National Institute of Business and Industrial Chaplains in Houston.

2. Slow Your Pace

In our industrial, technological world, people often are asked to work at the same pace as machines, says Lewis Richmond, a former Buddhist monk and author of *Work as a Spiritual Practice*. That's not realistic over the long term. While you may not be able to lighten your workload, skip meetings, or postpone deadlines, you can find moments throughout the day to pause and mentally collect yourself.

For example, Richmond works in front of a computer all day. Once an hour he turns off the display screen and sits quietly for one minute in his chair, "staring at the welcome gray of the screen," he says.

Another option: Develop some habits that will help you slow down. Answer the telephone on the third ring, not the first. Instead of dashing down the hall to the copy machine, walk at 85 percent of your normal pace. When you take steps like this, you'll notice that your mind also stops racing. "These moments are spiritual because they are part of your inner life," says Richmond.

❧

A WORKER'S JOY PSALM

My Friend, hear my prayer, I fear today's plate is too full; too long is my to-do list with its down-to-the-wire work; so I need your help.

Dear Friend, as you are continually calling me to share in your life and work, I now invite you to come and share with me every work and event of this my day, the scheduled and expected things, as well as all the unexpected.

Beloved Friend, help me to load my every task with a full-hearted love and remind me of this prayer throughout the day so each labor may be a source of delight, an occasion of playtime with you.

—Edward M. Hays

---

3. Breathe

In Latin, one of the meanings of the word *spiritus* is *breath*. "Breathing is a bridge to a spiritual connection with ourselves," says Dr. Kurth. Yet many of us don't breathe deeply enough, especially under the pressures of our jobs. Then, when our breathing becomes fast and shallow, we feel stress. The following deep-breathing exercise will calm you on a physical, emotional, and spiritual level.

As you inhale, visualize yourself slowly breathing in a cloud of pure, white air. When you exhale, picture a cloud of dark air leaving your body with all the negative stuff in it. Repeat this pattern at least three times. While you're doing it, you may want to focus on an affirmative statement, such as *I am peaceful* or *God, my time is in your hands.*

4. Sharpen Your Ax

It's noon and you find yourself at your desk eating lunch while returning phone calls and wading through a stack of mail. Multitasking may seem great in theory, but the reality is that people are *not* more productive workers when they're doing three things at once. "Our brains are made to shut down every so often," says Dr. Kurth. It's a point she likes to illustrate with the following story.

Two woodcutters were having a contest to see who was the best in the land. The first one doggedly chopped down tree after tree. When he looked up, he noticed that the other woodcutter was stopping every hour to sharpen his ax and take a break. "Ah," he thought, "I will surely win the contest." Yet when the stacks of wood were measured at the end of the day, not only had the rested woodcutter cut more wood, but it was also more cleanly cut.

The moral of the story: You need to stop and take care of yourself to be productive, says Dr. Kurth.

Meditation is one way to sharpen your ax, says Schweitzer, who taught the technique to stressed-out workers at GPU Energy, a public utility company located in Reading, Pennsylvania. The training proved so helpful that some of the staff now meditate once or twice a day at work. In fact, an unused storeroom was recently converted into a quiet room specifically for that purpose.

Cultivating Your Inner Power

Just as physical exercise strengthens your body, spiritual exercise can strengthen your soul against the pressure encountered in the workplace, says Father William J. Byron, S.J., pastor of Holy Trinity Parish in Washington, D.C., and author of *Answers from Within: Spiritual Guidelines for Managing Setbacks in Work and Life*.

"Spirituality is your invisible means of support, your ever-reliable resource in keeping yourself and your career on track when the going gets rough," says Father Byron.

How do you incorporate your faith life into your work life?

1. Develop Your Spiritual Muscles

Fitness-conscious people work out regularly—sometimes every day. If you're concerned about spiritual fitness you should be just as conscious about "working in," says Father Byron. This means committing to daily prayer and reflective reading, he says. Also, you should remind yourself about the need to listen for God's voice in the circumstances of your day.

2. Find a Moment for Prayer

The bricks and mortar of your faith foundation are constructed from dozens of moments in the course of the day when you have the opportunity to pause in prayer. Let your commute become a quiet time when you converse with God, suggests Dr. Kurth. Stuck on hold or waiting for your computer to boot up? Use that time for a moment of prayer. Walking down the

A BUSY FRANTIC LIFE

How is it, my God, that you have given me this hectic busy life when I have so little time to enjoy your presence? Throughout the day people are waiting to speak with me, and even at meals I have to continue talking to people about their needs and problems. During sleep itself I am still thinking and dreaming about the multitude of concerns that surround me. I do all this not for my own sake, but for yours. To me my present pattern of life is a torment; I only hope that for you it is truly a sacrifice of love. I know that you are constantly beside me, yet I am usually so busy that I ignore you. If you want me to remain so busy, please force me to think about and love you even in the midst of such hectic activity. If you do not want me so busy, please release me from it, showing how others can take over my responsibilities.

—*Saint Teresa of Avila*

hall? Say a prayer to yourself, instead of thinking about how you're going to meet your goals for the day.

If your day is normally too hectic to allow for a few moments of calm, then it is important to set aside periods for reflection before and after work. Park your car at the end of the lot and use the extra minutes of walking for quiet contemplation.

3. Become Mindful

In the Zen Buddhist tradition, one of the first tasks assigned to novice monks is raking sand. Why? Because it's a very basic way for work to be experienced as a form of prayer, says Don McCormick, Ph.D., associate professor of management and business at the University of Redlands in California. The monks are told to pay close attention to body sensations, the sights, and the sounds as the rake is dragged through the coarse granules. When a thought intrudes, they note it and then gently push it away by returning their minds to the task.

"When we become more mindful of our everyday tasks, they can become a form of prayer," says Dr. McCormick. At home, you might start with a simple task like washing the dishes. Pay attention to each movement you make. Don't think about 10 other chores that you need to do. Simply focus on the task at hand.

Any task at work can also become a form of prayer—from signing a pile of papers to interacting with a customer—if you are mindful that everything you do has meaning.

4. Create Sacred Work Space

You probably don't have a picture of your boss on your nightstand. On the other hand, you probably do have a picture of your family on your desk at work. Why? Because it reminds you of what matters in your life, what has the most meaning. In the daily demands of work life, it's easy to feel disconnected from our faith life. Creating a small piece of sacred space in your work setting helps you remain centered, says Richmond.

Any object that has personal meaning can be used to create a feeling of sacredness—a collection of rocks, an inspirational quote, a copy of the Bible, or photographs. "Plants are good because you need to take care of them," says Richmond.

5. Talk with Others

If your coworkers will welcome it, engage them in conversation about spiritual issues. By doing so, you are inviting the presence of God into the workplace, says Dr. Kurth.

"You discover that there are more people interested in creating work that is meaningful and nourishing than you thought, and you not only get the support you need, but you also inspire and contribute to each others' growth," explains Dr. Kurth.

Finding Satisfaction in Your Job

Integrating work and spirituality is not about becoming more productive or profitable. Your ultimate goal is to turn a negative, pressure-filled situation into a more positive, peaceful one by living your faith in the workplace, says Dr. Kurth.

"As you gradually live more authentically by the values and ideas that you espouse, you not only experience more peace and meaning in your life but also have more of an impact on those around you," she says.

The end result is you feel more satisfied with your work. The effect is almost like having a new job. Here are three ways to renew your pleasure.

1. Look at the Big Picture

Job pressures build when you focus too closely on your own agenda. Instead, focus on the greater good in your work—view your work as service to God, suggests Judi Neal, Ph.D., director of the Center for Spirit at Work in West Haven, Connecticut.

There are two ways of meeting difficulties: you alter the difficulties, or you alter yourself to meet them.

—Phyllis Bottome

Make a list of the talents and gifts that you bring to your work. "We need to understand what our gifts are and how we are here to serve. Then each day becomes a new opportunity to share our gifts and be of service," Dr. Neal says.

2. Rediscover Your Passion

When your job means no more than a paycheck to you, it's time to rediscover your passion and look for ways to integrate it into your workday.

Dr. Neal coached a stressed-out executive at a telephone company who was helping to write health care plans for the organization. "It was okay, but it wasn't quite enough," explains Dr. Neal. "He couldn't figure out what was missing from his job." She asked him about his childhood and found out that he'd had tuberculosis. Because of his condition, he spent a year living away from his family. Through that conversation he realized that he was passionate about helping children and parents stay connected when a child is ill. And that became his goal. His work took on new focus. He began serving on volunteer panels and writing new policies for his company.

3. Discover Your Power

On-the-job pressure can also result from feeling like you have no control over your situation. A sense of uncertainty creates anxiety and erodes morale. This is where your inner power can take over.

"Regardless of our rank and station at work, we are each the chief executive of our inner lives," says Richmond. "No one can hand a pink slip to our soul."

To restore your own sense of control, make a list of areas at work where you have power and another list of all those areas where you feel you do not have power. Then complement each "do not have power" item with an inner power that can substitute, says Richmond. For instance, next to "I don't set my own salary" you might list " I do have inner power over my attitude about money."

Losing Your Job

Don't let the loss of a job devastate you. With optimism, persistence, and faith, you can use the experience as a blessing in disguise, a chance to start over, to become a new being.

Ask most people who they are and they'll tell you what they do: "I am a carpenter, a teacher, a truck driver, or a lawyer," they may say. In so many cases, the line between a person's identity and his labors is imaginary. That's what makes losing a job so hard.

"We have a good deal more than a paycheck invested in what we do for a living," says C. Wayne Dewar, a financial planner and founder of an unemployment support group at St. Matthew's United Methodist Church in Charlotte, North Carolina. "We ask our work to validate us as contributing members of society, to show that we deserve to be here, that we're productive, that we're carrying our load. When that gets taken away from us, it hits us hard."

Yes, losing a job affects everything about your life, from your family and your lifestyle to your sense of pride and self-esteem. But it needn't be something to be ashamed of, nor is it something from which you can't recover. As pastors and counselors point out, it can even have its blessings, offering you the opportunity for a new start, maybe in a new field of work, or even in a new town or state.

However, to get through this transition successfully, you need to concentrate on three areas.

- Use your faith in God to ride out the emotional turmoil.
- Turn to friends for advice and encouragement.
- Develop a good strategic plan for getting back into the job market.

There is always another chance. The thing that we call failure is not the falling down, but the staying down.

—Mary Pickford

Facing the Feelings

The loss of a job is like a death experience, says the Reverend John Vaughn, executive director of the Peace Development Fund in Amherst, Massachusetts. Just as with a death you're likely to mourn, get angry, feel lost and alone, and question why God has allowed this to happen.

This is normal, say counselors, and you shouldn't try to suppress it. Instead, admit what you're feeling and let it out.

"Venting your feelings is a little like cleaning out old pipes or going through detox," says Reverend Vaughn. "It gets a lot of poison out, clears your head and heart, and positions you with the right attitude to land that next job."

Here are five ways to get over painful feelings and get yourself going again.

1. Take Your Anger to God

"In prayer, tell God how angry you are that this is happening to you. You may even be angry at Him, in which case you should say so," says Reverend Vaughn. If you have doubts about turning your anger on God, read Psalm 22 ("My God, my God, why hast thou forsaken me?") and then Psalm 23 ("The Lord is my shepherd . . ."). These will remind you that God gives you the freedom to express your anger and still provides the support you need in hard times.

2. Talk through Your Shame

If you're feeling ashamed you've lost your job, share your feelings with your pastor, your spouse, and perhaps other people who have been through a similar experience. "If you talk it over with someone you trust, the other person can assure you that there's no need to carry that shame with you," says Dewar.

Besides, losing a job isn't all that unusual these days. "People used to be assured of employment until they were ready to retire, but now there's so much more volatility in the workplace that no one has that assurance anymore," says

❧

HELP ME THROUGH THIS CRISIS

Lord, make possible for me by grace what is impossible to me by nature. You know that I am not able to endure very much, and that I am downcast by the slightest difficulty. Grant that for your sake I may come to love and desire any hardship that puts me to the test, for salvation is brought to my soul when I undergo suffering and trouble for you.

—*Thomas à Kempis*

the Reverend Asa Hunt, executive pastor of the First Presbyterian Church in Houston. "People who lose their jobs should be reminded that they may simply be the victims of a new way of doing business and that their situation might have little or nothing to do with their own abilities."

3. Take Responsibility, If It's Appropriate

If you think you've been let go because of poor work performance, talk it over with a counselor or pastor. "Confession is good for the soul," says the Reverend Thomas Brown, doctor of theology, an adjunct professor of pastoral care and dean at the Interdenominational Theological Seminary in Atlanta. "If you've been unhappy at work, maybe it's shown through in the way you dressed, the level of work you did, the attitude you took. The only way to prevent this from happening again is to be able to say, 'You know what, I didn't like that job, and I didn't do my best work there.' Then, you can start with a clean slate."

4. Redefine Yourself

Meditate on Paul's passage in the Epistle to the Romans: "For we hold that a man is justified by faith, apart from works of law" (Romans 3:28, RSV). "What this little verse reminds us is that we are children of God, alive in our faith," says Reverend Hunt, "and that God's love for us is in no way dependent upon our works. It relieves an enormous burden when you remember that God is at work even if you are not."

❧

LORD, I NEED A JOB

I'm trying not to be anxious about this, Lord, but I'm coming to you with my need for a job. You understand all that has brought me to this crossroad. It's a scary place to be. Forgive my failures, Lord, and help me avoid those mistakes in the future.

I know you've not given me a spirit of fear. Your Word says you have given me a spirit of "power and of love and of a sound mind" (2 Timothy 1:7, NKJV). Help me to move ahead with confidence in you, trusting you to guide me and give me favor to find the right job. Thank you, Lord. Amen.

—*Quin Sherrer and Ruthanne Garlock*

5. Don't Panic

Remind yourself every day that you are in a transition time, with a beginning, a middle, and an end, says Reverend Vaughn. "Unemployment isn't for life, so there's no need to panic. Keep yourself calm and focused and, if need be, talk about your fears with your pastor and ask that he or she help allay them for you."

Creating a Security Blanket

Losing a job can be a terribly lonely experience, says Dewar, because "we think we're the only person this has ever happened to. We see others going to work each morning and coming home at night, and we feel as though we're living in a whole other world from them."

This isn't true, of course, but when you're struggling with a whole range of conflicting feelings it helps to get reinforcement, and strength, from others.

1. Give Yourself over to God

Pray repeatedly to yourself, "Thy will be done."

"We often acknowledge God's presence in our lives when things are going well," says Reverend Hunt, "but you really *need* that reminder when they're not. By saying this little prayer you stay focused on your ultimate source of security and find assurance in the knowledge that as you try to help yourself, God will help you as well."

2. Talk to Others Who've Been Out of Work

Ask your pastor or friends if they know anyone who lost their job and has since gotten another one, then go talk to those people. "By hearing someone else's story, you can derive hope that yours too will have a happy ending," says Reverend Hunt.

3. Join a Support Group

Many communities have established support groups for people looking for jobs, says Reverend Vaughn. "It is a place to pray together, lift up individual concerns, offer encouragement to one another, and be reminded that what you are going through is not your burden alone," he says.

4. Find the Joy in Your Life

Before bed each night, ask yourself if there was at least one moment of joy in your day's activities and record it in a journal. "Whether it's your daughter's report card, a whiff of spring air, or a promising job lead, when you remind yourself of the things that are right with your life, you are strengthened to deal with those that you're trying to right," says Reverend Hunt.

5. Give Your Time to Others

Set aside a little time each week to volunteer for a charity or your church or synagogue. "Volunteering alleviates your boredom, but more than that it re-

GIVE ME WORK

Give me work
Till my life shall end
And life
Till my work is done.

—*Inscription from the grave of Winifred Holtby*

❧

GRANT ME A JOB WORTH DOING

What is the work you would have me do, Lord? Please guide me that I may find a job that is worth doing so that I may live full of purpose and joy in serving you, my creator, and helping in this world, whether it be in small ways or with wider responsibilities.

—Phyllis Lovelock

---

minds you that others are in need as well, and that you have something to offer," says Dewar. "It is immeasurably strengthening to your ego."

Planning Your Future

A man flies into a new city, runs out of the terminal, jumps in a cab, and tells the driver, "Drive like mad, it's urgent!" So the driver speeds off as fast as his car will take them, until, about 20 minutes into the ride, the passenger says, "Where in the world are you taking me?" to which the driver answers, "Beats me. You only told me it was urgent; you didn't tell me where you wanted to go."

The lesson here is that urgency alone won't get you far, particularly in a search for a new job. You need to wed urgency to strategy and fortify the two with a strong faith if you want to make your job search as swift and painless as possible. To this end counselors and pastors suggest six steps you'll want to take.

1. Gather Your Resources

Make a list of income, savings, and expenses. Make another list of people who are willing and able to help you—family members who might lend you money, friends and church members who might help you learn about jobs, counselors who might offer to talk about your options. "Family and friends are here for you as God's angels in your midst," says Reverend Vaughn. "You should use them."

2. Spread the Word

Let people know you're looking for work. "So many jobs are obtained because of people you know, or people who know people you know," says Reverend Vaughn, "and while it's not always easy to share your situation with others, you have to trust that they care about you and are willing to look out for you."

3. Design a Resume

Develop a resume that emphasizes the skills and talents you've acquired over the years, not simply your past job experience. "By doing this," says Reverend Hunt, "you make yourself marketable in a wide variety of professions, not just the one you've left. In most cases people have more talents than they know." Some churches also have career counselors in their ranks, and you can ask your pastor if he or she knows of one who'd be willing to help you out.

Prayer Miracles

God Is My Copilot

Five years ago I was clinically depressed and out of work. I needed a good freelance job that had the flexible hours I needed to care for my son, decent pay (to continue my therapy), and a relatively short commute. The therapist I was seeing, who also happened to be a Presbyterian minister, told me to just tell God what I needed. She said that God listens and will help us if we just ask. It might not be the kind of help we want or expect, but it's ultimately the kind of help we need.

Well, the thought of just "telling" God what I needed sounded sacrilegious. But I was desperate, so I just started to tell God what I needed. I didn't sit back and wait for my prayers to be answered, however. I kept up an active job search, went on interviews, and sent out resumes. In a couple months I landed a job at a company that was "working-mom" friendly at a good salary with an okay commute.

I've always had a deep faith in God and always believed God looked out for me, but this experience changed my way of thinking. I now have a copilot instead of flying stand-by.

Marie Corfield
Flemington, New Jersey

---

4. Make Finding a Job Your Job

Get up each morning at the same time you would for work. Dress as if you're going to work. Define how many hours you're going to give each day to looking for work. Have business cards printed up with your name, address, phone number, fax number, and e-mail address to give out to prospective employers. "The discipline of doing this is good for the soul," says Reverend Hunt.

"It clarifies your sense of purpose, your occupation. It keeps you from drifting into a netherworld of depression, daytime TV, and wasted days."

Our greatest glory is not in never falling, But in rising every time we fall.

—*Confucius*

5. Find a Mentor

If you're looking to move into a new career and don't yet have the necessary skills, ask your friends and your pastor if they know of anyone who does that kind of work. Then see if that person would be willing to let you work with them—without salary—a few hours a week so you can learn more about their trade. "You'd be surprised how many people are eager to tutor others in their craft," says Dewar. "Not only is it flattering, it's a way of feeling useful to another human being as well."

6. Retool Your Skills

If need be, get additional training. See if your local community college has training programs in areas you're interested in—computers, marketing, entrepreneurship, and so on—and use your time to make yourself more marketable than you were when you first lost your job.

Changing Jobs

Moving from an unsatisfying job to one that meets your spiritual, psychological, and personal needs can be a rebirth. But like any birth, it succeeds best if you approach it with stamina, trust, courage, and prayer.

It's easy to think of your paycheck as a source of security in an otherwise insecure world. Every two weeks, rain or shine, it pops up on your desk, pays your bills, and keeps you and your family chugging along until the next one comes.

But what if you're earning that paycheck in a job that leaves you stressed and miserable? What if your career leaves you feeling unfulfilled? Then it may be time to start over.

Making a job or career change is a bold move that most people approach with what Saint Paul called "fear and trembling." But if you do decide to start afresh, acting deliberately and prayerfully can keep the turbulence to a minimum, say counselors and pastors. They suggest you take three steps when orchestrating a change of this magnitude.

- Make sure moving on is right for you.
- Plan carefully so the change is both successful and as painless as possible.
- Call upon your faith to see you through the transition.

Examining Your Reasons

Sometimes the desire to leave a position is clearly justified: If you're working for an unethical company or making too little to support yourself, there's no reason to stay where you are. But if your decision is not as clear-cut you should carefully consider why you want to leave before resolving to move on.

Here are four things you can do to reach a conclusion.

Make your own destiny,
Don't wait for it
to come to you,
Life is not a rehearsal!

—*Unknown*

1. Check Your Attitude

Ask yourself how you really feel about your job, suggests Stephen M. Pollan, a career advisor based in New York City and coauthor of *Starting Over: How to Change Careers or Start Your Own Business, Live Rich*, and *Die Broke*. Specifically, are you bored with what you're doing? Do you dread waking up in the morning and going to work? Do you say to yourself, "I have to go *there* again?" "The bottom line is, if you don't look forward to going to your job, you may be ready to think about transitioning yourself into another line of work," says Pollan.

2. Measure Your Stress

Ask yourself if your career contributes to your sense of peace or detracts from it, advises the Reverend Thomas Brown, doctor of theology, adjunct professor of pastoral care and dean at the Interdenominational Theological Seminary in Atlanta. "God tells us to 'seek peace and pursue it,' and we need to take that quite seriously," he suggests.

One way to seek peace is by making an "ecomap," suggests the Reverend Erik Kolbell, former minister with the United Church of Christ in New York City and a psychotherapist. Take a blank piece of paper and draw a circle in the center signifying you. Next, around the edges of the paper write words that represent pieces of your work life: your hours, boss, coworkers, commute, salary, and so on. Then, draw a line from you to each piece and make the line representative of how you feel about it; a jagged line between you and your boss might represent stress, a faint or broken line to a coworker might stand for an alienated relationship, a thick bold line to your salary could represent anger that it's not higher than it is. Finally, look at the whole picture. See what, if anything, is right with your work environment and what's wrong. This can help you determine if you can "fix" what you perceive as problems, live with the status

My Will Is to Do Your Will

Lord, you know what I desire, but I desire it only if it is your will that I should have it. If it is not your will, good Lord, do not be displeased, for my will is to do your will.

Amen.

—*Lady Julian of Norwich*

quo, or whether for your own peace it's time to think about moving on, says Reverend Kolbell.

3. Consider What God Wants for You

Pray for God's help in discerning what will fulfill you. "Our culture and especially our workplace put a premium on being 'successful,' making a lot of money and reaching a high level of prestige in our field, but the Bible simply asks us to do what makes us whole," says the Reverend Asa Hunt, executive pastor of the First Presbyterian Church in Houston. "One thing we can do to interrupt our culturally biased way of thinking is to pray, 'Lord, help me find happiness. If success follows, that's fine, and if it doesn't that's fine too.' Such a prayer gives us a different outlook on what our career is supposed to mean."

4. Talk to a Pro

If you're feeling dissatisfied but are unsure whether another job or career will be any better, speak to a career counselor. A counselor can introduce you to new possibilities, and many can administer tests that measure your interests and aptitudes and match them with career fields.

Planning a New Path

Okay. You know it's time to leave. What do you do now? Above all, you must plan carefully.

GRANT ME CONTENTMENT
IN THIS JOB

Lord . . . grant that my new work may be enjoyable for me and that I may be able to serve You and others in richer measure through this change of jobs. Whoever You bless is blessed indeed. Therefore I pray You, crown my action with Your gracious benediction. Make me faithful in every duty. Give me a kind and loving heart that I may get along well with my new associates. Give me respect for my superiors, and let me be fair to those whose work I am to direct. In all actions help me to show that I love You and serve You.

—From My Prayer Book

You want to do everything in your power to prepare and execute a move. If you do, you'll have greater peace of mind about this major change in your life.

"A plan of attack puts you in control," says Pollan. "It keeps you from panicking. And it has a logic to it; it makes sense to you. In this way, it's a very, very comforting thing to have."

Experts agree it's always good to devise your strategy with the help of a career counselor who can design a plan for you the same way an architect designs a house. But even if you're working with a professional, there are a few things you want to keep in mind.

1. Do Your Math

"Ideally you want to hold onto your present job while you're preparing to move because it provides a steady stream of income for you and will keep you from taking any other job in desperation," says Pollan. But if you anticipate you'll have to leave your current job to find another one, you should draw up a family budget that will take into consideration sources of revenue (savings, other income, possible loans) and expenses, including fixed expenses, such as your rent or mortgage, and expenses you may be able to trim. Your goal should be to budget well enough to keep solvent for at least 6 months, suggests Pollan.

2. Examine Your Options

Look at all the potential ways you can make a career change, and consider the advantages and disadvantages of each. According to Pollan there are seven possibilities for moving from your current job. You can:

- Move to another job in your current career and industry (such as a lawyer going to another firm).
- Stay in the same career but work in a different industry (a corporate lawyer going to work for an environmental group).
- Work in the same industry but in a different career (a law clerk becoming a lawyer).
- Move to a new career in a new industry (a lawyer becoming an elementary school teacher).
- Start your own business in your current industry (an associate in a law firm hanging out her own shingle).
- Start your own business in a different industry (a lawyer opening a restaurant).
- Go back to school and get a part-time job (a lawyer going to medical school and working nights in the university's law library).

If nothing else, making this list will clarify what options appeal to you, what are in reach, and what you don't want to consider.

3. Find a Mentor

When you think you know what kind of career you want, find someone who's already in it and ask if that person would agree to meet with you a few times to teach you the pluses and minuses of the work. If no one comes to mind,

BE MY GUIDE, LORD

O Lord, you are my redemption, also be my protector; direct my mind by your gracious presence, and watch over my path with guiding love; that, among the snares which lie hidden in this path in which I walk, I may so pass onwards with my heart fixed on you, that by the track of faith I may come to be where you would have me.

—*Mozarabic Sacramentary*

FINDING HIS TRUE LOVE

Bill T. felt unfulfilled and miserable selling satellite dishes, yet he stayed with the job because of what he called "the golden handcuffs" of high salary and good benefits. But when his misery finally got the better of him he decided to make a change.

While seeing a pastoral counselor, Bill was racking his brain trying to think of what he could do that would pay as much as his current position but be more fulfilling. The counselor put this question to him: "What is the one thing you've ever done in your adult life that you really and truly enjoyed?"

In a heartbeat, Bill answered, "I used to be a disc jockey on a small radio station and I loved it. Unfortunately, DJs don't make as much as I do, and I don't know how to get into the business anyway."

But he did know someone who worked at a local station and, more importantly, when he spoke with his wife about it he learned that she would be quite content living on less money provided he came home each night a happy man.

Four months later, Bill was hired as the station's program manager. "Best pay cut I ever took," he now says.

---

ask friends and your pastor if they know of someone who would do this for you. "You'll be surprised how many people are willing to take this on," says Pollan.

4. Develop a Support System

Ask your family, friends, and pastor to serve as your support system as you start your move; ask them to pray for you, and call on them for encouragement and advice. "It can be lonely going off to start a new career, and not a little unsettling," says Father Andre Papineau, S.D.S., author of *Breaking Up, Down, and Through: Discovering Spiritual and Psychological Opportunities in Your Transitions.* "Sometimes just a gentle pat on the back from someone who cares about us is all we need to keep ourselves going."

Banish Your Doubts

Making a transition to a new career can be exciting. You'll have the opportunity to meet interesting new people, learn new skills, and grow emotionally and intellectually. But you also may find this an unsettling period when your thoughts are invaded by self-doubt and worry about your ability to master a new job. This is when your faith can help you through.

We should not let our fears hold us back from pursuing our hopes.

—*John F. Kennedy*

Pastors and counselors suggest four ways you can put your doubts to rest.

1. Seek God's Support

Ask God to help you during the rough spots you're likely to encounter while learning your new job, says Dr. Brown. When you pray, "remind yourself that there will be rapids and churning water to go through. And that beyond the rapids the water will one day be calm again," he says.

2. Confess Your Doubts

Bring God your doubts and ask Him for confidence. "When you make so bold a move as a career change, you need to give yourself permission for doubts to creep in from time to time," says C. Wayne Dewar, financial planner and founder of an unemployment support group at St. Matthew's United Methodist Church in Charlotte, North Carolina. "When you turn them over to God, you relieve yourself of the guilt you might feel for having them."

3. Play Your Part

Recite the prayer "God helps me when I help myself" each morning when you start your day, suggests the Reverend John Vaughn, executive director of the Peace Development Fund in Amherst, Massachusetts. "Faith is a partnership between us and God," he says, "and by reciting this prayer we remind ourselves of both our responsibility and God's."

4. Find Peace in Solitude

Sit quietly for 10 to 20 minutes each day. "Before Jesus did anything important he always went off by himself," says Father Papineau. "In quiet solitude we can meditate on the biblical adage, 'Be still and know that I am God,' which will deepen our trust that God will look out for us in our transition."

Being a Valuable Team Member

More and more, businesses are requiring workers to handle projects cooperatively, as members of small teams. Here's how you can use your spiritual beliefs and practical steps to make your team a success.

harged with designing an eco-friendly copier, a team of workers at Xerox Corporation in Rochester, New York, turned to an ancient spiritual tradition, the Native American talking stick, for inspiration and guidance.

Team members would begin meetings by acknowledging that they were called together by the spirit for a higher purpose and that the talking stick was there to help them discover that purpose.

At first, the group would sit in silence. Then, as someone felt moved to comment, that person would take the talking stick and speak. Others in the room would listen openly. Only if they too felt moved by the spirit would they take a turn with the talking stick.

"At first things moved very slowly, and very awkwardly," says Judi Neal, Ph.D., director of the Center for Spirit and Work in West Haven, Connecticut, who participated in one of the meetings. "And then, suddenly there was this huge spark that hit the group. Clarity came, and so did a passion for action."

Whether through an approach like this or a more mainstream religious route, faith and spirituality can indeed move a team to a whole new level of creativity. You can play a key role in helping your team reach new heights—if you take these steps.

- Foster the spirit of teamwork.
- Cooperate to accomplish goals.
- Find creative ways to overcome differences.

[C]reating a successful team . . . is essentially a spiritual act. It requires the individuals involved to surrender their self-interest for the greater good so that the whole adds up to more than the sum of its parts.

—Phil Jackson

Building Team Spirit

At the heart of high-performing teams is spirit. We're not talking about team spirit in the rah-rah sense.

Instead, the spirit behind most successful team efforts is service to the greater good, says Barry Heermann, Ph.D, author of *Building Team Spirit* and president of the Expanded Learning Institute in Del Mar, California.

The key to developing this sense of spirit is to work with other team members to build relationships and trust with each other, says Dr. Heermann, who has advised companies like AT&T, NCR, and Lexis/Nexis. You can help develop trust and strong relationships in three ways.

1. Always Start with a Prayer

When you gather with other workers to work on a project, always ask for God's help to make the work a success.

For example, when she attends department meetings, Dr. Neal will often sit silently for several moments, first to become more aware of how the team is interacting, and then to pray for guidance. "I will say, 'What is it that I can do here to help the group? Please give me guidance.' And I'll find that I get the answer," she says.

2. Be There to Serve

In his first epistle, the Apostle Peter urged people to help one another, saying, "God has given each of you some special abilities; be sure to use

---

HELP ME CONTRIBUTE, LORD

Dear God,

Before I go to work today, please lift my mind to the realm of Truth.

May I remember and not forget throughout the day that my only work is to love, for Your Sake, that the world might be renewed.

I think of my workplace—the people, the circumstances, the situations—and I surrender them to you.

I remember, Lord, that this is but a veil across a truer truth.

I withdraw my judgments, my interpretations, my agendas.

I ask only to be a healing force.

This business is but a front for a temple, a healing place where all shall be lifted above the insanity of a frightened world.

So may it be that I contribute to this healing, to this upliftment, with my efforts and my resources.

And that is all I ask.

—*Marianne Williamson*

---

them to help each other, passing on to others God's many kinds of blessings" (1 Peter 4:10, LIV). You should follow this advice when you gather with your coworkers. "There's an old saying that there's no limit to the good results you can produce as long as you're unconcerned about who gets the credit," says Father William J. Byron, S.J., pastor of Holy Trinity Parish in Washington, D.C., author of *Answers from Within: Spiritual Guidelines for Managing Setbacks in Work and Life*. "Act accordingly and watch your creativity unfold."

3. Inspire with Your Vision

Is your group stalled on some project? You can motivate the members by sharing your hopes for the group's success.

We frequently underestimate people and don't challenge them with our dreams for God's work in the world. Yet when we tell our coworkers our hopes, we inspire them to accomplish higher goals. Sharing your vision also can help your team clarify its purpose and get excited about the possibilities of working together, says Dr. Heermann.

Putting Your Plan to Action

Once a team comes up with a shared vision, the members need to move on to the nitty gritty—getting the work done. Of course working together as a team involves collaboration and cooperation.

"In order to achieve high performance the team needs to function as a harmonious unit," says Dr. Heermann. Here's how you can contribute to team harmony.

1. Stake Your Claim

Take advantage of your unique talents. During this what-can-get-done-and-when phase of a project, team members iron out who's going to do what. To play a valuable part in this process, you should volunteer for those tasks that excite you or that you know your skills will help you do well. "If team members do what they feel passionate about, the team will be more successful," says Dr. Heermann.

2. Help Others

An old African proverb says, "God gives nothing to those who keep their arms crossed." When you open your arms and reach out to help others, God will bless you with spiritual rewards, says Father Byron.

To raise awareness of each team member's individual needs, Dr. Heermann suggests this exercise. Have all the team members write down their job duties on a large sheet of white paper, and then give everyone four markers: green, red, blue, and orange. Then ask everyone to underline the duties they feel passionate about in green, the things they could get rid of in red, duties where the learning curve is steep in blue, and areas where they could use help in orange. Finally, stick all the papers up on the wall and review what everyone has said.

If you can suggest another employee, a book, a Web site, or some other re-

❧

BLESS OUR WORK

My God, Father and Saviour, since you have commanded us to work in order to meet our needs, sanctify our labor that it may bring nourishment to our souls as well as to our bodies. Make us constantly aware that our efforts are worthless unless guided by your light and strengthened by your hand. Make us faithful to the particular tasks for which you have bestowed upon us the necessary gifts, taking from us any envy or jealousy at the vocations of others.

Above all may every temporal grace be matched by spiritual grace, that in both body and soul we may live to your glory.

—*John Calvin*

source that will help people reduce their learning curve, point them toward it. If you see opportunities to trade the things you find difficult for parts of someone else's job, make the switch. If you know you can provide knowledge that will help someone else, volunteer it.

When people share like this, "they see how they can help each other and support each other," says Dr. Heermann. "It helps bring the team together."

3. Celebrate Everyone's Accomplishments

Many teams bypass this step entirely, says Dr. Heermann. Yet acknowledging success along the way can ignite and nurture a team. It's also what motivates the team to work effectively in the future. "Members feel appreciated and acknowledged within the team, and they have a sense of unbounded energy—the ability to move mountains," he says.

You can celebrate accomplishments in simple ways by going out to lunch together or just by thanking each other for hard work and good contributions.

Dr. Heermann's favorite celebrating exercise is what he calls a recognition circle. During the first part, team members discuss the importance of recognition and how to communicate it. In the second part, one team member is identified, and then his or her contributions to the team are discussed. That person sits and generously receives the good words. "Often people come into this exercise thinking that it's trite or superficial. By the end, the spirit is palpable," says Dr. Heermann.

Managing Team Turmoil

Breakdowns occur on the best of teams. Members can get frustrated with the performance of other team members or other people in the company. They can disagree on how to best serve the client or customer. It's hard to avoid this stage, but if you deal with the issues smartly you can prevent a disruption from damaging your work environment.

How? "Successful teams venture into the dark side and let go of the bad stuff," says Dr. Heermann. Letting go allows team members to start fresh. Also, it keeps past issues from infecting future projects, he says. Here are three suggestions for working through this critical stage.

1. Keep the Communication Lines Open

Dr. Heermann has reviewed dozens of studies on teamwork from all types of business and industry, and he has found that members of successful teams have one clear advantage work groups that fail lack: They communicate freely

HELP US THINK OF OTHERS

O God, you have bound us together in this bundle of life; give us grace to understand how our lives depend on the courage, the industry, the honesty and integrity of our fellow men; that we may be mindful of their needs, grateful for their faithfulness, and faithful in our responsibilities to them; through Jesus Christ our Lord.

—Reinhold Neibuhr

and speak their minds, rather than getting caught up in petty games. This helps them get right to the bottom of troubling issues.

The key, however, is voicing concerns in a constructive way. Say you're in a meeting where there's a lot of cross-talking and interruption, a lot of high energy and people not listening to each other. It's coming to a point where the meeting is chaotic and going nowhere. You could yell for everyone to shut up, walk out in disgust, or sit quietly while the group disintegrates. Or, you could call for a moment of silence.

> *Express the limitless power of soul in anything you take up. Every position you hold in life will be the stepping stone to a higher one if you strive to climb upward.*
>
> —*Paramahansa Yogananda*

"It's a courageous thing to do, but it's fairly simple and it makes a difference," says Dr. Neal. How would you do this? "I would say something like, 'This group is feeling way too chaotic right now. I suggest we just stop talking for a few minutes and see what happens.'

"Propose it as an experiment," she adds. Because everybody may not share your approach to things, it's better not to use spiritually laden language. Say things in a nonthreatening, straightforward way. If you tend to be shy, rehearse in your head what you might say.

2. Learn to See the Other Person's Side

You may think of people who do things differently from you or have different work styles or thinking styles as *difficult*. But you might be allowing a surface perception to influence your feelings, says Krista Kurth, Ph.D., codirector of Renewal Resources, a management consulting firm in Potomac, Maryland.

Prayer can help shift that perception and give you strength to deal with the situation, says Dr. Kurth. Pray for the ability to see the other team member's point of view. Or, if it's clear that the other person is being difficult, ask God to guide you toward an honest conversation with the person and explain your concerns. For instance, to a person who constantly interrupts others in the group you might say, "When you interrupt during meetings, it frustrates me."

3. Use a Symbol

Getting together for a team meeting can trigger a number of difficult situations—heated arguments, someone dominating the conversation, or simply an inability to stay focused on the task at hand. To bring things back under control try this tactic, which was used by a workgroup at AT&T, says Dr. Neal.

Put a bowl of clear marbles in the center of the meeting table. Any team member who notices that the group is having difficulty can reach in the bowl and take out a marble. This is a sign for everyone in the room to pause and pull back for moment in silence, explains Dr. Neal. The person who grabs the marble can either speak out about the concern or just sit in silence.

"By grabbing that marble they're saying, 'I'm concerned about the team right now, and let's just take a moment to let things settle down and get peaceful.' When that person feels satisfied with the shift in the group, they'll put the marble back," says Dr. Neal.

VISUALIZATION

Picturing Perfect Prayer

On a crowded subway car in New York City, a man sits with his eyes closed, a faint smile on his lips. Physically, he is careening down a dark tunnel between Times Square and 59th Street, but mentally and spiritually he is seated at a wooden table in a primitive cabin high on a snow-covered mountain. Seated across from the man at the wooden table is Jesus Christ. The man stares reverently into Jesus' eyes. Jesus stares lovingly back, smiling.

The train pulls to a stop. The man opens his eyes, stretches, gathers his things, and walks off the subway car. He feels calm, blessed, and ready to start his day.

This is an example of praying with images, or visualization. The idea is to create an image in your mind that helps you connect with God. The range of possible images is limited only by your imagination. You can "visualize" the taste of an orange wedge dipped in buckwheat honey or the sound of a tinkling fountain in a Japanese rock garden. You can envision yourself sitting at the foot of a Buddha, gliding in a canoe with an Iroquois medicine man, or walking in heaven with a loved one who has died.

While it is possible to pray with images anywhere, you can best get a feel for this ancient technique by setting aside some quiet time when you can sit in a quiet space. Begin by trying to relax, says Carolyn Bohler, Ph.D., professor of pastoral theology at United Theological Seminary in Dayton, Ohio, and author of *Opening to God: Guided Imagery Meditations on Scripture*. Take several deep breaths and focus your attention by becoming aware of where you are sitting

334

and how your body feels. Dr. Bohler recommends sitting up straight, either in a chair or cross-legged on the floor. Lying down is fine, but you'll be more likely to fall asleep.

Probably the easiest way to enjoy visual prayer is to picture a place of natural beauty—a beach you remember from childhood, for example, or a favorite forest path—and then imagine yourself walking there. "Take a prayer vacation," says Dr. Bohler.

It can also be useful to simply try to quiet your conscious mind and allow images to float to the surface from your subconscious. Such images can give you clues about what's going on in your heart. Say, for example, that an image of a spinning wheel comes to mind. Thinking about what that means, you begin to realize that you're feeling stuck in your life—that you're "spinning your wheels." Now you can use this information to work on what's really bothering you, Dr. Bohler says.

You can also use visual prayer to consciously think of God in relation to various situations in your life that may be troubling you in some way. Say you had an argument with your husband this morning. Hold up in your mind's eye a visual image of you and your husband communicating and sharing in the presence of a holy figure.

For meditations on specific situations such as this, Dr. Bohler feels it's very important that you choose images that will lead you toward solutions, rather than images that focus only on the problem itself.

"Focus on what you do want, rather than on what you don't want," she says. "See whether the image might suggest some positive form of action."

Visual prayer need not be focused on any goal other than simply growing closer to God. One technique that can be particularly helpful in that regard is to visualize a specific passage from scripture. Some people picture themselves within the scene the passage depicts, walking alongside the biblical characters, even talking to them. You also can turn to books, such as Dr. Bohler's *Opening to God*, that provide "guided" meditations of various kinds.

Part 8

YOUR FINANCIAL LIFE

Buying or Selling a House

ༀ

Acquiring a new home or selling an old one is likely to be a challenging financial situation. Here's how to use your faith and a prayerful attitude to get through this frazzling time.

When Joseph, Mary, and Jesus needed to move, they had some help making the decision. An angel appeared to Joseph in a dream and told him to take his family and escape to Egypt to protect the young Jesus from King Herod's wrath. Then eventually, the angel of the Lord directed them to Nazareth.

It would be nice if a higher power could offer specific instructions when you're thinking about moving, but it doesn't always work that way. You have to make your own judgment about buying or selling a house. Often, this process can put you under stress as you determine whether you really need to make a move, how much you can afford to spend or what you should ask for your current home, and how you should conduct yourself during the entire process.

But if you follow some basic principles and God's guidance, you can make it through the process with your sanity and soul intact, say pastors and counselors. Here's how.

- Do it for the right reasons.
- Take the proper financial steps.
- Maintain your spiritual and peaceful perspective.

Make the Right Decision

Buying or selling a house affects your family, your job, and your financial future. To make the right move, you need sound guidance from two sources: yourself and your faith. Take these steps to help you choose the correct path.

> *Right choice, which will bring most happiness and least pain . . . is a choice inspired by the Spirit.*
>
> —*Bhagavan Das*

1. Ask Yourself Why

In today's world, a house has become much more than a place of shelter. It's evolved for some into a financial and social status symbol. With this as their rationale, some people decide to move only because they think a bigger and better house will elevate their own standing in life.

As you consider buying or selling a house, have a heart to heart talk with yourself and your spouse about why. "Are you looking for a nice, decent place to live? Or are you looking at something to impress people with your financial earning power?" asks Walton M. Padelford, Ph.D., chair of the McAfee School of Business at Union University in Jackson, Tennessee. "To me, the second choice is not a good motive."

Write out the reasons why you want to move. Perhaps you have a new job and the commute is hard, or your family is outgrowing your current home. Then with your family, discuss if the reasons are valid, rational, and spiritually sound.

2. Search for the Spiritual Go Ahead

After all the tabulations are complete, go off to your room or church and very quietly pray about the decision you are about to make. Even if it all works out on paper, if spiritually you don't feel right about it, don't do it. "A house may seem just right, but then you pray about it and you get what I call a 'check in spirit,'" says Mike Taylor, a former pastor and staff writer for Christian Financial Concepts, a nonprofit organization in Gainesville, Georgia, dedicated to teaching the biblical principles of handling money. "If you don't have peace

GOD, HELP ME MAKE THE RIGHT DECISION

Heavenly Father, You know all things and see the end from the beginning. You are never at a loss as to what to do next. The wonders of Your creation and the miracles of Your all-knowing direction of the affairs of all people and nations testify to the infinite wisdom with which You order all things.

I humbly confess that I am often confused by the problems in my life. Sometimes I do not seem to know which way to turn. I pray You, therefore, to enlighten me by Your Holy Spirit that I may recognize what is Your will in every situation; give me the courage to decide every issue accordingly and to leave the final outcome to Your direction.

Amen.

—From My Prayer Book

about it, don't move ahead." If it is truly the right decision, God will grant you a sense of serenity about your move, says Taylor. "You must do your homework when it comes to finances, but you also need that peace from God," he adds.

Figure Out the Financials

Having a house of your dreams shouldn't come at the expense of everything else in your life. "God is faithful in supplying our needs. But our responsibility is to live in the context of whatever He supplies," Taylor says. While you do want a nice home, keep in mind that a house's basic purpose is to provide shelter for your family. To stay within the means God gave you, follow this three-step process in determining what you can afford.

❧

A Prayer for the New Owners

May the person who is going to live in this house have many children, may he be rich, may he be honest to people and good to the poor; may he not suffer from disease or any other kind of trouble; may he be safe all these years.

—*Kenyan blessing*

---

1. Assess What You Need

If you don't have an idea of what you want and need when you start out, greed and desire can take over for prudence and common sense. You may end up bidding on a gorgeous five-bedroom, three-bathroom house, when all you need is a three-bedroom, one-bath condo.

So before you start looking, talk with your family and write down everything you need in a house. If you have kids at home, how many bedrooms must you have? Can you do with a one-car garage? This assessment will help protect you from making a commitment that may stretch you to unreasonable financial limits, Dr. Padelford says.

If you are selling, calculate how much you need to get from the sale, then find out the market value of your house by looking at what other similar houses in your neighborhood sold for. Between the two, you should come up with a fair and reasonable asking price, Dr. Padelford says.

2. Follow a Financial Guideline

Depending on your income level, Christian Financial Concepts recommends a housing allowance that is between 26 to 40 percent of your net income—meaning the money you have left after you've paid your taxes and tithe, Taylor says. For example, say you make $3,000 a month. The suggested percentage for housing allowance at that income level is 36 percent. After taxes and tithing, you have an estimated $2,175 a month left. Based on the guideline, your total housing allowance is $783 a month—and only a portion of that can be used for the mortgage payment. The rest of the housing allowance covers property taxes, insurance, utilities, and so on.

3. Consider All Your Expenses

Often when families calculate what they can afford per month in mortgage payments, they don't consider the emergency expenses of home ownership. But when a pipe bursts or there's a colder than expected winter, they realize they have stretched themselves too thin. "That's the biggest mistake we see families make," Taylor says. So Taylor recommends that you estimate all your housing costs—insurance, upkeep, utilities, plus a little extra for unexpected emergencies. After you've added that all up, then figure out what you can afford per month.

If you prefer, a reputable real estate broker or banker can help you develop an estimate. Or if you have access to the Internet, you can visit the Christian Financial Concepts' online budget/mortgage guide at www.cfcministry.org for advice. "You can play with the numbers by going into our Web site under 'Online Tools.' Click under 'Budget Guide.' Simply enter your income level, along with estimated taxes and gifts to the church, and the software automatically creates a budget for your income level," says Taylor.

> *Whenever you are to do a thing, though it can never be known but to yourself, ask yourself how you would act were all the world looking at you and act accordingly.*
>
> —*Thomas Jefferson*

Act in a Fair and Spiritual Manner

Since selling or buying a house is stressful for both sides, tensions can arise during negotiations. Seemingly normal, nice people transform into crazed creatures, and bargaining can turn as tense as meetings between warring tribes. Obviously, this isn't the spiritual way of dealing with the situation. To keep your spiritual perspective throughout, try these suggestions.

1. Do Unto Others

How would you like it if you bought a house to find out that the former owners lied about the condition of the plumbing? Or how would you feel if someone came through your home on a walk-through and called it a decorative nightmare? Not very good, that's for sure. So during the buying or selling process, keep Matthew's Golden Rule in mind: In everything do to others as you would have done to you. Before you speak or take any action, first ask yourself is this how you'd like to be treated, says William Raabe, Ph.D., professor of business at Samford University, a Baptist-affiliated school in Birmingham, Alabama.

2. Pray for Patience

A lot can go wrong for both buyer and seller during a house transaction. Inspectors can find unknown problems, mortgages can get held up, real estate agents can miss appointments. "Buying a house is such a complex transaction. It's a matter of how many things will go wrong," Dr. Raabe says. Accept from the outset that things may go astray. Before you start negotiations, pray to God for the patience and calm needed to get through the transaction, Dr. Raabe says. If during the process you feel like you're losing control, repeat this mantra to recenter yourself: "God is with me. Everything will work out for the best."

Managing Your
Money

Computers. Fancy cars. Designer clothing. With all the spending temptations these days, it's hard to get through the month without wiping out your paycheck. Here's how to prayerfully develop a financial plan your family can live with.

If you don't think religion and money advice mix, take a quick look at the Book of Proverbs.

"The wages of the righteous bring them life, but the income of the wicked brings them punishment" (Proverbs 10:16, NIV).

"Dishonest money dwindles away; but he who gathers money little by little makes it grow" (Proverbs 13:11, NIV).

Throughout the Bible, you'll find suggestions on handling your finances, which is why the Bible is a favorite among money managers, says Tom Bray, a certified public accountant from Kingsville, Maryland, and a counselor who specializes in getting people out of debt using biblical principles.

In fact, money and faith can work hand in hand. Money can help you accomplish your spiritual duties. Meanwhile, your beliefs can dictate just how you manage and use your money so that you stay true to your morals. How can you do all this in a world that seems to build a wall between the financial and the spiritual?

- Establish spiritually sound financial priorities.
- Protect yourself from materialism.
- Invest wisely and spiritually.
- Make finances a family affair.

Mapping Out Your Destination

Before you take a trip, you must pick a final destination. Managing your money starts the same way. You need to figure out your secular and spiritual money goals before you can start saving and investing. Pastors and counselors suggest the following three-step process:

> *Money is the cause of good things to a good man, and evil things to a bad man . . .*
>
> —*Philo*

1. Meet the Needs of Your Family First

Before anything, you must take care of your family, as even the Bible makes clear: "But anyone who won't care for his own relatives when they need help, especially those living in his own family, has no right to say he is a Christian. Such a person is worse than the heathen" (1 Timothy 5:8, LB).

Start by writing out a list of your true basic needs: shelter, food, clothing, and such. And include money for retirement and college expenses for your kids. Then calculate how much they will cost. You can figure your current expenses by looking at your spending and bills for the last 6 to 12 months and developing an average. As for retirement and education, you may want to meet with a financial planner or consult one of the many good financial planning books available.

When identifying your family's needs, practice prudence. While you do need shelter, you don't need a mansion. While your children do need clothing, they don't always need the latest designer styles. If you have extra money for luxuries later, that's fine. But your first priority is to the basic needs of your family, says Bray.

2. Select Your Spiritual Spending Goals

In terms of your spiritual priorities, calculate how much you'd like to give to your church or synagogue and other charitable groups—whether it be a percentage of your total income or a set amount. Then set aside that amount as

---

GUIDE OUR WAY WITH MONEY, GOD

Help us to earn money honestly
To spend a little wisely
To save some prudently
And to give generously.

—*From* Prayers for Children and Young People

---

soon as you get your paycheck, much as you would do with a savings goal, says Mike Taylor, a staff writer for Christian Financial Concepts in Gainesville, Georgia.

3. Prioritize the Little Things in Life

Do you need a new car? Would you like to take the family to Disney World? As long as you've met your family and spiritual goals, it's fine to want and to work for these other joys of life. To figure what your focus should be, write out a list of the nonessentials you'd like and work with your family to decide which are major needs and which can wait awhile. Let's say your old television set is fine, but a bit dated, while the family car is getting old and less reliable. If you and your family decide a car is more important then it moves to the top of your list. Once you have the goal of a car written out it crystallizes your savings plan, Bray says.

You may even want to set up a separate savings account for these items. This will keep your savings priority clear and make it less likely that you will tap the money for spur-of-the-moment purchases.

Turning Off the Materialism Switch

For many people today, the old-fashioned method of saving for the things they want has gone by the wayside. With today's easy credit, they can get whatever they desire, right now—even if they can't afford it. This is a particular

---

For More Abundant Living

Blessed Lord and Savior Jesus Christ, You have warned me that "a man's life does not consist in the abundance of his possessions." Teach me to realize that happiness in life does not depend on the measure of material things I may call my own, but on the use I, as a good steward, make of what You have committed to my care.

—From My Prayer Book

---

temptation, says Taylor, when people are in a spiritual or emotional crisis. "They try to resolve their problems with material goods. But you can't settle a spiritual issue with something material," Taylor says. To really manage your money in a fiscally and spiritually responsible way, you must shun this materialism and stay out of debt. Here are four ways to block out impulse spending.

1. Burn Out the Boob Tube

We live in an age where people watch the Super Bowl as much for the commercials as the game. These 30-second mini-movies invade our homes and consciousness screaming at you to "BUY, BUY, BUY."

The best way to fight back? Turn the TV off. "Cultivate other habits like reading a book," says Walton M. Padelford, Ph.D., chair of the McAfee School of Business at Union University in Jackson, Tennessee.

2. Can the Credit Card

Obviously, misusing a credit card can lead to an ocean of debt. But even for people who pay off their balance each month, credit cards are a danger. Research has shown that when using a credit card, people spend 33 percent more than they would if they used cash.

What can you do to counter this? Get rid of all your credit cards except one to hold for emergencies. Then when you want to buy something, make yourself go to the bank, take out the cash, and then go to the store. This gives you plenty of time to evaluate whether you really need the thing you want to purchase. If the item can't stand up to this test, you know it's not really worth buying, Bray says.

3. Get Two or Three Bids

If you want to buy an expensive item, compare the price at two or three places. This ensures you'll get the best deal, and it requires time and effort. "That takes a few days and takes away the impulse buy," Bray says. If you don't feel up to the comparison shopping, then you probably don't need the item.

4. Practice Self-Control

In Galatians 5:22–23, it says that self-control is a fruit of the Holy Spirit (NIV). If the pull of materialism seems too strong, pray directly to the Holy Spirit. Ask for the gift of self-restraint and willpower as you fend off the constant commercialism of this world. "God calls us to live within the confines that He has set up for us," Taylor says.

Building Your Treasure

In the parable of the three servants, the master gives one servant five talents, one two talents, and yet another one talent. The first two servants double their money, but the third servant buries his talent for fear that otherwise he'll lose it. His unwillingness to take a risk incurs the master's wrath: "You wicked lazy servant. . . . You should have put my money on deposit with the bankers, so that when I returned I would have received it back with interest" (Matthew 25:24–25, NIV).

As this story makes clear, the Bible teaches that it is good to make your money grow. It's the means to help you achieve the goals you set for your family and your faith. The key is to save and invest—without compromising your morals—by using steps like these.

A Sacred Trust

Help me, O God, to spend wisely and to buy fairly, remembering that money and the things of this world are a trust for which I shall have to account to you.

—*Malcolm L. Playfoot*

1. Make Saving a Habit

The key to successful saving or investing is to make it part of your regular routine. So even if you only have a small amount left over after you pay your bills each month, allocate a portion of it to savings, Dr. Padelford says. Then as your income grows, increase how much you save or invest each month. Your ultimate goal should be to save at least 10 percent of your income, Dr. Padelford says. This will prepare you for major expenses, such as college costs, as well as for retirement.

2. Keep Your Head about You

Get-rich-quick schemes may look good, but usually there's a downside—a big downside. If you fall for the promise of quick returns on risky stocks or day trading over the Internet, you could lose all your money, putting you and your family's financial future at stake. "Don't be reckless with your investments," says William Raabe, Ph.D., a certified public accountant and professor of business at Samford University in Birmingham, Alabama.

3. Let Your Investments Reflect Your Values

If you intend to invest in a stock or mutual fund, you naturally will want to check out the company's financial status. But it's just as important to look into what the company makes or does and the policies under which it operates. If a company sells a potentially harmful product, treats workers inhumanely, or doesn't reflect the religious ideals that you have, don't invest in it. "There are plenty of opportunities to invest in groups that are socially responsible as well as profitable," Dr. Raabe says.

In fact, there are more than 35 faith-based investment funds that represent all types of religions. A qualified financial planner will help you find and evaluate a faith-based fund.

Keep It All in the Family

Because you and your spouse may have completely different financial personalities, conflict over how to spend and how to save may cause major discord. But there are ways to limit the distress. Here's how.

1. Develop a Thorough Budget

You want to save every penny; your spouse feels like money burns a hole in his pocket. Can you ever agree? Probably not. And that's why you need a budget, Taylor says.

With a budget, you plan out what you need to spend and what you want to save each month. Don't stop there, though. Also allot each spouse a certain amount of do-as-you-will spending money. That way the spender has money to burn, but knows exactly what the limit is. And the saver feels better knowing that the spending partner isn't going wild, Taylor says. "What a budget does is puts restraints on the spender. It doesn't mean they cannot spend; it just directs and controls the spending," Taylor says.

> *As long as money is our servant it works for us, the moment it becomes our master we work for it.*
>
> —*Alice H. Rice*

2. Pray Together

When you and your spouse don't agree on how to manage money or are on the cusp of making a major financial decision, join together in prayer. "The best way to resolve spiritual conflicts—and money management is a spiritual conflict—is to pray," Taylor says. Pray for one another, so that God helps you draw on each other's financial strengths and offset your weaknesses. Also, ask God for guidance and the power to do what is best for your entire family—not just what you want at the moment.

3. Just Say No

How's this for an amazing statistic: Children ages 4 to 12 will spend or influence more than $550 billion of retail spending each year. That's because companies are skipping you and marketing right to your children, making them feel like they need every new toy and designer outfit that comes down the pike. And when they turn their pleas on you, you're more likely to cave in and buy what they want.

While most parents want to give their kids everything, you're not doing the children or yourself any favors by buying them whatever they want. Doing without things on occasion is "a good life lesson," says Taylor. If your children demand the latest and greatest toys and clothes, explain to them that you cannot afford it. If that doesn't work, tell them outright, "No; you can't have it because I said so."

"The bottom line is that you are the authority figure. You can't have kids demanding things from their parents," Taylor says.

Coping with
Financial Crisis

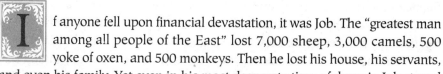

Whether it's caused by losing a job, a medical emergency, or getting over your head in debt, a financial crisis can overwhelm you and your family. Using prayer and sacrifice can help you emerge from the ruins.

I f anyone fell upon financial devastation, it was Job. The "greatest man among all people of the East" lost 7,000 sheep, 3,000 camels, 500 yoke of oxen, and 500 monkeys. Then he lost his house, his servants, and even his family. Yet even in his most desperate time of despair, Job stayed true to his faith and trusted in God.

His reward? "The Lord made him prosperous again and gave him twice as much as he had before" (Job 42:10, NIV).

Perhaps you feel like Job right now. Perhaps you fear your financial problems will take away everything precious to you. Don't give in to a feeling of hopelessness. Just like Job, you can use perseverance and faith in yourself and God to get you through this desolate time and back on your way to security. The key, say counselors and pastors, is to take charge of your situation—financially and spiritually—by following these steps.

- Bring your spending under control.
- Slowly but surely pay off debts.
- Keep your faith.

Ending the Spending Cycle

People teetering near financial ruin often seek advice from Walton M. Padelford, Ph.D., chair of the McAfee School of Business at Union University in Jackson, Tennessee. He's glad to advise them, but when he tells them what they have to give up to get back on their feet, many of them balk. "They say, 'I can't give up cable, I won't give up my online access.' It is amazing how locked in people get even on the brink of bankruptcy," he says.

> *If you are swept off your feet, it's time to get on your knees.*
>
> —*Fred Beck*

It's hard to turn away from the comforts of modern life. But if you are in debt or fear some change in your life may soon prevent you from keeping up with your bills, the first thing you must do is cut back on your spending.

Here are four ways to take control.

1. Follow the Money Trail

Before you can decide what to sacrifice, you must first figure out how you're spending money now. For one month, track every dime you pay out and then compare it to how much your family is bringing in. When some families do this they are horrified to learn that they routinely spend $200 a month on such nonessentials as fast food, says Mike Taylor, a former pastor and staff writer for Christian Financial Concepts in Gainesville, Georgia.

2. Separate "Wants" from "Needs"

Once you identify all your expenses, go through them with your family to select which ones you can eliminate. This may require some real soul-searching, but you need to separate what you absolutely need to survive from material goods that are mere luxuries. "You may need to take radical steps: Cut the TV cable, sell the television," Dr. Padelford says.

3. Avoid Temptation

Even with the best plan, getting out of debt will not work if you keep charging and spending money you don't have. To break this mold, you have to change

'TIS A GIFT TO BE SIMPLE

'Tis a gift to be simple,

'Tis a gift to be free,

'Tis a gift to come down where we ought to be,

And when we find ourselves in the place just right

'Twill be in the valley of love and delight.

—*Shaker hymn*

your patterns. First off, that means staying away from shopping centers and outlet malls. "If I am an alcoholic, the worst place I can be is in a bar. If I have trouble controlling my spending, the worst place I can be is at a mall," Taylor says.

Beyond this, you need to throw out the mail order catalogs and avoid fliers or circulars promoting sales. And tear up your credit cards, except for one you set aside for emergency use only.

In today's consumer world, it may be hard to turn away from ads promising perfection if you only buy such-and-such product. If this is the case, turn off the TV, get rid of your popular magazines, and read an ad-free book, suggests Dr. Padelford.

3. Pray for Strength

Cutting out the extras, walking instead of driving, scaling down your grocery expenses—decisions like these are tough medicine. But keep in mind that making these sacrifices now means you are taking steps to secure your future. In making these difficult decisions, look to God for support. "Turn to God for the strength to do these things. These are hard steps to take. But God will help you," Dr. Padelford says.

Putting Your Debt on a Diet

In Proverbs it says: "The borrower is the slave of the lender" (Proverbs 22:7, NRSV). That's exactly what happens when you go into debt—you become beholden to your bills instead of to your family or your financial future. "People who are massively in debt have lost their freedom," Taylor says.

And don't look to bankruptcy as a solution. It not only ruins your credit rating for 10 years or more, but it goes against what God expects you to do. "The wicked borrow, and do not pay back" (Psalm 37:21, NRSV). While paying down a massive debt may seem impossible right now, with God's help you can tackle it a piece at a time and regain your freedom through four steps.

1. Ask the Lord for Guidance

In these times, it's real tempting to ask God for a $10,000 check in the mail. That's not likely to happen, and it isn't a correct use of prayer, either. Instead, turn to God for the guidance and wisdom you'll need to get out of debt. "It's not enough to sit back and pray that God is going to bail you out of this problem. Pray for the direction and ability to put a plan into practice," Dr. Padelford says.

2. Talk to Your Creditors

In the end, your creditors would rather be paid late than not at all. So tell them the truth: that you want to pay but can't right now. "Most of them are decent and will work out something with you," says Tom Bray, a certified public accountant from Kingsville, Maryland, and a counselor who specializes in get-

BLESS US, O LORD!

Bless us, O Lord,

in this coming year,

May dew and rain

be a source of blessing,

Bless to our use the fruits of the earth

and let the earth rejoice in them.

And bless all that we do

and the work of our hands.

—From the Amidah

ting people out of debt using biblical principles. Once you've explained your situation, work with them to work up a feasible payment schedule.

If you think you'll have trouble negotiating with your creditors or working out a payment schedule, turn to one of the several nonprofit groups that can advise you for free or at a low cost. (See "When You Need Outside Help.")

3. Develop a Payment Plan

One of the major roadblocks to getting out of debt is the hefty interest you have to pay. Even if you're not making new purchases, that interest keeps accumulating on your old bills, putting you further and further in debt each month. To get out of this spiral, you need to develop a payment plan.

Here's one Taylor recommends: Separate out the bills with the highest interest rates, then pick the one among this group that has the lowest balance and concentrate on paying it off first. Continue to pay at least the minimum on

WHEN YOU NEED OUTSIDE HELP

When the piles of bills are higher than your door and the phone won't stop ringing with bill collectors, it may be time to call for help. Many agencies—some religiously affiliated and some not—help people who are in debt. They help you negotiate with creditors, consolidate your debt, and serve you in other ways. For more information, contact the following:

Christian Credit Counselors
851 S. Coast Highway 101
Encinitas, CA 92024

The National Foundation for Consumer Credit
Suite 100, 8611 2nd Avenue
Silver Spring, MD 20910

Christian Financial Concepts
601 Broad Street SE
Gainesville, GA 30501

A Prayer for Peace

Why can't I ever find peace, God? I've been fighting for so long, and each time I think I'm done, a new battle arises. Will my struggles ever end? Renew my strength, God. Restore my hope. Give me the courage to stare down adversity and the faith to face whatever may come without fear and without despair.

Amen.

—*Rabbi Naomi Levy*

each of your other bills, but concentrate extra money you collect each month and put it toward that one high-interest bill, Taylor says. When you retire that bill, use the money you'd been allocating for that payment to start paying off your next high-interest bill. Continue this way until all your bills are paid off.

4. Start a Savings Account

As soon as you are able, you need to set up a savings account. A savings account will help keep you out of debt in the future when unexpected expenses pop up. "If something goes bad, you won't have to pull out the plastic to pay for it," Taylor says. He recommends an ultimate goal of saving the equivalent of 3 to 6 months of your net income—your paycheck after taxes.

Keep the Faith

While weathering the storm of a financial crisis, some people pull away from their faith. "Because of financial mismanagement they feel they can't serve God. They get discouraged and depressed and sometimes leave the church," Bray says. Yet this is one of the times you need God and your faith the most. As it says in Hebrews, "You can never please God without faith, without depending on him" (Hebrews 11:6, LIV). Your prayers and faith will provide you with the wisdom to get out of your situation, as well as the support to help you

Prayer Miracles

Prayer Helped Me Get through a Financial Crisis

After my dad passed away, I moved my business to Little Rock, Arkansas, so I could be close to my mother. My business was soon near bankruptcy and I was strapped with two homes (my new home and my old one) that I could not afford to maintain and could not sell due to a slow real estate market. The pain and humiliation of my monetary and business failures, grief over my dad, and the fear of an uncertain future pushed me to the breaking point. But "weakness was turned to strength" (Hebrews 11:34, NIV). I prayed to God to see me through this horrible time, and He did in ways I never dreamed possible. God did not wave a magic wand and make everything better overnight; however, slowly but surely I was able to recover, first selling one home and then the other. I always had just enough to make ends meet. I transitioned out of my business and after some floundering finally found a wonderful job that I love and that pays me well. My life went from being one of turmoil and grief to one of peace and joy.

Susan Fitzgerald
Little Rock, Arkansas

persevere in this storm. Here are some suggestions for staying grounded with God.

Trust in God

When in a financial dilemma, many people can't fathom that there's a way out—even with God's help. Yet one of the definitions of the word *faith* is "belief and trust." Just by having faith, you already accept that God is present and will help you. "That's what faith is about—that's what keeps us going when the chips are down. I am not in this alone. God is with me. I will make it through this," Taylor says.

If you find your faith faltering, go to a trusted friend in your church or confide in a pastor or priest. Lay out what is going on in your life, and ask them to help you get through this time, Dr. Padelford says. Many times, they can guide you out of financial trouble, but they can also provide religious and spiritual support for you if you start to lose your way.

Continue to Be Generous

Despite your financial burden, be as generous as you can, as did the widow Jesus spoke of: "Jesus saw the rich putting their gifts in the treasury. He also saw a poor widow put in two very small copper coins. 'I tell you the truth,' he says, 'this poor widow has put in more than the others. . . . [S]he out of poverty put in all she had to live on'" (Luke 21:1–4, NIV).

If you absolutely cannot give of your money, donate your time or expertise to your church and other charity organizations, Dr. Padelford says. Many times, what you give will be made up in other ways.

Accept the Challenge

In ways you often cannot understand, God sometime uses bad events to strengthen you. "Through trial God helps to shape and refine our character," Taylor says. Instead of becoming hostile because of your financial troubles, take the opportunity to learn, grow, and improve because of it. "That's the question: Will you let it make you bitter or better?" Bray says.

We turn to God for help when our foundations are shaking, only to learn it is God who is shaking them.

—Charles C. West

PRAYER-WALKING

In Step with God

When people talk about walking with the Lord, they don't necessarily mean it literally. Nonetheless, prayer-walking can be a powerful method of communing with the Divine—and a healthy one, too.

Prayer-walking takes advantage of the linkage that exists between your mind, your body, and your spirit, says Carolyn Scott Kortge, author of *The Spirited Walker: Fitness Walking for Clarity, Balance and Spiritual Connection*. The natural rhythm of walking and breathing helps focus your mind on the present moment, she says, sweeping away the jumble of thoughts that keep you from noticing that you are surrounded by miracles. When you add a rhythmic prayer to the rhythm of your moving and breathing, you can swing open a doorway to the holy, leaving you profoundly aware of your connection to the Divine power that surrounds you.

For Kortge, a spirited walk usually moves gradually through four distinct stages.

1. Focus: As she begins walking, she repeats, to herself, a gentle phrase that serves to focus her in the moment. A favorite is: "I am here, I am grateful/I am here, I am happy."

Like all the phrases she uses in her walks, these fall naturally into sync with the cadence of her walking and her breathing. "That rhythm is very important," she says. "It is physically, biologically soothing."

2. Observe: After 5 minutes or so of repeating this first phrase (more or less, depending on the length of the walk), Kortge shifts into what she calls a "sensory scan" stage. She begins by repeating a phrase such as "I am here and I am seeing," focusing her attention on what she sees. After a couple of minutes, she'll move to another sense: "I am here and I am hearing," focusing on what she hears. This continues as she works her way through what her body feels and what she smells.

3. Pray: Now 10 minutes or so into her walk, Kortge moves into a sort contemplative prayer, repeating a phrase that focuses her awareness on being in the presence of the Divine. She often chooses a Buddhist saying— "om mani padme hom"—which refers to the spirit of God in all things. Other people use such phrases as "God be with me," "Thy will be done," or simply, "Amen."

In his book *The Complete Guide to Prayer-Walking: A Simple Path to Body-and-Soul Fitness*, author Linus Mundy suggests rhythmically repeating favorite passages of scripture. Lines from favorite hymns are also an option. Make up a prayer if you want to. The possibilities are literally endless, as long as they fit into the rhythm of your walking and breathing and as long as they give you some positive sense of connection to your higher power.

4. Rejoice: When she reaches the last couple of blocks of her walk, Kortge shifts into a cool-down phase, repeating "I give thanks" as she slows her physical pace and her breathing. Early on in her development as a walker, she says, she was mostly giving thanks for being done with her workout. Over time her prayer of gratitude came to encompass all her blessings, from the fresh air she breathes to the house she has to live in to the husband who loves her.

Kortge walks 4 or 5 days a week, usually, for periods of time ranging from 45 minutes to an hour. There are plenty of books available that discuss walking techniques in some detail, including hers. She cites two basic training tips as essential: good, supportive shoes and an erect posture that allows you to breathe deeply.

Part 9

YOUR HOME LIFE

Standards That Clash

*Compulsive cleaners versus pack rats. Penny-pinchers versus
spendthrifts. Differing views on the way to live are bound to
create conflicts at home, but with a little prayerful thinking you
can stop them before they lead to wars.*

As a reward for a hard week's worth of work, Tom and Maureen decided they'd dine out each Friday, figuring it would be a nice relaxing break. It started out that way. Then they discovered that whenever it came time to leave the tip, the evening inevitably dissolved into a clash of views.

Tom, a buttoned-down, bottom-line accountant, saw the tip as a measure of the quality of service—good service, good tip; poor service, poor tip. Maureen, a former waitress, saw it as an opportunity to reward people who struggled in difficult, low-paying jobs. She favored generous tips regardless of service. Try as they might, the couple never could strike a happy medium. And instead of enjoying dinner, they began to dread it because they knew each night would end with an unhappy drive home.

Conflicts like this are a common part of family life, whether they involve different views on tips, how clean the house should be, or whether the family stereo should broadcast bebop or heavy metal. They're to be expected. But that doesn't mean they have to be acrimonious.

Pastors and counselors say there are prayerful ways you can resolve the things you *don't* like in a person you *do* love. The keys:

- Search for the value in the other person's point of view.
- Open yourself up to compromise, and have faith that the other person will do the same.

The Art of Listening

You can have everything you want, if you just help enough other people get what they want.

—*Zig Ziglar*

Joan and Steve are at an impasse. On occasional weeknights, Steve still likes to go out and have a good time with his college buddies, and while Joan doesn't begrudge him his evenings out, she gets upset when he doesn't come home until one or two in the morning. It worries her, and if the kids wake up and see that dad's not home yet, it worries them too.

Steve, on the other hand, doesn't see what all the fuss is about. He's spent time with these guys his entire adult life, has always stayed out late with them, and has always found his way back home. What's more, he considers meeting a curfew something children do, not spouses and parents.

They both have a case, say experts, and what they need to realize is that the way out of this box is not to stress the legitimacy of their own position but to try to see the legitimacy of the other person's. Here's how.

1. Communicate through Prayer

If you and another family member can't see eye to eye on an issue, pray together and talk to one another as well as to God. "When you have a clash of values or tastes, pray out loud and ask God to open your mind to what the other person needs and wants," suggests Sue Patton Thoele, a psychotherapist from Boulder, Colorado, and author of *Heart-Centered Marriage*. "One way to reinforce your commitment to listen is to put your hand on the other person's heart and, as you pray, say, 'I pray this from the depths of my heart.' This helps everyone appreciate that you're trying to hear one another's deepest longings."

2. Tell the Whole Story

Talk candidly about the things you want to change—and explain why. This helps the other person understand why an issue is so important to you, says Gary Brainerd, Ph.D., a clinical psychologist and workshop leader from Los Angeles. He offers an example of how well this can work. "A couple was living in a handsome neighborhood, and the wife complained that their yard looked overgrown,"

A Prayer for Cooperation

O Lord, you have brought all your faithful people into a single universal family, stretching across heaven and earth. Bind us together with a spiritual love which is stronger than any human love, that in serving one another we may neither count the cost nor seek reward, but think only of the common good.

—Mozarabic Sacramentary

says Dr. Brainerd. "She thought the lawn should be mowed more often, while her husband, who did the mowing, thought once a week was sufficient. They couldn't get together on this until she finally told him that she had grown up ashamed of her family's poverty, that their yard was always the shabbiest on the block, and that those old feelings of shame were stirred up when she looked at their lawn."

Once the husband heard her candid comments, he was more than willing to give her what she wanted, says Dr. Brainerd.

3. Switch Points of View

When you can't seem to discuss your way out of an impasse, try reversing roles. "Sometimes it even helps to change seats," says Lew Richfield, Ph.D., a marriage and family therapist practicing in West Los Angeles. "Take on the other person's argument, state it to them as clearly and persuasively as possible, and ask them to do the same for your point of view." This technique helps you better appreciate what the other person needs, he says.

4. Search for Common Ground

If you can't reconcile your views on an issue, set aside all the points on which you *don't* agree and write up a list of the ones on which you *do*, suggests Lowell Erdahl, bishop emeritus of the St. Paul, Minnesota, area synod of the Evangelical Lutheran Church of America. For example, you may not be able to agree as a family where you want to go on vacation, but you may find you all want a place that offers peace and quiet or natural adventures. "Hopefully,

HELP ME ADMIT WHEN I'M WRONG

Lord,

Why is it so difficult

To make peace with each other?

No wonder there are wars.

Is it pride that holds my mouth tight shut,

A childish feeling

that I am not the one who should apologize?

It wasn't my fault?

In these flare-ups

What does it matter whose fault it is?

The only thing that matters is love and harmony,

Lord, turning my back in anger is weakness,

It reduces me as a human being,

Give me the courage,

the stature

to say, "I'm sorry."

—Frank Topping

listing similarities will help you to find other points of agreement, and you can begin to develop a solution," says Bishop Erdahl.

Give a Little, Get a Little

It would be nice to live in a world where everything was black or white— where every family conflict ended with one person happily yielding to the other's point of view. The truth: That isn't gonna happen.

More than likely, if you want to gain ground you'll have to give ground—

to compromise. How can you do that successfully, so everyone feels they've been treated fairly? It's a matter of acting prayerfully and accepting that the common goal—a happy home—is greater than any one person's self-interest, says Dr. Richfield.

He and the other experts offer five tips to help you reach meaningful compromises.

1. Rank Your Desires

Have each family member make a chart of what they want and assign to each item a number from 1 to 10, representing the intensity of the desire. Make

GETTING DOWN TO BUSINESS

Some of the toughest conflicts around the home are those that involve keeping the place clean. This can be a particular problem if one spouse is a neatnik and the other sloppy or if both of them are in a pitched battle against kids who leave dirty clothes and dishes and book bags around the house. What's the solution?

Take a lesson from the business world, suggests Jean Newhouse, a therapist specializing in individual and family treatment practicing in New York City. "Families are based on love but they also operate like a small business," says Newhouse, "and when it comes to dividing up the chores, we need to think of it that way."

Newhouse offer three suggestions for treating cleaning as a business. First, parents and children should make a list of what jobs they're particularly talented at, whether it's washing dishes, straightening furniture, or weeding gardens. This becomes their "family resume." Next, after looking at each others' lists, they should each make a second list, this time of jobs they are willing to learn how to do. This is their "on-the-job training." Finally, they need to look at which jobs are still not accounted for and begin to divide them up evenly amongst themselves. "This is the grunt work that no one likes but is indispensable to the running of the 'business,'" she says.

Prayer Miracles

Prayer Opened My Son-in-Law's Eyes

My *daughter Donna and her husband, David, had been struggling with finances for years and the strain had gotten to Donna. She called one day and said she was considering leaving David. He had insisted that she not work because their two kids were so young, and she felt the stress of a one-paycheck, one-car family. Immediately upon hanging up from my daughter's call, I got on my knees and asked the Lord to strengthen David, to give him the financial support the family needed. I also asked the Lord to make David aware that he needed to mend his marriage by putting the Lord first and going back to church. I prayed until I felt the comfort of the Holy Ghost telling me everything was gong to be okay.*

The next day Donna told me David had come home from work and said that he knew he needed to start going back to church and put the Lord first in their life if he wanted to keep his family. He also apologized for hurting Donna's feelings and making her feel inadequate.

Today, Donna and her family are strong in church. David has a fantastic job and Donna is working also. This is a miracle grown out of what could have been a tragedy but for the power of prayer.

Janette Tatum
Little Rock, Arkansas

1 "no big deal," 10 "I think I'll die if I don't have this," and see who is willing to yield on which points. "Often," says Dr. Richfield, "you find that a number of issues that mean a lot to you are quite disposable to others, and they're more than willing to concede to you."

2. Make a Small Concession

See if there's a way you can budge a bit from what you want. "When you each relinquish just a small part of your argument," says Bishop Erdahl, "when you each can say, 'well, maybe I'm being 2 percent stubborn on this point,' it often has the effect of spiraling everyone down from a mood of contention to one of cooperation."

3. Put Your Brains to Work

If it seems you're at an impasse, look for creative solutions to your problem. For example, Tom and Maureen, the couple that argued over tips, finally solved their problem by thinking outside the box. They decided to take turns taking each other out. On the Fridays Tom paid, he was free to leave whatever tip his accountant's mind deemed the service deserved, while on the evenings Maureen paid, she left as much as her compassionate heart desired. The result: No more spoiled dinners, no more fights.

4. Keep It Light

Apply the sense of humor that God gives all of us to lighten your conflicts. One example: "A father and son were at loggerheads about how often the boy was supposed to clean up his room," says Thoele, "and on one occasion the boy really let it get bad. Knowing that his dad would pitch a fit over it but not having time to clean the entire room, he took his dirty clothes and used them to spell out 'Will Clean Tonight.' The dad loved it and, of course, cut the boy some slack."

> *If a relationship is built on "what am I getting?" all is lost.*
>
> —*Ossie Davis*

5. Show Your Appreciation

When another family member has given you what you want, let the person know you're thankful. "It's simple; do unto others as you would have them do unto you," says Bishop Erdahl. "Whether it's with flowers, a note of thanks, or a promise to concede when there's something they want badly, when you acknowledge a compromise it will beget further compromises."

When Acceptance Is the Only Course

Sometimes there's just no possibility for compromise. Each of you is just too entrenched in your view to make a change. What do you do then? Ask God to give you the power to love each other as Jesus taught, suggests Bishop Erdahl.

"Jesus taught two kinds of love," says Bishop Erdahl. "Eros, which is 'love because,' meaning I love you because of your personality, or your looks, or your generosity, etc., and agape, which is 'love despite,' or, I love you despite the fact that you snore, or leave your clothes on the stairway, or whatever." When you're stuck in a conflict, each of you should pray, "Dear God, please give me the love of agape." Then you can know you're both trying to love each other despite your faults and foibles.

Creating Prayerful Surroundings

Designing a sacred space and filling it with icons, mementos, and spiritual symbols does more than embellish your home. It focuses your prayer life and deepens your relationship with God.

very object on the long window ledge above her kitchen stove reminds Peg Streep, author of *Spiritual Gardening* and *Altars Made Easy*, of her spiritual life and relationship to God. A hammered tin shrine of the Virgin of Guadelupe stands side-by-side with an African Ashanti wood statue of a nursing mother. Nearby, beneath the foliage of a potted plant, an ancient goddess stands in the earth—just as her creators intended 30,000 years ago. Nestled in between are tiny, carved wooden animals. And in the center of the collection—a baby picture of her only child.

"The shrine is a place of strength for me," says Streep. "It reminds me that the ordinary day-to-day acts of feeding my family and giving them my energies are meaningful."

Sacred, prayerful surroundings like this are a source of spiritual renewal for many people, often because they promote a connection to God in a busy world that seems designed to hamper it. Increasingly we may be plugged into the world around us—through computers, telephones, and faxes, yet these machines can leave us feeling more isolated. Prayerful surroundings help us bridge that isolation.

If you yearn for a sacred place where you can worship, take heart. Creating a space is easy if you follow these steps.

- Choose a special spot and make it sacred.
- Practice prayerful acts in your new space.
- Cultivate prayerful surrounding everywhere.

Create Your Own Sacred Space

In a recent *House & Garden* magazine survey, people were asked what they considered necessities for their home. Only half mentioned features like a security system, a home computer, or multiple phone lines. At the top of the list? A quiet place for meditation and spiritual contemplation, said 82 percent of the respondents.

Creating prayerful surroundings is not decorating. It is a process of discovering what has meaning for you and giving it a physical form. You may already do this unconsciously. Children, for instance, create their own altars all the time. Near their beds you'll often find a collection of favorite objects carefully arranged, explains Streep. This simple act is a way to find comfort and identity.

"The very act of creating sacred space makes us spiritually receptive," says Streep. Here's how to develop your sacred space.

When our life is filled with the desire to see the holiness in everyday things, something magical begins to happen: Ordinary life becomes extra-ordinary, and the very process of living begins to nourish our soul!

—*Rabbi Harold S. Kushner*

1. Select a Space

Any room—or any corner of a room—can become imbibed with the Divine. You can transform a shelf or windowsill, a tabletop, a quiet corner of a room, even a walk-in closet into areas for prayer and meditation, says Ruthann Valentine, doctor of ministry, a pastoral psychotherapist in Monroeville, Pennsylvania. Many people select a room where they spend the most time.

There are, however, a few general points to ponder. Consider whether you want the space to be communal or private. Ask yourself: Will I be comfortable here? How do I feel here? What kind of associations does this room bring forth?

THE PRAYERFUL GARDEN

Abba, Abba-Father
Help me to plant
A garden for You
Mystical Flowers
Seeded by virtues
Nourished by loving
Strengthened by trials
Your life and your water
Giving it life
Blooming inside me
For You to enjoy
Abba, Abba-Father
Within this garden
May together we live
I as your child
You as my God

—Desiree Brassette

---

2. Fill It with Objects of Meaning

Objects in and of themselves aren't sacred. It's the feeling that they awaken in you that is sacred. Although a crucifix, a star of David, or other traditional icons may be the first things that come to mind, don't stop there. Choose objects that remind you of the fullness of life. A memento of a trip or an emotionally important occasion or a photograph of a loved one are powerful visual reminders that your life is filled with many gifts. "You are surrounding yourself with objects that are meaningful to you," says Streep.

3. Stir Your Senses

Objects that can be handled—a string of beads or a smooth rock, for example—are a way to bolster yourself with the power of touch, says Streep. Also, you can use the power of scent—from candles, incense, or flowers—to ready yourself for prayer. "It has long been known that scents have the ability to influence how we feel and think. Each of us has deep-seated associations with scent and smell," she says.

4. Reconnect to Family Traditions

Rediscover the sacred traditions of your grandparents, suggests Streep. Perhaps your grandparents started every meal with a prayer of thanks. For them, the kitchen table was a communal sacred space. Rekindling traditions like these can touch a deep place in you.

Kindling the Spirit in Your Space

The rhythm of modern life simply isn't conducive to prayer. In the juggling act of everyday life, taking time for prayer and meditation can seem like one more ball to keep up in the air. It's not.

Just as a good night's sleep recharges physical energy, time spent in your sacred space will replenish your spiritual energy. Think of that energy as a weaver's cloth, explains Dr. Valentine. Your everyday obligations pull at the fibers and stretch the cloth out of shape. A period of prayer and reflection in your sacred space realigns the threads until the cloth is once again smooth and square. You feel more peaceful. Your thoughts are no longer racing. Even your posture can improve.

How can you make best use of your space?

1. Make Time Every Day

To remind yourself of God's grace, you need to set aside time for prayer and spiritual renewal when you start and when you end each day. In the morning, you might read an uplifting scripture passage, and in the evening you might record the day's events in a journal for reflection, suggests Dr. Valentine.

2. Establish a Ritual

Ritual helps prepare you for prayer, explains Dr. Valentine. You might want to light a candle to remember a loved one, have a moment of silence, or take a few deep breaths.

3. Say the Rosary

The Catholic, Hindu, Buddhist, and Muslim traditions all use prayer beads and the ritual of repetition. "As a tool of meditation, repetition is meant to free up the mind so that it focuses solely on the act of prayer," says Streep.

SHOW ME THE SPIRITUAL AROUND ME

O Great Spirit, Whose voice I hear in the winds, And whose breath gives life to all the world, Hear me! I need your strength and wisdom.

Let Me Walk in Beauty, and make my eyes ever behold the red and purple sunset,

Make My Hands respect things you have made and my ears sharp to hear your voice.

Make Me Wise so that I may understand the things you have taught my people.

Let Me Learn the Lessons you have hidden in every leaf and rock.

I Seek Strength, not to be greater than my brother, but to fight my greatest enemy—myself.

—Native American prayer

---

4. Sound It Out

Soothing sounds such as chimes, soft music, or a bubbling fountain can add energy to your spiritual space, says Dan Dwyer, codirector of the Windrise Spirituality Center in Metamora, Michigan. Sound also helps remove distracting noises that can impair spiritual openness, such as the hum of a refrigerator or the din of traffic.

Carving a Sacred Niche Anywhere

In his *Spiritual Exercises*, St. Ignatius of Loyola urges us to look for God in all things. Simply put: Your life takes on greater meaning when you are aware of the sacred in everyday life. Yet many people tend to ignore that advice.

"In our society we tend to discriminate about what space is sacred—the church is considered, the kitchen is not," says Dwyer. But, he adds, "We carry within us the capacity to rename everything sacred."

Here are some suggestions for expanding your sacred space.

1. Hide an Altar

Place a special object in a place where only you will notice it—a tiny figurine above a door molding, a photograph inside a closet, or a beautiful marble in a chink in a stone wall, for example—says Jean McMann, author of *Altars and Icons: Sacred Spaces in Everyday Life*. These will inspire and refresh you privately. Looking where you normally don't look keeps your eyes alert. You begin to see more in your surroundings.

> *Nowhere can you retire with more quietness or more freedom than within your own spirit. Constantly give yourself this retreat, and renew yourself.*
>
> —*Marcus Aurelius*

2. Work with Spirit

Try incorporating a small-scale altar into your workspace as a reminder that your spiritual needs should be tended no matter where you are physically, says Streep. Choose objects that remind you of the things in your life that nurture your spirit—a Bible, a cherished photo, a dish of river pebbles, even a bouquet of flowers can bring spiritual energy into your work sphere. Select a spot for your sacred space based on your own needs. For example, if you spend long hours on the telephone or in front of a computer screen, pick a spot where you can literally turn away from your work and rest your eyes and spirit for a moment.

3. Calm the Road Rage

Make your daily commute a spiritual journey, suggests Dwyer. He recalls a client who found his sacred space in his car. The man spent several hours on the road each week. It made perfect sense to use those solitary hours for spiritual reflection, explains Dwyer. So, the man built a miniature altar on the dashboard, turned off the radio, and became more mindful about his actions in the car.

4. Honor the Sacred in Nature

You may spend most of your days indoors deprived of natural light and no longer feeling a connection to sun and growth, earth and harvest—all God's works. Go outside. Gaze at the stars. Listen to the trill of a bird. Pay attention to the delicate shadows cast by the sun. Appreciate the beauty of a bright flower blossom.

Surviving Disasters

When catastrophe strikes, it can expose your doubts about safety, fairness, and virtually every other aspect of your life. How can you recover? Turn to prayer, faith, and a renewal of your relationship with God.

It's a sunny August day in Salt Lake City, just before 1:00 P.M. Workers are installing a temporary pavilion for a convention at the Delta Center, while all around people are heading to and from lunch. Suddenly, a tornado rips through the downtown. Within seconds winds rise to more than 150 miles per hour, ripping through the pavilion, peeling part of the roof off the convention center, stripping windows from glass office towers, and damaging more than 120 homes. It's the strongest tornado ever to hit Utah; by the time it leaves, a half-mile-wide section of center city is devastated, one convention worker is dead, and another 100 people are injured.

"We had no warning: The skies didn't darken, the temperature didn't change. It just struck—like a thief in the night," recalls the Reverend Ron Hodges, pastor of Christ United Methodist Church in Salt Lake City.

Often, natural disasters are like this. They surprise you, disrupt and devastate your life, then move on. The only truth they leave behind is this: "There are no guarantees in life, even for the most diligently faithful among us," says Reverend Hodges. "The rain truly falls on the just and the unjust alike."

How can you make sense of such senseless acts? How can you get beyond them? Counselors and pastors recommend three ways.

- Affirm your faith.
- Rebuild your life in logical steps.
- Find satisfaction in helping others.

Keeping the Faith

If disaster strikes your life, your first reaction may be to question why: Why didn't God protect you and your faithful family and friends, and why would a loving, all-powerful God let such a horrible thing occur? The truth is, disasters are simply a part of our sometimes random life on Earth, says Reverend Hodges. "God does not protect some and inflict others. God didn't choose for our tornado to hit one side of Salt Lake City and not the other, to destroy one family's home and leave another's intact."

Nevertheless, that doesn't mean God is absent when disaster strikes. "It makes no sense to ask God to take away our pain, because that is part of life, that is our 'crucifixion,'" says the Reverend Edward Gunter, doctor of ministry, pastor of St. James United Methodist Church in Tarboro, North Carolina, a city devastated by floods after several hurricanes pounded the area in the fall of 1999. "We ask only that He help us endure it, as He helped Jesus endure *His.*"

We do not say, "I am with God and therefore nothing bad will happen to me." We say, "I am with God and therefore whatever might happen to me, God will see me through it."

—*Reverend Ron Hodges*

But how do we reach out to God when our world is falling in upon us?

1. Let Out Your Anger

If you feel God has let you down, say so. "We sell God short if we think He's not willing to hear our laments and our anger," says Dr. Gunter. "Prayer can be a shout of protest to the heavens, an angry missive in your journal, or maybe a loud conversation in the pastor's office about the paradox of a loving God who allows selective suffering. If you feel it, you ought to speak it. It's your obligation to yourself."

2. Draw Closer to God

Sit in silence and meditate on the words, "Lord, just be with me." "No matter how disillusioned or angry you might be with God, silence can have an

MY VOICE IS SILENT NOW

Strengthen me, O Lord,

for Your servant is bowed to the dust.

The voice that used to sing Your praise is silent now. . . .

Raise me up, do not leave me alone.

I need my health to sing Your praise,

and help Your people lead holy lives.

I plead with You: You are my strength,

do not desert me, do not leave me alone.

I grew weak amid the storm,

and betrayed Your love,

but I long to return to You.

—*Gregory of Nazianzus*

enormously healing effect, especially when there's been great, dramatic tumult in your life," says the Reverend Mychal Judge, chaplain to the New York City Fire Department. "It calms you down, centers you, brings God closer."

3. Admit Your Uncertainties

Pray daily, "Lord, I do not know what the future holds, but I know Who holds the future," suggests Reverend Hodges. "By repeating this little prayer you confirm in your heart that no matter what happens today, God is there."

4. Encourage Yourself

If your faith flags, recite this little verse from Charles Gerkin, Ph.D., former professor of pastoral theology at Candler Seminary in Atlanta: "Be not discouraged, for God is with you." "I started reciting this to myself shortly after a bad fall left me a near invalid," says Dr. Gerkin, "and I found that it lifted my spirits. Then as I met up with others who were suffering I would pray it aloud with them and it lifted theirs as well."

Picking Up the Pieces

Disasters can make you feel powerless, as though you're no match for a mighty flood, a raging fire, or a mammoth earthquake. You see how easily nature can uproot whole homes, reducing a lifetime of labor to rubble. Your emotions are like a roller coaster, and just when you think the ride's over, up they come again in unpredictable ways.

But it's precisely because of that feeling of powerlessness that you need to find ways to exert "mastery" over the crisis, says Thomas M. Haizlip, M.D., director of the division of child and adolescent psychiatry at the University of North Carolina Medical Center in Chapel Hill and leader of disaster relief teams. By this, he means taking a series of steps calculated to assert as much power as you can over your situation, so that you don't feel overwhelmed or incapacitated by it.

"You can do this in stages, beginning with the recognition that whatever has caused you your grief is not in and of itself bad," Dr. Haizlip says. "Your house burns down, but you begin to 'master' fire again by reminding yourself that it is a good and necessary thing as well as a potential enemy. It's a simple mindset, but it helps remind you that you do have a level of control in these situations."

Pastors and counselors offer these other useful tools for gaining "mastery" over disaster.

1. Describe Your Pain

You're likely to have mixed feelings for a long time after a disaster. To come to grips with them, keep a daily journal of your emotions and talk to other survivors. "Posttraumatic stress is the most common psychological fallout from disasters," says Dr. Haizlip. "It's dangerous because you start out in the first week or so feeling as though you've gotten on top of the problem, but then, about 2 or 3 weeks later, when your guard is down, it hits you again. And if you're not expecting it, it will come out in insidious ways—anger directed at people you love, rebelliousness, maybe even substance abuse. The best way to ward it off is to surround yourself with the people you love and for all of you to keep talking honestly about what you're feeling and why."

2. Build a Shield for the Future

As a family, discuss how you can make yourselves safer than you were before the disaster. "In North Carolina, after Hurricane Floyd devastated the eastern third of the state, people found a measure of comfort in making themselves more secure against future floods," says Dr. Haizlip. "This could be any-

PROTECT US, LORD

Almighty God,
you know us to be set in the midst of so many
and great dangers,
that, because of the frailty of our nature,
we cannot always stand upright.
Give us such strength and protection
as may support us in all dangers
and carry us through all temptations;
through Jesus Christ our Lord

—*From* The Alternative Service Book

thing from laying in sand bags and mapping out and rehearsing escape routes to waterproofing the basement of their home."

3. Look at the Bigger Picture

Make a list of the *things* you lost and the *people* you didn't. "This puts your life into perspective," says Dr. Gunter. "Victims of the Tarboro flood were more grateful for having their loved ones survive than they were upset about having their homes ruined."

4. Be Realistic

Don't expect life to return to normal quickly. If you do, you could end up disappointed. "It's too easy to have your hopes dashed if rebuilding takes longer than you anticipate," says Dr. Gunter. If you want to get a realistic sense of when things are going to be okay again, ask a disaster expert who's on the scene.

5. Rebuild Your Life

Piece by piece, begin to restore whatever was lost. "We encourage people to begin fixing up their home and their lives quickly, not only because they have to get on with life but also because it reduces their feeling of despair and powerlessness," says Dr. Haizlip. "It's a perfect time to prevail upon whatever assistance is out there—from churches to friends to the government—and put it to work for you."

6. Get Back into a Routine

Even if your home has been destroyed, resume as normal a family schedule as your circumstances will allow. "Kids should be getting up and going to school at the regular time, adults should be going off to work, families should be attending their regular worship services on weekends, all of which restores a sense of security in a very turbulent time," says Dr. Haizlip.

Doing Well by Doing Good

Experts believe another way you can help your own recovery is by assisting other people in theirs. It gives you a feeling of purpose and an opportunity to make something "right." In addition, it softens the irrational blame you might put on yourself because another family endured greater suffering than yours. As Dr. Haizlip says, "Altruism is itself a healing balm for the person who administers it. It relieves us of guilt, distracts us from our misery, and as the adage goes, lights one light instead of cursing the darkness."

I Don't Understand, Lord

I don't at all understand the tough times I'm going through right now, Lord. But I release to you my own desires and expectations in this situation. I declare your lordship over my life, and I choose to believe that you love me. Show me the attitudes I need to change, and enable me to do it. Thank you that in the unseen realm, you are working in people and events in a way that ultimately will bring you glory. Lord, my faith is in you, not in my circumstances. Help me see these things from your viewpoint and then walk in your peace. Amen.

—Quin Sherrer and Ruthanne Garlock

Here are some things pastors and counselors suggest you might do to help your own healing process.

1. Do Something Charitable

Since the house is on fire let us warm ourselves.

—*Italian proverb*

Do at least one good deed for someone outside your own family each day. Volunteer at an emergency shelter, pray with another family, make a donation to the relief effort, or pick up someone else's kids at school for them. Whatever you do it will be life-enhancing, says Reverend Hodges. "Good deeds are, as St. John put it, the light that the darkness will not consume. So when you help someone else, you're declaring that the light continues to shine on you and that your own actions turn hope into reality."

2. Get Children Involved

Use the disaster as an opportunity to empower your own children by encouraging them to donate toys, pray for their friends, or perhaps volunteer in the cleanup efforts. "Kids not only need to know their parents will take care of them," says Dr. Haizlip, "they also need to know that they, too, have a contribution to make to their community, that they're important to its lifeblood."

3. Get Your Church Involved

Ask your church leaders to organize groups of relief volunteers. "When our town was flooded," says Dr. Gunter, "it forced us to look beyond our church walls and see our connectedness to the community in ways that we might not have thought of before. Because everyone was suffering, issues of class, race, wealth, religious affiliation, and the like—issues that might at one time have separated us from one another—became irrelevant. We truly experienced one another as God's children, no one any different than another. It was a great blessing."

Moving Away

Whether you're leaving by choice or necessity, moving from a home you've lived in for years can cause stress and emotional strain. But with prayer and a spiritual perspective, you can make the best of this intense time.

Once their three kids grew up and moved away, Seymour and Josie Hyde decided that it was time for them to move on as well. There was too much house for just the two of them.

So they sold the old homestead and purchased a smaller place in a nearby community. But rather than quietly leaving, Seymour and Josie made their move a spiritual experience. They drew upon Native American tradition and held a day-long celebration to both mourn and celebrate the change in their lives.

"They made a virtue of necessity," says Drew Leder, M.D., Ph.D., professor of philosophy at Loyola College in Baltimore, who shares the Hydes' story in his book *Spiritual Passages: Embracing Life's Sacred Journey.*

If you're preparing to leave the house you've called home for years, you can ease the strain by following Seymour and Josie's example and making the move a spiritual experience. The key is to follow three steps.

- Use prayer and practical steps to face the troubling emotions you may experience.
- Plan a meaningful and spiritually enriching goodbye.
- Embrace your new life.

Weathering Emotional Upheaval

Moving has become commonplace in our society. If your business wants you to go to Topeka, Kansas, you pick up and go. But while your possessions are easily transportable, your life is not.

What lies behind us and what lies before us are tiny matters compared to what lies within us.

—*Ralph Waldo Emerson*

When you dismantle the outer part of your life, you also disrupt your interior life. The truth is, on the scale of life's traumas, moving ranks somewhere between filing your income tax return and getting a divorce.

Here's how to weather the upheaval.

1. Sideline Stress

Physical and emotional stress is a logical by-product of the upheaval that you experience during a move, says Arlene Alpert, a therapist in Jupiter, Florida, and author of *Moving without Madness*. You're likely to get less sleep and exercise as you deal with the hectic activities that accompany a move. Plus, you may not eat the way you usually do. Altogether, these changes can lead to immense fatigue, headaches, backaches, and indigestion.

To minimize stress, plan for enough rest and relaxation during the chaotic weeks that surround a move, says Alpert. Set aside time each day for quiet leisure, or take a walk around the neighborhood to say goodbye to friends. Also, you can try deep breathing exercises, which increase oxygen to the brain, the body, and the immune system, says Alpert. Inhale to the count of two through your nose. Hold it for two counts and then slowly breathe out through your mouth letting out a sigh to the count of four. Repeat five to ten times.

2. Turn to Prayer

If you're feeling overwhelmed by the pressure of your move or fears about what will come next, tell God what is troubling you, suggests Everett L. Worthington Jr., Ph.D., chairman of the psychology department at Virginia Commonwealth University in Richmond and executive director of the Campaign for Forgiveness Research. Not only will you feel better for putting your concerns into words, but praying to God has calming effects, he says.

3. Mourn Your Loss

In many ways leaving your home is like experiencing a death, says Dr. Leder. Life as you know it is about to be forever changed. Your place of familiar security is stripped away. At the same time, you face the loss of social and emo-

FINDING JOY IN MOVING

Thank you, God, for this new home, for the excitement of moving, for the challenge of making this place a "home."

Thank you that wherever I go, whatever I do, whatever happens you are by my side.

Lord Jesus, help me to put aside those fears, doubts, and any second thoughts I am having and help me to enjoy this home, to make it a place where your peace reigns.

—*Christian Publicity Organisation*

tional connections that have sustained you—friends, neighbors, and church.

"When you leave all that behind, your old self is dying in a certain sense, and a new self will be born," says Dr. Leder. Reactions to this process can range from mild sadness to full-blown depression. It's important to give yourself permission to experience the sadness. You might want to do this by taking an afternoon to visit special places one last time and say goodbye.

4. Pay Special Attention to Your Children

Children experience very strong emotions when they have to move. To ease their fears, talk with them about their feelings, or read them a book about moving. Alpert says there are several designed specifically for children, such as *Alexander, Who's Not (Do You Hear Me? I Mean It!) Going to Move* by Judith Viorst. And, even though life may be in an uproar, try to stick to familiar routines, such as having dinner together at night or going to church on Sundays.

Creating a Meaningful Goodbye

There are rituals to mark most of life's significant occasions—birth, marriage, and death. But other than packing your possessions onto a truck and hauling them away, there isn't much ceremony involved in the act of moving.

Yet one of the best ways to cope with a move is to acknowledge and cele-

❧

WHEN WE SAY GOODBYE

Lord,

when it is time to say "goodbye"

to friends, family, or places we love

give us courage

to move on to new experiences,

to make new associations

and to allow our children the freedom

to create their own journeys in life.

Where families face division and separation

so that individuals can rediscover their own identity

please be near to sustain and guide.

—*From* Further Everyday Prayers

brate it, as Seymour and Josie Hyde did. To make your move a spiritual journey, gather friends and family at your house. Then try one or all of these rituals.

1. Make Gifts of Unneeded Things

Hold a ceremony to "gift away" possessions that you no longer need and tell the recipient what the object meant to you. "The presentation of each gift should be accompanied by its story," says Dr. Leder. "You're not celebrating a pile of objects, but a shared life."

2. Donate Others to the Needy

You might want to also gather together items for a local charity. Speak briefly about the organization that you've chosen, and then say a prayer asking that the gifts bring blessings to the needy, suggests Dr. Leder.

3. Make the Rounds

Make a ceremonial trip to each room, suggests Dr. Leder. Just as each room has its own special purpose, each also evokes a set of memories—nights spent on the porch swing gazing at the stars, a quiet space where you prayed each morning, the kitchen where you cooked dinner for 20 every Thanksgiving.

4. Thank Your House

When it's time to say goodbye, say a prayer for your house. At their ceremony, Seymour and Josie read a prayer that they had written together, says Dr. Leder. "Bless this fine house and all that it's given us. We give it back to the bountiful universe. May this house always bless whoever comes within its walls, and may it always have a place in our hearts."

> *All things change . . .*
> *but God remains!*
>
> —*Mrs. Humphry Ward*

Building a New Nest

In the Bible, Sarah and Abraham were summoned out of their land by God. At an advanced age, they left behind everything—even their names—to follow a new direction. In the process, they were transformed.

While your move is sure to elicit feelings of loss and sadness, as it did for Sarah and Abraham, moving also holds promise for rebirth.

"We leave behind the habitual on a journey that can also be a spiritual journey," says Dr. Leder.

Here are some ways to welcome the Spirit into your new home.

1. Bless Your New Home

Hold a family prayer service to ask for God's blessing in your new home, says the Reverend David Stevens, associate pastor of Holy Spirit Church in Sioux Falls, South Dakota. Gather family members at the front door, a place symbolic of welcoming God into our new life. Start with a reading from the Bible such as this verse from Luke 10:5, "When you enter a house, first say, 'Peace to this house'" (NIV).

Then go through each room. Describe the activities that will go on in each room and ask for God's blessing.

Return to the front door to end the service by reciting the Lord's Prayer.

2. Make a Fresh Start

Your new environment presents you with the opportunity to cultivate a new you, says Dr. Leder. Make a list of negative things about yourself that you want to leave behind, and then choose some positive pursuits you'll adopt to take their place. For instance, moving into your new home might be an ideal time to start a new hobby like gardening.

Problems
with Neighbors

Whether it involves an encroaching fence, a howling dog, or some other irritating issue, difficulties with a neighbor can lead to ill feelings that last for years—if you let them. Instead, use a prayerful approach to put the problem to rest.

I t's two o'clock in the morning and you've been jarred from a sound sleep by your neighbor's barking dog—for the third time in a week.

Your neighbor's house is an eyesore and an embarrassment. His lawn is knee-high in weeds, and the porch has become a repository for cast-off, broken-down furniture.

There's a worn path across your lawn—a shortcut for your neighbor's kids who walk through on their way to and from school.

Problems like these are part of life when people live close together. But if left to fester, they can cause stress, damage relationships, and make everyone dread coming home at night.

If you're caught up in an issue with a neighbor and want to address it without creating hard feelings, the best way to handle it is to follow a three-step approach built on the teachings of the Bible, say experts.

- Use prayer to consider all sides of the issue.
- Seek a peaceful resolution on your own.
- If that fails, invite others to help you solve the problem.

First, Put It to Prayer

Hatred is never ended by hatred but by love.

—*Buddha*

Conflict with someone isn't necessarily bad or destructive. In fact, there are usually spiritual lessons to be learned in any problem that you encounter, says Charles A. Turnbo, president of Positive Solutions, a nonprofit Christian agency that offers counseling and family mediation in Evergreen, Colorado. But you must take the steps to learn those lessons.

The first temptation when you're involved in a conflict with a neighbor is to rush to take action. "What we normally want to do is straighten our neighbor out," says Turnbo.

Before you take action, however, you should reframe the problem using these biblical principles of peacemaking. It's the spiritual equivalent of taking two deep breaths and counting to 10.

1. Maintain the Right Attitude

The apostle Paul urged the Corinthians, "So whether you eat or drink or whatever you do, do it all for the glory of God" (1 Corinthians 10:31, NIV). He wasn't referring to 1 hour a week spent in church, says Turnbo. He wanted them to show honor to God in all their day-to-day activities, especially when resolving conflict.

If you're having a problem with a neighbor, you need to approach it first with a loving, merciful, and forgiving attitude. Instead of focusing on your own desires (*I want to cut down that tree that keeps dropping leaves in my yard*) or dwelling on what others may do (*They never rake up their leaves, so they blow in my yard*), pray for an answer to this question: *How would God want me to handle this problem?* "Prayer tends to reorient our heart and soften our approach to the problem," says Turnbo.

2. Get the Log out of Your Eye

One of the most challenging peacemaking principles set forth in the Bible is to look at your own role in creating the problem. As the Book of Matthew instructs, "[F]irst take the plank out of your own eye, and then you will see clearly to remove the speck from your brother's eye" (Matthew 7:5, NIV).

HELP US OVERLOOK THE LITTLE PROBLEMS

Lord, you taught us that all who come our way are our neighbors. But hear our prayer for those with whom we come in daily contact because they live close to us. Help us to be good neighbors to them. Give us the grace to overlook petty annoyances and to build on all that is positive in our relationship, that we may love them as we love ourselves, with genuine forbearance and kindness. For Jesus' sake, Amen.

—*From* The Doubleday Prayer Collection

When you're embroiled in a dispute with a neighbor, there are two kinds of "logs" that you need to look for. First, you should consider whether you've had a critical, negative, or overly sensitive attitude that is contributing to the problem. Second, if you are at fault in some way, you should admit your own part in the situation and apologize. It's not always easy for people to see their own faults, admits Turnbo, so you may want to talk with an objective friend who can help you take an honest look at your actions.

3. Reconcile and Repair the Relationship

When faced with a conflict, there may be a strong temptation to either avoid it by denying the problem or to attack it, such as by filing a lawsuit. Neither way reflects biblical peacemaking principles. In each of these scenarios, your relationship with your neighbor will suffer.

As you're prayerfully reflecting on how you want to resolve the problem, keep in mind that your goal is to actively pursue reconciliation in the relationship. Have an open heart to forgive and make peace, says Turnbo.

We Can Work It Out

You'll probably feel awkward approaching your neighbor about a problem—especially if you feel the neighbor *is* the cause of the problem. In a situation like this, it's easy for both parties to end up saying things that they later regret.

Instead of playing the role of wronged neighbor, play the role of peacemaker, working from this point of view: "Let there be peace on earth, and let it begin with me," suggests Turnbo. Approach your neighbor with kindness and concern, he advises. Your goal is to preserve your relationship with your neighbor, not to win a battle.

These are the three basic approaches to take.

1. Let It Pass

Minor problems, such as leaves blowing into your yard from a neighbor's pile or neighborhood kids occasionally tromping across your lawn, are often best resolved by simply overlooking them and forgiving your neighbor, says Turnbo. As Proverbs 19:11 makes clear, "A man's wisdom gives him patience; it is to his glory to overlook an offense" (NIV).

Note that this is not the same as avoiding the problem because you're uncomfortable discussing it with your neighbor. Treating a problem that way can lead you to feel resentful or angry. When you overlook an issue in the biblical sense, you're saying it just isn't significant enough to warrant your anger. For instance, Turnbo and his wife agreed to overlook an incident when a neighbor's barking dog woke them up in the middle of the night. "Our relationship is more important than a moment of inconvenience," he said.

To determine whether you should overlook your problems, ask yourself questions like these: Is this problem hurting other people, or has it permanently damaged our relationship? Is it something that only happens occasionally?

2. Talk It Through

If, however, your neighbor's dog is keeping you up every night and people have been asking why you have dark circles under your eyes, you probably need to talk to your neighbor.

Pick a time and place when you can speak privately, and plan your words carefully. "Many times we assault with powerful words," says Turnbo. If you're uncomfortable with a face-to-face meeting send your neighbor a note or leave a telephone message. In any case, begin the discussion with positive words. You might say, "I really value our relationship," or "We haven't talked in awhile, I hope everything is okay. We heard your dog the other night and were wondering if anything was wrong."

If the initial conversation does not resolve the issue, don't give up. Review what was said and done, and look for alternative ways to approach the problem a second time.

LET US ACT IN LOVE

O Lord, grant that this night we may sleep in peace. And that in the morning our awakening may also be in peace. May our daytime be cloaked in your peace.

Protect us and inspire us to think and act only out of love.

Keep far from us all evil; may our paths be free from all obstacles from when we go out until we return home.

—*From the Babylonian Talmud*

---

3. Negotiate a Compromise

More serious issues that affect more than one neighbor or that relate to money or property should be resolved by prayerfully negotiating solutions that meet the interests of all those involved, says Turnbo. Follow the Bible's lead in this case: "Each of you should look not only to your own interests, but also to the interests of others" (Philippians 2:4, NIV). In other words, try to resolve the situation in a cooperative, not competitive, manner. Look for solutions that will benefit everyone involved.

If, for example, a tree straddles a property line: One neighbor wants more sunlight and decides to chop the tree down. But the other neighbor enjoys the privacy provided by the branches and leaves of the tree. Perhaps they could reach a compromise, says Ron Mock, director of the Center for Peace Learning at George Fox University in Newberg, Oregon. Have a professional service prune the tree to allow more sunlight into one yard, yet still preserve enough vegetation to allow the other neighbor to enjoy the privacy.

Calling In Outside Help

When careful attempts to work it out on your own have failed, consider contacting a professional mediator—a person trained to work with both sides to resolve the dispute.

Mediation can be as informal as sitting down together for a cup of coffee or as complicated as arranging an all-day meeting with several witnesses. Unlike litigation, which pits one person against another, mediation involves a cooperative effort to reach an agreement. The best benefit: It also normally preserves the relationship.

"The idea is to make it not so much a tug-of-war as working from the same side of the table," says Mock. "Mediation is aimed at understanding the other person."

To locate a mediator, ask your pastor if your church offers mediation services, check in the Yellow Pages of your telephone book, or go to www.mediate.com if you have access to the Internet. This Web site explains the various types of mediation services and provides an online referral service.

> *It is folly to punish your neighbor by fire when you live next door.*
>
> —*Publilius Syrus*

When you meet with the mediator, you will want to follow some basic rules to improve the chance that you and your neighbor come to an agreement.

1. Tell Your Story, Then Listen

The mediator will set some ground rules: no gossip, no slander, no interrupting. Then you and your neighbor each will be asked to tell your version of the story and to describe what you would like to accomplish. During this time, you should strive to understand your neighbor's point of view, says Mock.

Unlike a courtroom, where attorneys are trained to challenge you, mediation provides a safe environment where there is no need to attack or defend.

2. Identify the Problem

When you're caught in a conflict, sometimes you lose sight of the issues. If that's the case in your disagreement, the mediator will help you and your neighbor clearly and objectively define the issues. Again, it is important to listen objectively and try to look at the issue as your neighbor does.

3. Explore Solutions

Once you've defined the issues, the mediator will ask you and your neighbor to brainstorm possible solutions to each one. The mediator will then help you evaluate each option and encourage you and your neighbor to come to an agreement that is perceived as just and equitable. After all, that is what God would want you to do, as it says in Micah. "And what does the LORD require of you? To act justly and to love mercy and to walk humbly with your God" (Micah 6:8, NIV).

PRAYER-JOURNALING

Correspondence from the Heart

Having trouble getting in touch with God? Try writing a letter.

That's one way to look at writing a spiritual journal: as a letter to God. "When I keep a journal, I listen to the still, small voice within," says Mike Heller, Ph.D., who has taught journal-writing at Pendle Hill, a Quaker center for study and contemplation near Philadelphia. "The writing becomes a bridge for the spirit. I'm connecting to something that feels transcendent."

Spiritual journaling occupies an honored position in Quaker history. From about 1600 to 1900, many Quakers compiled journals that traced how their faith in God developed over the course of their lives. These personal narratives were collected and published after their deaths as a record of the Spirit's work within the community. Since 1900 the practice of journal-writing has faded, but Dr. Heller and others are working to bring it back, as are teachers in other denominations who have discovered the powerful spiritual connection journaling can provide.

There are no rules to writing a spiritual journal, emphasizes Dr. Heller. One of the greatest joys of writing a journal is that it's *yours*. You needn't show it to anybody, if you don't want to. Nor need you be overly concerned with the elegance of the writing. The point isn't to win prizes for composition, but to get in touch with what's going on in your heart.

You may wish to choose a special notebook or folder for your journal; this helps bestow a sense of ritual to the time you spend with it, Dr. Heller says. When you write is up to you. Some teachers recommend you spend a half-hour a day, five days a week. Many people like to write first thing in the morning or last thing at night. Dr. Heller carries his journal with him so that he can jot down a few lines whenever he has a few idle minutes or whenever inspiration strikes. Some days he'll make five entries; other days none.

Before you begin writing, try sitting for a few moments in front of the open page. Simply contemplating that blank page is a powerful spiritual tool, Dr. Heller says. It helps quiet the surface noise of the mind and allows you to turn your attention inward.

What do you write about? Dr. Heller encourages his students to focus on one thing—a memory, a feeling, a problem, an event—and write what they feel about it. A prayer journal, by definition, will make a point of considering matters of spirit and faith. Some people begin their daily journal entries by writing down a favorite prayer. Others begin with the salutation "Dear God" or "Dear Jesus."

Don't be concerned if you find yourself focusing on problems in your journal, Dr. Heller says. This is natural. Part of the value of journaling is the help it can give you in working through negative feelings. On the other hand, many people find it beneficial to simply write down five things they're grateful for every day.

Another exercise Dr. Heller recommends, taking a page from the Quakers, is trying to recall how the Spirit has moved within you since childhood. You might also try to recall moments when you were troubled by some form of injustice you encountered. (The Quakers are known for their social and political activism.) But again, the point isn't to write a dissertation, just to let what's hidden deep inside bubble up to the surface.

At the end of your writing session, you may take what you've written and offer it up to God in prayer if you wish, although Dr. Heller doesn't feel that's a necessary step.

For him, the very act of writing in his journal is a form of prayer.

Part 10

YOUR EMOTIONAL LIFE

Controlling Anger

Giving in to anger will corrode the human heart, but there are strong spiritual weapons you can use to defeat this powerful negative emotion.

he teenage girl sat in the counselor's office and unleashed bitterly hostile remarks about virtually every authority figure in her life, from her parents to her teachers to the police. The therapist decided he'd probe a little.

"You seem very angry at your parents," he ventured.

He still remembers the cold, flat look in her eyes as she answered.

"I don't get angry," she said. "I get even."

She was wrong, of course: She was incredibly angry. The fact that her anger manifested itself as a sort of icy rage only underscores the fact that anger can appear in any number of guises. Whether you're infuriated or irritated, fearful or belligerent, violent or vengeful, anger is often the fuel beneath it all. Small wonder that anger is a theme that crops up throughout the Bible—and throughout our daily lives. "We all struggle with anger," says David Powlison, Ph.D., a counselor at the Christian Counseling and Educational Foundation in Glenside, Pennsylvania. "It's a central part of human nature."

For just that reason, religious and secular thinkers have devoted a huge amount of attention to dealing with anger. Their studies have shown that you can control anger prayerfully with the following three-pronged approach.

- Recognize when you have an anger problem.
- Take a series of specific steps to avoid anger-provoking situations and defuse them once they occur.
- Reach out to others for comfort and support.

Some pursue happiness;
others create it.

—*Anonymous*

Examining Your Anger

Everybody gets angry once in awhile. But for people with an anger *problem*, anger is an obsession that infects—and wrecks—their lives.

The destructive force of anger can not only damage your relationships with others and peace of mind, but it also affects your health, writes leading anger expert Redford Williams, M.D., director of the Behavioral Medicine Research Center at Duke University Medical Center in Durham, North Carolina. People who are consistently angry tend to drink more, smoke more, eat more, and exercise less. Their systems are also regularly flooded with stress hormones that increase their heart rates, constrict their blood vessels, and inhibit their immune systems. The result is an open door to heart disease, cancer, and a host of chronic illnesses.

About 20 percent of the population experiences levels of hostility regularly enough to threaten their health, Dr. Williams says in his book *Anger Kills*. Are you one of them? Your answers to three questions will tell you, he says.

- Do you automatically seek to blame somebody when faced with everyday frustrations, from traffic jams to noisy neighbors?
- Do you get angry at the person or persons you blame for these frustrations?
- Does your anger sometimes spill over into aggressive action?

If this chain reaction of angry responses fits you, then you may well have an anger problem. The question then is, what can you do about it?

The answer: plenty.

Who's In Charge Here?

From a religious point of view, says Dr. Powlison, anger poses a central question—perhaps *the* central question. Who's in control here, God or you?

If you put yourself in charge, once offended you will take it upon yourself to play all the roles in the courtroom of the mind: victim, accuser, prosecutor,

❦

THE SAINT FRANCIS PRAYER FOR PEACE

Lord, make me an instrument of your peace.

Where there is hatred, let me sow love,

Where there is injury, pardon,

Where there is doubt, faith,

Where there is despair, hope.

Where there is darkness, light,

Where there is sadness, joy.

O Divine Master, grant that I may not so much seek

to be consoled as to console,

not so much to be understood as to understand,

not so much to be loved as to love;

for it is in giving that we receive,

it is in pardoning that we are pardoned,

it is in dying that we awake to eternal life.

—A prayer often associated with Saint Francis of Assisi

judge, even hangman. The only role you'll leave unfilled is attorney for the defense.

The antidote for this angry, destructive drama is clear: Turn to God. Here are five steps for making that crucial shift from what Dr. Powlison calls a "horizontal" orientation—between you and the supposed offender—to a "vertical" one—between you and God.

1. Arm Yourself with Prayer

Since you can be blindsided by anger at any time during the day, it makes sense to arm yourself against anger as well by praying throughout the day. Pray a "preventive" prayer each morning, Dr. Powlison suggests, asking for God's help in avoiding anger no matter what occurs in the coming hours. Pray at night to assess your progress and to ask God's forgiveness for your lapses.

Q&A: Isn't There a Place for Righteous Anger?

Q: I'm disgusted by the poor facilities my grandson has at school. Don't I have a right to be angry and complain?

A: Yes, you do, says David Powlison, Ph.D., a counselor at the Christian Counseling and Educational Foundation in Glenside, Pennsylvania. What you're describing is "holy anger"—anger that inspires struggles to fight injustice—and that is certainly justified.

Even Jesus saw a need for holy anger. An example from the Bible occurred when he overturned the tables of the moneychangers in the temple. More contemporary examples include Martin Luther King Jr.'s struggle for civil rights and the crusade of Mothers Against Drunk Driving (MADD).

"The acronym MADD was chosen for a reason, I'm sure," Dr. Powlison says. "They are saying, 'This is wrong; this is an outrage.' Now, if you look at each individual member of that organization, I'm sure you would find many who are motivated by their anger in a righteous way, to correct an injustice, while others, I suspect, are motivated by hostility and a desire for vengeance. There *is* a line there.

"At best, though, MADD and other such organizations are motivated by a need to bring justice to a fallen world."

For a model prayer, look no further than that recommended by Jesus Christ Himself: the Lord's Prayer, Dr. Powlison suggests. Another excellent option is the famous Saint Francis Prayer, he says, which takes direct aim at one of the prime producers of anger: the human tendency to put our own gratification first.

2. Recognize Your Triggers

Recovering alcoholics are taught to avoid "people, places, and things" that may tempt them to drink, like bars and old drinking buddies. The same strategy can work against anger, Dr. Powlison says.

All of us have certain things that provoke us—therapists call them "triggers." You won't be able to avoid them entirely, but you can minimize their impact. If a brother-in-law's political views push your buttons, try to avoid getting into long conversations with him during family get-togethers, for example.

To help crystallize what you need to avoid, make a list of your anger triggers, suggests Carla Perez, M.D., a psychiatrist in San Francisco who has written extensively on controlling compulsive behavior. "You have to know what the enemy is before you can go after it," she says.

3. Step Back

Okay, somebody has ticked you off. What do you do then?

A key tool for making sure anger doesn't get the best of you is to interrupt it. How? By distracting yourself until the first explosive flash passes. The classic distraction techniques are counting to 10 or taking a "time-out" walk around the block, but there are plenty of other variations. Shouting "Stop!" to yourself as loud as you can and then singing a favorite song, also at the top of your lungs, is one example. Another is to imagine your anger as a balloon filled with hot air that you envision slowly leaking away. Use your imagination: The point is to give yourself some breathing room in which to let the force of your anger dissipate.

Taking a time-out also provides you with the perfect opportunity to reach out to God for some spiritual first aid: An instant application of prayer at the

---

GOD, ADJUST MY ATTITUDE

Heavenly Father, your Word renews my mind and prayer changes the attitudes of my heart. . . . I want to get rid of all resentment and bitterness in my life, because I know a root of bitterness can spring up unexpectedly, thereby bringing defilement to many.

Teach me your ways, Father, because I know your way is perfect. . . . Help me to trust you with all my heart instead of leaning upon my own understanding. In all my ways I will acknowledge you and I know you will direct my paths. . . .

When I see someone overtaken in a fault, instead of judging or criticizing that person, I ask you to help me to restore him/her in the spirit of meekness, considering myself, lest I also be tempted. . . .

Lead and strengthen me to walk in the fruit of love, joy, peace, patience, kindness, goodness, faithfulness, gentleness, and self-control. Father, I praise you for bringing forth this fruit in my life.

—*Clift Richards and Lloyd Hildebrand*

❧

HELP ME MEND THIS RELATIONSHIP

Lord, give me the wisdom to help repair breaches and mend broken relationships. I don't want to be a party to dissension and strife. Help me break down walls of enmity and be a peacemaker. I want to be pleasing to you and a good example to others. Keep my mouth from deceit and malice. Help me, with the strength only you can provide, to walk in your compassion. Amen.

—*Quin Sherrer and Ruthanne Garlock*

moment of crisis can make all the difference. Dr. Powlison suggests saying something as simple as the following: "God, be merciful and help me: I don't want to be ruled by this anger. I tend to wander, Lord, and I know it. I need your help."

4. Analyze before Acting

One way to avoid going over the edge when provoked is to step back and examine what's going on. Dr. Williams suggests you ask yourself four questions that will help you decide how to handle the situation effectively.

1. Is the situation that is making me angry important?
2. Is the reaction I'm having appropriate to the facts of the actual situation?
3. Is there anything I can do about the situation?

If the answer to those three questions is "yes," Dr. Williams says, then ask yourself this:

4. Is it worth it to take whatever action would be necessary to change the situation?

Often the answer to that last question will be "no," Dr. Williams says. For example, if your boss is acting inappropriately in ways that have a significant impact on your work life and your emotions, telling him off probably isn't going to serve your best interests in the long run. It may, however, be constructive to take another form of action, such as beginning to search for another job.

5. Step Forward

Once you've gained control of your own immediate emotional response to an anger-provoking situation, Dr. Powlison suggests taking the next step: Try to defuse the tension between you and whoever else is involved by making some sort of conciliatory, peacemaking gesture.

"If it's your spouse or a friend," Dr. Powlison says, "try putting an arm around their shoulder and saying, 'Forgive me for my tone of voice there—the way I said that wasn't right.' Or, 'I was getting defensive—let me rephrase that.'" Such an action can initiate what Dr. Powlison calls "a gracious cycle," as opposed to the "vicious cycle" that anger typically creates.

> *Keep your words sweet, in case you have to eat them.*
>
> —*Unknown*

Be aware that behaving gracefully is a spiritual discipline that the other person may not be willing to practice. Still, even if you're the only one showing grace, your behavior may have a positive influence. One man, a client of Dr. Powlison's, was being mistreated horribly by his boss. Instead of complaining or quitting, he aimed a "love offensive" at her, going out of his way to treat her as kindly and generously as possible. His guide was Saint Paul's instructions in Romans 12: "Bless those who persecute you. . . . [I]f your enemies are hungry, feed them; if they are thirsty, give them something to drink" (Romans 12:20, NRSV). After a month or so, the woman came into his office and broke into tears, saying how sorry she was for treating him so badly.

Share the Struggle

Anger is one of those emotions that flourishes in the dark, Dr. Powlison says. For that reason, sharing your angry impulses with those you trust—whether that be a spouse, friends, a religious leader, a congregation, or a support group—can shine a light on the beast that lurks within. "I know a lot of argumentative people," Dr. Powlison says, "but I've never seen anyone act openly hostile in church, and I've rarely seen it happen in counseling. The very fact of bringing another person into the picture can serve as a check on angry outbursts."

Talking about the things that make us angry relieves some of the pressure that's building up inside, Dr. Powlison adds. However, if you decide to take this route, you need to make sure you're releasing tension constructively, not angrily, belligerently venting emotion in a temper tantrum, Dr. Powlinson says. Research has shown that blowing off steam in that way often makes people madder than they were in the first place.

Fighting Temptation

Temptation is an enemy that can attack you at every turn.
Here's how to use your spiritual armor to defeat it.

You might call it the Super Bowl of Temptation.

In one corner, Jesus Christ. In the other, Satan, a.k.a. "the tempter."

Jesus had been weakened by 40 days and nights of fasting in the desert when Satan, true to his wily reputation, appeared. Quickly, he threw temptation's greatest hits at the hungry Messiah: power, privilege, and wealth.

Jesus could have all these, Satan said, on one condition: "Bow down and worship me."

"Away from me, Satan!" Jesus replied. "For it is written: 'Worship the Lord your God, and serve him only'" (Matthew 4:1–11, NIV).

Does your willpower match that? Probably not—at least not always. Ever since Adam nibbled the apple with Eve, humans have been assailed by temptation. And like Adam and Eve, we frequently fall. We may eat too much, lust after our neighbor's fancy car, steal a few pens from the office, go to a casino and lose more money than we can afford to lose, or scheme a little too ambitiously for that promotion we really want.

Each of us has different definitions of what constitutes a temptation and a sin. At the same time we all know that there are lines we shouldn't cross, and we all sometimes cross them. "Temptation hits all of us," says the Reverend Richard Ganz, Ph.D., pastor of the Ottawa Reformed Presbyterian Church in Almonte, Canada, and author of *The Secret of Self Control*. "It's what we *do* with that temptation that matters. We can't avoid temptations, but we can be delivered from them."

How?

- Figure out what tempts you and why.
- Put on your spiritual armor.
- Wage spiritual warfare against temptation.

Know Thine Enemy

Whether you consider Satan a reality or a metaphor, sometimes it can seem as if temptation is placed directly in your path. Example: You're on a diet and somebody offers you one of your favorite chocolates. Or you're struggling to stay faithful to your wife and the prettiest girl in the office starts smiling in your direction. Or you've vowed not to succumb to anger and somebody crowds into line in front of you at the supermarket. The first step in fighting temptations like these is to identify your weak spots and determine what's triggering them.

Here are some steps to take that will help you accomplish that goal.

> *Be strong in the Lord and in his mighty power. Put on the full armor of God so that you can take your stand against the devil's schemes.*
>
> —*Ephesians 6:10–11 (NIV)*

1. Make a List

Take an inventory of what tempts you and write it down, suggests Paul Tripp, doctor of ministry and counseling, director of Changing Lives Ministries in Glenside, Pennsylvania. Is your weakness food? If so, what kind of food? If you crave power, take a look at precisely how that desire infects your life.

Once you've got your major weak spots on paper, go back to each and look for patterns that will help you identify when and under what circumstances you are most vulnerable. Do you tend to crave chocolate at night when you're lonely? Do you get angriest at people when you're in a hurry? "Heighten your insight into how you get ensnared," Dr. Tripp recommends. "You can't defend against something you can't see."

2. Look for the Source

Often our temptations stem from painful experiences in our past, says Paul Meier, M.D., cofounder and medical director of the New Life chain of Christian

LEAD ME TO RIGHTEOUSNESS

O Lord, I pray
that you will inspire my heart
to do what is worthy of you.
Do not let me fall into sin.
Do not allow my lower instincts to prevail.
Stretch out your hand and lead me
into the ways of righteousness
and of your holy laws.
Put temptation far from me.
Make my stubborn heart humble and obedient,
that I might return to you
along the path that you desire;
so that it may come to pass
for me and my sons as
you promised, and as is written:
"the Lord will turn your heart
and the hearts of your sons
to perfect love,
to the Lord your God,
and then you will enjoy true life."

—From the Talmud

counseling clinics headquartered in Plano, Texas, and author of numerous books on psychology and faith. For example, many people who grew up in abusive households have a deep sense of shame inculcated in their hearts. Such people often indulge temptations such as overeating or engaging in extramarital sexual relations to dull the pain of that shame, Dr. Meier says.

If you can, trace the deeper feelings you may be trying to avoid by giving in to temptation, Dr. Meier suggests. If you can't discover them on your own, a therapist can help you successfully root out the source of your weaknesses.

Put On Your Spiritual Armor

Once you've drawn a bead on your enemy, it's time to prepare for battle. Your weapons of defense? Prayer, scripture reading, worship, service, the support of a faith community and of faithful friends—all the basic spiritual disciplines, says Dr. Meier.

Here are some specific suggestions for strengthening your spiritual shield.

1. Use the Two-Prayer Approach

The first way to beat your weaknesses is to confess them to God and pray to God to help you resist them, says Dr. Tripp.

Two avenues of prayer can be useful here, he says. One is to ask God ahead of time, whenever you pray, to give you strength against the temptations that assail you, especially those you have identified as most troublesome.

The second avenue is to prepare a prayer and have it at hand so you can utter it at the moment temptation strikes. Say, for example, you struggle with pornography, and on your way home from work you happen to walk past a newsstand that has lurid magazines on display. Before taking another step, use your prayer to ask God to help clear your mind of the lustful thoughts even this brief temptation has generated, Dr. Tripp says.

Prayers of repetition—prayers that consist of a word or short phrase, repeated over and over—can be especially helpful for getting through those tense moments when temptation strikes, adds Carolyn Bohler, Ph.D., professor of pastoral theology and counseling at United Theological Seminary in Dayton, Ohio.

Try repeating the phrase "Infinite patience be" quietly and soothingly to yourself, for example. For an even simpler version, try the word "Calm," Dr. Bohler suggests.

2. Visualize a Guardian

When temptation strikes, it can help to visualize in your mind's eye the supporting presence of a holy guardian at your side, Dr. Bohler says. Different images are helpful to different people, she adds. You might picture Jesus walking along, gently holding your arm. Dr. Bohler likes to think of God as a large mother figure who is embracing her warmly from behind.

❧

RESISTING TEMPTATION

Lord, your Word assures me that no temptation I face is irresistible.
Thank you for your promise that you are faithful to give me strength
to overcome the enemy's enticement. Father, I confess that when I
have yielded to temptation, it was because I failed to keep my heart
fixed upon you. Forgive me, Lord, for going my own selfish way.
Help me to turn away from the world's fascination and to walk in
your love. Amen.

—*Quin Sherrer and Ruthanne Garlock*

3. Wield the Word

Scripture can also be a helpful shield against a temptation attack, says Dr. Ganz. Keep a favorite passage memorized and repeat it to yourself whenever you feel the need. He recommends the Bible's "wisdom literature"—Psalms, Proverbs, and Ecclesiastes—as especially strong sources of defense against temptation.

4. Practice Moderation

We've all heard that an idle mind is the Devil's playground, and there's some truth to that, says Dr. Meier. If you're sitting around doing nothing all day, it's more likely your mind will start drifting toward thoughts that will eventually lead you astray.

On the other hand, Dr. Meier points out, many people set themselves up for a fall by being *too* busy. "Stress and frantic activity can be tiring and can lower your resistance to temptation," he says. "Busyness can also be a way to avoid being in touch with your feelings, which also makes you vulnerable to temptation."

The solution is a healthy balance, Dr. Meier says. Keep yourself engaged in productive activity, but don't overdo it. Take breaks, get enough rest, and leave time in your daily schedule to sit still, pray, and meditate.

Shaping Up Your Willpower

You may have noticed that staying in good physical condition takes on a kind of momentum. When you've been exercising regularly, it's much easier to keep exercising than it is if you haven't been exercising at all. Resisting temptation is like that, too, Dr. Bohler points out. A temptation resisted once is a temptation that's easier to resist the next time around.

For that reason, one of the best ways to improve your ability to resist temptation is to practice resisting temptation. "Exercising the will is not discussed very often these days," Dr. Bohler says, "but it's important to remember that we do have a will, that it can be good and powerful, and that we can actually work to strengthen it."

Here are some specific tools that can help you get your will into shape.

1. Enlist Your Friends

Resistance to temptation is weakest when we're isolated, says Dr. Meier. Therefore, it can help when temptation strikes to call or visit loving friends, family, and a faith community for support.

A prayer partner can be an especially important resource, Dr. Meier says. The ideal prayer partner is a friend of your sex with whom you can stay in close contact. Talk with that partner at least once a week, either in person or on the

KEEP ME ON THE STRAIGHT PATH, GOD

I beseech Thee, my most gracious God, preserve me from the cares of this life, lest I should be too much entangled therein; also from the many necessities of the body, lest I should be ensnared by pleasure; and from whatsoever is an obstacle to the soul, lest, being broken with troubles, I should be overthrown. Give me the strength to resist, patience to endure, and constancy to persevere. Amen.

—Thomas à Kempis

phone. Make a habit of telling him or her your most persistent temptations, and provide a running account of how successfully you've coped with them. Pray together for the strength to continue the fight.

2. Satisfy Your Real Needs

> *The more one yields to desire, the more insatiable it will become.*
>
> —*Mahabharata*

People often use temptations to fill emotional "holes" in their souls, Dr. Meier says. One good way to counter temptations is to find legitimate ways to fulfill those same emotional needs.

For example, if you tend to overeat because you feel unloved, try getting involved in your church's shelter program for homeless people. By giving love, you get love back, Dr. Meier points out. In the process, the pull of temptation fades into the background.

3. Make Another List

You've already made a list that identifies the temptations that bedevil you most. Now, Dr. Bohler suggests, make a second list: one that specifically identifies things you can do when temptation strikes. For example, if you tend to sit around watching TV all weekend, your list of possible evasive tactics might include calling friends (have a list of phone numbers handy), taking a walk, listening to music, dancing around the living room, gardening, crocheting a sweater, writing a letter, paying a bill, or taking a bubble bath.

Fighting Obsessions and Compulsions

Are you plagued by obsessive thoughts and compulsive behaviors? Then turn to God and modern medicine for help. With them on your side, you can banish these demons.

John is an insurance agent from New York who reads carefully—much too carefully.

"When I read," he explains, "if I feel like I didn't get the *exact* meaning of a sentence, I have to reread it. Language is very structured, with the commas and the parentheses and everything, and sometimes you need to reread it, to make sure you're getting the meaning right. I can reread something 5, 10 times, and then go on to the next sentence and read that 5 or 10 times. It's kind of tortuous."

In truth, John's reading problem is worse than torturous: It's debilitating. Imagine trying to do your homework in high school and college reading at that pace. John did, just as he has tried to function with the 30 or so other types of obsessive thoughts and behaviors that have plagued him, off and on, since he was 11 years old.

John is one of an estimated four million Americans who struggles with obsessive-compulsive disorder, or OCD. People with the obsessive part of the condition have thoughts they can't get out of their minds; those with compulsions have behaviors they feel forced to repeat, like John's tendency to reread continuously. For many of these people the disorder is so all-consuming that they are barely able to function.

Have patience with all things, but chiefly have patience with yourself. Do not lose courage in considering your own imperfections, but instantly set about remedying them—every day begin the task anew.

—*Saint Francis de Sales*

If you feel you may share this condition, take heart: There are steps you can take to address it.

- Learn to identify the obsessive or compulsive characteristics that are affecting you.
- Seek treatment.
- Pray and practice "behavior modification" techniques.

Understanding OCD

Experts used to think that people with OCD had a psychological problem—that their habits represented a type of mental breakdown or neurosis. Now they know that obsessive-compulsive disorder is a physiological disease that results from physical changes in the operation of the brain.

What actually causes OCD is still something of a mystery. "We do know there's a genetic link, so it travels in families, and that it involves a brain chemical called serotonin," says Bobby Miller, M.D., a neurologist and psychiatrist with the New Hope Christian Counseling Center in Huntington, West Virginia. "We also know that it affects the limbic system, the part of the brain that controls emotion and thought. Somehow the wires get crossed."

Everyone has a few habits or pet peeves that they tend to focus on—that's perfectly normal. But for people with OCD, the brain gets stuck on certain thoughts or behaviors until they interfere with life, says Gail Steketee, Ph.D., a professor of social work at Boston University and a nationally recognized expert in OCD.

How can you tell if your habits are normal or symptoms of OCD?

1. Look for the Classic Symptoms

Certain types of thoughts and behaviors are common fixations for people with OCD. Here's a list of OCD's "greatest hits," compiled by Frank Minirth,

HEAL ME, GOD

O Lord, I know not what to ask of thee. Thou alone knowest what are my true needs. Thou lovest me more than I myself know how to love. Help me to see my real needs which are concealed from me. I dare not ask either a cross or consolation. I can only wait on thee. My heart is open to thee. Visit and help me, for thy great mercy's sake. Strike me and heal me, cast me down and raise me up. . . . Teach me how to pray. Pray thou thyself in me.

—*Metropolitan Philaret of Moscow*

M.D., founder and president of The Minirth Clinic in Richardson, Texas, and author or coauthor of 50 books that integrate psychiatric and Christian principles.

Obsessions of contamination: Many people with OCD wash their hands or scrub countertops over and over, out of fear that otherwise they'll be exposed to germs. Other common fears involve exposure to dirt, bodily waste, AIDS, and pollution.

Obsessions of aggression: People with this symptom fear they'll act on unwanted impulses or cause an accident. One person was obsessed with the thought that he might hit a pedestrian with his car; another couldn't stop himself from fantasizing about stabbing babies. These fears were totally unfounded, but they persisted nonetheless.

Compulsions of repeating: Virtually any routine activity, from washing hands to tapping fingers on a desk, can become a compulsion for someone with OCD. John's "sentence checking" obsession is typical.

Religious obsessions and compulsions: Religious obsessions often center on imagined sins—one extremely religious patient of Dr. Minirth was on the verge of committing suicide because he was plagued with what he considered to be blasphemous thoughts. Religious compulsions can involve rituals such as reading the Torah or reciting the Rosary over and over and over again or attending evangelists' services and compulsively "giving yourself over to Jesus" at service after service, Dr. Miller says.

Actually, religious disorders are very common among people with OCD, in

LISTEN TO YOUR HEART

Some religious people are prone to obsessive behavior because they believe that God and Satan speak to them through their thoughts. If they have evil thoughts, it's tempting to assume such thoughts prove that Satan has taken control.

Don't believe it, says Bobby Miller, M.D., a neurologist and psychiatrist with the New Hope Christian Counseling Center in Huntington, West Virginia. "People with obsessive-compulsive disorder have a dissonance between what's in their hearts and what's in their heads," he says. "Their heads can be filled with thoughts that are venomous, poisonous, murderous, and blasphemous, while their hearts can be filled with love, sincerity, empathy, compassion, and purity. They need to recognize that difference, and listen to their hearts. They're not demon-possessed or lacking in faith. They simply have an illness called OCD."

Dr. Miller often shares with his OCD patients this passage from Proverbs: "For as he thinketh in his heart, so is he" (23:7, KJV).

part because people with OCD tend to be unusually sincere and conscientious, says Dr. Minirth. It's believed that such prominent religious figures as Martin Luther and John Bunyan, the author of *The Pilgrim's Progress*, may well have suffered from OCD.

2. Do Your Homework

Read the available material on OCD to get a better sense of the disorder. There are a number of good books that can help. Dr. Miller recommends *Brain Lock: Free Yourself from Obsessive-Compulsive Behavior*, by Jeffery M. Schwartz with Beverly Beyette. Another source of information is the Obsessive-Compulsive Foundation, 337 Notch Hill Road, North Branford, CT 06471.

3. Ask Your Relatives

Talking with your family also can help you determine whether or not you have OCD because the genetic link for the condition is strong. Poll family members to see if they also experience symptoms. Finding a family history of OCD can make you feel less odd for having it yourself. "Sharing OCD with your family helps break the isolation people often feel," says Bonnie Cushing, a clinical social worker and family therapist based in Montclair, New Jersey. "It's no longer a question of, 'What's the matter with *me?*'"

Treating OCD

Because OCD is now recognized as a physiological disease, the most effective tool doctors have for treating it is medication. For that reason, the first thing you should do is talk to your doctor about the options. There are at least

---

GRANT ME SILENCE

O Lord,
the Scripture says,
"There is a time for silence
and a time for speech."
Saviour, teach me
the silence of humility,
the silence of wisdom,
the silence of love,
the silence of perfection,
the silence that speaks without words,
the silence of faith.
Lord teach me to silence my own heart
that I may listen to the gentle movement
of the Holy Spirit within me
and sense the depths which are of God.

—Unknown

a half dozen medicines which have been approved for OCD, Dr. Miller says, and the likelihood of success if you use them is high. However, side effects such as insomnia and dry mouth can be a problem. This is why some OCD patients, like John, try eventually to get off the drugs. Sometimes the symptoms return, sometimes they don't.

Many patients combine medication with prayer, self-help techniques, and behavioral counseling. These methods are particularly useful in controlling intrusive thoughts, such as fears of picking up germs from kitchen counters, that can evolve into serious obsessions, says Dr. Steketee. To control behaviors like this, try these techniques.

1. Relax Your Mind

There's an odd thing about obsessions: Trying to control them only increases them. Therefore the best way to fight OCD is to *not* fight it.

"Try to adopt an attitude of mental passivity, a sort of blank mind," suggests Dr. Steketee. "If you have an obsessive thought, try to just observe it. As you do, ask yourself, 'Hmm. What's that about?'" The goal is to watch your obsession as a disinterested observer. This helps you stop the repetitive thought process, Dr. Steketee says.

You can reach this passive, peaceful state of mind through prayer, Dr. Miller believes. As you pray, just surrender yourself to God's will. "*Allow* the obsession, rather than fighting it," he says. A scripture passage Dr. Minirth recommends is 1 John 3:20. Be reassured, it says, "whenever our hearts condemn us; for God is greater than our hearts, and he knows everything" (NRSV).

Be aware, however, that prayer can easily become another obsession. If you feel that this is happening to you, give up prayer and concentrate on professional help.

2. Reduce Stress

Stressful situations can precipitate or aggravate OCD, Dr. Minirth says. So try not to overtax yourself with work or family pressures.

Talking to God is one way to help minimize stress, including the stress caused by OCD itself. John, the insurance salesman, regularly shares his frustrations about OCD with God, and he feels that doing so helps him cope much more peacefully. "Lots of times I feel terrified because I don't know how long this will go on," he says. "Praying lessens that and makes me feel hopeful again."

3. Try "Behavior Modification"

Brain scans of OCD patients show that practicing such behavior modification techniques as "thought stopping" can actually change the physiology of the brain, says Dr. Minirth. For that reason, the most effective OCD treatments combine behavior modification with medication.

Behavior modification actively enlists the power of the mind in its own defense, Dr. Minirth says. While one part of the mind wants to obsess on some thought or behavior, you apply conscious effort to try to break free of those obsessive thoughts and behaviors. Often the point is to simply catch yourself in the act of obsessing and, through these techniques, jar the brain off its obsessive-compulsive track. Dr. Minirth believes that this conscious effort physically summons various chemical changes in the brain that can counteract OCD.

It is our attitude at the beginning that more than anything else produces a successful outcome.

—*Earl Nightingale*

Some caution is in order, however. Practicing thought stopping and the other forms of behavior modification listed here can cause you to become obsessed with your obsession. Some experts advise against using them for that reason. It's important, if you do try them, to monitor yourself and to seek professional help if you sense your thoughts or behaviors are getting out of control.

Types of behavior modification including the following:

Thought stopping: If you feel an obsession or compulsion kicking in, tell yourself, "Stop!"

Labeling: When you catch yourself in an obsessive thought or compulsive behavior, mentally put a name to it. Say to yourself, "Now, you're obsessing."

Limiting: Allot yourself a specific, short amount of time to think about your obsessions. For example, if you obsessively worry about whether God has granted you salvation, only let yourself think about it for 10 minutes each day, at 5:00 P.M.

Toughening: If you have an obsession about something like contamination, gradually expose yourself to it. Let that countertop go unscrubbed for a day, for example, then run your hand over it.

Diverting: Force yourself to perform some other specific act before you allow yourself to complete an obsessive act. For example, if you feel you must check the locks on your front door three times when you come in the house, force yourself to first go in the kitchen and put on a pot of water before checking them. Or check them once, then go do some task and come back. Vary these interruptions so that they don't become incorporated into the obsessive ritual.

Coping
with Addictions

Addiction to alcohol, drugs, gambling, or food can sneak up on you and turn life into a nightmare. You can beat an addiction, however, with help from God and the wisdom of those who have been there before you.

New York stockbroker, down on his luck, sat in his kitchen one bleak November morning, drinking. He was making a mental list of the several places in the apartment where he had extra gin stashed when the phone rang.

An old school friend asked if he could come by for a visit. Sure, said the stockbroker, remembering that this was one drinking buddy who never had any trouble keeping up. But this time was different. The old school buddy was sober, had been for 2 months. More than that, he seemed filled with an inner vitality that suggested he would be staying sober for a good long time. To his amazement, the stockbroker realized he was witnessing a miracle.

"My friend sat before me, and he made the point-blank declaration that God had done for him what he could not do for himself," the stockbroker later wrote.

"His human will had failed. Doctors had pronounced him incurable. Society was about to lock him up. Like myself, he had admitted complete defeat.

Then he had, in effect, been raised from the dead, suddenly taken from the scrap heap to a level of life better than the best he had ever known!"

It wasn't long after this exchange that the stockbroker surrendered himself to God—and successfully quit drinking after years of alcoholic despair. The stockbroker's name was Bill Wilson. He became the cofounder of Alcoholics Anonymous (A.A.).

Bill Wilson's story has inspired millions of people to triumph in their own struggles against addiction—and not only alcoholics. People with a whole range of addiction problems, from gambling and narcotics to tobacco and food, have followed A.A.'s Twelve Step path to freedom.

> *A habit cannot be tossed out the window, it must be coaxed down the stairs a step at a time.*
>
> —*Mark Twain*

Whether your own road to recovery lies in the 12 steps or in some other approach, the success of Bill Wilson and countless other addicts proves that you *can* beat your addiction, if you make certain moves.

- Honestly assess whether you have an addiction.
- Draw strength from your faith and other recovering addicts.
- Never give up your fight.

Are You an Addict?

The symptoms, severity, and remedies for various addictions differ from one addiction to another, says Jacqueline Hudak, director of Family Therapy Associates of Monmouth County in Red Bank, New Jersey. But there also are some important underlying similarities among them all, Hudak says. Take progression, for example. With any addiction, the longer you are involved, the greater the amount of substance or behavior you need to achieve the same effect.

Another similarity is that no matter what the addiction, once addicts ingest the substance or engage in the behavior, they continue to do so and defend their behavior despite negative consequences. This is the "powerlessness" emphasized in A.A.'s first step, and it explains why successful recovery usually depends on total abstinence. You have to stop using the addictive substance or engaging in the addictive behavior entirely.

Another quality most addicts have in common is that they are in "denial" about their problem, says Bill Lagerstrom, founder and director of Lazarus Ministries, a lay ministry program focusing on the spiritual development of people in recovery from addictions, based at St. Francis Xavier Church in New York

THE TWELVE STEPS

Here are the famous Twelve Steps of Alcoholics Anonymous, used with slight alterations (including the substitution of other words for "alcohol" in the first step) by many other addiction recovery groups.

1. We admitted we were powerless over alcohol—that our lives had become unmanageable.

2. Came to believe that a Power greater than ourselves could restore us to sanity.

3. Made a decision to turn our will and our lives over to the care of God as we understood Him.

4. Made a searching and fearless moral inventory of ourselves.

5. Admitted to God, to ourselves, and to another human being the exact nature of our wrongs.

6. Were entirely ready to have God remove all these defects of character.

7. Humbly asked Him to remove our shortcomings.

8. Made a list of all persons we had harmed, and became willing to make amends to them all.

9. Made direct amends to such people wherever possible, except when to do so would injure them or others.

10. Continued to take personal inventory and when we were wrong promptly admitted it.

11. Sought through prayer and meditation to improve our conscious contact with God as we understood Him, praying only for knowledge of His will for us and the power to carry that out.

12. Having had a spiritual awakening as the result of these steps, we tried to carry this message to alcoholics, and to practice these principles in all our affairs.

City. That means they can lose their jobs, their health, their relationships, even their homes and still find a way to convince themselves that they don't have an addiction. Most addicts will continue to deny they need help, Lagerstrom says, until they hit what A.A. calls a "bottom"—a point at which the impact of the addiction is so obvious that the hard shell of denial finally cracks. This is why A.A. stresses that you need to *admit* you are powerless over the addiction before you can begin recovering.

You don't have to lose everything to reach a point where you're ready to admit that you have a problem with addiction. The steps that follow can help overcome the deceptive powers of denial and lead you to an answer.

1. Ask God for Guidance

If you're wondering whether you have a problem with addiction, the first person to whom you should take that question is God, says Tom Windels, executive director and counselor at Ephraim Resources, a Christian-based, nonprofit counseling service in Appleton, Wisconsin. On your knees, ask God to help break down your denial. Here is the sort of prayer Windels suggests: "God, I think I may have a problem here. Expose it to me, God, help me see. Show me. Bring me the truth."

Listen quietly for God's answers, Windels adds. Take a long walk or spend a quiet hour in a peaceful park—without engaging in your addiction. This will make you more receptive to God's response.

2. Listen to Those around You

Chances are that if you have a problem with addiction, your closest friends and family have been warning you about it for years. Chances are also that you haven't been listening. Now is the time to open yourself up to their opinions, suggests Windels.

Another way to gather information on whether you qualify as an addict is to attend meetings of a Twelve Step group that is dedicated to the addiction you're struggling with, says Ernest Kurtz, Ph.D., a visiting scholar at the University of Michigan in Ann Arbor who has written a history of A.A. Most such groups have what are called "open" meetings, meaning they are open to people who are not yet certain that they are addicts. "You can sit in these meetings without saying a word to anyone, if you want," Dr. Kurtz says.

Listening to the discussion that goes on in these meetings will teach you a tremendous amount about the thoughts and feelings that are characteristic of addiction. To find a group, check the Yellow Pages of your phone book under headings such as "alcoholism" or "drug abuse," or ask your pastor to refer you to a group.

A Prayer for Healing

Dear God,

My body is sick and I am so scared, so weak, so sad.

Please heal me, Lord.

Whatever the words I am supposed to say, whatever the thoughts that would set me free,

I am willing to have them shine into my mind.

For I wish to be released.

Please give me a miracle.

Please give me hope.

Please give me peace.

Lift me up beyond the regions of my pain and despair.

Prepare each cell to be born anew into health and happiness, peace, and love.

For You are the power, not this sickness.

You are the truth, not this illusion.

You are my salvation, not the doctor.

I am willing to rise, to let go all false thinking, to release this false condition.

For this is not freedom, and I wish to be free.

This is not peaceful, and I desire peace.

This is not Your will for me, that I would suffer or feel pain.

I accept Your will for me,

I accept Your healing,

I accept Your love.

Please, dear God, help me.

Take me home.

Amen.

—Marianne Williamson

3. Talk to a Professional

If for any reason you are uncomfortable with Twelve Step meetings, other options are available, says Tim Sheehan, Ph.D., regional vice president of Minnesota Recovery Services, parent organization of the famous Hazelden Foundation. These include talking to a counselor at a community health center, a psychotherapist, a clinical psychologist, or your family physician.

4. Read Wise Words

Another easy way to get at least a beginning idea of what addiction is all about, Dr. Kurtz suggests, is to find copies of the basic texts of A.A., *Alcoholics Anonymous* (called "The Big Book") and the primer on the A.A. program, *Twelve Steps and Twelve Traditions*. Although A.A. literature is focused exclusively on alcohol, much of what it says applies to addictions across the board.

5. Examine the Evidence

A common misperception about addiction, says Hudak, is that it is defined by the *quantity* of alcohol, drugs, food, or whatever you use. Far more important, she says, is the *effect* the substance or behavior is having on the quality of your life, regardless of the quantity. In other words, how much pain is your habit causing you?

For that reason, it is important to examine as carefully as possible what you're actually doing to yourself. Denial makes it difficult for most people to honestly appraise themselves, but it's worth trying. You never know, says Dr. Kurtz, when you might be ready to face the truth.

Many public health agencies offer checklists that can guide you in this sort of self-examination. For example, this list, published by the National Clearinghouse for Alcohol and Drug Information, suggests you have a problem with drugs or alcohol if:

- You can't predict whether or not you will use drugs or get drunk on any day or at any occasion.
- You believe that in order to have fun you need to drink and/or use drugs.
- You turn to alcohol and/or drugs after a confrontation or argument or to relieve uncomfortable feelings.
- You drink more or use more drugs to get the same effect that you used to get with smaller amounts.
- You drink and/or use drugs alone.
- You remember how last night began, but not how it ended, so you're worried you may have a problem.
- You have trouble at work or in school because of your drinking or drug use.

- You make promises to yourself or others that you'll stop getting drunk or using drugs.
- You feel alone, scared, miserable, and depressed.

If you have experienced *any* of these problems, says the Clearinghouse, you may need help dealing with an addiction.

Getting Help

When Bill Wilson struggled to get sober in the late 1920s, he and the people around him assumed he kept drinking either because he was an undisciplined lout or because he was insane. Since that time doctors have come to a quite different conclusion, says Hudak: Addiction is a disease, a disease that progresses along predictable patterns and produces measurable physiological effects. (Different addictions may fit this definition differently: Tobacco addiction will have different physiological effects than cocaine addiction or gambling addiction.)

Seeing addiction as a disease helps people understand that addicts can't just quit by making up their mind to quit: They need help. "It's really the same as with any other disease," says Dr. Sheehan. "You don't cure *yourself* of chronic heart disease or hypertension either. A successful recovery doesn't occur in a vacuum. Some sort of partnership is required."

Here are two ways to get the help you need.

1. Lean on a Higher Power

"Nowhere in medicine has the faith factor proved more powerful than in the field of addiction recovery," write Dale A. Matthews, M.D., and Connie Clark, collaborators on *The Faith Factor: Proof of the Healing Power of Prayer.* Study after study documents that addicts who have experienced a spiritual awakening are more likely to beat their addiction than addicts who haven't, the authors say.

For example, the authors cite a 1981 study of 248 men with long histories of opiate abuse (mostly heroin) that found that those who attended religious treatment programs were almost 10 times as likely as those attending nonreligious treatment programs to remain abstinent from heroin for 1 year after the program ended.

There is no requirement in A.A. that its members believe in God. Nonetheless, reliance on a Higher Power is a central part of the 12-step programs, Dr. Kurtz says, and most addicts who follow the 12-step approach consider prayer and meditation to be key to their recovery. A lot of this goes back to that cen-

TRUE FAITHFULNESS

Lord, since you have taken from me all earthly favours, I can now see that you have left me with a spiritual gift beyond price, which every dog has by nature. You have made me faithful to you even at times of the greatest distress, bereft of all comforts. This faithfulness I cherish more fervently than all the riches of the world.

—Mechthild of Magdeburg

tral issue of powerlessness. "The addict usually sees himself or herself as the center of the universe, and that has to change," Dr. Kurtz says. "Exactly how you define your Higher Power is less important than realizing the basic point that there *is* a Higher Power, and you're not it."

Many recovering addicts make a point of praying each morning as a means of establishing their relationship to their Higher Power before they do anything else. In fact, many recovery programs that use the Twelve Step approach now have morning meditation books of their own. Many addicts also make a habit of repeating to themselves the serenity prayer as they go through the day:

God, grant me the serenity to accept the things I cannot change,
Courage to change the things I can,
And wisdom to know the difference.

2. Lean on Others

Often in A.A. meetings, you hear that recovery hinges on two fundamentals: "Don't drink, and go to meetings." That's an indication of how important group support is in staying sober. "Being involved in a community of recovering people is absolutely key," says Lagerstrom.

Twelve-step meetings offer one choice, but there are other options. Many churches sponsor "accountability" groups aimed at providing support for people struggling with various problems, says Windels.

Wherever you turn for support, however, it's best to find someone who has had personal experience dealing with your particular addiction, Windels believes. "People who have traveled the same road you're on can tell you which

Prayer Miracles

Prayer Helped Me Beat Addiction to Food

When I was young I was very thin and ate whatever I wanted. But after I got married I began to gain weight, until I reached 254 pounds. The morning the scale showed 254, I went to the Lord in prayer. I had asked God to curb my appetite and speed up my metabolism many times before. But this time I asked Him to forgive me for the sin of idolizing food. Immediately I felt a sense of His presence and I had faith that He would give me the strength. That very day I started eating low-fat foods and exercising, and with the willpower He has given me, I have turned away from gluttony. Now, 3 years later, I have lost 104 pounds and my goal is to lose 6 more. I know my success is because of the support of my family and friends and because my Heavenly Father is my salvation. As it says in Psalm 20:4 (NIV), "May he give you the desire of your heart and make all your plans succeed." He has done this for me.

Linda Keeter
Edenton, North Carolina

way to go," he says. "Look for someone who seems to have a strong grasp on recovery."

Besides finding a community of fellow addicts, it's also important to reach out to a broader spiritual community, Lagerstrom believes. A.A. is meant to be "a bridge back to life." Many recovering addicts find it helpful to get involved in a religious community to help them stay connected in a healthy way, to God and to other people.

Doing the Good Work

Addicts who think they can quit their addiction and be instantly fine are kidding themselves, Lagerstrom says. Lasting recovery requires more work than that, as indicated by the fact that there are 12 steps, not 1. Here are three ways you can make sure you stay on the straight path.

1. Clean Your House

Much of the additional work of recovery is devoted to what addicts call "cleaning house." This means you take a systematic look at the impact your addiction has had on you and those around you. Also as part of this process you should examine your "character defects"—jealousy, resentments, dishonesty, and cowardice are a few prime examples—to see where you need to make improvements.

WHEN YOU CAN'T STOP EATING

If you're a recovering alcoholic, the key to controlling your condition is staying away from alcohol completely. Recovering drug addicts, similarly, must end drug use entirely. But what if you're addicted to food?

"Alcoholics can keep booze out of their houses, they can stay out of bars, and they don't need to hang around with people who drink," says Tom Windels, a recovering food addict, executive director and counselor at Ephraim Resources, a Christian-based, nonprofit counseling service in Appleton, Wisconsin. "Food is a different story. You have to eat at least a couple of times a day—and food is everywhere."

So how do you control it? Windels suggests taking the following three steps:

1. Pray for God's Guidance

This is especially important when it comes to food disorders, Windels says, because there is such a vast amount of conflicting information floating around about dieting and weight loss. It's best to approach the area carefully, and faithfully, he says.

2. Get Help

Just like alcoholics, food addicts will have a harder time quitting on their own. Seek the counsel of someone you know who has successfully dealt with an eating disorder or attend an Overeaters Anonymous meeting. For a reference to a counselor who has experience treating disorders, contact the International Association of Eating Disorders Professionals, 427 Center Point Circle, Suite 1819, Altamonte Springs, FL 32701.

3. Be Accountable

Find someone you can trust and give that person permission to ask you very specific questions about your eating. Talk to that person at least once a week.

The goal is to build yourself into the kind of person who is able to face the world head on, rather than the sort of person who seeks to escape into an addiction at the first sign of trouble. Learning to take "life on life's terms" is how they put it in A.A.

> *He can who thinks he can,*
> *And he can't who thinks*
> *he can't.*
> *This is an*
> *indisputable law.*
>
> —*Henry Ford*

Several of A.A.'s Twelve Steps are aimed at helping you "clean house." One (step four) is called a "personal inventory." Here the idea is to carefully and honestly review your past behavior to see where you have harmed others and where you are harboring resentments against people you feel have harmed you. Letting go of these resentments is a vital step in maintaining sobriety, A.A. says, as is facing the damage you've inflicted on those around you.

Another part of the process of cleaning house (steps eight and nine) involves making "amends" to people you have harmed. This entails an honest confession to each person you've hurt, along with a commitment to behave honorably in the future.

2. Stay with It

"Why do you have to keep going to those meetings?" is a question addicts in 12-step recovery programs are used to hearing. The reason, says Windels, is that the danger of relapse is always there. Consistently practicing all the tenets of the program—attending meetings, continuing your self-examination, seeking God's guidance through regular prayer and meditation—is the best way to keep that from happening. "The spirit may be willing, but the flesh is weak," Windels says, "so constant vigilance is required."

3. Pass It On

Bill Wilson found he could not stay sober himself unless he passed on the message of A.A. to other alcoholics, and the idea of service remains at the heart of the A.A. program. "Giving back what you've received is really what it's all about," says Lagerstrom. "The goal is always to give it away to another alcoholic."

There is no ready clinical explanation for why service to others is so vital, although Lagerstrom believes part of its magic is the proof it offers of the progress you've made in your own recovery. And, of course, service to others is one of the most basic spiritual principles there is.

Battling Depression

This quiet killer weighs down the hearts of millions of Americans, yet it is a problem that can be dealt with. Here's how you can bring the light of the Spirit into your heart of darkness.

America has a scary secret.

Its name is depression.

This insidious disease affects more than 17 million people in this country, about one-third of whom don't know they have it and two-thirds of whom aren't seeking treatment.

For each of them depression is a tragedy, made all the more so because the vast majority of depressed people who get treatment improve, usually within weeks.

If you are sunk in the dark pit of depression, don't allow yourself to suffer needlessly. Instead, suggest pastors and counselors, follow these steps to combat it.

- Learn the symptoms and causes of the disease.
- Seek immediate professional help—when it is called for.
- Use your faith and other remedies to battle back.

Unmasking the Beast

The first thing you need to know about genuine depression is that it is a serious condition. It's not overactive self-pity or just a mood that you can shake off if you put your mind to it. It also is not a sign of weakness or something you should be ashamed of, although many depressed people are ashamed.

Depression is not a sin. It's a disease, and like any other it should be treated—and treated quickly—for without care, depression can last for weeks, months, even years, says Michele Novotni, Ph.D., a professor of graduate counseling at Eastern College in St. Davids, Pennsylvania, and author of *Making Up with God.*

> *Do not let your hearts be troubled and do not be afraid.*
>
> —*John 14:27 (NRSV)*

How do you know if you are depressed? The National Institute of Mental Health lists the following symptoms.

- Persistent sad or "empty" mood
- Feelings of guilt, worthlessness, or helplessness
- Loss of interest or pleasure in hobbies and activities that you once enjoyed
- Insomnia, early morning waking, or oversleeping
- Loss of appetite or overeating, with consequent weight loss or weight gain
- Decreased energy, fatigue, feeling "slowed down"
- Restlessness or irritability
- Thoughts of death or suicide
- Difficulty concentrating, remembering, or making decisions
- Persistent physical symptoms that do not respond to treatment, including headaches, digestive problems, and chronic pain

You need not display all these symptoms to qualify as depressed. In fact, you don't need to feel sad, empty, or dejected all the time. Many people who have chronic mild depression are simply sad more days than not, or just have a sense they're going through the motions most of the time, rather than enjoying life.

There are many causes of depression. Some people have chemical imbalances in their brains that make them vulnerable to the disease. (Since these imbalances can be inherited, depression often runs in families.) Drug addiction, alcoholism, poor nutrition, medications, and serious illness can also cause or contribute to depression. For that reason, it's a good idea to start your fight against depression with a thorough physical checkup.

Beyond these physical causes, there are psychological reasons for depression. They include everything from stress, money problems, a difficult marriage, and low self-esteem to being scarred by a childhood trauma (being sexually abused, having an alcoholic parent) or going through some sort of trauma as an adult (losing everything in a flood, being the victim of a crime).

GOD, TAKE THIS PAIN

Dear God,

    The pain of this life is more than I can bear.

    I feel as though death would be better.

    My thoughts are dark, my sorrows huge.

    I feel as though I shall not endure, and there is no one and nothing to turn to now.

    My hurt is so big,

    I cannot handle this.

    If You can, dear God, please do.

    If You can, please do.

    Amen.

—Marianne Williamson

When to Seek Professional Help

If you are suffering from depression, a vital question you'll want to address is whether or not you need professional help. The answer is a definite "yes" if:

- You are considering suicide.
- You are unable to function.

Take any thoughts of suicide extremely seriously, says Dr. Novotni. Call a suicide hotline, go a hospital emergency room, or contact a psychiatrist, a therapist, or other mental health professional immediately. The urgency only increases, she says, if you find yourself making specific plans, such as "I'll take a bottle of pills and not wake up tomorrow," or "I'll go in the garage, close the door, and start up my car." If a period of several weeks goes by when you feel you don't have the strength to get your work done or talk to people, you also should seek professional help. "That's true even if you have a good reason to be depressed," Dr. Novotni says. "There should be some upward movement." If you feel paralyzed by your depression, seek help from a licensed social

DEEP PEACE

Deep peace of the running wave to you,
Deep peace of the flowing air to you,
Deep peace of the quiet earth to you,
Deep peace of the shining stars to you,
Deep peace of the Son of Peace to you.
Amen.

—Celtic oral tradition

worker, a psychiatrist, your general practitioner, or a knowledgeable pastor.

For either symptom, doctors and counselors can offer a host of therapies that really do work, especially when used in combination with one another. They include medications and various forms of psychological counseling.

Putting Gloom to Flight

If your depression hasn't reached the stage where professional treatment seems necessary, there are a number of steps you can take on your own to feel better.

High on the list of antidepression weapons are faith and prayer. Study after study has shown that religious people are less apt to be depressed in various situations—when they've lost a spouse, when they're hospitalized, when they've been diagnosed with AIDS, when they're stressed—than people who are not religious.

In one case, a study of more than 1,000 patients in a Veterans Administration hospital found that those patients who stated that their religion was very helpful to them in coping with their illnesses were much less likely to suffer from depression than those who did not mention using religion to cope.

Dr. Novotni has seen proof of faith's power in her own practice as well. "Most depressed people are feeling helpless and alone," says Dr. Novotni, "and there's nothing stronger than faith in addressing both those problems. There is hope, and we're not alone."

Here are some specific ways you can tap the power of faith and other self-help methods to overcome your depression.

1. Ask for Help

Tell the truth about how you're feeling to those around you. This in itself is a spiritual act, says Bonnie Cushing, a clinical social worker and family therapist based in Montclair, New Jersey. By breaking the silence, you dispel the veil of denial, shame, and secrecy beneath which depression flourishes. "The amount of energy it takes to keep up a false front is energy you could be using to heal yourself," she says.

Speaking out also will bring you the support and assistance you need from others. Numerous studies have shown that people in stressful situations suffer less from depression if they are surrounded by friends and family. In fact, reaching out to your loved ones for support is even more important in most cases than reaching out to counselors and other professionals, says David Powlison, Ph.D., a counselor at the Christian Counseling and Educational Foundation in Glenside, Pennsylvania.

"The most helpful people are wise folks who are already a part of your life," he says. "Turn first to trusted friends and family, pastors, small group leaders, the people who know and love you. They are the ones you can be candid with and who will hang in with you for the long haul."

LEAD ME, LORD

Father,
I am seeking:
I am hesitant and uncertain,
but will you, O God,
watch over each step of mine
and guide me.

—*Saint Augustine*

This said, Dr. Powlinson cautions that you be careful from whom you seek advice. Look for "upbeat" people, Dr. Powlison suggests, and be especially careful to avoid friends or family members who also are depressed. He quotes Proverbs 13:20, "He who walks with the wise grows wise, but a companion of fools suffers harm" (NIV).

2. Pray Out Loud

One of the glories of prayer is that you can always bring to God all your feelings, no matter how embarrassing or shameful you might think they are.

The Bible, especially the Book of Psalms, is filled with passages that describe the faithful bringing their darkest emotions to God in complete honesty, Dr. Powlison says. He points to Psalm 88:1–9 (NIV) as an example.

O Lord, the God who saves me, day and night I cry out before you.
May my prayer come before you; turn your ear to my cry.
For my soul is full of trouble and my life draws near the grave.
I am counted among those who go down to the pit; I am like a man without strength.
I am set apart with the dead, like the slain who lie in the grave, whom you remember no more, who are cut off from your care.
You have put me in the lowest pit, in the darkest depths.
Your wrath lies heavily upon me; you have overwhelmed me with all your waves.
You have taken from me my closest friends and have made me repulsive to them. I am confined and cannot escape;
My eyes are dim with grief. I call to you, O Lord, every day; I spread out my hands to you.

"This is probably the single darkest psalm in the Psalter," says Dr. Powlison, "but even here the psalmist turns repeatedly to God, asking that he be lifted and saved."

Another message implicit in many of the psalms, Dr. Powlison adds, is that it can be helpful for the depressed person to pray aloud. "Many of the psalms talk about 'lifting up my voice,' and that's an indication they were literally prayed aloud," he says. "Praying aloud can help you get past that sense that it's hard to tell whether you're praying or just thinking to yourself."

3. Seek Inspiration

Some severely depressed people have trouble mustering the motivation to pray, says Dr. Novotni. If this is a problem for you, connect spiritually by looking at religious art, listening to religious music, or reading religious poetry,

THINK AGAIN

If you're feeling depressed, be especially on the watch for "thinking errors," says Aaron T. Beck, M.D., a faculty member of the Center for Psychotherapy Research at the University of Pennsylvania in Philadelphia. This means a negative pattern of thinking that can lead to depression.

Here are the 10 most common types of thinking errors.

- **Catastrophizing**: Believing the worst-case scenario. Example: "If my boss doesn't like this report, I will be instantly fired."

- **All or nothing**: Seeing things as either black or white. Example: "If I don't win this tennis match, I'll be a total failure."

- **Discounting the positive**: Refusing to accept favorable feedback. Example: If somebody gives you a compliment, you immediately think they must be lying.

- **Labeling**: Putting other people or events into disparaging categories. Example: "Look at how dressed up she is. What a flirt."

- **Mental filtering**: Listening only to what you're expecting to hear—the worst.

- **Mind reading**: Imagining that you know what people are thinking about you, and being convinced it's got to be negative.

- **Overgeneralization**: A tendency to make sweeping statements. Example: "All men are pigs," or "I'll never get it right."

- **Personalization**: Thinking that things are directed at you personally when they're not or that you're responsible for things when you're not.

- **Emotional reasoning**: Believing that just because you feel something, it must be so.

- **Should and must statements**: Examples: "You must do it my way or else," or "You should have known how to do it."

Prayer Miracles

Prayer Helped End My Depression

In 1994 I left my full-time job at a bank because of stress and plunged head-first into the black abyss called depression. I slept all day and cried when I was awake. I lost weight and looked terrible. I hated myself, my life, and everything in general.

Then one day as I sat weeping, I began to pray. I prayed to be healed for my family's sake. I prayed for guidance and strength. I prayed for an answer to this nightmare of an existence. Before long, I was praying on a regular basis, and I began reading the Bible and watching religious programs on TV to find answers and moral support. I was still suffering terribly from depression, but praying made me feel peaceful and hopeful.

Gradually, I began to feel better and was taken off all medication. I became a member of a church and met wonderful people there. I even found a job through a fellow church member.

Now I pray every night. I've changed to a healthy diet, drink eight glasses of water a day, exercise, and practice yoga. I am a new person and the best part is I've never had a relapse.

Did praying help? You bet it did! It gave me hope in a hopeless situation. It's opened a whole new world to me. I believe everything happens for a reason. When I pray now, my prayers are filled with thanks.

Joy Klassen
Lumby, British Columbia

she suggests. "The creative arts bypass the thinking process," Dr. Novotni says. "They can go directly to the heart and soul to help bring about healing."

4. Listen to God

Because depression is so isolating, depressed people tend to hear one voice and one voice only: their own, with all its negative thoughts. This isn't a good thing, Dr. Powlison says. The cure? Read scripture. This gives God an opportunity to join the conversation. "Ponder His word," Dr. Powlison says. "Turn it over in your heart. Let it rattle around." God's Word can heal you.

Another way to reach God is through meditation. This makes you receptive to God's voice while turning off your own. On a physical level, meditation can help counter the stress that exacerbates depression, says Cushing. On a spiritual level, it opens you up to the healing power of the Spirit, allowing you to draw on energy outside yourself.

Try meditating on a single word or phrase, like "Our Father who art in heaven," "Lord Jesus Christ, have mercy on me," "shalom," or "om." This will help clear your mind of distractions.

5. Do Service

Stuff envelopes at church or take care of the toddlers in a day care center, suggests Dr. Powlison. Get your mind off yourself, if you're able; help somebody who's worse off than you. Simply put, doing good feels good.

6. Use the "Natural" Approach

There are at least two "natural" remedies that every antidepression regimen should include: a healthy diet and regular exercise. Eat well-balanced meals with plenty of fruits and vegetables, and avoid coffee, alcohol, fats, and sweets. This keeps your body strong and in balance, which in turn can help keep depression at bay. Exercise causes your body to release endorphins into the system that act as natural antidepressants. Just about any type of exercise, from walking and running to lifting weights, can help, according to Andrew Weil, M.D., director of the program in integrative medicine of the College of Medicine at the University of Arizona in Tucson. He prescribes a brisk, 45-minute walk at least 5 days a week.

> *When I am depressed, somewhere deep inside, I know that I am denying the Presence of God.*
>
> —*Gerald Jampolsky*

7. Change Your Thought Pattern

Just as you can "program" yourself for depression by falling into negative patterns of thinking, you can fight depression with positive thoughts. Although some people seek professional counseling to help them correct negative thought patterns, it is also possible to work at overcoming them on your own, Dr. Novotni says. To do so, try to be aware of your negative thoughts as they arise, then challenge them by telling yourself they're false. See page 439 for a list of the 10 most common examples of negative thinking.

Overcoming Fear

Each of us is filled with fears, whether they're about small events in everyday life or big ones like death. But with faith, courage, practice, and planning, it's possible to leave your fears in the shadows and live in the light of hope.

he seminary student was terrified.

He was literally down to his last dollar and was still far from achieving the goals he had dreamed of so long: a divinity degree and the opportunity to earn his living preaching the Gospel.

Not knowing where to turn, he prayed to God and meditated on scripture. Suddenly, an image came to him of the ancient Israelites fleeing into the desert from Egypt. The Pharaoh's pursuing army was behind them and the Red Sea was before them. The people cried out in despair to Moses.

And Moses answered: "Do not be afraid, stand firm, and see the deliverance that the Lord will accomplish for you today."

The seminary student decided that heaven-sent image was good enough for him. He set aside his fear of failing and continued on with his study, living one day and one dollar at a time. Today, he's preaching professionally.

For as long as humans have walked the planet, fear has been a companion. It used to be that we worried mainly about things like starving, freezing, and furry creatures with sharp teeth; today it's the drunk driver and the man with a gun. Running out of firewood isn't life-threatening anymore, but unemployment sometimes is. We also contend today with a strange new class of fears called anxiety. Fear of meeting strangers. Fear of closed spaces. Fear of flying.

Whatever its source, fear can eat away at the edges of self-confidence, leaving you diminished in the process—unless you use your faith and a practical plan to tame it. Specifically, pastors and counselors suggest you take these steps to control your fears.

Fear knocked at the door. Faith answered. And lo, no one was there.

—*Anonymous*

- Bring your fears out into the open.
- Use faith to calm your mind and heart.
- Defeat your fears, one step at a time.

Putting Fear into Perspective

Did you ever notice how much scarier some problem seems when you wake up thinking about it in the middle of the night? Fear thrives in the dark, which is why the first step toward getting a handle on your fears is to bring them out in the open and look at them straight on.

"The worst fear is a hidden fear, the nagging fear at the back of your mind," says David Rensberger, Ph.D., a professor of New Testament studies at the Interdenominational Theological Center in Atlanta. "The way to deal with that is to lead it out in the center of your mind and get to know it. That allows you to put your fear in context. Often when you do that the fear shrinks—it doesn't seem so overwhelming."

Here are two steps that can cut what's scaring you down to size.

1. Write Them Down

"Get your fears out of your heart and head and put them onto paper," suggests the Reverend Robert Corin Morris, an Episcopal priest who directs the Interweave Center for Wholistic Living in Summit, New Jersey. This helps you decide which fears are real and which may be figments of your imagination.

If you have a hard time differentiating between real and imagined fears, try to write down the reasons behind each fear. If you can't figure out the reason for a fear, that's a clue that it may be unreasonable.

2. Know Your Enemy

If it's true that what scares us most is the unknown, then it stands to reason that knowing more will help you fear less. So, if you find a fear overwhelming, research it thoroughly and see if this helps shrink fears to a more manageable size.

❧

Victory over Fear

Heavenly Father, help me to lean on your strong arm when I am afraid. Give me a greater confidence in you, my Good Shepherd, so I can say I fear no evil. I desire to become totally secure in your love—the kind of love that never lets go. Help me to set aside worry and re-place it with trust. And to remember that Christ's resurrection destroys the enemy's power to make me afraid. Help me every day to walk in this new level of faith. I ask in Jesus' name, Amen.

—Quin Sherrer and Ruthanne Garlock

Say, for instance, you're been diagnosed with a serious disease. That disease will be much scarier if you don't know all the possible symptoms and outcomes. But if you go to the library or log on to the Internet and read up on it, then seek out other people who have had experience with the disease, you can combat the anxiety of confronting the unknown. "The more I know about my enemy, the less I need to live in fear of it," Reverend Morris says.

Summoning the Armies of Faith

Once you have your fears out in the light, they are vulnerable. Now's the time to unleash God on them.

Faith can be a highly effective weapon against fear—a fact documented by numerous medical studies. For example, a survey of 760 Midwestern women found that those who attended church more than once a month experienced significantly less anxiety than those who attended less frequently or not at all. Another study of nearly 3,000 people found that young and middle-age individuals who attended church at least once a week were significantly less likely to have anxiety-related disorders than those who did not attend church regularly. Both these studies were reported by Dale Matthews, M.D., of Washington, D.C., coauthor of *The Faith Factor: Proof of the Healing Power of Prayer.*

WHEN TO SEEK PROFESSIONAL HELP

Everyone has little fears and anxious episodes, but for some people fear is so great they're unable to function.

People who lose control of fears like this often have what is called an "anxiety disorder." Here are three of the most common types of anxiety disorder.

Generalized anxiety disorders: These are characterized by regular, repeated bouts of worry and tension, often without any specific cause. If you're always anticipating disaster and can't seem to shake your fears even though you realize they're excessive, you may have this disorder.

Panic attacks: If you have sudden bursts of intense fear accompanied by rapid heartbeat, dizziness, stomach pains, shortness of breath, and other physical symptoms or feelings of losing control, you may be having panic attacks. As with generalized anxiety disorders, there may or may not be a specific cause for your fears.

Phobias: These are intense, irrational fears of certain things or situations. Among the most common objects of phobias are dogs, closed-in places, heights, escalators, tunnels, and injuries involving blood. Also quite common is social phobia, which is an intense fear of becoming embarrassed or humiliated in social situations.

The key word in deciding whether you need professional help in dealing with your fear is "debilitating," says Steven E. Hyman, M.D., director of the National Institute of Mental Health in Bethesda, Maryland. "If you have feelings of fear most days, and they last for more than a few weeks—you should get treatment," he says.

To get help, ask your family doctor or your church leader for a referral to a mental health professional in your area or call your county mental health services organization.

The following three steps can help you maximize your faith defenses against fear.

1. Take Your Fears to the Lord

There is no better way to lift your fears than by taking them straight to God in prayer, says Reverend Morris. Tell God honestly and directly that you're afraid and ask for comfort and protection. That invites God to share your burden and to give you strength in the process. Also ask God for guidance in dealing constructively with your fears, Reverend Morris adds.

Many people of faith are reluctant to bring their fears to God in prayer because they feel guilty about having them, Dr. Rensberger says. The thinking is that the presence of fear demonstrates a lack of faith in God—and in a way that's true. If we each had perfect faith it *would* drive out fear, Dr. Rensberger agrees. But who among us is perfect? In our humanness, we struggle with faith, and as a result we struggle with fear. Rest assured that God understands that all too well.

2. Work on the Fundamentals

If you want to maintain a solid base of serenity, it's important to regularly practice the fundamentals of faith: regular prayer, regular worship, regular

Q&A: Can Fear Be Healthy?

Q: Is there such a thing as healthy fear?

A: Definitely, says the Reverend Robert Corin Morris, director of the Interweave Center for Wholistic Living in Summit, New Jersey. Healthy fear protects us from danger, he points out. Without it, we might walk off cliffs or in front of cars. Healthy fear reminds us that it's time to replace the batteries in the smoke detector.

It's also healthy to have what Reverend Morris calls "holy fear." That's an appropriate appreciation of the sovereign majesty of God and of our human limits in comparison to that majesty. Appreciating those limits encourages us to live with the proper balance and humility. Ignoring them—whether by eating too many cheeseburgers or by polluting the earth's atmosphere—can lead to disaster.

Holy fear also encourages us to ponder the God who created this glorious, mysterious, and sometimes savage universe we inhabit and to wonder what that God might have in mind for us. "Holy fear is something that can lead us to knowledge," Reverend Morris says. "It's an invitation to learn something."

TAKE AWAY THESE UNFOUNDED FEARS

Most loving Father,
Preserve us from faithless fears and worldly anxieties
and grant that no clouds of this mortal life
May hide from us the light of that love which is immortal
And which you have manifested unto us in your Son
Jesus Christ our Lord.

—William Bright

reading of scripture, and regular service to others. Consistency counts, Dr. Rensberger says. It's like taking your vitamins regularly: You build up your resistance over time, so that when you're exposed to some virus that might compromise your immunity, your defense system is strong.

"You can't always whip courage up on the spur of the moment," Dr. Rensberger says. "A constancy of relationship with God builds up your confidence in God's reliability and presence."

3. Follow the Leader

Watching heroes inspires us to be heroic, too, says S. J. Rachman, Ph.D., professor of psychology at the University of British Columbia in Vancouver and author of *Fear and Courage.* "Watching somebody else behave bravely in a situation that's worrying you will definitely help," he says.

One good place to turn for heroic role models is the Bible. Jesus, Abraham, Moses, Mary, Paul, and many other figures in scripture have provided inspiration and hope for millions of believers, Dr. Rensberger says.

Taking On Your Fears

Once you've marshaled your faith resources behind you, it's time to challenge your fears more directly. Of course, you don't really have to—you can cower in the corner, afraid to come out into life. But that's not how God wants you to live.

Remember the Bible story in Matthew when Jesus walks on the water? He

Prayer Miracles

Prayer Took Away My Fear

One year ago I began to experience episodes of panic that were so extreme they rendered me incapable of performing my job, of interacting with friends and family, of caring for my spouse and children, and virtually unable to leave my home. I spent most days and nights alone in my room surrounded by fear.

A doctor diagnosed my condition as panic attack and prescribed some medicine. Along with educating myself about this condition, I began to look to the Lord for strength to persevere. I met a woman who had a similar condition, and she introduced me to a tape of spiritual songs that she thought might help change my state of mind. The tape helped buoy my spirits so that I began to attend church more regularly. I spent more time in quiet solitude praying to the Lord. I really began to listen at church and understand that we are not alone in this life. The Lord is with us always and loves us tremendously; we just have to be wise enough to put our trust in Him.

I slowly began to resume my regular activities and knew in my heart that I had a new agenda in life. I now start and end each day with the Lord. I thank Him for watching over us and keeping us safe, ask Him to bless us, and praise all He has accomplished.

Deborah A. LaBonte
Laurel, Maryland

is walking toward his disciples, whose boat is being tossed on a churning sea. Peter, seeing his Savior approach, wants to leave the boat to meet him.

"Lord," he cries out, "if it be thou, bid me come unto thee on the water."

"Come," Jesus says.

The message is clear: Each of us has work to do in the world, and we can accomplish miracles if our faith doesn't fail us.

You've already made a list of your fears and prayed to have them lifted. Now you need to make a specific plan for confronting and overcoming them once and for all. Two specific steps can help you realize that goal.

1. Focus on the Details

It's easy to get overwhelmed by the big picture. Whether it's looking at all the questions you have to answer on a tax return or noticing how steep the drop is from that cliff you've got to climb, the sheer immensity of a challenge can make you want to turn and run.

There's a simple solution to the big picture dilemma: Don't look at it. Take the answers on the tax return one at a time, or focus all your attention on the next step you have to take on the way up the cliff. Alcoholics use this principle when they talk about staying sober "one day at a time." Ditto the ancient sages when they talked about the journey of a thousand miles beginning with just one step. And this is how high-wire walkers operate; it will work for you, too.

2. Practice Confidence

Athletes who compete seriously in any sport spend literally thousands of hours practicing the fundamentals. That way when the crunch comes they are able to perform almost without thinking about it. The same principle applies to confronting fear. If you practice handling your fears confidently, they will almost certainly dissipate. They may never disappear—many seasoned stage actors still get nervous just before the curtain goes up—but never again will you be frozen by full-blown terror.

> *Deep faith eliminates fear.*
>
> —*Lech Walesa*

A classic example of how preparation sheds fear is public speaking. Practicing your speech in front of a mirror in your bedroom can prepare you to more calmly deliver it in front of an audience. Similarly, the more experience you have speaking in front of groups, the more at ease you become.

When it comes time to actually confront your fear, don't forget to take God with you. Again, speaking in public is a good example. "Visualize yourself giving the speech and invite God to be present with you as you do," Reverend Morris says. "Keep practicing, so that when you actually give the speech, you'll carry that image with you, almost as a prayer."

Dealing with Disappointment

❧

Life is filled with disappointments, large and small, and coming to terms with them is one of the greatest spiritual challenges. Thankfully, through prayer and acceptance you can meet that challenge and emerge more connected to God.

e was a successful cattleman with a huge farm and a happy family. Everything, it seemed, was going his way. Then things turned sour—in a very big way.

Virtually overnight his seven sons and three daughters died, many of his workers were killed, and his herds—more than 15,000 animals in all—perished. Then just when it seemed things couldn't get worse, he broke out in painful sores from his head to his toes.

In utter disappointment, this man we know as Job cried out to the Lord:

Let the day perish in which I was born, . . .
Let that day be darkness!
. . . My groanings are poured out like water.
I am not at ease, nor am I quiet; I have no rest; but trouble comes (Job 3:3–4, 24–26, NRSV).

Who among us has not shared the anguish Job felt over the disappointments of life? It's one thing to understand intellectually that things don't always work out as you'd planned, it's another to actually feel the pain of dreams not realized, potential unfulfilled.

Disappointments don't have to be on the magnitude of Job's to be a struggle, either. Sometimes daily discouragements can be just as hard to take: the promotion you didn't get at work, the noisy neighbors who are turning your dream home into a nightmare, the snotty attitude your kids seem to be developing. Over time, these sorts of disappointments can mount up, gradually chipping away at your spiritual composure. If you're not careful, the day may come when you find your spirit poisoned, your whole outlook on life embittered.

Some people complain because God put thorns on roses, while others praise Him for putting roses among thorns.

—Anonymous

Thankfully, there are spiritual ways you can battle that bitterness and defeat disappointment. The keys:

- Take your disappointment to God.
- Seek God's purpose in your life.
- Practice accepting the things you cannot change.
- Move on with the life God has planned for you.

Grieving with God

As in other times of spiritual need, the first step toward coming to terms with disappointment is to bring your sorrow to God in prayer. There are five steps that can be especially helpful in getting your healing started.

1. Comfort Yourself

In times of suffering, there is no better place to turn for comfort than the psalms, says Robert DeVries, Ph.D., doctor of ministry, professor of church education at Calvin Theological Seminary in Grand Rapids, Michigan. In particular he suggests reading the psalms of lament, which most directly express anguish over personal loss. These include Psalms 3, 4, 13, 22, 31, 39, 57, 69, 88, and 139. Among the most famous and heart-rending laments of all time is the opening verse of Psalm 22, which Jesus repeated on the cross: "My God, my God, why hast thou forsaken me?"

Meditating on the psalms of lament and praying with them can help you realize you're not alone in your suffering, Dr. DeVries says. They tell you that it is perfectly acceptable—as well as immensely comforting—to express your anguish to God in the strongest possible terms. It may also be helpful to note, he adds, that in almost every instance the lament psalms lead to some sense of resolution between the sufferer and God.

2. Talk It Out

Another way to find comfort is to share your pain with others, says the Reverend Siang-Yang Tan, Ph.D., professor of psychology at Fuller Theological Seminary in Pasadena, California, and author of several books, including *Managing Chronic Pain*. Talk about your disappointments with good friends, or with a therapist, if the disruption of your emotional stability is substantial. "Allow others to come alongside to share the load," he suggests.

3. Mourn Your Loss

Part of coming to terms with disappointment is simply admitting how deeply it hurts and grieving the loss, says Elaine M. Prevallet, Ph.D., member of the Sisters of Loretto religious community and director of the Knobs Haven Retreat Center in Nerinx, Kentucky. Usually we associate the word "grieving" with the death of a loved one, but it is also possible to grieve for the loss of a

What Would **Jesus** Do?

Until the resurrection, most people would have said that the ministry of Jesus Christ came to a somewhat disappointing conclusion. Arrest, trial, and crucifixion don't satisfy the usual standards of worldly success, and even Jesus struggled to accept this ignoble end.

The fact that he did struggle to accept it can be a comfort for those who are dealing with disappointments of their own. *How* he handled that struggle, as recorded in the Book of Matthew, can serve as a useful model as well.

The night He was to be arrested, Jesus came with His disciples to the garden at Gethsemane.

"I am deeply grieved," He told his companions, *"even to death."*

Then He went off by himself to pray, throwing Himself prostrate on the ground.

"My Father," Jesus said. *"If it is possible, let this cup pass from me; yet not what I want but what you want."*

(Matthew 26:36–39, NRSV)

GOD'S LOVE

If you seek peace,
you will have none.
If you seek life,
you will lose it.
If you seek wealth,
you will find poverty of soul.
If you seek adventure,
you will be unfulfilled.
If you seek joy,
you will ache with sorrow.
If you seek love,
you will despair in loneliness.
If you seek God,
you will find God.
You will have peace
that surpasses understanding,
gain eternal life,
find true wealth,
be fulfilled,
worship in joy,
and revel in God's love.

—Susan Gerrish

dream or of some emotionally meaningful part of your life: Perhaps you have cherished the hope that your daughter would graduate from a prestigious school, but she's refused to even apply, or perhaps you have coveted a job in management, but time and again you've been passed over.

These are genuine losses, and they deserve to be mourned. Take quiet walks, Dr. Prevallet suggests, and ask God in prayer for comfort and healing. Tell trusted friends what you're going through. Get plenty of rest. Most of all, simply give yourself time to allow the grieving process to unfold naturally and completely.

4. Look for Role Models

The Bible is filled with stories of disappointment and loss, says Dr. DeVries. Reading the scriptures' accounts of figures who suffered yet carried on can provide powerful inspiration when you are struggling with your own trials and tribulations. In addition to the story of Job, Old Testament examples include Abraham, Moses, and the prophets. In the New Testament, the reactions of Jesus' followers to His crucifixion are especially powerful examples of people struggling with extraordinary disappointment.

5. Reassure Yourself of God's Love

In times of disappointment, there's a temptation to forget one of the most fundamental facts of faith: that God loves you, says Dr. Tan.

It is also important to remember, Dr. Tan adds, that one day you will be delivered from your disappointments, no matter how great they may seem right now. Yes, you'll still feel pain in the present moment, but the prospect of ultimate relief can be reassuring. "We can bank on God's promise," he says. "One day, there will be no more tears."

What Will Be, Will Be

Acknowledging, expressing, and mourning your disappointment are all key first steps in the spiritual process of coming to terms with it. Once you've completed those steps, it is time to begin the hard work of acceptance. That means accepting your life for what it is, even when it falls short of what you'd hoped.

This is tough for most of us. We are raised on advertisements, sports slogans, and inspirational speeches that tell us we can have it all—the fancy cars, the beautiful house, the great vacations, the perfect waistline—if only we *want* it badly enough. In truth, Dr. Tan points out, we *can't* have it all, and to pretend we can is a setup for disappointment. "Dreams do not always come true," he says. "I'm not saying that you shouldn't try, but we have to be realistic. We live within human limits."

Another reason we find disappointments so difficult to deal with is our lust to control what happens in our lives—to have things our way, says Dr. Prevallet. We become attached to our vision of the way things should be. For example, you might have expected that by the age of 50 your family would be living off an income of $100,000 a year, but now it's clear that's not in the cards. Disappointment teaches all of us that the world—and God—sometimes have different ideas about what we need or deserve.

Here are five specific steps to take that will help you accept the disappointments in your life.

1. Examine Your Expectations

It's one of life's more relentless spiritual axioms: The more you allow yourself to expect something, the more you set yourself up for disappointment. Try not to fall into this trap. If something or somebody has let you down, take a look at what you expected and try to determine whether or not your expectation was realistic, Dr. Tan says. If you're a writer, should you expect that your first novel will be instantly accepted for publication and win the Pulitzer prize? Probably not.

2. Forgive Those Who Disappoint You

Of course, there are times when your expectation may be realistic and someone genuinely lets you down. You have a right to expect that your spouse will tell you the truth, for example. It's also reasonable to assume that your business partner won't embezzle money from the company account.

What if your legitimate expectations aren't fulfilled? You may need to take appropriate measures to protect yourself against future violations of trust, but you also need to work on forgiving the other person, says Dr. DeVries. This is not the same as forgetting, he stresses. If your disappointment was severe, you may remember it for years. Nonetheless, Dr. DeVries says, you can learn to keep your hurt in a place in your heart where it doesn't continually rule your thoughts and emotions, even though it may be necessary to reaffirm your forgiveness on a daily basis.

One way to start forgiving: Write a letter to the offending party explaining how you feel, suggests Dr. DeVries. Then throw away the letter. Another option: Write about your disappointment in a journal or in a letter to yourself.

Don't forget to apply these same principles to disappointments you have with yourself. Many of us have higher expectations of ourselves than of anyone, and many of us find it difficult to forgive ourselves when we fail. Give yourself a break, advises Dr. Tan. "It's important to realize that we're good at some things and not so good at others," he says. "That's fine—that's the way

YOUR WILL, LORD, NOT OURS

Blessed are you, O Lord, Almighty God,

to whom our inmost thoughts are revealed:

you know our needs much better than we ourselves can ask or
imagine.

Sovereign Lord and ever-loving Redeemer,

in the richness of your mercy give us pure hearts

to call upon your holy name;

lead us not into temptation but deliver us from evil

and order all things for our good.

Because all glory, honor, and praise are yours by right,

Father, Son, and Holy Spirit, now and for ever, to the ages of ages.
Amen.

—*Russian Orthodox Church*

God made us. A level of self-acceptance and realistic expectations will help in overcoming unnecessary disappointment."

3. Meditate on God's Plan for You

There is an old saying that if you want to make God laugh, tell God your plans.

The point is that God has plans—for you and for everybody else—and they may be quite different from what you had in mind.

Disappointments may be God's way of telling you that you're on the wrong path, Dr. Tan believes. "There's a saying that disappointments are actually '*His* appointments,'" he says.

In that case, you need to reevaluate your goals, your expectations, and your plans to bring them more into line with God's. "Go back to square one," says Dr. Prevallet. "Say to yourself, 'Okay, my life is in God's hands. What direction should I take now?'"

On the other hand, your disappointment may involve the loss of something you legitimately need. Perhaps you're convinced that your calling is to start a church ministry for the homeless, but your pastor doesn't like the idea and vetoes it. If you're still convinced your plan is a solid one, don't give up: Figure out what it will take to make it happen.

One thing to remember in the case of thwarted dreams is that there are many different ways of approaching a goal, says the Reverend Robert Corin Morris, an Episcopal priest who directs the Interweave Center for Wholistic Living in Summit, New Jersey. So, if your church doesn't support your idea of that homeless ministry, maybe the church around the corner will. "It's not necessary to get boxed in with disappointment," he says. "Once you get in touch with what brings you joy, there are lots of different ways to fulfill that dream."

4. Discover Your True Desires

Sometimes you don't *really* want what you *think* you want, points out Reverend Morris. You may desire a candy bar, for example, when what you really want is a feeling of comfort. You may desire dinner and a movie, when what you really want is to share some quality time with a special person. You may

LETTING GO

Take, Lord, all my liberty,

my memory, my understanding,

and my whole will.

You have given me all that I have,

all that I am,

and I surrender all to Your Divine will.

Give me only Your love and Your grace.

With this I am rich enough,

and I have no more to ask.

Amen.

—Ignatius of Loyola

Prayer Miracles

A Backdoor Answer to Prayer

While I was the minister of music at a large church in Corpus Christi, Texas, I completely lost my singing voice and then my speaking voice to spasmodic dysphonia. I received treatments that helped for periods of time, but eventually I lost my voice again.

Over the years I had held services of healing, during which people experienced miraculous healing. At the same time, I had many people pray for me to be healed. I have even been prayed for at my own healing services in which others have been healed. But my voice never was healed. Many, including myself, have asked why.

I continued praying to God to show me a way, then I found it was before my eyes the whole time. For years I wrote as a means of expressing myself when I couldn't speak. People often told me I should be writing. I have stated many times that I would like to be a professional writer. Now I have the incredible opportunity to do what I have always wanted to do. And now that I am writing daily I am discovering that there are realities and understandings deep within me.

In an odd twist of answered prayers, God has not only given me my heart's desire, but has also opened windows within me. I have found both my passion in life and the continuing opportunity to help others find meaning when life unexpectedly runs a stop sign and wrecks.

When you pray, don't just watch the front door. Throw open the windows and watch the back door. God may have another plan.

Terry Thomlinson
South Sioux City, Nebraska

desire success in your career when what you really want is to feel that you have value.

Disappointment offers an opportunity to learn what deeper needs may lie beneath your surface desires, Reverend Morris says. He recommends you bring your desires, whatever they might be, directly to God in prayer. "The practice of stating your needs and desires in the presence of God can help you begin sifting through them," he says. "I'm not suggesting that we get everything we ask for, but prayer can help you be more aware of what it is you're truly asking for. Prayer, meditation, and journaling are all techniques that can help you dig deeper for what you really want."

5. Let Go

For the truly religious person, the ultimate desire at the bottom of all other desires is that God's will be done. If something is happening in your life that is disappointing, it may be that God has willed it to be so. Your task then is to surrender to God's will, which is perhaps the most profound spiritual discipline of all.

"We need to consciously cultivate the ability to acknowledge and accept disappointment, to say to ourselves, peacefully, 'I wanted it to be this way; it's not that way; I can let it go,'" says Reverend Morris.

Perhaps the best way to learn to accept is through prayerful meditation, suggests Reverend Morris. One acquaintance of his, when confronted by disappointment, concentrates on taking deep breaths and repeating to herself a sort of mantra: "This is what is."

Letting go of your disappointment can serve as one of the most powerful possible tools for spiritual insight, adds Dr. Prevallet. God often works in our lives to strip away encumbrances that stand between us and the Divine. Try to see disappointment as a purifying process. Painful as it may be as it occurs, it can result in the long run in a deeper unity with God, and more peace. That's why Dr. Prevallet calls disappointment "a privileged occasion for self-knowledge."

> *Do not allow yourselves to be disheartened by any failure as long as you have done your best.*
>
> —*Mother Teresa*

Again, meditating and reflecting prayerfully can help you take note of any guidance God may offer and help you grow closer to God.

Moving On

Just as it's important to mourn and accept disappointments, it's also important at some point to put them behind you and move on. "You don't want to run away from the pain that accompanies disappointment," says Dr. Tan, "but neither do you want to stew in it forever. After you confront your disappointment, try to take your mind off it. Exercise, listen to other people, read scripture, pray—there are many things you can do to continue constructively with your life. You need to remember that 'this, too, will pass.'"

One of the most direct ways to put personal disappointments behind you is to turn your attention toward serving others, says Dr. DeVries. "Don't allow yourself to dwell on your own circumstance," he says. "Go visit some inmates in prison or clean up a neighbor's yard. It is in serving that we receive, and one of the ways of breaking out of disappointment is to make a real contribution to someone else's life. That's true partly because you find out in helping others how good God has been to you."

Finding Balance

Trying to give too much of your time and emotional energy to family, friends, jobs, and causes can take the joy out of life. If you've fallen victim to this plight, use prayer, spiritual regeneration and common sense to renew yourself.

Katherine Brown-Saltzman, R.N., was stuck in a giving mode—every waking hour of the day.

As an oncology nurse at the UCLA Medical Center, she cared full-time for cancer patients who were suffering or dying. After work, she cleaned house, cooked meals, and tended to the other needs of her husband and two children. Then when she was done with all that she wrote scientific articles, volunteered, and nurtured friends.

Finally after 13 years of giving her all, she felt utterly drained and started thinking about leaving the job she loved. Worse, she found herself turning off her emotions—and sometimes avoiding people who might want her help.

Thankfully, the solution was clear: If Brown-Saltzman wanted to continue her natural, giving ways, she had to develop a better balance between her needs and those of the people who wanted her help. So, she began taking twice-annual silent retreats and longer vacations. She incorporated her faith into her work by praying with her patients. She learned to leave work at work—to stop feeling guilty when she couldn't accomplish everything on her to-do list and to really rest on the weekends.

Today, she feels energized and restored—so much so that she has become an advocate for balanced living and has created a retreat program called Circle of Caring to help other overcommitted health care workers get control over their lives.

Perhaps you're caught up in a similar web of overwork and "overgiving." Perhaps between your demanding job and demanding private life, you never quite feel like you're on top of things. It happens to many people of faith who try to follow Jesus' decree that "It is more blessed to give than to receive."

This isn't healthy—emotionally or physically, say counselors. Instead, you need to allow yourself more free time—and more *me* time. If you do, says Brown-Saltzman, "it's like taking care of the temple. It's the difference between having a home that's in total disarray and chaos and a home that's in order."

> *I will work in my own way, according to the light that is in me.*
>
> —*Lydia Maria Child*

How do you put your house in order?

- Create some equilibrium between work and rest.
- Find your real purpose in life and follow it.
- Learn to say no when you're overbooked.

Let's look at some ways you can accomplish each of these changes.

Bringing Balance into Your Life

Many of us are committed to our jobs, to developing ourselves, and to helping others. These are all wonderful traits. But you need to balance them with their opposites: rest, play, and receiving. Otherwise, you burn out or succumb to stress, which has been linked with dozens of ailments, from emotional problems to heart disease.

Here are six ways to make sure you balance your needs.

1. At the End of the Work Week, Light a Candle

Candle-lighting has served as a symbolic link with God for centuries. It can give you a feeling of peace and help you meditate or pray. Most importantly, this simple act can help you make the transition from work to rest.

2. Extend Your Vacation

Take the time you're entitled to. If you can, take more than a week at a time.

Brown-Saltzman tries to vacation for an entire month. She knows if she takes just 1 week she barely gets thoughts of work out of her mind before she has to go back again. Two weeks gives her just enough time to feel rested. But

PRAYERFUL RETREATS

If you're feeling overwhelmed by all the obligations in your life, you may want to consider making a spiritual retreat. These mini-vacations provide time for quiet contemplation and relaxation, a breather from your hectic life. Going on a spiritual retreat can renew your enthusiasm and focus. Here are four that counselors recommend.

1. The Pathwork Transformation Program teaches you how to feed your soul, enrich your heart, and strengthen your courage. Write to Sevenoaks Pathwork Center, Route 1, Box 86, Madison, VA 22727.

2. The Dwelling Place offers opportunities for spiritual renewal on its 17-acre wooded property. Write to The Dwelling Place, HC-01, Box 126, 2824 Dwelling Place Road, Brooksville, MS 39739-9537.

3. Inward Bound Retreat focuses on bringing you more in touch with yourself and with nature. Write to Inward Bound Retreat, 11298 County Road 14, Del Norte, CO 81132.

4. The Lindenwood Conference and Retreat Center, run by the Poor Handmaids of Jesus Christ, promotes personal growth, faith enrichment, and education. Write to Lindenwood, 9601 Union Road, P.O. Box 1, Donaldson, IN 46513-0001.

in 4 weeks she can get into a restful state *and* enjoy quality time with her family. In fact, during that month off, she usually spends some time alone first.

3. Relearn How to Play

When you spend much of your time running from one activity to another, you keep your brain on analytical mode, just constantly solving immediate problems. To relax, you need to balance analytical thinking with playful thinking. You can put yourself in a frame of mind for playful thinking by, well, playing—really playing—with young children.

Make pictures with finger paints, mold clay, blow bubbles. Activities like these not only give you quality time with your children or grandchildren, but they also take you to a restful part of your brain where you're more open to creative ideas. Other options if there aren't any young kids around: Go on a nature hike. Star gaze or bird watch. Sing songs.

You can even incorporate such forms of play into your job. Take a short doodling break during your work day. Go for a quick walk outside and listen to the birds. Close your office door and read a passage from a Dr. Seuss book—out loud. Tell a joke to one of your coworkers.

4. Take Instead of Give

People of faith often get into the giving trap by donating their spare time to various committees and activities at church or in the community. Of course, giving *is* good, but not when you give so much that it leaves you mentally and physically exhausted. Instead, you need to regularly take time for yourself. One way to do this is to go on a retreat like Brown-Saltzman's Circle of Caring. There, organizers handle every need so visitors can concentrate on learning how to relax.

You can also renew yourself by participating in women's and men's groups, Bible study, prayer groups, and other gatherings where people come together to share their needs and concerns.

5. Escape from the Helper Trap

Women especially get caught in this situation, with children, spouses, in-laws, and others expecting them to meet their many needs. If you feel over-

RESTORE MY WEARY SOUL

Father, I have grown weary in the journey of life, and in the process I feel that I've lost so much. I come to you now, asking you to restore to me the joy of your salvation, and to help me to recover from the mistakes and losses that have accumulated in my life. . . .

Lord, I draw close to you now and I receive the refreshing that comes from being in your presence. Thank you for your blessing of rest, renewal, recovery, refreshing, and total restoration.

—Clift Richards and Lloyd Hildebrand

whelmed, ask for help, says Brown-Saltzman. Ask your spouse to share the housework or to entertain the kids for the evening. Or tell someone from your faith community that you are feeling overwhelmed. Chances are, prepared dinners will start arriving at your doorstep.

6. Always Have Your Sabbath

Just because church services are held on Sunday doesn't mean that's *your* Sabbath. If your Sunday is packed with cooking, chores, church meetings, and Sunday school teaching, then you may feel just as drained as you do after a day of work. If so, then Saturday or another day should be your day of prayerful rest. Sleep late. Go for a walk and contemplate the beauty of nature. Lounge around with a good book.

Finding Your Real Purpose

Christopher Neck started his adult life as an accountant, and he hated every minute of it. It wasn't that accounting was a bad profession; it was simply a bad profession for him because he found no meaning in crunching numbers all day long. So, he followed his inner nudging and went back to school for a master's degree in business administration and then his doctorate in management.

Then one day during his Ph.D. program while filling in for a professor who was out sick, he discovered his true career: teaching. He simply felt exhilarated after every class. Today, Neck, Ph.D., is an associate professor of management at Virginia Tech in Blacksburg and author of *Medicine for the Mind* and *Mastering Self-Leadership*. He says he still thrives on teaching. "I get a high many times a week that some people never get in their entire lives," he says.

The high comes from following his inner purpose, says Dr. Neck. Pastors refer to it as a "calling." Others might call it destiny. Whatever your name for it, it's the thing that you do that makes you feel like life is truly worth living.

Once you start following your inner purpose, the rest of your life mysteriously falls into place, says Dr. Neck. Suddenly you know which tasks to take on and which to turn down. You feel at one with yourself, your career, your family, and your acts of charity. In short, your life is filled with a balance.

So, how do you find your purpose?

1. Recall Your "Majestic Moments"

These are times in your past when you felt exhilarated by what you were doing. For instance, the first majestic moment Dr. Neck can remember dates back to ninth grade. His speech class teacher gave him a slip of paper with the word "bowling" written on it and told him to talk about that word for 5 minutes. "At first I thought, 'Five minutes! That's an eternity!' I had only bowled once before. But then as I started talking, the time just flew. When I was done, all I could think was, 'Wow,'" says Dr. Neck.

Try to remember your own "wow" or "majestic moments." What common link runs through them? For Dr. Neck, the common link was talking in front of large groups of people. Once you pinpoint your link, you're well on your way to discovering your God-given talent.

2. Take Risks

If meditating on your majestic moments makes you feel strongly that you are on the wrong career path, gather the courage to forge a new career. But first, make sure you know where you are headed. Before you quit your current job, experiment with the new skills that you dream of. Take on part-time, freelance, or volunteer jobs. "Do a trial run and see what happens," suggests Dr. Neck. Also, seek out others

Prayer Miracles

The Miracle of Roses

I *was getting ready to leave the hospital for a long weekend and checked in with one cancer patient, a spiritual woman whom I had grown close to. She had previously had a bone marrow transplant, but was back in the hospital because of complications with her liver.*

She was so sick that her doctor didn't know whether she would make it through the weekend. Well, this woman adored roses. When I went to see her, the roses in her room were dead and my first thought was, "She needs new roses." On the elevator, I ran into a volunteer who was delivering flowers. She gave me some roses and said, "You look like you could use these." They were an answer to my prayer.

I brought them back to the woman's room and while I was there, I ran into one of her family members who had also been given a rose. Everywhere I went that day I was surrounded with roses. I took it as a sign that this woman, whether she lived or died, was being surrounded by God's love.

When I returned to work that Monday, she not only was still alive, but she was healing! Her liver enzymes were returning to normal, she was conscious, and all of the complications were being reversed!

Katherine Brown-Saltzman, R.N.
Los Angeles, California

who have taken similar risks. Get their advice on what to expect.

3. Sprinkle Your Day with Meaning

If you don't have the luxury of quitting your job or going back to school as Dr. Neck did, you can still find a way to make your work meaningful. "Not

BALANCING HOME AND WORK

Lord, I'm doing my best to balance home and work. Sometimes I feel there's not enough of me to go around in meeting all the demands. Both my energy and my clock run out before I can get it all done. And when I get really frazzled, the people I love most bear the brunt of my frustration. Help me, Lord, to draw from your strength and peace in ordering my priorities. Help me to use my tongue wisely and always with kindness (Proverbs 31:26). Equip me to be the best I can be, both at home and on the job, and bring people into my life who can help me with what I need to do. Thank you for your provision, Lord. Amen.

—Quin Sherrer and Ruthanne Garlock

everyone loves their entire job, but within their job they find some way to make a difference," says Dr. Neck. "It's not the company mission that needs to be important. It's your mission that's important." For example, you might find satisfaction in bringing in flowers to brighten a coworker's day or in complimenting at least one colleague a day.

4. Periodically Reexamine Your Purpose

Whenever you feel overloaded, take a new look at your inner purpose. Have you agreed to tasks that deviate from it? Or has your inner purpose simply changed? That can happen as you age. If you feel confused about what to do, pray or meditate over your dilemma. Or talk to a religious counselor, friend, or career counselor who can help you get back on track.

Learning to Say No

There's one problem when your life is aligned around your inner purpose. You tend to feel so exhilarated that you can sometimes take on too much.

That still happens to Brown-Saltzman, even with all of her concentration on leading a balanced life. She feels so attached to her patients that she sometimes stays at work too late, then rushes to meet her other commitments and ends up feeling drained again.

If you feel caught in a consuming spiral of obligations, counselors say there's just one solution: You just have to look at your to-do list and start paring.

For example, think about your ties at church. Are you on a committee because you really care about it or because someone asked you and you didn't know how to say no? If it's the latter, then maybe it's time to bow out. Your goal should be to serve in a way that complements your talents as well as nourishes your soul.

How do you reduce your obligations without feeling guilty? Turn the problem over to God, suggests Margaret Stockwell, a spiritual counselor in Buenos Aires, Argentina. If God wants you to do more, God will grant you the energy, she says. If God doesn't, you know you're doing more than God is asking. "We keep running around doing more and more until we are exhausted, perhaps afraid we haven't done enough for God. Yet, God wants a balance in our lives of worship, work, rest, and play. He is in it all!" says Stockwell.

> *Do everything with a mind that lets go. If you let go a little, you will have a little peace. If you let go a lot, you will have a lot of peace. If you let go completely, you will know complete peace and freedom.*
>
> —*Achaan Chah*

Staying Balanced

Have you ever seen a wobble board? It's a flat piece of wood that's mounted to a ball. Podiatrists often ask people with weak ankles to stand on them to improve the balancing muscles in their feet. Try standing on one and you'll often wobble from one side to another. For brief seconds, you may succeed in keeping the board balanced, then one side tips to the floor again.

This is much the same as staying balanced in life. For brief moments you achieve perfect harmony. But in essence, you are usually in a state of unbalance. That's okay. In fact, that's human nature, explains Father Larry Gillick, S.J., director of the Deglman Center for Ignatian Spirituality at Creighton University in Omaha, Nebraska. Just keep trying. Eventually you'll be able to keep yourself in a balanced state for longer and longer periods of time. That's a true blessing.

Managing Stress

Are all the pressures in your life leaving you worn and frazzled? There are three spiritual ways to reduce those sagging feelings, and they all start with you.

Rushing to get to work on time. Keeping an eye on your ever-so-wandering 2 year old. Trying to sleep even though your neighbor's kids are still playing loudly outside.

The stress that comes with situations like these can make you anxious and irritable and can seriously damage your health—if you let it. But there are simple, prayerful ways to eliminate stress, or reduce it if eliminating it isn't possible.

Stress links back to our cave-dwelling days, the days when we needed a quickened heart rate, dilated pupils, warm muscles, and shallow breathing to outrun big hairy sharp-toothed animals who took one look at us and thought "dinner!"

In modern times, however, stress is more likely to be a curse than your salvation. When you're worried about the safety of your loved ones, your health, your job security, your self-esteem, or a hundred other things, the stress hormones cortisol and adrenaline kick in, sapping energy, lowering your immunity, and setting you up for a host of diseases. High blood pressure, headaches, panic attacks, ulcers, insomnia, cancer, and other conditions all have been linked to stress, says Steven M. Tovian, Ph.D., director of health psychology and chief psychologist at Evanston Hospital in Illinois.

How can you as a spiritual person turn off stress and develop a sense of peace in an ever-so-fast-paced world? You have three options.

- Change the situation.
- Change how you perceive the situation.
- Change how you react to the situation.

Here are some specific tips for using each strategy.

Make It All Go Away

Sometimes this solution to stress is easy. If the daily traffic jam makes you jittery about being late to work, simply change things by leaving 10 minutes earlier. But if the cause of your stress is more complex—say you're unhappy that you haven't gotten further in your career—beating it may mean changing your idea of what's important.

Everything can be taken from man except the last of the human freedoms, his ability to choose . . . his own way. Remember this choice of attitude when you are feeling overwhelmed by your circumstances.

—Viktor E. Frankl

Morrie Schwartz favored this method. The central character in Mitch Albom's acclaimed book *Tuesdays with Morrie*, Schwartz was dying of Lou Gehrig's disease. But he was dying well, offering love and wisdom to everyone who visited. He told one visitor: "Everyone is in such a hurry. . . . People haven't found meaning in their lives, so they're running all the time looking for it. They think [all they need is] the next car, the next house, the next job. Then they find those things are empty, too, and they keep running."

Clearly, chasing the wrong things doesn't work. But that doesn't mean you should stop chasing altogether—just make sure your goal is something that fills your life with meaning and helps you find a purpose. Here are some specific suggestions.

1. Make Every Minute Count

The next time you find yourself in a hurry, stop and ask yourself, "How do I want to use my time if each minute is a sacred gift?" suggests Gwen White, a spiritual counselor in Newport, Rhode Island, who offers workshops on stress management and spiritual life retreats throughout the country. "Suddenly time has a different value," she says.

When you start evaluating your day in this way, you'll realize that many

Q&A: How Can I Handle "Faith Stress"?

Q: I'm worried that I don't put enough time and effort into prayer and the other aspects of my faith. What can I do to prevent this from being a source of stress?

A: There is no such thing as "enough." When you suffer from this spiritual inferiority, you are always in a losing position, says Father Larry Gillick, S.J., director of the Deglman Center for Ignatian Spirituality at Creighton University in Omaha, Nebraska.

Indeed, there is no such thing as not praying enough, not doing enough good deeds, or not going to church often enough. "Humans are by nature limited beings, and God loves us the way He finds us," says Father Gillick. With prayer, God will help you extend your limits. But if you create an artificial, human goal of praying five times a day or never missing a church service, you will always be disappointed. Instead of feeling inferior about your relationship with God, accept it. Revere it. Then do something good in the world.

Your good deeds do not have to change the world. You don't have to mirror or better the efforts of others in your faith community. Think of it this way. God gave all of us cans of paint and a brush to color the world. We all have different colors, different sized brushes, and different sized cans. Don't worry that your can is different. Instead, use it to paint your unique picture.

time-consuming activities no longer pass the time test. As you eliminate them, you'll curb your stress, too.

2. Get with the Plan

Often, the conflict of wanting to do two things at once results from a deep inner battle between a drive for self-gratification and a drive to follow your higher purpose, says Donovan Thesenga, director of Sevenoaks Pathwork Center in Madison, Virginia, and coauthor of *Surrender to God Within*.

Knowing when you're conflicted is easy. You feel awful. Figuring out which is the right path to follow, however, takes more prayerful inner searching. You can stay aligned with your higher purpose by praying regularly a few times each day. For instance, Thesenga does brief 10-second prayers throughout the day simply to remind himself of his purpose. Periodically, he says to himself,

"I commit again to be a man of God.

"I commit again to making this the focus of my life."

That way, when feeling rushed to run errands, he can easily relax by recalling that his life "has deeper significance than going to work to earn the money to buy the toothpaste. When I remember to do these brief prayers, it dispels all of my problems. I don't worry. I don't feel as perturbed," says Thesenga.

3. Find Purpose in Everyday Activities

Your job may be a source of stress in your life. But maybe you're not ready to find a job that better suits you. Or maybe you're not financially able to take such a risk. That doesn't mean you can't make some small, meaningful changes that will relieve your stress, says Christopher Neck, Ph.D., an associate professor of management at Virginia Tech in Blacksburg and author of *Medicine for the Mind*.

Try this exercise: Think about what you actually do at work. Then brainstorm some techniques for making your work more rewarding. You may find you can accomplish the same tasks in ways that would give you a feeling of competence, self-control, and purpose. For example, Dr. Neck recalls one highway toll collector who added meaning to her job by smiling, chatting, and generally trying to make each motorist she dealt with have a nice day. The task brought purpose to her work and, in turn, reduced stress. Motorists soon got used to her smile and would even change lanes just to have her say hello to them.

4. Focus on Your Real Needs

We have many false needs in life: The drive to climb the corporate ladder. The desire to keep up with the Joneses. The obsession with making and saving money. None of those things bring true happiness, says Father Larry Gillick, S.J., director of the Deglman Center for Ignatian Spirituality at Creighton University in Omaha, Nebraska. "If you identify your self-worth by what you own, by how important your title at work sounds to others, or by how much esteem you hold at church, your life will always have stress. Prestige, power, and titles

What Would **Jesus** Do?

Do you fear the worry and stress in your life is about to overwhelm you? Try to follow Jesus' example on the night when He knew a crowd would come to capture Him and take Him to his death. He concentrated on the present, on the work that had to be done. He concentrated on loving his disciples, on telling them what they would need to know later.

As they all sat around the table, Jesus continued to teach. He said: *"Peace I leave with you, my peace I give unto you: not as the world giveth, give I unto you. Let not your heart be troubled, neither let it be afraid."*

(John 14:27, KJV)

A PRAYER FOR RELIEF

Lord, when we think only of our own wants and desires, we are impatient to have them satisfied, yet in our hearts we know that such satisfaction will crumble to dust. Give us that spirit of hope which can enable us to want what you want, and to wait patiently on your time, in the knowledge that in you alone comes true and lasting pleasure.

—*Mozarabic Sacramentary*

---

never satisfy. You will always want more because you are chasing after a false God. And envy is the root of your problem."

What are your real needs? Food and shelter, for sure. Other than that, Saint Paul summed up our real needs best in his first letter to the church of Corinth: "The greatest of these is love."

Or in Morrie Schwartz's words, "You know what really gives you satisfaction? . . . Offering others what you have to give."

Change the Way You Look at Things

What you think can greatly influence how you feel. Going back to that example of a traffic jam, if you're caught in traffic, worrying about being late for work will raise your stress level. But, you can stop stress in its tracks if instead you tell yourself, "This is no big deal. It's not like I'm going to get fired for getting caught in traffic."

Here are three other thought processes that tend to cause stress and tips on how to turn them around.

1. All-Or-Nothing Thinking

In his book *Don't Sweat the Small Stuff* Richard Carlson, Ph.D., writes, "I've yet to meet an absolute perfectionist whose life was filled with inner peace."

Perfectionistic thinking causes stress by setting you up for failure. Say you

PRAYER FOR MYSELF

Dearly beloved God,

In whom I lay my trust,

Please give me new life.

Fill every cell of my being, transform each thought, cleanse every heartbeat,

That I might be as You would have me be.

Take away the darkness of my past.

Fill me with Your blessing and graciousness.

Allow me rebirth from the many deaths I have endured in this life.

Dear God,

I have been through the wars.

Where I have been weak, please make me strong.

Where I perceive myself as guilty, please show me my innocence.

Where I block my healing or full empowerment or full experience of love and joy, please show me my wound and take from me its sting.

May I experience the beauty, the abundance, the power, and the joy that is Your wish for all mankind,

That I may be a vessel for these things in the lives of others.

Amen.

—Marianne Williamson

want to lose 10 pounds by July 4. As Independence Day draws near, you'll feel stress about meeting your goal. Yet you're the only person who even knows about that goal!

The next time you find yourself worrying because you might miss a deadline, because you might not pay all of your bills on time, because you notice a small spaghetti sauce stain on your shirt, or because you simply can't get everything on your to-do list done, turn off those perfectionist tendencies and meditate on the second commandment as explained by Jesus to the Pharisees, "Love your neighbor as yourself" (Matthew 22:39, NIV), then apply it to yourself, suggests Margaret Stockwell, a spiritual counselor in Buenos Aires, Argentina. Self-love is incredibly important, and it's something many people forget to do, she says.

Here's another way to think about perfectionism. Imagine yourself at one end of a dark room and a candle at the other. The closer you get to that candle, the more your imperfections—stains on your shirt, wrinkled pants, and so on—will show. You have three options. You can hide in the corner, blow out the candle and stumble around in the darkness, or let your flaws show. "Live with your shortcomings. To be human is to be limited. We're fragile. Pray and revere your limitations. Don't hide them," says Father Gillick.

2. Mind-Reading

We do this when we imagine we know what other people are thinking about us. For instance, one day Dr. Neck's boss walked by and didn't even acknowledge his presence. Dr. Neck began trying to figure out what he had done to get his boss angry with him. It turns out that his boss was late for a meeting with the dean and was preoccupied with his thoughts. He didn't even notice Dr. Neck.

The next time you catch yourself worrying about what other people think about you, remind yourself of three things.

- It's possible you're misreading the situation.
- People spend very little time thinking about other people. In fact, they spend most of their time thinking about themselves.
- It doesn't matter what so-and-so thinks about you. What really matters is how you feel about yourself.

3. Fortune-Telling

This is a psychologist's word for worrying, says Dr. Neck. When you look into the future—"I missed a deadline at work, therefore my boss will be mad at me, therefore I won't get that raise I need"—you fret about things that may never occur. "Mark Twain put it best when he said, 'I have been through some terrible things in my life, some of which actually happened.'"

The next time you find yourself caught in this thought trap, try one of these tips.

- Bring yourself back to the present. You only have control over the present. Concentrate on what you can do right now to alleviate what you fear will happen later.
- Question your predictions. Ask yourself "is it possible" questions, like: "Is it possible that my boss really doesn't hate the report I wrote, but is just having a bad morning?" or "Is it possible that my neighbor really isn't out to get me, but instead doesn't know he left the dog out again?"

Also, ask yourself, "What's the worst thing that could happen if (blank) happens?" For instance, if you are worried about getting laid off, is it more likely you'll get another job or more likely you'll end up homeless?

At the heart of the cyclone tearing the sky Is a place of central calm; So here in the roar of mortal things, I have a place where my spirit sings, In the hollow of God's palm.

—*Edwin Markhan*

Changing Yourself

If you can develop and practice a prayerful, meditative attitude, stressful events won't evoke such a strong bodily reaction. You have many ways to do this. You can practice deep breathing or yoga or tai chi. Of course, you can pray. Here is just one prayerful meditation to try on a regular basis.

Imagine a restful place. It's a place that you would love to go, one that gives you a sense of rest and well-being. See the trees, water, birds, and sunlight. Imagine the smells. The tastes. The sounds. Once you have a strong picture in your mind's eye of this restful place, imagine that place is at the center of your heart.

"That's your source of being," explains White. "Eventually you won't have to work hard to go to this place. It becomes a part of you. It becomes your center. It's the place where God waits."

Once you can easily travel to this restful place, bring God along for the ride by adding prayer to the journey. "Your inner world is one of peace. You can get to it any time, any place, and any situation. It's a great gift. In a sense, it's home," says White.

PRAYERS OF
PRAISE

Giving Thanks for God's Gifts

Lying on your back in a field at night, looking up at the blanket of stars in the Milky Way, it's hard not to be overwhelmed by the infinite majesty and mystery of the universe. In such moments it's easy to praise God—in fact, it would be hard not to.

The wonder of God can stir your heart on a less spectacular scale, too.

- A smile on the face of a child
- The smooth flow of the bark on a stand of birch trees
- The sound of a clarinet solo in a Mozart symphony

All these things and many, many more remind us that life is a miraculous, wondrous thing and that praise of our Creator is definitely in order. How odd it is, then, that in many people's worship lives prayers of praise seem to be more a rarity than a staple.

The reason for that goes back to childhood, says Libby Farmer, Ph.D., a psychotherapist with the Full Life Counseling Service in Bowling Green, Kentucky. "We were taught when we were little that you use prayer when you're hurting: 'Tell God about it and he'll heal you,'" she explains. "Those are prayers of petition, and they are definitely a part of our relationship with God, but they aren't the whole story."

As people's spiritual lives mature, Dr. Farmer has found, they develop a growing appreciation of God's gifts, and prayers of praise become more important. "The intent of a prayer of praise in my mind is to adore God," she says. "We give God what is rightfully His: respect, adoration, and love."

476

If you'd like to add more praise to your prayer life, Dr. Farmer has several suggestions. Many of the psalms are great "praise starters," she says. Psalm 100 is an example. "Make a joyful noise to the Lord, all the earth," it begins. "Worship the Lord with gladness; come into his presence with singing" (Psalm 100:1–2, NRSV).

Another way to praise God is to make a list of the various names for God that you find in the Bible. Each day, take one of those names and improvise a prayer based upon the attributes it describes. For example, the Old Testament mentions "God the provider." A prayer on that theme might go something like this, Dr. Farmer says:

"Lord, I appreciate the daily bread you bring us, the daily needs you provide, the ordinary things that you do, the way you choose day in and day out to keep coming into my life and meeting me at every point of need."

For a more meditative approach, Dr. Farmer suggests you try to dedicate your entire person, part by part, to the praise and glory of God. Envision that you are bringing God into yourself with what you see, for example, and that the spirit of God is going out through your eyes as you look at the world. Open your hands to take in the glory of God and think of how your hands can express through their labors your celebration of God's gifts.

You may notice that there seems to be a natural connection between praise, gratitude, and joy. This makes perfect sense, in Dr. Farmer's view.

"When I am able to take my eyes off what I want from God and focus on Him," she says, "I can just sit there and say, 'Thank you, Lord. Thank you.'"

Part 11

YOUR FAITH LIFE

Building Your
Faith Life

❦

*Feeling out of touch with God or filled with doubt? You can
open wide the lines of Divine communication by practicing these
fundamentals of a spiritual life.*

The Reverend Sam Shoemaker was fed up.

As pastor of the prestigious Calvary Episcopal Church in Pittsburgh during the 1950s, he was trying to get more people to make a commitment to God. But the response from the prominent businessmen in his congregation was lukewarm. So one night, at a country club dinner, he threw down a spiritual challenge.

He asked the businessmen around the table to take a test of faith that would prove God exists. For 30 straight days the men were to pray: "Lord, if You're real, make Yourself known to me." They were to say the prayer first thing in the morning and any other time they thought of it during the day. At the end of the time, the men were to gather again to discuss what had happened.

The result was—you guessed it—miraculous. Every single man in the group reported that he had been directly and deeply touched by the Holy Spirit.

The businessmen weren't about to walk away after that. They formed prayer groups, and those groups eventually grew into a movement that came to be known as the Pittsburgh Experiment. It is still flourishing today.

At the heart of the Pittsburgh Experiment was a simple but extremely powerful message that can transform your spiritual life as radically as it did those complacent businessmen's a half-century ago: Knock and the door will be opened.

How exactly do you knock? How can you clear away your doubts and strengthen your connection to God?

Take the first step in faith. You don't have to see the whole staircase, just take the first step.

—*Martin Luther King Jr.*

- Practice the fundamentals of prayer daily.
- Gather with other believers to reinforce your faith.
- Perform Godly service.

Just Do It

Improving your connection to God is a lot like improving your tennis game: The more faithfully you practice the fundamentals, the better the results.

"Godly people are disciplined people," writes Donald S. Whitney, doctor of ministry, in his book *Spiritual Disciplines for the Christian Life*. "I've never known a man or woman who came to spiritual maturity except through discipline."

Don't let the word *discipline* intimidate you: Like any exercise, spiritual discipline is easy if you take it in small doses. The Pittsburgh Experiment succeeded because it offered lukewarm believers a simple program they could follow for a short period of time, says the Reverend Paul F. Everett, a Presbyterian minister who was executive director of the Pittsburgh Experiment for nearly 30 years. The John Wesley Great Experiment, a Methodist program of spiritual growth, is based on a similar keep-it-simple approach (see page 484).

To start on your spiritual fitness program, practice these fundamentals.

1. Give Your Mornings to God

To connect with God, dedicate time every morning to prayer, scripture, and reflection. The combination of those three activities is a key. In fact, Dr. Whitney says that meditating and praying on scripture is the single most powerful spiritual tool he's ever found.

Keep the amount of scripture you read short. The point is to savor God's Word and let it germinate in your heart, not to finish in a hurry. The Reverend Danny E. Morris, a retired Methodist minister and the author of *A Life That Really Matters: The Story of the John Wesley Great Experiment*, recommends choosing Bible passages that are no longer than nine verses. You'll also get more out of the experience, he feels, if you follow a planned reading schedule, rather than picking passages at random.

2. Keep a Journal

Whether you jot your thoughts down in a series of spiral notebooks or buy a diary with fancy leather binding, try to write an entry every day. Record such things as daily events, prayer requests, thoughts on scripture, or hopes you have for the future—almost anything that pertains to your daily walk with God. This will help you chart the path your faith journey is taking and reveal the patterns as they unfold.

3. Retreat from the World

God often speaks to us in whispers, but the noise of the modern world drowns God out. The stress and clamor of daily life also keeps us from listening to

Prayer Miracles

Faith and Prayer Saved My Life

After my divorce I turned to drugs and drinking to try to kill the throbbing ache that filled my entire body and soul. It became so bad that my ex-husband ended up taking me to court and taking away custody of our son. With my son gone, I felt I had no reason left to be alive.

Then I received a book about God's love. I read it in one sitting and then honestly prayed to God about the mess my life was in. I heard the Lord telling me to start a prayer journal where I could write to Him. I started asking Him to help me get through the day and to help me correct the thinking that had gotten me into this mess. It wasn't easy at first, but I hung in there and little things began to happen that strengthened my faith. Today, I have a good job and career. I graduated from college this past spring and am now working toward an even higher degree. I share a nice home with a friend and have a nice car and money in the bank. Everything I have in my life I attribute to prayer, for in the process of asking God for things, we initiate a subconscious process that helps us make our wishes come true.

Sherril Fretwell
Waynesboro, Virginia

our own hearts. To reconnect—with God and with yourself—schedule a silent, weeklong retreat at one of the hundreds of retreat houses around the country.

Once you're settled into a retreat, you'll find that your perspective on life slowly comes back into focus, partly because you're becoming physically rested, partly because your spiritual balance is being regained.

If a long retreat isn't possible, enjoy a miniretreat at the nearest park or in a quiet room tucked away in the back corner of your church, Dr. Whitney suggests. Even 15 minutes of silence will help, if that's all you can manage. Sit qui-

A Stairway to Heaven

On the surface, the John Wesley Great Experiment seems like a simple set of spiritual exercises. But many people who take part in the experiment say it helps them get closer to God and irrevocably changes their lives.

The Experiment got its start in Tallahassee, Florida, in 1965 when Sam E. Teague, a Sunday school teacher, prayed for help reaching the teenage members of his church.

Alone in his office, Teague put his head down on his desk and said, "O God, show me how to challenge these young people so they can have a life that matters!"

Instantly, his prayer was answered with such a torrent of ideas that he scarcely had time to write them down. Within minutes he'd developed a 1-month program that would energize the people who participated. All the people had to do was commit to five acts of faith.

1. Learn how to pray.

2. Work at least 2 hours in the church each week.

3. Give God a tenth of their earnings.

etly—without static, without distraction, and without interruption—as you focus on God through the Word or prayer.

Gather Ye Together

As valuable a tool as spiritual retreats can be, they still should be considered a seasoning in your basic spiritual diet, Dr. Whitney believes, not the main course. The joyfulness of group worship, and the anchor it provides, should be staples of your faith. Here are the two primary ways to share your spiritual life.

4. Spend from 5:30 to 6:00 each morning in prayer and the study of scripture.

5. Tell others about their faith in God.

Teague issued a challenge to the congregation and the first group to answer consisted of 22 parishioners. One of them was the pastor of Teague's church, the Reverend Danny E. Morris, who later wrote a book about the experience, *A Life That Really Matters: The Story of the John Wesley Great Experiment.*

Reverend Morris says the first group's experience not only invigorated their spiritual lives but also brought spiritual vitality to the entire congregation. Attendance soared, and contributions increased enough to move the church from a deficit to a surplus.

"The experiment blew the lid off the church," Reverend Morris says. "It took us to a new level of dedication to the Gospel and a clearer sense of what the church is all about."

Since then, some 200,000 copies of Reverend Morris's book have been published and Sam Teague's challenge has been taken up by literally tens of thousands of participants, proving that the 30-day challenge can open the way for changes that last a lifetime.

1. The Intimate Gathering

Get together with a small group of believers (between 5 and 15 people is typical) and talk about God. Whether it's a Bible study group, a support group, or a weekly prayer group, millions of people have found the small group to be one of the most powerful spiritual tools there is.

Why? First of all, says Reverend Everett, a group this size affords just the right combination of collegiality and intimacy. You can see and hear the Holy Spirit working in the other members of your group over time, up close. You also have the opportunity to tell others what's going on with you. The group's feedback—and prayers—can be, literally, a godsend. Last but not least, you can listen to what others are going through and learn from them.

A Pathway through Scripture

You probably can't go wrong reading scripture, but doing so with a guide can be more fulfilling than just opening up to a page at random and diving in.

Here are the Bible readings chosen for participants in the John Wesley Great Experiment. "They have a distinct rhythmic pattern," says the Reverend Danny E. Morris, author of *A Life That Really Matters: The Story of the John Wesley Great Experiment.* "One passage may challenge, the next may affirm, the next may comfort, and the next may arouse. Together, they provide a unique personal invitation to put God first."

Day 1: 2 Chronicles 7:14

Day 2: James 4:16

Day 3: 1 John 1:9

Day 4: John 15:6–7

Day 5: Mark 11:24

Day 6: Philippians 4:6

Day 7: 1 John 5:14

Day 8: Jeremiah 29:13

Day 9: Matthew 6:7–13

Day 10: Matthew 18:19

Day 11: Isaiah 65:23–24

Day 12: Matthew 6:6

2. Raise the Roof

Attend church regularly. There's no substitute for the massive infusion of spiritual energy you can get from attending a spirited worship service. This is especially true if the service involves singing and a meaningful ceremony such as communion. Regular church attendance also makes you part of a loving, sup-

Day 13: Luke 11:9–10

Day 14: Isaiah 58:9–11

Day 15: Psalm 127:1

Day 16: Psalm 66:18

Day 17: Isaiah 59:1–3

Day 18: Proverbs 28:9–10

Day 19: Matthew 8:24–27

Day 20: John 6:47

Day 21: Ecclesiastes 8:1–8

Day 22: Psalm 55:22

Day 23: John 14:27

Day 24: Psalm 1:1–8

Day 25: John 14:1

Day 26: Matthew 6:25–33

Day 27: Psalm 23:1–6

Day 28: Mark 12:30

Day 29: Hebrews 12:1

Day 30: John 4:14

Day 31: Matthew 5:13–16

portive community—a vital antidote to the indifference with which the world at large so often confronts us.

Another spiritual benefit available in group worship is the insight you gain from listening to the sermon, Reverend Everett says. The real life issues you grapple with in small group discussions need to be leavened with the

GIVE MY PRAYERS NEW LIFE

May I invest each word of my spoken prayers

with a whole and sincere heart.

With a heart full of fire,

may I strive to live out all that I pray,

finding a musician's delight

in the rhythm and sounds of my prayer words,

savoring the flavor of an unquenchable love

in my prayers to you, my Beloved.

O Divine Mystery, may I pray best in my closet,

hidden from view except from you.

May I feel the Spirit's spur in my side

speedily rousing me to become my prayer.

May I feel the Spirit's wind filling my soul

with a holy windmill power.

May I pray not only for what I know I can do

but also for what I would long to do in you.

May my habit of heartfelt prayer

bring me ever closer to your blessed side.

—*Edward M. Hays*

disciplined theological reflections that a good preacher, priest, or rabbi can provide.

Extend Yourself

When the first Christian monasteries were started about the third century A.D., it was thought that the best way to worship God was to get as far away from civilization as possible. The "desert fathers" devoted their days to worship and prayer—and nothing else. About 100 years later a monk named Basil of Caesarea came along and pointed out that the monastics were overlooking a crucial element of the Christian program: service to others. So Basil began building monasteries not in the wilds of the desert but on the edges of cities, where the monks could offer hospitality to travelers, care for the sick and needy, and religious instruction.

The idea that a faithful life includes service has been carried down through the centuries, and it lives today in the soup kitchens, shelters, and prison outreach ministries run by countless churches throughout the country. The rewards for this supposedly selfless work are abundant: Simply put, service can supercharge your spiritual life.

There are innumerable ways to harness the spiritual power of service. The John Wesley Great Experiment specifies the following two as particularly powerful:

Q&A: Am I Wrong to Question My Faith?

Q: I sometimes have doubts about God; is that a bad thing?

A: Not at all, says Carolyn Bohler, Ph.D., professor of pastoral theology and counseling at United Theological Seminary in Dayton, Ohio. Doubts can be a route to great spiritual wisdom, she says, because they are signs we take what we believe and what we don't believe seriously. The key is to use doubt as a stimulus for investigation. Go ahead and reject religious ideas you find unacceptable—but then go on and search for ideas that ring true.

Let's say, for example, that you're not moved by the images of God you grew up with—you're having trouble taking seriously the stern old man with the long white beard. Rather than getting stuck with that image, take the opportunity to meditate on what image of God *does* make sense to you. "You're free to come up with an idea that touches your spirit," Dr. Bohler says.

Although the major religions teach that there is but one God, Dr. Bohler points out that this does not mean there can be only one *metaphor* for God. She likes to imagine God as a great Jazz Band Leader, for example, standing amongst the human band, nodding to each of us when our turn comes to play our riffs, orchestrating all the instruments so that the end result is harmonious. A woman friend of Dr. Bohler's, by contrast, was suffering from diabetes, and she took comfort in imagining God as a sort of Divine Physical Therapist.

"It's perfectly okay to have a half dozen metaphors for God, or more," Dr. Bohler says. "God is happy to be all those things for us, I think. They're simply images that help us to experience God."

1. Give 2 Hours

As an experiment, try devoting at least 2 hours of service in your church each week for a month, Reverend Morris suggests. Exactly how you participate is limited only by your imagination; possibilities range from visiting hospital patients or teaching a Sunday school class to singing in the choir or volunteering in the church office.

God does not die on the day when we cease to believe in a personal deity, but we die on the day when our lives cease to be illumined by the steady radiance, renewed daily, of a wonder, the source of which is beyond all reason.

—Dag Hammarskjöld

"Often people think of making a commitment to service as a lifetime experience, and it is that," says Reverend Morris, "but you don't have to quit your job and become a missionary to make that happen. The 2-hour commitment is a way of saying, 'Here's a little short-term thing that you can do that will make a difference.' You go from being an onlooker to being a participant."

2. Show Them the Money

Donating a regular amount of your income to the church—10 percent is the figure most churches recommend—is more than simply putting your money where your mouth is, Dr. Whitney says. Tithing demonstrates a recognition of your debt to God, an eagerness to serve God's purposes, and a recognition that, ultimately, whatever you have belongs to God.

A key element of tithing, Reverend Morris has found, is the idea that in dedicating money to God you *put God first*. To drive this point home, Reverend Morris suggests that you make your check to the church the first one you write every month.

To make the impact even more direct, Dr. Whitney suggests that you take your gift with you to church on Sunday and place it in the collection basket. The immediacy of giving in person, rather than sending it through the mail, places the act of giving exactly where it belongs: in the context of worship.

As with performing service, you will find that tithing gives you back much more than you put in. "Money begins to take on spiritual dimensions far beyond what you've ever imagined," Reverend Morris says.

Coping with Sin

The guilt you feel after acting in a sinful way can overwhelm you—if you let it. Thankfully, through prayer and practical steps you can let go of your feelings and come clean before God, your family, and your friends.

he church service was nearing its end when the pastor made an announcement. A long-time member had asked for a few moments to talk to the congregation. With that the woman rose in her pew and spoke.

"I have a confession to make," she said. "I have been a regular gossip in this church, and I have hurt many of you and I have damaged your relationships. My gossip has been so widespread that I thought it was important to say this to all of you. I need your forgiveness, and I need your help in holding me accountable so that I won't sin again."

One worshiper who witnessed this woman's confession remembers it as one of the most moving events he'd ever experienced in church. "There wasn't a dry eye in the place," says Paul Tripp, doctor of ministry and counseling, director of Changing Lives Ministries at the Christian Counseling and Education Foundation in Glenside, Pennsylvania. "And at the end of her confession a stream of people were waiting to talk with this woman and hug her and to tell her that, yes, they forgave her."

We're all human. Being human, sooner or later we end up doing something like this woman did that we regret. When we do, we shudder with guilt and shame, embarrassed at how unworthy we must appear in the eyes of our friends and family—not to mention in the eyes of our Creator.

If you find yourself feeling this way, don't let the guilt of sin overwhelm you. Instead, take the following steps to acknowledge the sin and to seek forgiveness and redemption.

By the presence of good, evil is cast out, just as by the presence of light, the darkness disappears.

—*Earnest Holmes*

- Honestly examine whether you've sinned.
- Accept responsibility if you have.
- Repent, fully and completely.
- Pray thankfully for being cleansed.

Take an Honest Look

If you feel burdened with sin, it's important first to make sure that the guilt you're assuming is rightly yours, says Paul Meier, M.D., cofounder and medical director of the New Life chain of Christian counseling clinics headquartered in Plano, Texas, and author of numerous books on psychology and faith. That's not always the case.

A person who has suffered through an abusive childhood, for example, may be filled with unjustified feelings of guilt and shame, even when she has done nothing sinful, says Dr. Meier. Likewise, it is possible to feel guilt for doing something that really isn't a sin, like overindulging at a holiday meal. Here are four steps to take in assessing whether the sinfulness you're feeling is real.

1. Pray to God

As always, the first action to take in addressing a problem is praying. Ask God for guidance and strength in discerning whether you've truly sinned.

2. Run a Check

If you're unsure an act you've committed is sinful, see how it stands up to the following checklist compiled in *The Handbook of Bible Application: A Guide for Applying the Bible to Everyday Life.*

- **Sinful behavior often begins as a delightful and fun action.** The woeful consequences only become apparent later.
- **Sin's effects spread.** Sinners love to draw others into the sinful webs they're weaving.
- **Sin usually causes guilt.** God has placed something inside people that tells when they've sinned. It's called a conscience.

PURIFY THIS SOUL

O Light everlasting, surpassing all created light! Pour forth from heaven the glorious rays of your light, and pierce the dark depths of my soul. Purify, gladden and enlighten my soul, that it may turn to you in joy. I know that the shadow of sin still hangs over me. I know that I fight against your light, preferring the gloom of worldly pride to the bright sunshine of true humility. Yet you, who can make the raging sea calm, can bring peace to my soul. You, who turn night into day, can bring gladness to my miserable soul. Act now! Banish darkness at this very moment! Inspire my soul with your love at the next breath I take!

—*Thomas à Kempis*

- **Sin creates a barrier between sinners and God.** Just as Adam and Eve hid from God after they'd sinned in the Garden of Eden, so do believers turn away from God in shame when they do something they know isn't right.
- **Sinful behavior is almost always covered by excuses.** Rather than admit something is wrong, sinners supply a reason justifying their sins; it's never their fault.
- **Sin often leads to more sin.** Think of the slippery slope.

3. Share Your Story

Tell trusted, prayerful friends what happened and ask their opinions of whether you've sinned, suggests Dr. Meier. Say you feel guilty because you think you may have been overly rude when you failed to return a salesman's phone call. Your friends can tell you your guilt is misplaced and that not calling back is a perfectly appropriate way of saying, "I'm not interested."

4. Seek a Counselor's Help

Many people become overwhelmed or obsessed with feelings of guilt. This is definitely not what God intended, says Dr. Tripp. "If your guilt ends in anxiety or depression or if it paralyzes you, you're doing something wrong," he says.

You should be able to confront your guilt, deal with it constructively, and move on. If you feel stuck in guilt or remorse, speak to a counselor, your pastor, or someone else with professional training who can help you sort things out, Dr. Tripp suggests.

Also, if you feel stuck, take comfort in the fact that God not only knows you've sinned, God expects you to sin, and forgives you. "We don't have to persuade God to forgive us," says Carolyn Bohler, Ph.D., professor of pastoral theology and counseling at United Theological Seminary in Dayton, Ohio.

"God already has. The challenge for us is to accept that we've been forgiven."

Expose Sin to the Light

The moment Adam and Eve tasted the forbidden fruit in the Garden of Eden, they shamefully tried to cover up their nakedness and hide themselves from the eyes of God. Then, when God confronted them with their sin, each denied responsibility—Adam blaming Eve, Eve blaming the serpent.

This is a textbook case of how *not* to react when you've sinned. If you want to get past your sin and prepare for paradise, take these steps instead.

1. Confess to God

Sin places a wedge between you and God that needs to be removed before your relationship can be restored, Dr. Tripp says. Come out of hiding. If you have sinned, go before God in prayer and say so, flat out.

Dr. Tripp calls this the "vertical" confession. "God's help is available to

GOD, FORGIVE ME

Lord, you have come into the world to save sinners—no matter what the world thinks of sin: all have sinned and come short of your glory. You have come to seek and to save the lost sheep like me. I accept your salvation, Lord. I come to be forgiven.

—*From* The Prisoner's Lantern

Q&A: What Should I Say to a Sinner?

Q: A friend recently confessed she had been dishonest with me. I didn't know what to say about her sin, so I didn't say anything. What should I have said?

A: "If you're receiving a confession from someone, it's best not to reassure them by saying things like, 'That's okay,' or 'It's all right,' or even 'I understand,'" says Paul Tripp, doctor of ministry and counseling, director of Changing Lives Ministries at the Christian Counseling and Education Foundation in Glenside, Pennsylvania. "The person is coming to you with a sense that it's *not* all right, it's *not* okay. If God has produced a sense of guilt in someone, you need to acknowledge that it's wrong. Saying 'that's okay' only leaves the person hanging.

"The way to cancel the debt the person feels is to say the words, 'I forgive you.' The wrong needs to be honestly and humbly acknowledged—from both sides."

those who are willing to own responsibility," he says. "There's no help available for those who won't accept responsibility."

2. Confess to Those You've Sinned Against

Sin places a wedge between people that needs to be removed in order for the relationship to be restored, Dr. Tripp says. Confessing directly to those you have harmed is the first step toward that restoration.

This is "horizontal" confession, Dr. Tripp says, and it needs to include all those who have been affected by the sin, both directly and indirectly. That's what the woman in Dr. Tripp's church did. She felt her gossiping had damaged the entire congregation, so she needed to confess to all the parishioners. Similarly, if, say, you gamble heavily and your gambling places a financial strain on the entire family, you need to confess your sin to the entire family. You also need to specifically ask for their forgiveness.

3. Confess to Those Who've Passed On

If the person you have harmed is no longer living, Dr. Bohler suggests you confess to him or her through a visualization prayer. This involves holding a conversation with the deceased person in your imagination.

Don't try to push this imagined conversation to some immediate conclusion, Dr. Bohler adds. Simply make your confession and see where the images flow from there. It may take many sessions of visualizing prayer before you resolve your feelings of guilt.

4. Make Amends

Personal acts of atonement can help release your feelings of guilt, Dr. Meier says. For example, a close friend of Dr. Meier paid for an abortion during his college days. Now a committed Christian and a gifted public speaker, the friend makes speeches against abortion whenever he can. "He calls it 'giving back a gift to God,'" Dr. Meier says. "He knows he's been forgiven by God, and he's forgiven himself, but he likes to make a contribution in an area where he's experienced weakness in the past."

Go All the Way

Recovering from sin does not end with an apology, says Dr. Tripp. You need to repair the relationship as much as possible, to make it right. "True confession ought to end in a changed person," Dr. Tripp says.

Here are some suggestions for achieving that goal.

1. Be Vigilant

When you've sinned, Dr. Tripp says, you have a responsibility in the future to be watchful, lest you repeat the wrong. So after confessing your sin, ask yourself, "What do I need to do to keep myself from being in this situation again?" Dr. Tripp suggests.

LEAD ME BACK TO YOU

Teach me, God, to have eyes to see all that is false and destructive. Help me to stay far from the forces that can lead me astray. Remind me that I have the power to shatter the false gods that lead me far away from You. The false gods that tempt me with false promises. May I learn to choose wisely, even when in pain, to choose not the path of false comfort but the road that will lead me back to You.

Amen.

—Rabbi Naomi Levy

2. Confess Completely

Too often we allow ourselves to confess only part of our sin lives—the sins we get caught in. Dr. Tripp calls these "Jimmy Swaggart confessions," after the TV preacher who tearfully confessed to sexual improprieties in 1988. Later it turned out he'd apparently had other sexual indiscretions—which made his tearful confession look pretty phony.

True confession means full confession: You don't hold back.

3. Commit to Change

The truly repentant sinner vows to change, Dr. Tripp says, and honestly looks at what needs to be done to make that change happen. Ask yourself, "If what I did before was wrong, what does right look like?"

> *Just as you used to be slaves to all kinds of sin, so now you must let yourselves be slaves to all that is right and holy.*
>
> —*Romans 6:19 (LIV)*

4. Change

Often people convince themselves that a commitment to change equals the change itself, Dr. Tripp says. That's because the process of confessing a sin and promising to behave differently in the future is in itself satisfying.

Don't kid yourself. You have to actually begin to live in a different way, if you want to change for the better.

Give Thanks and Go Forward

True repentance will leave you feeling cleansed, a feeling you may wish to acknowledge in worship. How? One way is to say a silent prayer of thanksgiving the next time you receive communion, Dr. Bohler says. Another is to devise a cleansing ceremony of your own. Here's a suggestion for one such ceremony.

Wash Your Sins Clean

Kneel in prayer with a bowl of clean water in front of you. As you thank God for accepting you as you are, dip your fingers in the water and bring them to your forehead. Think of your sins as being washed clean. Meditate on the cleansing power of the Holy Spirit.

Building Your Faith Community

Without proper nurturing, churches can grow stale, lose their focus, and gradually fade away. Don't let that happen. Keep your congregation fresh, inspired, and doing God's work.

lat, tired, and uninspired.

Does that describe your church?

If so, you're far from alone, according to one of the country's leading consultants on congregational health, the Reverend Peter L. Steinke, doctor of religion, a Lutheran pastor, author, and head of Bridgebuilder Ministries, based in Austin, Texas. In a 1999 cover story in *Christian Century* magazine, he wrote, "We often hear that two-thirds to three-fourths of American congregations are in decline or at a plateau with regard to membership. They are . . . immobilized by a flat growth line and in many cases by dwindling resources of time and money."

A bleak picture—on the surface. But Dr. Steinke and many others who help congregations revive troubled churches say it doesn't have to be that way. In fact, you can view problems at church as incredible opportunities to set your faith community on a new course, to build it to new heights, even to give it a spiritual rebirth that's just as profound as the one a new believer undergoes.

How can you achieve all this?

- Ask God to inspire your church, its leaders, and its ministries.
- Start Bible study or discussion groups to give your church an intimate feel.
- Develop a clear mission for your church.
- Energize your leaders and your meetings.

Let us go forth to lead the land we love, asking His blessing and His help, but knowing that here on earth God's work must truly be our own.

—*John F. Kennedy*

Filled with the Spirit

Like a human body, a church community is a living organism, Dr. Steinke believes, and you keep both healthy in much the same way: by nourishing the mind, the body, and the spirit and keeping balance among them.

Here are some specific ways to achieve this goal.

1. Pray for Your Faith Community

If your community is indeed an organism, then you can consider daily prayer the vitamin supplement that helps it ward off spiritual illness, says the Reverend Danny E. Morris, who created and for 20 years was the executive director of the Academy for Spiritual Formation in Nashville. Pray for your church the way you would pray for your family, Reverend Morris says, specifically asking God to preserve its faith and its vitality.

2. Pray for Your Leaders

Ask God to "raise up" effective, vigorous, and inspiring leaders. Although each member of the church can contribute to its overall vitality, leaders are the ones who are most responsible for keeping a genuine passion for God flowing through the congregation—and out into the world at large, Reverend Morris says. Your prayers can help bring such leaders to the fore and can help sustain them as they go about their crucial work in the church.

3. Pray for Clarity

Ask God to guide you as you investigate the types of improvements or changes your faith community needs to make and the role individual members

MAKE THIS CHURCH A SPIRITUAL HAVEN

O God, make the door of this house wide enough
to receive all who need human love and fellowship,
and a heavenly Father's care;
and narrow enough to shut out all envy, pride and hate.
Make its threshold smooth enough
to be no stumbling block to children or to straying feet,
but rugged enough to turn back the tempter's power;
make it a gateway to thine eternal kingdom.

—Thomas Ken

should take to keep the church thriving. With God's guidance, Reverend Morris says, you can move forward confidently, with a clear vision of your goals in sight.

4. Pray for Strength

Pray that God grants you and the other members the strength you'll need to pursue your church's mission.

Getting Intimate

A busy businessman once approached the Reverend Paul F. Everett, former executive director of the Pittsburgh Experiment and now minister at large for the Peale Center in Pauling, New York, to talk about his spiritual life. "I only have time to attend church on Sunday morning," Reverend Everett recalls the man saying. "The minister really has to perform so I will get all my spiritual needs for the week filled then."

Reverend Everett says that his response to this businessman is not what the man wanted to hear. "Sitting in a pew for 1 hour a week on Sunday morning, expecting you'll get all your spiritual needs met, is not possible. Being in a relationship with God is not for 1 hour on Sunday morning. It is a daily experience of growing in that relationship and learning to listen to the ways in which God leads and guides you through the Holy Spirit," he says. Then, "when Sunday morning comes you will be equipped to really hear what the Lord has to say to you."

The same logic holds true for your church community. If you want to be part of an inspiring church, you need to become passionately involved with the congregation, Reverend Everett says. How?

Gather in Small Groups

Join with fellow parishioners in small discussion and action groups. Intimate groups have become a major inspirational focus of churches across the country, says Reverend Everett. This is happening for good reason: In a world that is increasingly overwhelming and impersonal, sitting down with 5 or 10 other people who have interests and needs similar to yours can renew you spiritually.

Seek out small groups within your church, Reverend Everett suggests. If your church hasn't got any, start one yourself. The most common example—and also the most important one—is Bible study, he says. Most churches also offer other types of small group involvement, whether they be outreach pro-

OPEN OUR MINDS AND HEARTS

I pray that we may at all times keep our minds open to new ideas and shun dogma; that we may grow in our understanding of the nature of all living beings and our connectedness with the natural world; that we may become ever more filled with generosity of spirit and true compassion and love for all life. . . .

I pray that we may learn the peace that comes with forgiving and the strength we gain in loving; that we may learn to take nothing for granted in this life; that we may learn to see and understand with our hearts; that we may learn to join in our being.

—Jane Goodall

grams for various ministry projects or discussion groups for singles, divorced people, widows and widowers, or those with other special interests.

"Small groups provide the intimacy that is lacking in corporate worship," Reverend Everett says. "The risk of drifting away from the congregation at some point is significantly reduced if you get involved in one."

Equally important, Reverend Everett says, is that the spark that is kindled in individual believers' hearts in those small groups can invigorate the entire church.

Motivated by a Mission

A healthy congregation is one that is going somewhere. That means it has a clear mission and that it is directing the bulk of its energies toward accomplishing that mission.

"A lot of churches get into trouble because they don't know what their ultimate purpose and their ultimate values are," Reverend Morris says. "Usually they want to be an extension of God's will in the community, however they define that. But too often they get sidetracked into focusing on other, lesser things—like building a new church, or competing socially with other churches in town. As time goes on, they begin to lose touch with the more central qualities."

If you're unclear of your church's mission, you can bet others in your congregation may need some clarification, too. Here's how you and the members of your faith community can define a mission and motivate everyone to work toward it.

1. Get It on Paper

If your church does not already have a mission statement, talk to your church leaders about composing one. The entire faith community should be encouraged to participate in drafting such a statement, which will define your community's spiritual values and mandate—the things it stands for. For example, the mission statement for Reverend Morris's church declares that it is a church committed to Jesus Christ, to do His will, in His Spirit, educating people in the Christian faith and working to draw all people into the kingdom of God.

2. Set Some Goals

The next step is for your church community to develop specific goals that will help it realize its mission. These goals should be specific and positive, Dr. Steinke says. Two possible examples: feeding the homeless in your community

THE ULTIMATE MISSION STATEMENT

Lord,

when I am famished,

give me someone who needs food;

when I am thirsty,

send me someone who needs water;

when I am cold,

send me someone to warm;

when I am hurting,

send me someone to console;

when my cross becomes heavy,

give me another's cross to share;

when I am poor,

lead someone needy to me;

when I have no time,

give me someone to help for a moment;

when I am humiliated,

give me someone to praise;

when I am discouraged,

send me someone to encourage;

when I need another's understanding,

give me someone who needs mine;

when I need somebody to take care of me,

send me someone to care for;

when I think of myself,

turn my thoughts toward another.

—Japanese prayer

and ensuring that your Sunday school thoroughly teaches your denomination's religious traditions.

Again, the whole community should be involved in drafting and approving the goals, although the groundwork can be laid by leadership committees and the church's professional staff.

3. Stay Flexible

To stay alive in the modern world, churches must become "learning organizations," which react to changes in the make-up of the membership and the needs of the surrounding community, Dr. Steinke says. So revisit your written mission statement from time to time to make sure it is still appropriate. This will ensure your faith community remains vital to the people it serves.

A Faith Community Built on Strength

Successful churches don't run on automatic pilot. They need both energetic leaders and energizing meetings to keep the faith community inspired and on course.

The problem, Reverend Morris says, is that too many churches fail to take

Q&A: Does Declining Membership Mean We're Doomed?

Q: Our congregation has been losing members. To help boost attendance, we're considering spending a significant amount of money on a publicity campaign. Is this a good idea?

A: Situations vary from congregation to congregation, but in general you shouldn't assume that a successful church has to be a growing church, says the Reverend Peter L. Steinke, doctor of religion, a Lutheran pastor, author of *Healthy Congregations*, and head of Bridgebuilder Ministries, based in Austin, Texas, which trains people to work with churches in trouble.

"Growth can come in terms of complexity and depth just as much as it can in terms of numbers," he says. In his book, Dr. Steinke describes a church in South Dakota that slowly declined in membership from 46 to 25 members over a period of 15 years. During that same period, the amount of money it collected for its mission work increased every year—proof that the church was healthy despite its shrinking numbers.

these two issues seriously enough. They allow important positions to pass by default to people who don't really want them or to go to people who want them for the wrong reasons. And they let meetings become dull or contentious. Both of these failures can sap the life from a faith community.

Your church can avoid this fate by taking the following steps to keep on a course that is purposeful and filled with love.

1. Cut Unnecessary Jobs

This advice may seem at odds with the idea of developing more leaders, but the truth is, "there are too many jobs in most churches," says Reverend Morris, "and the people in them often don't do that much. As a result, the church goes limping along with perfunctory leaders in perfunctory positions doing perfunctory work."

> *In every community, there is work to be done. In every nation, there are wounds to heal. In every heart, there is the power to do it.*
>
> —*Marianne Williamson*

So before appointing someone to a position, ask whether it truly needs to be filled. If the right person for the job can't be found, Reverend Morris says, leave the position open. What describes the right person? Someone capable of leading out of a genuine, living commitment to the principles of his or her faith, rather than from a need for power, control, companionship, or applause, Reverend Morris says.

2. Hold Worshipful Meetings

Successful meetings not only keep your faith community informed, they also reaffirm your beliefs in God and your church. So approach each meeting with those goals in mind, as do the Society of Friends—the Quakers.

Quaker business meetings are conducted as a form of worship, says Thomas Jeavons, general secretary of the Philadelphia Yearly Meeting of the Religious Society of Friends. Consequently, the goal of a Quaker business meeting isn't to reach consensus—"consensus" implies a decision mutually arrived at by *human* minds—but to listen for and respond to *God's* will.

Toward that end, Quakers open their business meetings with a period of prayerful silence. A clerk then guides the group through the agenda. If there's a disagreement, the meeting may be stopped for another period of prayerful silence, until the group gets a sense it again is moving with God's will.

Does it work? "Sometimes yes, sometimes no," Jeavons says. "The usual human frailties enter into it. But many times I've seen meetings wrestle with issues that seemed impossible to resolve, where people had very firm ideas about what had to be done—ideas that were in total conflict with one other. Nonetheless, when they entered into the spirit of worship, new solutions emerged which were not only satisfactory, but exciting."

3. Assess Your Progress

Reverend Morris often uses the Quaker approach in the Methodist churches he works with, but at the end of meetings he adds a fillip of his own. All those attending are asked to meditate on the following three very specific questions.

- What impact has this meeting had on this congregation?
- What impact has this meeting had on the community?
- What impact has this meeting had on the kingdom of God?

After a minute or two, Reverend Morris asks each person attending to say a brief silent prayer before adjournment. Whether it's a prayer of thanksgiving or of repentance depends on how each of them has answered the three questions.

Being a Prayerful Citizen

❧

There is much wrong in the world, but through your prayers
and your actions, you can help heal the hurts.

hen Eleanor started dating the man she would later marry, she felt it was important that he witness firsthand the human suffering she saw daily as a volunteer worker in some of New York City's poorest slums. So she insisted on taking him on a tour.

This was in the early 1900s, and the poverty and desperation the couple encountered was overwhelming, especially for Eleanor's beau, a young man from a wealthy, sheltered background. He told her he'd had no idea such conditions existed, and he vowed to do what he could to improve them.

It turned out he could do a lot. His name was Franklin Delano Roosevelt, and as president of the United States he would establish many of the programs that to this day provide a social safety net for America's poor.

Roosevelt set an incredible example, but you don't need to be FDR to help change the world for the better. In fact, two of the most effective tools you have in your personal arsenal are prayer and a prayerful attitude, says Walter Wink, Ph.D., one of the nation's most respected writers on the relationship between religion and social justice.

How can you use these skills in the world of social and political affairs?

Dr. Wink and others who have studied that question suggest taking three steps.

- Pray for change.
- Stand up for what's right.
- Pitch in.

Pray for Change

Growing up in conservative Texas in the 1940s, Dr. Wink learned that prayer can be just as much a "detour" from responsible citizenship as a road to it. "There were people all around me who prayed a lot," he recalls, "but that never caused them to think they should do anything about racial segregation. Somehow the Holy Spirit was able to inform them about the needs of their own souls, but never said anything to them about social problems."

Don't let your prayer be a social sleeping pill, Dr. Wink urges. Instead, use your prayer as a vehicle for constructive change. Here's how.

> *And what does the Lord require of you? To act justly and to love mercy and to walk humbly with your God.*
>
> —*Micah 6:8 (NIV)*

1. Face the Pain

Make a point to go where the suffering is, as Franklin and Eleanor did, suggests Dr. Wink. Simply taking a public bus through your city's poorer neighborhoods can teach you a lot about life in the sorts of places it is too easy for most people to ignore.

2. Pray for Insight

Ask God to help you understand the social and political problems that face you, your family, your town, your state, and your nation, suggests Dr. Wink.

3. Pray for Intercession

When it comes to ending injustice, the most direct prayer is simply to ask God to actively step in to correct it. These intercessory prayers can "break loose miracles" in the world, Dr. Wink believes. "In many situations, all we can do is pray," he adds, "but we can do so with confidence that for the Holy Spirit, nothing is impossible." For example, in a gentle form of intercessory prayer practiced by the Quakers, members of the congregation ask God to fill the people involved in an issue with holy light. The hope is that such an infusion of the Holy Spirit will bring healing grace to the problem.

LEAD US TO A NEW TIME

*Professing unshakable reliance upon you our God, and human re-
liance upon one another, we, women and men of your creation,
joined in love, open wide the window of a new time in which the sun
will refresh equally the rich and the poor, the animals of the sea and
the birds of the air, the plants of the earth and the stones of the
ages—indeed, all creation.*

*May our trust in your providence and in each other lead us to act
justly, to love tenderly, to walk humbly, and to live together in peace
on this earth. Amen.*

—*Sister Mary Ann Coyle, S.L.*

4. Pray Together

If you're trying to bring about a miracle, the intensity of the prayer makes
a difference, Dr. Wink believes, and therefore he thinks groups praying together
can potentially pack a much harder punch than individuals can alone.

He especially recommends extended sessions of prayer in small groups of,
say, 10 or 12 people. "In a church service you might devote 30 seconds to
praying on an issue," he says, "but in a small group you can spend half an hour
if you want to."

5. Pray for Your Leaders

Often it seems we need to pray that God will protect us *from* our leaders,
but in fact praying *for* our leaders is a constructive and useful form of intercessory prayer, says Ron Sider, Ph.D., professor of theology and culture at Eastern
Baptist Theological Seminary in Wynnewood, Pennsylvania, and president of
Evangelicals for Social Action.

Such prayer can take many forms, Dr. Sider says: We can pray that our
leaders be guided by the will of God, that they have compassion for the poor, that
they have courage to make the difficult decisions that will lead us in the right direction. We can pray that the forces of evil in the world be defeated, and we can
pray that God's spirit will flow through our government and business institutions.

FOR THE RULERS OF THE NATIONS

Today, O God, I hold before you the rulers of the nations—Kings, Queens, Presidents, Prime Ministers—all who are in positions of supreme leadership.

I can be quick to criticize: help me, Lord, to first enter their dilemma. On most issues of state I have the luxury of withholding judgment, of not committing myself, of sitting on the fence. Even when I have an opinion, it has little influence and seldom any consequence. Not so with the rulers of the nations. To the extent that they really lead, they must make decisions, even if they are poor ones.

Help these leaders, O God, in the loneliness of their decisions. Put wise counselors around them.

Take, I pray, the bits and pieces of virtue that are in each ruler and cause them to grow and mature. And take all destructive motives and cause them to vanish like smoke in the wind.

Lord, I know that many—perhaps most—rulers do not know you, nor do they seek you. But you seek them! Help them see how good right decisions are. And where decisions must be made that are not in their own interest, deepen their sense of duty. Having seen the light, give them the courage to walk in the light.

Amen.

—*Richard J. Foster*

Stand Up for What's Right

Alongside the horror of Nazi Holocaust during World War II stands an equally horrible mystery: How could so many decent citizens stand by and let 6 million Jews be slaughtered?

A famous quote from a German pastor of that period suggests that those decent people simply didn't see a reason to open their mouths. "[The Nazis] first came for the Communists, and I didn't speak up because I wasn't a Communist," said Pastor Martin Niemöller. "Then they came for the Jews, and I didn't speak up because I wasn't a Jew. Then they came for the trade unionists, and I didn't speak up because I wasn't a trade unionist. Then they came for the Catholics, and I didn't speak up because I was a Protestant. Then they came for me, and by that time there was no one left to speak up for anyone."

The point is clear: Silence in the face of evil is itself an evil. Here are three ways you can speak out against what's wrong.

1. Call a Sin a Sin

Evil often hides behind denial and rationalization, says Dr. Sider. You can blow its cover simply by naming the sin. If your church isn't addressing some need, speak out. Write a letter to the editor to protest an improper action by the city council if it's needed. Stop a conversation to object when someone you know uses a racist slur.

Just remember, Dr. Sider adds, you can accuse someone of taking the side of evil on an issue without necessarily calling that person evil. God commands us to forgive the unjust as well as to fight the injustice.

2. Take a Stand

Sometimes it's tempting to dodge hard choices on political issues by committing yourself only to safe generalities, Dr. Sider says. It doesn't cost much to speak out against heroin addiction, for example, given that the pro-heroin lobby is pretty weak.

But if you're serious about achieving real change, you need to fight for what's needed, even if it means you'll have to sacrifice something like your tax money to solve the problem. "It simply won't do to say, 'I'm committed to justice in general,' and then refuse to be in favor of concrete steps to move in that direction," Dr. Sider says.

3. Light a Candle

Even if you're not a natural activist you can play a role in raising an alarm about social injustice, Dr. Wink says.

The Trappist monk Thomas Merton practiced this approach, he believes. Through "incandescent prayer" in a monastery, Merton gained a profound moral perspective on race issues and on the Vietnam War. By communicating his views to the world through his writings, Dr. Wink says, Merton helped galvanize others to join forces against those injustices.

If quiet reflection is your forte, pray meditatively on issues that concern

---

A Prayer for Social Justice

Grant, O God, that your holy and life-giving Spirit may so move every human heart (and especially the hearts of the people of this land), that barriers which divide us may crumble, suspicions disappear, and hatreds cease; that our divisions being healed, we may live in justice and peace; through Jesus Christ our Lord. Amen.

—*From the* Book of Common Prayer

---

you, spot areas of injustice that are being overlooked, and then find a way to communicate your insights to people who can put them into action. Sending thoughtful letters to your congressperson or senator can have an impact, for example, as can sending a note to your pastor.

Pitch In

It would be comforting to think that as godly people all we really need to do is sit in our churches or in our bedrooms and pray that God take care of the world's problems. Think again.

"We are called not only to pray for God to bring about the change we think necessary, but also to do everything in our power to make that change possible," says Dr. Sider. "We are called upon to put 'legs' on our prayer."

Three steps will help you confront that responsibility.

1. Act Locally

Chances are you will be most effective in the place you know best, which is close to home, says the Reverend John Dear, S.J., executive director of the Fellowship of Reconciliation, one of the oldest and largest interfaith peace organizations in the world. "Go where you're planted," he says. "Whether it's in your family, your school, or your church, see where help is needed and then act."

2. Plug In

Are you looking for a social action program you can participate in? The possibilities, like the needs, are endless. To find out how you can help, perhaps the best place is to start by talking to your own pastor, priest, or rabbi, says the Reverend Erik Kolbell, master of divinity, a former Congregational minister in New York City who has worked in social justice ministries for 17 years. Virtually every religious group has a list of projects and programs.

Another good point of entry, Reverend Kolbell says, is your denomination's state or national headquarters: Most faiths have an Office of Church in Society, or some office with a similar title, which coordinates its members' charitable activities. Many cities have lists of local charities, and many states have interfaith organizations that can also steer you to organizations.

How far you go in life depends on you being tender with the young, compassionate with the aged, sympathetic with the striving and tolerant of the weak and the strong. Because someday in life you will have been all of these.

—*George Washington Carver*

3. Pay Your Dues

Social justice isn't free, and you can contribute toward its cost with money as well as time and labor. But don't just send off a check. Take some time to research the organization you're contributing to, Reverend Kolbell says. Make sure that the majority of the money it receives goes to help people in need, rather than paying for advertising, fancy offices, and fat salaries for the program administrators.

Many offices of the Better Business Bureau audit nonprofit groups in their area to see how they spend money. Contact your local office. For information on national charities, write the bureau's Philanthropic Advisory Service, 4200 Wilson Boulevard, Suite 800, Arlington, VA 22203-1838 or visit their Web site at www.bbb.org/about/pas.asp. You also can ask the social organization itself for a copy of its annual report, which should contain figures on how its budget is allocated.

Handling Problems
at Church

*From complaints about the pastor to arguments over social
causes, conflicts at church are extremely common and extremely
disruptive. But with the guidance of God and some forthright
action, you can use a conflict to strengthen your church.*

he church seemed happy and healthy on the surface. Then one
Sunday, the pastor abruptly announced he was taking a new job in a
distant city. Within 2 weeks, he was gone, and shortly after that allegations began to surface: embezzlement, sexual improprieties.

The interim pastor who took over found a congregation in shock, lashing
out not only at the departed pastor and his wife, but also at the church, at God,
and at each other. "At first there was a lot of denial," he recalls. "People were
saying this must be some kind of mistake. When it was clear it wasn't a mistake, you saw people go through every conceivable emotion—anger, frustration, grief, disgust. You name it, they went through it."

One woman whose wedding ring had been blessed by the disgraced pastor
felt she could no longer wear it. A couple whose baby had been baptized by
him thought about having the service done again in another church. Many
people left the parish. "I felt raped," said one woman who had been a member
of the parish for years. "We entrusted our spiritual lives to this man. All of a

sudden someone yanked on the rug and we were on the floor. It was a visceral feeling—a kick in the stomach."

An extreme reaction? Not necessarily, say counselors who deal with troubled churches on a regular basis. When conflicts hit houses of worship, the pain they create can take on extraordinary dimensions, challenging the idea of the church as a safe haven where people work together for God.

If we pray, we will believe;

If we believe, we will love;

If we love, we will serve.

—*Mother Teresa*

Sadly, counselors say, conflict is far from a rarity in American churches today. Look around and you'll see parishioners fighting with pastors and arguing over everything from church rituals to how the soup kitchen should be run.

These sorts of conflicts can poison the atmosphere in your worship community—if you let them. Don't. Instead, take three steps.

- Approach the problem prayerfully.
- Play an active role in restoring your church to health.
- Bring the conflict to a formal close.

The Prayerful Approach

When conflicts break out in church, remember that this is the most obvious place to practice what your faith preaches. Specifically, that means responding to the problem prayerfully—"differently than the world does," says Anne Bachle Fifer, an attorney based in Grand Rapids, Michigan, who helps mediate congregational conflicts. You can fulfill that mission in the following ways.

1. Glorify God

No matter what the problem, your first priority in approaching a conflict should be to keep the glory of God, suggests Fifer. This will help prevent the conflict from escalating and damaging the church. When she works as a church mediator, Fifer uses the conflict-resolution program of Peacemaker Ministries, a Christian counseling group based in Billings, Montana. "Glorify God" is the first principle of its "Peacemaker's Pledge," which reads as follows:

"Instead of focusing on our own desires or dwelling on what others may do, we seek to please and honor God—by depending on His wisdom, power, and love; by faithfully obeying His commands; and by seeking to maintain a loving, merciful, and forgiving attitude."

LORD, BRING US TOGETHER

O God, make up the dissensions which divide us from each other, and bring us back into a unity of love, which may bear some likeness to thy divine nature. And as thou art above all things, make us one by the unanimity of a good mind, that through the embrace of charity and the bonds of affection, we may be spiritually one.

—*Liturgy of Saint Dionysius*

2. Look for the Higher Purpose

Another way in which you can use a difficult situation to glorify God is by realizing that God sometimes uses conflict to strengthen a church. It's much like the way your body's immune system grows stronger after it's been exposed to a virus, says the Reverend Peter L. Steinke, doctor of religion, a nationally recognized authority on congregational discord. The body remembers the experience the next time a similar virus appears and is better prepared to defend itself.

So don't think of church conflict as a problem but rather as an opportunity to bring its mission more in line with God's will.

3. Pray for God's Guidance

Any attempt to solve church conflicts should include serious prayer; otherwise it probably will fail, says the Reverend Danny E. Morris, who created and for 20 years was the executive director of the Academy for Spiritual Formation in Nashville. He particularly recommends parishioners ask God to strengthen their spirit of reconciliation and repentance. You can say these prayers to yourself in church while the service is underway, he suggests. Also ask God for help in discerning how to deal with the conflict in ways that will best serve the church.

You may be tempted to try to get everyone who is involved in a dispute to attend a group prayer session, thinking that all the animosity will be washed away. Think again, Reverend Morris cautions. Many times proposing such a session serves only to exacerbate tensions and suspicions. There are, he stresses, no quick fixes to church conflicts, even through prayer.

4. Uncover the True Source of the Problem

From her experience, Fifer has seen that many times the issue that people think is dividing the church is not really the problem. She recalls one church where it seemed the people were angry at some small decision the pastor made. In reality, they were releasing repressed anger over the way they had been treated by the previous pastor, who had left under a cloud of suspicion.

It helps to be aware that church congregations often behave like families, says Karen B. Helmeke, Ph.D., who teaches at Western Michigan University in Kalamazoo: They can have hidden secrets, bad habits, and unresolved grief that extend back literally for generations. That's why it's a good idea to spend some time meditating on what the true, underlying issues of a conflict might be. "The first part of healing is understanding," she says. "Reflect back on your church's history and see what it will tell you about your current situation. Look for patterns that may shed some light on what's happening now. Those insights can suggest some new approaches that you can try."

A Plan of Action

Living a life of faith does not mean that you sit around praying all day, hoping God will take care of your problems. If you have conflict in your church, you need to acknowledge it and then actively address it.

Remember Dr. Steinke's virus analogy: A festering conflict is much like that

MAKE ME A PEACEMAKER

Strengthen me, Lord, to face the task, the crucifying task, of being a reconciler amongst guilt and fear, anxiety and anger.

Bring me, Lord, further to the point where I can accept life with all its problems and pains with gladness and exultation,

Not because of future perks in a future heaven,

But because I know that to be fully a man, to be fully human, I can do no other.

—Rex Chapman

virus. If left untreated, it too can gradually spread through the entire body, Dr. Steinke says. Eventually, it can become life-threatening.

Here are five ways to help your church face up to conflict.

1. Be a Truth-Teller

When you and other church members are at odds over something such as the theme of the annual fund drive, it's tempting to hope that somebody else— the pastor perhaps—will take care of it. Don't fall into this passivity trap, Dr. Steinke says. Get involved. This is the only way healing can begin.

The goal is not to throw your weight around or to insist on having your own way. Nor is it to find fault with others. Rather, Dr. Steinke says, the goal is to accept a measure of personal responsibility for the health of your faith community.

2. Practice Restraint

Speaking honestly is not the same thing as picking a fight. You should approach the other church members with a measure of civility, respect, and, yes, love. If you find those things are missing in the heat of the moment, then back off until the situation has calmed down.

Reverend Morris tells of one church meeting where the situation became so hostile that the pastor threw a folding chair across the room. "That meeting should have ended right then and there," says Reverend Morris. "Somebody should have said, 'Everybody go home, regroup, do whatever you need to do to get back on track. Because where we are now is not what church is about.'"

3. Use the Tools of Tradition

When you're locked in crisis, it's easy to forget that your church traditions may provide specific guidelines for resolving conflicts, Fifer says. For example, the Evangelical Lutheran Church in America provides its member churches with a constitution that spells out in detail the specific powers and responsibilities of the congregation as a whole, the pastor, and the Congregation Council. Such guidelines often represent centuries of accumulated wisdom on dealing with problems that are surprisingly similar to yours. Find out what conflict-solving mechanisms are recommended by your church's doctrine, and use them.

4. Use the Tools of Faith

It's also important to bring all the resources of your faith to bear on painful problems of your church, Dr. Steinke says. In addition to prayer, this includes reading scripture. You will be surprised how many lessons you will find there that will give you insight into the situation at hand. How might the story of the prodigal son, for example, be applied to church members who threaten to leave the church in the midst of a conflict? Matthew 18:15–17 provides another

OPEN OUR HEARTS, GOD

O God, we are one with you. You have made us one with you. You have taught us that if we are open to one another, you dwell in us. Help us to preserve this openness and to fight for it with all our hearts. Help us to realize that there can be no understanding where there is mutual rejection.

O God, in accepting one another wholeheartedly, fully, completely, we accept you, and we thank you, and we adore you, and we love you with our whole being, because our being is in your being, our spirit is rooted in your spirit. Fill us then with love, and let us be bound together with love as we go our diverse ways, united in this one spirit which makes you present in the world, and which makes you witness to the ultimate reality that is love. Love has overcome. Love is victorious.

—Thomas Merton

useful lesson: "If your brother sins against you, go and show him his fault, just between the two of you. If he listens to you, you have won your brother over. But if he will not listen, take one or two others along, so that every matter may be established by the testimony of two or three witnesses. If he refuses to listen to them, tell it to the church; and if he refuses to listen even to the church, treat him as you would a pagan or a tax collector" (NIV).

Also, try taking communion together to remind you and your fellow parishioners of your common grounding in faith. Or perform community service with other church members; this will remind you of your church's greater mission.

5. Tell the Story

The Bible shows how sharing a religious community's story can be a powerful force in unifying the faithful.

This same power can be used to address church conflict, says Reverend Morris. Here's how: Organize what Reverend Morris calls a "group tell." The idea is to get everyone involved in the crisis together in a room, then have each person give his or her account of what has happened. Obviously, such a session can be potentially explosive, Reverend Morris points out, so you need to observe certain ground rules.

- An outside, objective person should lead the session, perhaps another pastor from the community or a professional counselor.
- The session should start with a prayer to convey the message that this is not merely a gripe session—this is "worshipful work."
- The moderator should ensure that each person's account is focused and brief (no more than 2 or 3 minutes at a time, says Reverend Morris) and as free of anger, judgment, and recrimination as possible.

As each person describes his experience, a collective, composite picture of what has occurred should begin to emerge. Depending on the situation, this may take more than one session to accomplish; some stories can take a long time to unfold.

Once the narrative has been completed, Reverend Morris says, church members next should consider whether there is a scripture passage that might apply to what's happened. Discussing that can lead into a period of prayerful reflection on what God would have the church community do from this point forward. One point in particular you should consider, Reverend

What Would **Jesus** Do?

When things don't go our way in church (or out of church), we may be tempted to attack or ostracize those whose views or actions we find unacceptable. Jesus Christ taught a more tolerant approach.

"*The scribes and the Pharisees brought a woman who had been caught in adultery, and placing her in the midst they said to him, 'Teacher, this woman has been caught in the act of adultery. Now in the law Moses commanded us to stone such. What do you say about her?'*

"*This they said to test him, that they might have some charge to bring against him. Jesus bent down and wrote with his finger on the ground.*

"*And as they continued to ask him, he stood up and said to them, 'Let him who is without sin among you be the first to throw a stone at her.'*

"*And once more he bent down and wrote with his finger on the ground. But when they heard it, they went away, one by one, beginning with the eldest, and Jesus was left alone with the woman standing before him.*

"*Jesus looked up and said to her, 'Woman, where are they? Has no one condemned you?'*

"*She said, 'No one, Lord.'*

"*And Jesus said, 'Neither do I condemn you; go, and do not sin again.'*"

(John 8:3–11, RSV)

Morris says, is what new vision of the church's mission might emerge from all that's transpired.

Ending the Conflict

At some point, a church community that has struggled with conflict needs to agree to put the problem to rest—what counselors call "closure."

But you need to consider carefully before taking this step. "Sometimes people rush for closure because they don't want to deal with the pain," says Fifer. That's a mistake. The conflict is bound to boil to the surface again if you don't adequately deal with it before putting it to rest. If you're unsure whether to seek closure, then you and your fellow church members should pray for God's guidance.

Every act of self-control of the Christian is also a service to the fellowship. Every member serves the whole body, either to its health or to its destruction.

—Dietrich Bonhoeffer

Celebrate the End

If the time for closure has indeed come, you can mark the passage with a special liturgy. This doesn't signify that every member of the community has completely accepted the situation, Fifer says. Some people still may need to work through issues on their own. The service indicates, however, that the community as a whole has decided to move forward.

Closure services range from simple communion services to something more elaborate. One minister set a basket on the church's altar and encouraged members to deposit letters in it that described their feelings about the conflict and their prayers for the church's future. Another church set a basket of stones at the entry to its chapel so that members could pick one up as they arrived for the service. These stones represented all the judgments each person had made about other members of church in the heat of the controversy just past. During the service, the pastor read the story from the Book of John in which Jesus rescued an adulterous woman from being stoned by the crowd. After the reading, each member of the church then came forward and put his or her stone on a pile at the altar.

This pile of stones remained in the church permanently, Fifer says, as a reminder to the members of the congregation that they had laid down the wounding judgments they had once been ready to hurl.

LECTIO DIVINA

Reaching Out to God through the Study of the Divine Word

Have you ever found yourself reading the Bible without paying attention to what it's saying?

That won't happen if you use "lectio divina," an ancient technique for meditating on scripture that virtually guarantees you'll connect—with the Bible and also with God.

Lectio divina (pronounced "lex-ee-o da-veen-ah") is Latin for "divine reading." It has been practiced at least since the second century A.D., and probably longer than that, says the Reverend John Belmonte, S.J., a Jesuit priest in Chicago who has studied and written extensively about this form of prayer.

Lectio divina remains popular to this day because it is simple and easy to practice and at the same time profound in its results. To prepare, find a quiet, comfortable spot to settle in—someplace you can be undisturbed for a half hour or so—and choose a Bible passage to study.

This passage can be a sentence, a verse, or a few verses long. It can even be an entire parable or psalm. The point is to read a manageable section of the Bible that you can focus on intently in one sitting. Father Belmonte stresses that you should not simply skip through the Bible, picking out your favorite passages. Rather, your readings should be chosen in some systematic fashion so that over time you will read a variety of material, some of it familiar, some of it unfamiliar. For example, read your way straight through one of the four

522

Gospels or straight through the psalms, a little at a time. There are also systematic reading schedules available in many study Bibles and in the Catholic lectionary. Using a structured approach leaves God the option of surprising you with something you don't expect, Father Belmonte says.

Now you're ready to begin. The classic lectio divina proceeds through four steps. Move from one to the next as you feel ready to do so.

1. Reading ("*lectio*"): Read your chosen passage slowly and carefully several times, focusing your attention on what the text itself is saying. Try to understand objectively what the text is communicating, rather than thinking about what your reaction to the text is. "The point in the *lectio* stage is to let the text speak for itself," Father Belmonte says.

2. Meditation ("*meditatio*"): In this stage, you switch to pondering what the text means to you personally. What parts of the passage do you find particularly moving? Is there a character who you see as especially attractive or repellent? Why? What thoughts, images, or emotions does the passage bring up?

3. Prayer ("*oratio*"): Now is the time to bring all these thoughts and emotions to God in prayer. Communicate your thoughts and feelings about the passage to the Lord and listen in your heart to what God might be saying to you.

4. Contemplation ("*contemplatio*"): Ideally, at this point you will be able to move into a meditative state in which you are no longer *talking* with God but simply *being* with God. This is the destination in the lectio divina journey, Father Belmonte says. The Bible passage which helped carry you here now fades into the background and you rest peacefully in the Divine presence.

Experts List

James Abell, M.D., obstetrician and gynecologist for 45 years. Works at Prince George Hospital Center near Landover, Maryland.

Arlene Alpert, therapist in Jupiter, Florida, and author of *Moving without Madness*.

Herbert Anderson, Ph.D., former professor of pastoral theology at Catholic Theological Union in Chicago.

The Reverend Carl Arico, master of divinity, priest in the archdiocese of Newark, New Jersey. Has studied and practiced centering prayer for more than 25 years.

Brother Larry Backus, C.S.C., director of jail ministries for the Diocese of Albany, New York.

The Reverend Lex Baer, doctor of ministry, counselor at the Professional Pastoral-Counseling Institute in Cincinnati, Ohio.

Aaron T. Beck, M.D., faculty member of the Center for Psychotherapy Research at the University of Pennsylvania in Philadelphia.

Dorothy Becvar, Ph.D., marriage and family therapist and president and CEO of The Haelen Centers in St. Louis.

The Reverend John Belmonte, S.J., Jesuit priest in Chicago. Has studied and written extensively about lectio divina.

The Reverend Alison Boden, dean of Rockefeller Chapel at the University of Chicago.

Carolyn Bohler, Ph.D., professor of pastoral theology and counseling at United Theological Seminary in Dayton, Ohio, and author of *Opening to God: Guided Imagery Meditations on Scripture*.

Debra S. Borys, Ph.D., psychologist and assistant clinical professor of psychology at UCLA.

Gary Brainerd, Ph.D., clinical psychologist and workshop leader from Los Angeles.

Robert Brantley, managing director of The Brantley Group, a Christian counseling center in Baltimore.

Tom Bray, certified public accountant from Kingsville, Maryland, and counselor specializing in getting people out of debt using biblical principles.

The Reverend Peter Bridge, doctor of ministry, marriage and family therapist, pastoral counselor, and clinical director at The Samaritan Counseling Center in Philadelphia.

Mariah Britton, master of divinity, youth minister at The Riverside Church in New York City.

The Reverend Thomas Brown, doctor of theology, adjunct professor of pastoral care and dean at the Interdenominational Theological Seminary in Atlanta.

Katherine Brown-Saltzman, R.N., advocate for balanced living. Has created a retreat program called Circle of Caring to help overcommitted health care workers get control over their lives; also uses meditative prayer with her patients at UCLA Medical Center.

Father William J. Byron, S.J., pastor of Holy Trinity Parish in Washington, D.C., a former professor of ethics at Georgetown University, and author of *Answers from Within: Spiritual Guidelines for Managing Setbacks in Work and Life*.

Elizabeth J. Canham, doctor of ministry, Episcopal priest and director of the Stillpoint Ministries in Black Mountain, North Carolina.

Richard Carlson, Ph.D., author of *Don't Sweat the Small Stuff*.

Joyce Hutchinson Carpenter, R.N., director at Mercy Hospice–Johnston in Iowa and coauthor of *May I Walk You Home? Courage and Comfort for Caregivers of the Very Ill*.

Steve Carr, senior pastor of Calvary Chapel in Arroyo Grande, California, founder of Covenant Keepers, and author of *Married and How to Stay That Way*.

David Carroll of Tappan, New York, leader of seminars and workshops on grieving.

Barbara Castellano, codirector of the Ignatian Lay Volunteer Corps in Baltimore, a faith-based service program that matches volunteers age 50 and over with community needs.

Gary Chapman, Ph.D., of Winston-Salem, North Carolina, is a Christian marriage counselor, seminar leader, and author of *Toward a Growing Marriage, Loving Solutions,* and *The Five Love Languages.*

Connie Clark, contributor to *The Faith Factor: Proof of the Healing Power of Prayer.*

The Reverend Thomas E. Clarke, Jesuit priest and director of New Bethany Retreat in Highland Mills, New York. Has written and lectured about spirituality and prayer for more than 40 years.

William Clements, Ph.D., professor of pastoral care and counseling at the Claremont School of Theology in California.

Howard Clinebell, Ph.D., professor emeritus of pastoral care and counseling at the Claremont School of Theology in California.

Ruth Conard, master of divinity, pastor of assimilation at Woodridge Church in Medina, Minnesota, and leader of seminars on Christianity and parenthood.

Cassandra Cook, Ph.D., clinical psychologist at Columbia University's Parent Infant Program in New York City.

Bonnie Cushing, clinical social worker and family therapist based in Montclair, New Jersey.

Diana Dale, doctor of ministry, executive director of the National Institute of Business and Industrial Chaplains in Houston.

The Reverend John Davies, master of divinity, chaplain of Hospice Care in Westchester and Putnam counties in New York State.

Patricia H. Davis, Ph.D., associate professor of pastoral care at the Perkins School of Theology at Southern Methodist University in Dallas.

Dasarath Davison, Ph.D., executive coach and retreat leader in Newfield, New York, and author of *Wisdom at Work: The Awakening of Consciousness in the Workplace.*

The Reverend John Dear, S.J., executive director of the Fellowship of Reconciliation, one of the oldest and largest interfaith peace organizations in the world.

Robert DeVries, Ph.D., doctor of ministry, professor of church education at Calvin Theological Seminary in Grand Rapids, Michigan.

C. Wayne Dewar, financial planner and founder of an unemployment support group at St. Matthew's United Methodist Church in Charlotte, North Carolina.

Larry Dossey, M.D., of Santa Fe, New Mexico, author of *Healing Words, Re-inventing Medicine,* and many other books on the healing power of prayer.

Dan Dwyer, codirector of the Windrise Spirituality Center in Metamora, Michigan.

Lowell Erdahl, bishop emeritus of the St. Paul, Minnesota, area synod of the Evangelical Lutheran Church of America.

The Reverend Chris Erdman, master of divinity, senior pastor at University Presbyterian Church in Fresno, California.

The Reverend Fanny Erickson, director of the Ministry of Parish Life at New York City's Riverside Church.

The Reverend Paul F. Everett, Presbyterian minister at large for The Peale Center in Pauling, New York, and former executive director of the Pittsburgh Experiment.

Libby Farmer, Ph.D., psychotherapist with the Full Life Counseling Service in Bowling Green, Kentucky.

Kirk Farnsworth, Ph.D., psychologist and author of *Wounded Workers: Recovering from Heartache in the Workplace and the Church.*

David Feinstein, Ph.D., psychologist based in Ashland, Oregon, and coauthor of *Rituals for Living and Dying.*

Everett Ferguson, Ph.D., professor emeritus of church history at Abilene Christian University in Texas.

Anne Bachle Fifer, attorney based in Grand Rapids, Michigan, and mediator of congregational conflicts.

Guy Finley of Merlin, Oregon, author of *The Lost Secrets of Prayer.*

Rabbi Nancy Fuchs-Kreimer, Ph.D., director of the religious studies program at the Reconstructionist Rabbinical College in Philadelphia and leader of numerous seminars and workshops on the spiritual challenges of early parenthood.

The Reverend Richard Ganz, Ph.D., master of divinity, pastor of the Ottawa Reformed Presbyterian Church, president and professor of biblical psychology and counseling at the Ottawa Theological Hall in Almonte, Canada, and author of *The Secret of Self Control.*

James G. Garrick, M.D., director of the Center for Sports Medicine at Saint Francis Memorial Hospital in San Francisco.

Charles Gerkin, Ph.D., former professor of pastoral theology at Candler Seminary in Atlanta.

The Reverend Richard B. Gilbert, master of divinity, chaplain, Anglican priest, and director of the World Pastoral Care Center in Valparaiso, Indiana.

Father Larry Gillick, S.J., director of the Deglman Center for Ignatian Spirituality at Creighton University in Omaha, Nebraska.

John Gottman, Ph.D., professor of psychology at the University of Washington in Seattle and author of *The Seven Principles for Making Marriage Work.*

Stephen P. Greggo, Psy.D., partner in Christian Counseling Associates of Delmar, New York, and chairman of the department of pastoral counseling and psychology at Trinity Evangelical Divinity School in Deerfield, Illinois.

Romano Guardini, author of *The Art of Praying.*

The Reverend Edward Gunter, doctor of ministry, pastor of St. James United Methodist Church in Tarboro, North Carolina.

The Reverend Daniel Hahn, doctor of ministry, pastor to students and families at Mission Hills Church in Los Angeles.

Thomas M. Haizlip, M.D., director of the division of child and adolescent psychiatry at the University of North Carolina Medical Center in Chapel Hill and leader of disaster relief teams.

Delia Halverson of Ft. Myers, Florida, Christian education consultant and author of more than a dozen books on spirituality and family life, including *How Do Our Children Grow.*

Robert M. Hamma, editorial director of Ave Maria Press in Notre Dame, Indiana, and coauthor of *A Circle of Friends: Encountering the Caring Voices in Your Life.*

Sister Maureen Harrison, master of divinity, Religious Sister of Mercy, director of the Foundation for Religion and Mental Health of Wyoming Valley in West Pittston, Pennsylvania.

The Reverend Siegfried F. Haug, master of divinity, psychotherapist and director of the Farmington Valley Counseling Service in Simsbury, Connecticut.

Barry Heermann, Ph.D., author of *Building Team Spirit* and president of the Expanded Learning Institute in Del Mar, California.

Mike Heller, Ph.D., professor of English at Roanoke College in Salem, Virginia. Has taught journal-writing at Pendle Hill, a Quaker center for study and contemplation near Philadelphia.

Karen B. Helmeke, Ph.D., part-time faculty member at Western Michigan University in Kalamazoo.

Robert S. Henderson, doctor of ministry, director of the Pastoral Counseling Center in Glastonbury, Connecticut.

The Reverend Carter Heyward, Ph.D., Episcopal priest, professor at the Episcopal Divinity School in Cambridge, Massachusetts, and author of *Saving Jesus from Those Who Are Right*.

The Reverend William Hiebert, master of sacred theology, executive director of Marriage and Family Counseling Services in Rock Island, Illinois.

The Reverend Ron Hodges, pastor of Christ United Methodist Church in Salt Lake City.

The Reverend Colleen Holby, chaplain to Children's Village shelter in Dobbs Ferry, New York.

Mary Dyer Hubbard, Catholic chaplain and pastoral counselor with The Samaritan Counseling Center in Ambler, Pennsylvania.

Jacqueline Hudak, director of Family Therapy Associates of Monmouth County in Red Bank, New Jersey.

Olson Huff, M.D., pediatric medical director of The Ruth and Billy Graham Children's Health Center in Asheville, North Carolina, author of *The Window of Childhood*, and pediatrician. Has worked extensively with seriously and terminally ill children and their parents.

The Reverend Asa Hunt, executive pastor of the First Presbyterian Church in Houston.

Mary E. Hunt, Ph.D., master of divinity, master of theological studies, cofounder and codirector of the Women's Alliance for Theology, Ethics and Ritual (WATER) in Silver Spring, Maryland, and author of *Fierce Tenderness: A Feminist Theology of Friendship*.

Steven E. Hyman, M.D., director of the National Institute of Mental Health in Bethesda, Maryland.

Thomas Jeavons, general secretary of the Philadelphia Yearly Meeting of the Religious Society of Friends.

Rabbi Isaac Jeret of Congregation Beth Ahm in Verona, New Jersey.

Timothy Jones, master of divinity, from Nolensville, Tennessee, author of *Finding a Spiritual Friend* and *Awake My Soul: Practical Spirituality for Busy People*.

LaVerne K. Jordan, Ph.D., professor of psychology at Olivet Nazarene University in Bourbonnais, Illinois.

The Reverend Mychal Judge, O.F.M., Franciscan friar and chaplain to the New York City Fire Department.

S. Bryant Kendrick Jr., doctor of ministry, associate professor of medicine at Wake Forest University in Winston-Salem, North Carolina.

David Kessler, R.N., author of *The Rights of the Dying*. Has worked with dying patients for nearly 20 years.

Kathleen J. King, Ph.D., psychologist in Kansas City, Missouri. Has specialized in teen issues.

Dale Klamfoth, human resources consultant and area director of Drake Beam Morin in New York City.

The Reverend Erik Kolbell, former minister with the United Church of Christ in New York City and psychotherapist.

Arthur Kornhaber, M.D., founder and president of the Foundation for Grandparenting in Ojai, California.

Carolyn Scott Kortge, author of *The Spirited Walker: Fitness Walking for Clarity, Balance and Spiritual Connection*.

Krista Kurth, Ph.D., codirector of Renewal Resources, a management consulting firm in Potomac, Maryland, that helps people implement spiritual principles in the workplace.

Ernest Kurtz, Ph.D., visiting scholar at the University of Michigan in Ann Arbor and author of a history of Alcoholics Anonymous.

Bill Lagerstrom, founder and director of Lazarus Ministries, a lay ministry program focusing on the spiritual development of people in recovery from addictions based at St. Francis Xavier Church in New York City.

Robert Lauer, Ph.D., research professor at the United States International University in San Diego, ordained Presbyterian minister, and coauthor of *Watersheds: Mastering Life's Unpredictable Crises*.

The Reverend Mel Lawrenz, Ph.D., senior associate pastor of Elmbrook Church, director of the Elmbrook Christian Studies Center in Brookfield, Wisconsin, and coauthor of numerous books, including *Life After Grief*.

Drew Leder, M.D., Ph.D., professor of philosophy at Loyola College in Baltimore and author of *Spiritual Passages: Embracing Life's Sacred Journey*.

The Reverend Kenneth Leech, Anglican priest living in London and author of *True Prayer*.

The Reverend J. William Lentz, senior pastor at Wesley United Methodist Church in Bethlehem, Pennsylvania.

Andrew Lester, Ph.D., professor of pastoral theology and pastoral counseling at Brite Divinity School in Fort Worth, Texas.

David Maitland, Ph.D., chaplain emeritus at Carleton College in Northfield, Minnesota.

The Reverend Jennie Malewski, master of divinity, staff chaplain at The University of Kansas Medical Center in Kansas City.

The Reverend H. Scott Matheney, chaplain and dean of the chapel at Elmhurst College in suburban Chicago, university chaplain for nearly 20 years.

Dale Matthews, M.D., of Washington, D.C., coauthor of *The Faith Factor: Proof of the Healing Power of Prayer*.

Peg Elliott Mayo, clinical social worker and psychotherapist in Blodgett, Oregon, and coauthor of *Rituals for Living and Dying*.

Don McCormick, Ph.D., associate professor of

management and business at the University of Redlands in California.

Jean McMann, author of *Altars and Icons: Sacred Spaces in Everyday Life.*

Michael J. McManus, president and founder of Marriage Savers, a consulting group in Bethesda, Maryland, that helps churches establish marriage ministries.

Paul Meier, M.D., cofounder and medical director of the New Life chain of Christian counseling clinics headquartered in Plano, Texas, and author of numerous books on psychology and faith.

Amy Miller, Psy.D., New York City–based clinical psychologist. Works with adolescents as well as couples on the verge of parenthood.

Bobby Miller, M.D., neurologist and psychiatrist with the New Hope Christian Counseling Center in Huntington, West Virginia.

The Reverend Bruce Miller, pastor of St. Matthews-By-the-Sea in Fenwick Island, Delaware.

James E. Miller, doctor of ministry, of Willowgreen Productions in Fort Wayne, Indiana, author of *When You Know You're Dying.*

Frank Minirth, M.D., founder and president of The Minirth Clinic in Richardson, Texas, cofounder of the largest chain of psychiatric clinics in the world, and author or coauthor of 50 books that integrate psychiatric and Christian principles.

Jerry F. Mock, Ph.D., pastoral counselor in Carlisle, Pennsylvania.

Ron Mock, director of the Center for Peace Learning at George Fox University in Newberg, Oregon.

The Reverend Jeremy Montgomery, youth coordinator of the Boston area–based Ten Point Coalition, a group organized to prevent youth violence.

Harry R. Moody, Ph.D., national program director of Faith in Action in Pearl River, New York, and author of *The Five Stages of the Soul.*

The Reverend Danny E. Morris, retired Methodist minister who created and for 20 years was the executive director of the Academy for Spiritual Formation in Nashville.

The Reverend Robert Corin Morris, Episcopal priest and director of the Interweave Center for Wholistic Living in Summit, New Jersey.

The Reverend Norman J. Muckerman, master of divinity, Redemptorist priest in Liguori, Missouri, and editor of *Preparation for Death: Prayers and Consolations for the Final Journey.*

M. Robert Mulholland Jr., doctor of theology, vice president and chief academic officer of New Testament at Asbury Theological Seminary in Wimore, Kentucky.

Linus Mundy, author of *The Complete Guide to Prayer-Walking: A Simple Path to Body-and-Soul Fitness.*

Judi Neal, Ph.D., professor of management at the University of New Haven and director of the Center for Spirit at Work in West Haven, Connecticut.

Christopher Neck, Ph.D., associate professor of management at Virginia Tech in Blacksburg and author of *Medicine for the Mind* and *Mastering Self-Leadership.*

Jean Newhouse, therapist specializing in individual and family treatment practicing in New York City.

Kathleen Norris, author of *Dakota: A Spiritual Geography.*

Michele Novotni, Ph.D., professor of graduate counseling at Eastern College in St. Davids, Pennsylvania, and author of *Making Up with God.*

Gary J. Oliver, Ph.D., executive director of The Center for Marriage and Family Studies at John Brown University in Siloam Springs, Arkansas, and coauthor of *How to Bring Out the Best in Your Spouse.*

The Reverend Charles M. Olsen, Presbyterian minister and director of the Worshipful-Work Center for Transforming Religious Leadership, based in Kansas City, Missouri.

The Reverend W. Sanford Ostman, master of divinity, associate pastor at Wesley United Methodist Church in Bethlehem, Pennsylvania.

Walton M. Padelford, Ph.D., professor of economics and chair of the McAfee School of Business at Union University in Jackson, Tennessee.

The Reverend Marilyle Sweet Page, doctor of ministry, pastoral counselor and Episcopal priest in Rochester, New York.

Father Andre Papineau, S.D.S., associate professor of pastoral studies at Sacred Heart School of Theology in Milwaukee and author of *Breaking Up, Down, and Through: Discovering Spiritual and Psychological Opportunities in Your Transitions.*

Julie Parton, manager of the Crisis Pregnancy Ministry, Focus on the Family in Colorado Springs, Colorado.

The Reverend Stephanie Paulsell, Ph.D., director of ministry studies at the University of Chicago Divinity School.

Carla Perez, M.D., psychiatrist in San Francisco. Has written extensively on controlling compulsive behavior.

Stephen M. Pollan, career advisor based in New York City and coauthor of *Starting Over: How to Change Careers or Start Your Own Business, Live Rich,* and *Die Broke.*

David Powlison, Ph.D., master of divinity, is a lecturer in practical theology at Westminster Theological Seminary in Philadelphia and a counselor at the Christian Counseling and Educational Foundation in Glenside, Pennsylvania.

Elaine M. Prevallet, Ph.D.

William Raabe, Ph.D., certified public accountant and professor of business at Samford University, a Baptist-affiliated school in Birmingham, Alabama.

S. J. Rachman, Ph.D., psychology professor at the University of British Columbia in Vancouver and author of *Fear and Courage.*

David Rensberger, Ph.D., professor of New Testament studies at the Interdenominational Theological Center in Atlanta.

Lew Richfield, Ph.D., marriage and family therapist practicing in West Los Angeles.

Kent Richmond, doctor of sacred theology, chaplain at the Lutheran General Hospital in Park Ridge, Illinois.

Lewis Richmond, former Buddhist monk and the author of *Work as a Spiritual Practice.*

Douglas Rosenau, Ed.D., Christian psychologist in Atlanta and author of *A Celebration of Sex.*

Alan Ross, executive director of Samaritans, a New York City–based suicide prevention organization.

Joyce Rupp, retreat director, member of the Servants of Mary religious community in Des Moines, Iowa, author of *Praying Our Goodbyes*, and coauthor of *May I Walk You Home? Courage and Comfort for Caregivers of the Very Ill.*

Dorothy Madway Sampson, pre-retirement planning expert, retired social worker in La Jolla, California, and coauthor of *The Healing Journey through Retirement.*

Michael Santorsa, master of theology, retired human resources consultant from Pocasset, Massachusetts, and former Passionist priest.

Peter Schineller, author of *Ministerial Spirituality and Religious Life.*

Greg Schweitzer, stress management counselor and the owner of Stress Reduction Resources in Sinking Spring, Pennsylvania.

Michael Seiler, Ph.D., marital and sex therapist based in Chicago.

Tim Sheehan, Ph.D., regional vice president of Minnesota Recovery Services, parent organization of the famous Hazelden Foundation.

Ron Sider, Ph.D., professor of theology and culture at Eastern Baptist Theological Seminary in Wynnewood, Pennsylvania, and president of Evangelicals for Social Action.

Bernie S. Siegel, M.D., founder of Exceptional Cancer Patients, an organization for people with serious illnesses, and author of *Love, Medicine and Miracles.*

William E. Simon, executive director of William E. Simon & Sons, a venture capital/investment banking firm in Los Angeles.

Art Sprunger, Ph.D., psychologist and director of New Hope & Freedom Counseling Center in Geigertown, Pennsylvania.

Robert F. Stahmann, Ph.D., professor of marriage and family therapy at Brigham Young University in Provo, Utah.

The Reverend Peter L. Steinke, doctor of religion, Lutheran pastor, author of *Healthy Congregations*, and head of Bridgebuilder Ministries, based in Austin, Texas.

Gail Steketee, Ph.D., professor of social work at Boston University and nationally recognized expert in OCD.

The Reverend David Stevens, S.T.B., associate pastor of Holy Spirit Church in Sioux Falls, South Dakota.

Margaret Stockwell, spiritual counselor in Buenos Aires, Argentina.

Peg Streep, author of *Spiritual Gardening* and *Altars Made Easy.*

Father Placid Stroik, O.F.M., director of pastoral ministry for the international youth haven Covenant House in New York City.

Merton Strommen, Ph.D., cofounder of the Youth and Family Institute of Augsburg College in Minneapolis.

The Reverend Gregory Sutterlin, master of divinity, minister at Ascension Lutheran Church and psychotherapist in Franklin Square, New York.

Jim A. Talley, Ph.D., marital and family therapist in Oklahoma City and coauthor of *Reconcilable Differences.*

The Reverend Siang-Yang Tan, Ph.D., professor of psychology at Fuller Theological Seminary in Pasedena, California, senior pastor of the First Evangelical Church in Glendale, California, and author of several books, including *Managing Chronic Pain.*

Mike Taylor, former pastor and staff writer for Christian Financial Concepts, a nonprofit organization in Gainesville, Georgia, dedicated to teaching the biblical principles of handling money.

Donovan Thesenga, teacher of Pathwork, director of Sevenoaks Pathwork Center in Madison, Virginia, and coauthor of *Fear No Evil* and *Surrender to God Within.*

Sue Patton Thoele, psychotherapist from Boulder, Colorado, and author of *Heart-Centered Marriage.*

The Reverend Clayton L. Thomason, J.D., assistant professor of spirituality and ethics at Michigan State University in East Lansing and an Episcopal priest.

Steven M. Tovian, Ph.D., assistant professor of psychiatry and behavioral sciences at Northwestern University Medical School and director of health psychology and chief psychologist at Evanston Hospital in Illinois.

John Townsend, Ph.D., clinical psychologist in Newport Beach, California, and coauthor of *Boundaries* and *Safe People.*

Paul Tripp, doctor of ministry and counseling, director of Changing Lives Ministries at the Christian Counseling and Education Foundation in Glenside, Pennsylvania.

Charles A. Turnbo, president of Positive Solutions in Evergreen, Colorado.

Ruthann Valentine, doctor of ministry, pastoral psychotherapist in Monroeville, Pennsylvania.

The Reverend John Van Regenmorter, master of divinity, chaplain at Bethany Christian Services and director of Stepping Stones, Bethany's ministry for infertile couples in Grand Rapids, Michigan.

The Reverend John Vaughn, executive director of the Peace Development Fund in Amherst, Massachusetts.

Henry Virkler, Ph.D., professor of psychology at Palm Beach Atlantic College in West Palm Beach, Florida, and author of *Broken Promises.*

The Reverend Walter Wangerin Jr., doctor of letters, Lutheran minister, professor of theology and literature at Valparaiso University in Indiana, and author of *Whole Prayer: Speaking and Listening to God.*

Patricia Weenolsen, Ph.D., consultant in Seattle and author of *The Art of Dying.*

Andrew Weil, M.D., director of the program in integrative medicine of the College of Medicine at the University of Arizona in Tucson.

Laurence Welborn, Ph.D., associate professor of New Testament at United Theological Seminary in Dayton, Ohio.

Gwen White, spiritual counselor in Newport, Rhode Island, and leader of workshops on stress management and other topics and spiritual life retreats throughout the country.

Tom Whiteman, Ph.D., director of Fresh Start divorce recovery seminars in Paoli, Pennsylvania, and coauthor of *The Fresh Start Divorce Recovery Workbook.*

Donald S. Whitney, doctor of ministry, associate professor of spiritual formation at Midwestern Baptist Theological Seminary in Kansas City, Missouri, and author of *Spiritual Disciplines for the Christian Life.*

Redford Williams, M.D., director of the Behavioral Medicine Research Center at Duke University Medical Center in Durham, North Carolina, and author of *Anger Kills.*

Edward P. Wimberly, Ph.D., professor of pastoral care and counseling at the Interdenominational Theological Center in Atlanta and author of *Counseling African American Marriages and Families.*

Tom Windels, executive director and counselor at Ephraim Resources, a Christian-based, nonprofit counseling service in Appleton, Wisconsin.

Walter Wink, Ph.D., professor of biblical interpretation at Auburn Theological Seminary in New York City and one of the nation's most respected writers on the relationship between religion and social justice.

Daryle R. Woodward, Ph.D., owner and clinical director of MOVES (Men Overcoming Violence Effectively Services), one of Colorado's largest counseling centers for domestic violence.

Wilford Wooten, clinical social worker, marriage and family therapist, and director of the counseling department at Focus on the Family in Colorado Springs, Colorado.

Everett L. Worthington Jr., Ph.D., chairman of the psychology department at Virginia Commonwealth University, executive director of the Campaign for Forgiveness Research, and author of *Dimensions of Forgiveness: Psychological Research & Theological Perspectives, Hope-Focused Marriage Counseling,* and numerous other books.

The Reverent Don Wright, assistant pastor and student minister at Covenant United Methodist Church in LaGrange, Kentucky.

Susan Zonnebelt-Smeenge, R.N., Ed.D., clinical psychologist with the Pine Rest Christian Mental Health Services in Grand Rapids, Michigan, and coauthor of *Getting to the Other Side of Grief.*

Credits

Our thanks to all those who have granted us permission to reprint prayers, quotations, or other material in this book, as acknowledged below. We have made every effort to trace and contact copyright holders; our apologies to those whom we were unable to locate and for inadvertent omissions.

Prayers

Pages 9, 64, 85, 111, 144, 154, 161, 241, 257, 314, 383, 406, 412, 444, and 466: From *Prayers Women Pray* by Quin Sherrer and Ruthanne Garlock (Servant Publications, Box 8617, Ann Arbor, MI 48107). © 1998 by Quin Sherrer and Ruthanne Garlock. Reprinted by permission of the publisher.

Pages 32, 48, 72, 77, 94, 128, 328, 435, and 473: From *Illuminata: A Return to Prayer* by Marianne Williamson (New York: Random House). © 1994 by Marianne Williamson. Reprinted by permission of the publisher.

Pages 38, 113, 165, 219, and 267: From *I've Got to Talk to Somebody, God* by Marjorie Holmes (New York: Bantam Dell Doubleday Publishing Group). © 1968, 1969 by Marjorie Holmes Mighell. Reprinted by permission of the estate of Marjorie Holmes.

Pages 41, 62, 102, and 299: From *A Grateful Heart* edited by M. J. Ryan (Berkeley, Calif: Conari Press). © 1994 by M. J. Ryan. Reprinted by permission of the publisher.

Page 517 (retitled "Make Me a Peacemaker"): From *A Kind of Praying* by Rex Chapman (London: SCM Press). Reprinted by permission of the publisher.

Page 61: From *The Way of Passion: A Celebration of Rumi* by Andrew Harvey (Frog, Ltd., Berkeley, Calif.; 800-337-2665). © 1996 by Andrew Harvey. Reprinted by permission of the publisher.

Pages 73 and 510: From *Prayers from the Heart* by Richard J. Foster (New

York: HarperCollins). © 1994 by Richard J. Foster. Reprinted by permission of the publisher.

Pages 92, 230, 405, and 463: From *More Prayers That Prevail* by Clift Richards with Lloyd Hildebrand (Tulsa, Okla.: Victory House Publishers). © 1995 by K & C International. Reprinted by permission of the publisher.

Page 121 (retitled "Thanks for this Gift of Life"): From *The Prayers of African Religion* by J. S. Mbiti (London: Society for Promoting Christian Knowledge). Reprinted by permission of the publisher.

Pages 143, 341, and 348: From *My Prayer Book* (St. Louis: Concordia). © 1980 by Concordia Publishing House. Reprinted by permission of the publisher under license number 00:10-20.

Page 160 (retitled "Coming of Age"): From a Sioux rite of initiation of a young man, *U.S. Bureau of American Ethnology Bulletins 1-63, 1888–1956* (Washington, D.C.: Smithsonian Institution Press).

Pages 175, 192, 205, 258, 268, 279, 357, and 496: From *To Begin Again: The Journey toward Comfort, Strength, and Faith in Difficult Times* by Naomi Levy (New York: Alfred A. Knopf, a division of Random House). © 1998 by Naomi Levy. Reprinted by permission of the publisher.

Page 196: From *Daily Word for Healing: Blessing Your Life with Messages of Hope and Renewal* by Colleen Zuck, Janie Wright, and Elaine Meyer (Emmaus, Pa.: Daybreak Books, an imprint of Rodale Inc). © 2000 by Unity School of Christianity, publisher of *Daily Word*. Reprinted by permission of the publisher.

Page 212: From *A Prayer for Every Need*, by Norman Vincent Peale. © 1964 by the Foundation for Christian Living. Reprinted by permission of the Peale Center for Christian Living, the outreach division of Guideposts.

Page 214: From *Thoughts in Solitude* by Thomas Merton (New York: Farrar, Straus & Giroux). © 1956, 1958 by the Abbey of Our Lady of Gethsemani; © 1986 by the Trustees of the Thomas Merton Legacy Trust. Reprinted by permission of the publisher.

Page 246 (retitled "A Prayer for Inward Peace"): From *The Prayer Manual* by F. B. MacNutt (London: Cassell Plc).

Page 269: From *More Everyday Prayers* edited by Hazel Snashall (Birmingham, B.C.: Nation Christian Education Council). Reprinted by permission of the International Bible Reading Association

Page 274: From *Laughter, Silence and Shouting: An Anthology of Women's Prayers* by Kathy Keay (Oxford, England: Lion Publishing). © 1998 Lion Publishing.

Page 287: From *More Prayers of the Plain Man* by William Barclay (New York: HarperCollins). Reprinted by permission of W. J. Ronald Barclay.

Pages 306 and 488: From *Psalms for Zero Gravity: Prayers for Life's Emigrants* by Edward Hays. (Leavenworth, Kans.: Forest of Peace Publishing). © 1998 by Edward Hays. Reprinted by permission of the publisher.

Page 321: From *Enfolded in Love* by Julian of Norwich (New York: HarperCollins). © 1980 by The Julian Shrine. Reprinted by permission of the publisher.

Page 331: From *Justice and Mercy* by Reinhold Niebuhr, edited by Ursula M. Niebuhr (Louisville, Ky.: Westminster John Knox Press, a division of Presbyterian Publishing; originally published by Harper & Row). © 1974 by Ursula M. Niebuhr. Reprinted by permission of the estate of Reinhold Niebuhr.

Page 347: From *Prayers for Children and Young People* edited by Nancy Martin (Louisville, Ky.: Westminster John Knox Press, a division of Presbyterian Publishing). © 1975 by Nancy Martin.

Page 368: From *Lord of the Evening* by Frank Topping (Cambridge, England: Lutterworth Press).

Page 382: Collect from *The Alternative Service Book (1980).* © The Archbishops' Council of the Church of England. Reproduced by permission.

Page 387: From *The Doubleday Prayer Collection* compiled by Mary Batchelor (New York: Bantam Doubleday Dell Publishing Group). © 1992, 1996 by Mary Batchelor. Reprinted by permission of the Christian Publicity Organisation, Worthing, United Kingdom.

Page 453: From "God's Love," by Susan Gerrish, in *Graces: Prayers and Poems for Everyday Meals and Special Occasions* by June Cotner (San Francisco: HarperCollins). © 1994 by June Cotner. Reprinted by permission of Susan Gerrish Peterson.

Page 456: From *Praying with the Orthodox Tradition* by Paula Clifford et al. (London: Society for Promoting Christian Knowledge). © 1996.

Page 457: From *The Living Testament* by Ignatius of Loyola (New York: HarperCollins). Reprinted by permission of the publisher.

Page 494: From *The Prisoner's Lantern* (London: Keston College).

Page 500: From *Family Book of Prayer* by Tony Castle (Essex, England: McCrimmons Publishing). Reprinted by permission of the publisher.

Quotations and Excerpts

Page 14 (beginning "By offering God thanks for some good . . ."): From *True Prayer* by Kenneth Leech (Harrisburg, Pa.: Morehouse Publishing) © 1980, 1995 by Kenneth Leech. Reprinted by permission of the publisher.

Pages 18, 195, and 373: From *When Bad Things Happen to Good People* by Harold S. Kushner (New York: Avon Books; published by arrangement with Schocken Books, a division of Random House). © 1981, 1989 by Harold Kushner. Reprinted by permission of the publisher.

Page 164: From *The Prophet* by Kahlil Gibran (New York: Alfred A. Knopf, a division of Random House). © 1923 by Kahlil Gibran; © 1951 by Administrators C.T.A. of Kahlil Gibran Estate and Mary G. Gibran. Reprinted by permission of the publisher.

Page 174: From *Collected Poems* by Langston Hughes (New York: Alfred A. Knopf, a division of Random House). © 1994 by the estate of Langston Hughes. Reprinted by permission of the publisher.

Pages 185, 266, 273, 310, 416, 443, and 449: From *The Book of Positive Quotations* compiled by John Cook (New York: Gramercy Books, an imprint of

Random House Value Publishing; published by arrangement with Fairview Press). © 1993 by Rubicon Press.

Page 424: From *Twelve Steps and Twelve Traditions* and *Alcoholics Anonymous* (New York: Alcoholics Anonymous World Services). Reprinted by permission of Alcoholics Anonymous World Services, Inc. (A.A.W.S.). Permission to reprint the Twelve Steps and the excerpt does not mean that A.A.W.S. has reviewed or approved the contents of this publication, or that A.A.W.S. necessarily agrees with the views expressed herein. A.A. is a program of recovery from alcoholism *only*; use of the Twelve Steps and the excerpt in connection with programs and activities that are patterned after A.A. but that address other problems, or in any other non-A.A. context, does not imply otherwise.

Pages 492 and 493: From *The Handbook of Bible Application* edited by Neil S. Wilson (Wheaton, Ill.: Tyndale House Publishers). © 1992 by Tyndale House Publishers. Reprinted by permission of the publisher. All rights reserved.

Page 515: The first principle of the "Peacemaker's Pledge": From *The Peacemaker* by Ken Sande (Grand Rapids, Mich.: Baker Books). Reprinted by permission of Peacemaker Ministries (406-256-1583, www.HisPeace.org)

Bible Quotations

Scripture quotations marked (KJV) are taken from the King James Version of the Bible.

Scripture quotations marked (NKJV) are taken from the New King James Version, © 1979, 1980, 1982 by Thomas Nelson, Inc. Reprinted by permission. All rights reserved.

Scripture quotations marked (NIV) are taken from the Holy Bible, New International Version. © 1973, 1978, 1984 by the International Bible Society. Reprinted by permission of Zondervan Publishing House. All rights reserved.

Scripture quotations marked (RSV) are taken from the Revised Standard Version of the Bible, © 1952 (2nd edition, 1971) by the Division of Christian Education of the National Council of the Churches of Christ in the U.S.A. Reprinted by permission. All rights reserved.

Scripture quotations marked (NRSV) are taken from the New Revised Standard Version Bible, © 1989 by the Division of Christian Education of the National Council of the Churches of Christ in the U.S.A. Reprinted by permission. All rights reserved.

General Index

❧

Underscored page references indicate boxed text and marginalia.

535

G

Q

Quality time
  with friends, 268
  in marriage, 43
Quotations, inspiring
  by source
    Aelred of Rievaulx, 271
    Aquinas, Saint Thomas, 266
    Baldwin, James, 187
    Beck, Fred, 353
    Bergman, Ingmar, 209
    Bhagwan Shree Rajneesh,
      162
    Bolles, Richard N., 202
    Bonhoeffer, Dietrich, 35, 521
    Bottome, Phyllis, 310
    Bourne, Randolph, 273
    Boyse, J. F., 148
    Buddha, 391
    Buscaglia, Leo, 290
    Caddy, Eileen, 110
    Camus, Albert, 4
    Carter, Hodding, 167
    Carver, George Washington, 513
    Chah, Achaan, 467
    Child, Lydia Maria, 461
    Cocteau, Jean, 233
    Coffin Jr., William Sloane, 134
    Confucius, 318
    Das, Bhagavan, 340
    Davis, Ossie, 371
    de Sales, Saint Francis, 416
    Emerson, Ralph Waldo, 386
    Farnsworth, Kirk, 303
    Frankl, Viktor E., 469
    Gandhi, 6
    Gibran, Kahlil, 164
    Hammarskjöld, Dag, 211, 490
    Hodges, Rin, 379
    Holmes, Earnest, 492
    Holmes, John Andrew, 185
    Homer, 60
    Hughes, Langston, 174
    Humphrey, Hubert, 120
    Jackson, Phil, 327
    Jampolsky, Gerald, 441
    Jefferson, Thomas, 343

Kennedy, John F., 325, 499
Kennedy, Rose, 247
Keyes Jr., Ken, 78
King Jr., Martin Luther, 482
Kushner, Harold, 18, 195, 373
Lemley, Bill, 253
Lindbergh, Anne Morrow, 58
Linkletter, Art, 54
Mahabharata, 414
Marcus Aurelius, 377
Markhan, Edwin, 475
Montgomery, Jeremy, 150
Mother Teresa, 11, 16, 52, 70,
  240, 259, 459, 515
Niebuhr, Reinhold, 156
Nightingale, Earl, 421
Nouwen, Henri J. M., 282
Paddleford, Clementine, 86
Patterson, Saidie, 204
Philo, 346
Pickford, Mary, 312
Rajneesh, Bhagwan Shree, 162
Rice, Alice H., 351
Rilke, Rainer Maria, 30
Rosten, Leo C., 180
Sarandon, Susan, 158
Scott, Sir Walter, 224
Sheen, Fulton J., 67
Spock, Benjamin, 140
Stevenson, Robert Louis, 118
Strauss, Robert, 142
Sullivan, Anne, 182
Syrus, Publilius, 395
Thurber, James, 255
Turner, Dale, 193
Twain, Mark, 423
van Gogh, Vincent, 37
Vivekananda, 23
Walesa, Lech, 449
Walsch, Neale Donald, 13
Ward, Mrs. Humphry, 389
Washington, Booker T., 298
West, Charles C., 359
Whiteman, Tom, 88
Williamson, Marianne, 505
Yogananda, Paramahansa, 280,
  332
Ziglar, Zig, 366

R

T

Index of Bible Verses

Underscored page references indicate boxed text and marginalia.

Index of Inspiring Quotations

Underscored page references indicate boxed text and marginalia.

By source

By topic

Index of Prayer Titles

Underscored page references indicate boxed text and marginalia.